THE BEST
AMERICAN
MAGAZINE
WRITING

2006

THE BEST AMERICAN MAGAZINE WRITING

2006

Compiled by
the American
Society of
Magazine
Editors

Columbia University Press   New York

Columbia University Press
Publishers Since 1893
New York   Chichester, West Sussex
Copyright © 2006 American Society of Magazine Editors
All rights reserved
Library of Congress Cataloging-in-Publication Data
ISSN 1541–0978
ISBN 0–231–13993–4

Columbia University Press books are printed on permanent and durable
acid-free paper.
This book is printed on paper with recycled content.
Printed in the United States of America
p 10 9 8 7 6 5 4 3 2

Contents

fingered vulgarians" who filled its pages every month. Most proper magazines though, are composed of a chorus of voices, with the editor serving as the choirmaster. It is his or her job to pair the right singer with the right solo, to create the pace, to assemble the right harmonies.

In general, an effective magazine article needs at least one of three basic ingredients: access, disclosure, or narrative. A great article has to have at least two of these components, and a memorable one has all three—along with a distinctive style and a fresh way of looking at its subject. Business-class travel for the writer doesn't hurt, either.

Access lays the groundwork for one of the most satisfying experiences a reader can have—the sensation that he has entered a world foreign to his own, a realm rich in detail and character. Access doesn't necessarily mean the cooperation of a subject. In a war zone, for example, it can mean entering an area that journalists have yet to penetrate. While large news organizations can deploy teams of reporters to cover a major event, there is something to be said for the power of a single, intrepid journalist. The best ones will go to almost any lengths to find their story. They will remain tenacious in the face of resistant, hostile subjects. They will risk their lives. They will risk tedium. And the best will wait out the periods in which nothing seems to be happening at all, understanding that those rare moments of truth can emerge at any time.

Disclosure, that key second element, is the result of great reporting or interviewing techniques and can result in a story breaking news. It can also attend an article that advances the scholarship on a particular subject.

Then comes *narrative.* Anyone can relay a sequence of events. But only the best writers have an instinct for telling a story: building suspense, fleshing out characters, shaping the narrative arc of the tale at hand. A great article transcends reportage. In the right hands, narrative journalism can be as insightful and stirring as a novel. An A.P. wire story about fatalities on Mount Everest is a compelling news story about a tragic event. A beautifully written tick-tock account by Jon Krakauer of a doomed climb in *Outside* becomes a moving picture of humanity.

The articles and essays in this volume have been chosen because they are the best of the best. In an age of info-blather overload, these are triumphs of organization, perseverance, and intellect. Really, there is no need to pity this anthology. It has it all.

Mark Whitaker

Acknowledgments

Ever since the first American magazine, *The General Magazine and Historical Chronicle*, was published in 1741, magazines have been engaging, educating, inspiring, and entertaining readers. And for the last forty years now, the American Society of Magazine Editors has been honoring the best of the best of magazines at the National Magazine Awards, the "Oscars" of our industry. The award-winning and finalist pieces in this anthology represent some of the year's most dynamic, original, provocative, and influential magazine stories, written by some of the most eminent writers in America.

While the entire community of American magazines can claim paternity for the awards and for this book, a few people in particular deserve special credit. Foremost among them are Nicholas Lemann, dean of the Columbia "J" School, cosponsor of the awards, and NMA administrator Robin Blackburn, who does great work organizing the entries in preparation for judging. We are indebted to our book agent, David McCormick of McCormick & Williams, and to our publisher, Columbia University Press. And none of it would happen without the tireless dedication of Marlene Kahan, the executive director of ASME, who chose the stories that make up this anthology.

And, of course, Graydon Carter. As the editor in chief of *Vanity Fair*, Graydon has helped produce some of the most memorable and award-winning magazine journalism, feature writing, and commentary of the 1990s and 2000s, and he has served as one of the industry's most visible and articulate spokespeople. We are pleased that he agreed to write the introduction.

As you read the best of the best for 2006, we hope that you are touched by the special magic of magazine writing that enthralls and inspires all of us.

THE BEST
AMERICAN
MAGAZINE
WRITING

2006

The American Scholar

WINNER—FEATURE WRITING

In "Genome Tome," Priscilla Long asks the question, What are the reverberations of the recent discoveries about the human genome? In twenty-three luminous "chapters" that reflect a human's twenty-three chromosomes, Long uses a blend of poetry, scholarship, and personal narrative to map out the implications of our past and how they will construct our future.

Priscilla Long

Genome Tome

Twenty-three Ways of Looking at Our Ancestors

Suddenly all my ancestors are behind me.
Be still, they say. Watch and listen.
You are the result of the love of thousands.   **—Linda Hogan,**
   "Walking," from *Dwellings:*
   A Spiritual History of the Living Word

The scientific revolution known as the Human Genome Project began in 1990 as an international effort to map the human genome. With jubilation, scientists announced in June 2000 that they had completed a rough draft. By 2003, they had discovered most of the estimated 20,000 to 25,000 human genes found on our double-strand of twenty-three chromosomes. This essay is a montage with twenty-three chapters, one for each chromosome. It was inspired by a 2002 art exhibition titled "Gene(sis): Contemporary Art Explores the Human Genome" mounted here in Seattle at the University of Washington's Henry Art Gallery. The exhibition sent our town into a flurry of lectures mutating into poetry readings mutating into PowerPoint presentations on elementary genomics. But the deep origin of my obsession has to do with my own genome. I am an identical twin—one of nature's clones. . . .

1. Grandmother

Six million years before we were born (before any of us were born) there lived in Africa a great ape, which our species has named *Pan prior*. Out of *Pan prior* both the chimpanzees and our own line evolved. This grandmother ape, how shall we think of her? Shall we despise her as if she were a massive piece of crud in our shiny kitchen? Shall we deny that we have inherited her genes? Shall we strut about as if we ourselves were made of computer wire and light?

2. Corps of Discovery

The Human Genome Project is the Lewis and Clark Expedition of the twenty-first century. In 1804 Meriwether Lewis and William Clark and thirty-one other souls (the Corps of Volunteers for Northwest Discovery) traveled into a country that was to them entirely unknown. They traversed rivers, mountains, prairies, swamps, rapids, cataracts. They took specimens and made notes and drew maps. To map the human genome, from 20,000 to 25,000 genes strung along twenty-three pairs of chromosomes, is also to journey into the unknown. Lewis and Clark meant to befriend the Indians, but in the end, they cleared the way for the destruction of indigenous ways of life thousands of years old. As human genomes are mapped, as the genomes of mice and flowers and fleas are recorded, much will be revealed—the secrets of life itself. And make no mistake about it: much will also be destroyed.

3. Alba

Take the gene that produces florescence in the Northwest jellyfish. Inject the green gene into the fertilized egg of an albino rabbit. Get Alba. Alba, the green-glowing bunny. Alba, designed by an artist in Chicago, created by a lab in France. Alba, a work of art, a work of science. Alba, the white bunny with one strange gene. Alba's jellyfish gene makes Alba glow green. Oh Alba. Oh funny bunny. Oh unique creature, foundling, sentient being without fellow being. Oh freak without circus, star without sky, noise without sound. Alba the ur-orphan among the creatures of the earth, for what mother rabbit would accept into her litter a newborn that glowed like a green light bulb?

4. Recombinant Recipe: Milk-Silk

The spider web is the strongest natural fiber in existence. But for centuries attempts to raise spiders in the manner of raising silkworms have failed, due to the spiderly taste for other spiders. Spiders eat spiders eating spiders.

The genomic solution: introduce a spider gene into the goat genome. Spider-goats in their spider-goat barns are renewing the economy of rural Quebec. Spider-goats look like goats—curious eyes, heads cocked to one side, perky ears. Their milk, strained like cheese, spun like silk, produces a filmy fabric, lightweight, stronger than steel, softer than silk. So strong is milk-silk that a bullet fired at point-blank range bounces off, unable to penetrate. And beautiful it is.

Milk-silk is a natural fabric. It is as natural as daffodils or baby crows or maggots creeping in a cow pie. It is as natural as a spring breeze or a drop of spring rain. And, too, milk-silk is an unnatural fabric. It is as unnatural as a robot or a tack or an airplane taking off for Peru. Milk-silk is both natural and unnatural. Still, it is more natural than Nylon.

5. Next of Kin

Chimps have long arms for climbing and for swinging in trees, and they have opposable thumbs and opposable big toes. They knuckle walk—walk on all fours with their hands folded into fists. They are born with pale faces that gradually turn brown or black.

Chimps live in large sociable communities that have an alpha male and several (less dominant) alpha females. They express affection by grooming each other with obvious pleasure and elaborate precision (they can remove a speck from the eye or a splinter from a toe). They can be quite aggressive; communities have been known to go to war. Chimps are territorial, and when they happen upon an isolated foreign individual on their border, they kill. Like humans, they are capable of cannibalism, of infanticide. But chimps also laugh and kiss and hug. They dine on a diet that varies from plants to ants, using stick-utensils to work the ants out of the ant cupboard. During the day they spread out in small groups to forage for food. While they are thus scattered, the males drum, stamp, and hoot: the chimpanzee Global Positioning System. At night they gather and make nests high in the trees.

When a chimp is born, the other chimps come around offering to groom the mother for a chance to inspect her baby. Mother chimps are fiercely attached to their infants. Baby chimps suckle for three to five years. Adolescents stick with the family and help to baby-sit the little squirt. The baby requires a long time, five to seven years, to learn all the ways of chimpanzees from chimp talk (so to speak) to tickling to hunting food to building the nightly nest. A chimpanzee becomes an adult between eleven and thirteen years of age, and can live to age sixty.

In December 2003, a chimpanzee genome was read for the first time. Chimps are so genetically similar to humans that some scientists want to reclassify them to the *Homo* (hominid) genus. Others disagree, arguing that language and culture may have a minuscule genetic basis, but major species consequences.

6. Lament for Ham and Enos

In the late 1950s, the United States Air Force acquired sixty-five juvenile chimpanzees. Among them were Ham and Enos. No doubt Ham and Enos and the others had witnessed the slaughter of their mothers.

Let the new life begin. The Air Force used the chimps to gauge the effects of space travel on humans. The small chimps were spun in giant centrifuges. They were placed in decompression chambers to see how long it took them to lose consciousness. They were exposed to powerful G forces—forces due to acceleration felt by pilots or by riders on roller coasters.

Three-year-old Ham was the first chimpanzee to be rocketed into space. This occurred on January 31, 1961. NASA archives record "a series of harrowing mischances," but Ham returned alive. The results pleased astronauts and capsule engineers, and three months later Alan Shepard became the first American to be shot into space.

Enos, age five, was launched on November 29, 1961. Enos had undergone a meticulous year of training to perform certain operations upon receiving certain prompts. Upon launch, however, the capsule malfunctioned, and Enos received an electric shock each time he acted correctly. Nevertheless, he continued to make the moves he knew to be right, shock after shock after shock. He orbited earth two times and returned alive.

The following year John Glenn orbited earth three times. On March 1, 1962, in lower Manhattan, four million people greeted Glenn and two fellow astronauts with a huge ticker-tape parade, confetti falling like snow at Christmas.

Ham and Enos were transferred to "hazardous environments" duty. To test the new technology of seatbelts, they were strapped into sleds, whizzed along at thirty, fifty, one hundred mph, slammed into walls.

By the 1970s the Air Force, done with the chimps, leased them out for biomedical research. These highly sociable primates, now adults in their twenties, were stored in cement-block cells with bars in front, but with no windows between cells to provide contact with fellow chimps.

After such a life, Ham died. After such a life, Enos died.

7. Lucy in the Sky with Diamonds

The fossilized skeleton of Lucy, discovered in 1974 in Hadar, Ethiopia, was the oldest hominid remains then known. Lucy died 3.2 million years ago. While her discoverers, Donald Johanson and his team, were looking at her bones in amazement, a Beatles tape played in the background. They named Lucy after the Beatles song "Lucy in the Sky with Diamonds." Lucy was short, about four feet high, with long arms for climbing. She stood upright. That's the important thing. Her proper species name is *Australopithecus afarensis*. From her group, several species of hominids evolved. *Homo erectus* evolved. We evolved. That's the old story. It's a nice story. It has a nice beginning, middle, and end.

But it's probably not true. Bones speak, but they do not enunciate. Skulls and femurs and molars are measured and compared and recompared, and theories replace theories. Thighbones and skulls "from the same species" placed side by side look different, and fossilized bones, alas, do not produce DNA.

In 2000 the creation story got a new beginning. About six million years ago, our human ancestor split off from *Pan prior*. This missing link, this half-ape, half-hominid has been the longed-for find, the physical anthropologist's Holy Grail. In Kenya, in 2000, scientists Martin Pickford and Brigette Senut discovered a very few very old bones. *Orrorin tugenensis* lived six million years ago, the time our oldest human ancestor split off from *Pan prior*. These scientists claim that Lucy was not our direct ancestor but an offshoot that died out. That *Orrorin tugenensis* were our true ancestor hominids. This being stood upright, but also displayed the attributes of knuckle-walking, tree-climbing apes. Donald Johanson thinks they might be right.

After that (if that really was that), perhaps fifteen different species of humans evolved. From one million to three million years ago (before *Homo sapiens*), perhaps ten different human species lived simultaneously. There were side branches and extinctions. *Homo neanderthalensis* was one of the side branches, and these beings shared the earth with *Homo sapiens*, our people, who evolved, in Africa, not so very long ago, 150,000 years ago.

8. Mother

Our ancient mother, the mother of us all, lived in Africa some 150,000 years ago. She was one individual in a world population of *Homo sapiens*—recently evolved out of *Homo erectus*—amounting to 2,000 individuals at most. There were other females of course, but their lines died out long before historical times. Everyone alive today descends from this one woman, from one of her two daughters. This is the astonishing news revealed by the book of the human genome, the book whose pages we are just beginning to turn.

9. History and Geography

We are apes evolved into *Homo erectus*. We are Africans, *Homo sapiens* evolved from a group of *Homo erectus* who lived in Africa 150,000 years ago. Not so very long ago. Twelve thousand generations ago.

We are *Homo sapiens*, alone knowing. We know and we don't know. We wonder. We wonder where we came from. We wonder who we are. We wonder where we are going. We pose questions.

10. Questions

1. Are we, then, the greatest of the great apes?
2. Is human kindness more human than inhuman cruelty?
3. What makes a cell divide? Am I dividing against myself?
4. If we were once single-celled creatures, was I once a single-celled creature?

5. Identical twins: aren't we the pioneer clones?
6. How does Earth's age, 4.5 billion years, relate to our age?
7. If grammar is innate, is iambic pentameter innate?
8. If you could read the book of your genes, would anything there surprise you?
9. Would it surprise you to learn that you were mixed race?
10. Can humans and chimpanzees mate?
11. What will life look like after 500 years of genetic experiments?
12. Is human selection less natural than natural selection?
13. Where did we come from? Where are we going?
14. If a twin is not the same person, why would a clone be the same person?
15. Should art include the creation of life?
16. Is there a gene for creativity, and if so what protein does it express?
17. If a scientist creates a new species, is the scientist the parent? Who gets custody?
18. Do I belong to myself, in the cellular sense?
19. Who wrote the book of life?
20. Is my cell line mine? Is my genome mine?
21. Considering that more genetic variation exists within racial groups than between racial groups, what is race?
22. Was our first mother happy?
23. How can you say that?

11. The Grammar Gene

Linguist Noam Chomsky argues that grammar is not learned, that it somehow comes with our DNA. People in any language recognize grammatical structures, apart from the sounds or meanings of words. Grammar is innate, whereas diction and meanings are cultural and, over the slow centuries, in flux. Others argue that what is inherited isn't grammar, it's a propensity to search for patterns in speech. We move from "Mama!" to "Mama get ball!" to "I think Johnny went to the store to get milk, at least that's what he said he was going to do before he found out he won the lottery"— a construction that will forever elude the most brilliant chimps taught to "speak."

Did language evolve out of primate vocalizations? Or did it evolve out of an entirely different part of the brain, the part that can practice throwing to improve one's aim, the part that can plan to marry off one's unborn daughter to the as-yet unconceived son of the future king.

Our first mother had no words to speak. Our earliest *Homo sapiens* ancestors were anatomically identical to ourselves, but had no cognition. They had no symbols. They had our vocal chords, but no language. They were osteologically modern but neurologically archaic. They had our bones, but not our wits. About 50,000 years ago something changed. After that, there were bone flutes and symbolic marks and cave paintings. The *Homo sapiens* who painted on cave walls with charcoal and red ochre had metaphor, symbol, language. The change had to do with the brain growing, not larger, but more complex.

There is something about language that we inherit. Perhaps our mother taught us to speak, but she could never teach a chimp to speak, except in the most rudimentary way after years of work. We are born with something structural about language in our DNA.

The structure of language lurks below the meaning of words. Chomsky wrote, "Colorless green ideas sleep furiously." This grammatical sentence illustrates that grammar and meaning have about as much relationship to one another as strangers on a blind date. Grammar is the towny. This dude, this thug, knows the ins and outs of the place by heart. He runs the show, and he practically owns the territory. His date just blew into town. She's all fluttery in this gaudy multipart outfit she copped at various exotic bazaars and flea markets. Half the time she's got no idea what she's saying, but she's easy, in actual fact a slut willing to go along with just about anything.

Oh my.

12. Grammar Gene Mutation

Courtly cows dispense with diphthongs. Chocolate-covered theories crouch in corners. Corners rot uproariously. Refrigerators frig the worms. Catastrophe kisses the count of five. A statement digests its over-rehearsed rhinoceros. Bookworms excrete monogamous bunnies. Blue crud excites red ecstasy. All this during the furious sleeping of colorless green ideas.

13. The Ghazal Gene

The ghazal is an old poetic form, very old, very stringent, very strange. It is older than the sonnet. Or so writes the poet Agha Shahid Ali. According to Ali, *ghazal* is pronounced to rhyme with *muzzle* and the initial *gh* sound comes from deep in the throat like a French rolled *r*. Like a smoker quietly clearing his throat.

The ghazal goes back to seventh-century Arabia, perhaps earlier, in contrast to the sonnet, which goes back to thirteenth-century Italy. If grammar is genomic, could the ghazal be genomic?

A ghazal performs itself in couplets, five or more. The couplets have nothing to do with one another, except for a formal unity derived from a strict rhyme and repetition pattern. In the last couplet it is customary for the poet to mention him or herself by name, by pseudonym, or as "I." In all other couplets this is strictly illegal.

The ghazal is the form of choice for the incorrigible narcissist because it always returns to the subject of the poet, rather like a bore at a cocktail party.

The ghazal has been tortured and butchered in English, which pained Agha Shahid Ali and moved him to write a rant. This humorous but headstrong harangue precedes an anthology of good ghazals in English, *Ravishing DisUnities*.

Or maybe they're not so good. Some are exquisite. Others stand in complete violation of Ali's ground rules. What does it matter?

If you construct a ghazal on a subject, so that each couplet chews on the theme announced in the title like a meat chopper, or if you violate the form by using slant rhyme—say, *white/what* instead of *white/fight*—or if you violate the rule of no enjambment between couplets, the form disintegrates. The eerie magic of the ghazal, its ravishing disunity, its weird indirection, falls to pieces. The thing becomes awkward, stiff, forced like a too-fancy, out-of-date party dress purchased at a thrift shop, which, besides missing a button, is too tight and unsightly.

I have committed God-awful ghazals. At first, I missed the point about autonomy of the couplets. Then one day I was visited by the muse, Keeper of Classical Forms. Perhaps she was sent by Agha Shahid Ali, who died of a brain tumor on December 8, 2001. He was fifty-two years old.

I gutted my ghazals and began again.

14. Genome Ghazal

One earth, one ur-gene, in the beginning.
Mountain air. No green, in the beginning.

Black towers. Steel and glass. Blue dawn
downtown. Pristine in the beginning.

Old friend, did you slip into not-being,
or was death like a dream, in the beginning?

Dirt-obliterated bones, bits of bowls,
stone tools—unseen in the beginning.

Sibilant hiss, susurrus sigh—Priscilla—
What did it mean, in the beginning?

15. In the Beginning

When I was twelve, I took up bird watching. On the first day of my new hobby, I set out down the dirt road of our dairy farm noting in my tablet any bird I saw. Crow. Red-winged blackbird. Sparrow—I had no idea what kind. Turkey buzzards spiraling down. A cardinal flashing red in a black locust tree. That evening over supper, I read my list to my brother and sisters, and to my rather worn-down parents.

The next day my sister Pammy took up bird watching. She returned with a list twice as long. Besides my birds, she had recorded a wood thrush, a black-capped chickadee, and a yellow finch. Our mother put an immediate stop to Pammy's bird-watching hobby. She forbade Pammy to watch for birds or to put down the names of birds. Pammy was not even to speak of birds. Bird watching was my hobby, not Pammy's hobby.

Pamela is my identical twin. We each, like everybody else, have three trillion cells, give or take a few. Most of these cells have at their center a copy of our genome. My genome is identical to Pamela's genome. Therefore, Pamela and I feel we have something to interject into the debate on cloning. But here I speak for myself.

I speak for myself because I am looking out of my own eyes. I live in the Puget Sound region—a land of clouds, salmon, orca whales, congested traffic, and double-leaved bascule bridges. Like many Seattleites, I grumble at the excessive sunshine in mid-July. I like foghorns and ducks and snowcapped mountains. Rainy Seattle with its cafés and bookstores is a perfect reading-and-writing city, and I am happy here, happy as a coot bobbing on Green Lake. My place, the Pacific Northwest, affects who I am.

Genes don't even determine all physical characteristics. I have curly hair; Pamela has straight hair. That could be because of the weather, or maybe I have more kinky thoughts.

Once an old friend of mine, long out of contact, saw Pamela in Washington, D.C., jogging in Rock Creek Park.

"Priscilla!" she screamed.

"I'm not Priscilla!" Pamela called back. She waved, but did not bother to stop.

Years later I reunited with my friend, and she informed me of my mental lapse, my rudeness, my inexplicable behavior. I reminded her that I have a twin sister who may or may not have identical fingerprints. In any case, I'm not responsible—for anything.

In my memory, our childhood is fused. For years I told the story of how our mother taught us to read at the age of three. Once I told the story in the presence of my mother, who informed me that Pamela had learned to read at the age of three. I had exhibited zero interest in reading until I was six or seven. I must have thought, as Pammy was learning to read: Oh! Look! We can read!

Twins share the same genome, but they do not share the same environment. One twin dominates; the other carves a niche out of whatever space the dominant twin—in our case Pamela—leaves available. One may be more conservative, the other more deviant.

Our desires send us out on our various paths; they color the persons we become. Pamela grew up wanting to be a scientist, and at eight or nine this moved her to collect white mice and to experiment with questionable liquid mixtures in her chemistry laboratory. When she was sixteen (in the bad old days of 1959), she wrote to medical schools asking how she should prepare herself to be admitted. Each and every school wrote back: Girls need not apply. We are formed by our generation, our era, as much as by our genes.

But times changed. After Pamela graduated from college and worked for a decade as a social worker, she came to her senses and got a Ph.D. She is now a brilliant historian of Renaissance science and technology.

I wanted to be a poet, and that sent me down a different road.

If a twin is not the same person, why would a clone be the same person? How could you replace one twin with another? Each looks at the world through his or her own eyes. Place, choice, chance—all affect who a person is. Who could imagine that one person—that ineffable, multivarious, complicated, constantly changing complexity that is a single human being—could be the same as another?

Today Pamela and I are the best of friends, a mutual-aid society, career consultants, fashion consultants. I live by myself; she lives with her husband and receives visits from her college-age daughter. We both write books—utterly different sorts of books.

I'm not a bird watcher, but I like watching widgeons paddling about on Green Lake squeaking like a flock of bathtub toys. They look identical to me, probably because I do not take the time to distinguish their particulars. Pamela would do better. I think she has a Life List, and I think widgeons are on it.

16. Dolly

Dolly, cloned from an udder cell of a six-year-old sheep, was born on July 5, 1996. She looked very lamblike, with her white wool and curious eyes. Dolly the newborn had six-year-old cells. She soon went stiff with arthritis. She soon came down with lung disease. Sheep live for eleven or twelve years and in old age typically suffer arthritis and lung disease. Dolly's caretakers, considering her progressive lung disease, put her to sleep in February 2003. She was not yet seven years old.

Dolly illustrates the difficulties of reproductive cloning. She was just a lamb, like any other lamb, soft and woolly and frisky. But she was one cloning success out of hundreds of failed tries, and even then, she had complications and died young, if you count her age from the time she was born. Since Dolly, other large mammals have been cloned. One calf's hind end is fused into one back leg. Extreme abnormalities in cloned animals are routine. Life is not easy to create in the lab.

The idea of using reproductive cloning to clone human babies is fought, and it's fraught with the nightmare of grotesque "successes"—infants with severe abnormalities. Any cloned infant will enter a life of many problems and early death. The most heartwarming argument used in favor of reproductive cloning is that human cloning could provide the grief-stricken parents of terminally ill babies a copy of their lost child. It could give them their baby back.

I am here to speak as one of nature's clones. A genetically identical being is not the same being. A cloned baby would not return a dying baby to its parents. It would not erase the grief of losing a child. A cloned baby is a different baby. It is an identical twin, not the same little boy, not the same little girl. A cloned baby would start life in the wake of grief and death—already a vitally different life beginning. It would delete neither the death nor the grief over the death of the child that lived for only a short while. Imagining that a cloned baby could replace a lost child is as insensitive as the idiot persons who say to grieving parents, "You can always have another child!"

17. Stem-Cell Research

But stem-cell research is a different thing. Stem cells are fetal cells; no born child is involved. Stem cells are the body's ur-cells, the first to grow after the sperm and egg join. Stem cells are poised to become any body tissue, from liver to brain to skin. Stem-cell research holds the promise of curing paralysis, Alzheimer's, multiple sclerosis, Parkinson's. . . .

To my way of thinking, stem cells are not a human being but a potential human being. I do not disrespect the right-to-lifers, but I've always wondered why they don't go on a campaign to save the world's 18 million infants and toddlers who die every year, mostly from diarrhea—preventable deaths of born children.

18. The Ancient One

Looking into this petri dish, into this dish of our own cells, we can see, after a fashion, our ancestors. We can unravel their journeys. It is as if DNA were a telescope with multiple lenses pointed at the deep past, each lens revealing a different scene. The Human Genome Project, added to the archeological breakthrough of carbon dating, added to new archeological digs, added to the study of languages living and dead, added to the study of blood types, added to sonar sweeps of ocean floors that were once dry land, will rewrite the story of who we are and who our ancestors were.

We know now that *Homo sapiens* spread out from Africa. That is a long story. We know the species spread to Asia and to Europe. Another long story. Then some of them came to America.

The old story is that peoples out of some sort of Asian gene pool walked to the North American continent over the Bering land bridge, when the Bering Strait was iced over, some 12,000 to 13,000 years ago. These people, these ancient ones, evolved into American Indians, into South American Indians, into Cherokee and Crow and Sioux and Mayan. That's the old story. A newer old story is that they came earlier, in waves, and that some may have come by boat.

Kennewick Man threatened to rewrite the old story. Teenagers found a man's bones half-buried in a bank of the Columbia River, in eastern Washington on July 28, 1996, during Kennewick's annual unlimited hydroplane races. The bones were determined to be 8,400 years old, one of the oldest complete skeletons ever found in the Americas. Controversy flared when an archeologist working for the Benton County coroner's office declared that they were Caucasoid bones (a white man's bones). The skeleton had a narrow, elongated skull, like Europeans, unlike Native Americans. This would suggest that the ancestors of Europeans arrived in the Americas before the ancestors of Native Americans did.

However, genetic research has uncovered that Native Americans have a common ancestor with native peoples who now occupy south-central Asia. Several of these peoples have narrow, elongated skulls. The scientist who breezily declared in the first week of the find that the Kennewick Man's bones were white man's bones spoke in haste.

In the case between Native Americans who want to bury the Ancient One's old bones and certain scientists who want to examine them, the courts have ruled that Kennewick Man's bones may be studied. Although DNA has yet to be extracted (it's difficult and sometimes impossible to extract DNA from old bones), it is now considered quite far-fetched to think of Kennewick Man as European.

19. My Ancient Ones

My ancestors are European. They came out of Africa, just as all of our ancestors did. They lived for many generations in the cold steppes of Russia and in the cold steppes of eastern Europe. During these many generations, groups that would become Asian were moving east, probably along the seacoast. Eventually some arrived in North America. At the same time, groups that would become Caucasian were moving into what were then the steppes of Germany. The earth was becoming colder. *Homo sapiens* were hunting with more social cooperation than before. Neanderthal bones show that the Neanderthals were having a hard time. They were starving. This was about 20,000 years ago. The last ice age lasted a long time. Then it got warm again. Germany grew trees. Germany grew the Black Forest. Children played in the woods, got lost in the woods. The woodcutter's children, Hansel and Gretel, found their witch. . . .

20. The Courage of the Ancestors

Back in the forested hills and hollows of Old Germany, the Brothers Grimm went about collecting fairy tales, legends, riddles, ridiculous superstitions. This was in the early 1800s, but the stories they collected were of course much older, handed down from previous generations. Grimm's fairy tales are known the world over and can be compared to analogous fairy tales from just about every culture.

Their legends are less well known. One of them, Number 328 in the Brothers Grimm published collection, is titled "The Dead from the Graves Repel the Enemy." According to this legend, the town Wehrstadt got its name—related to the verb *wehren*, to repel—after this happened: The town suffered an attack by "foreign heathens" of vastly superior force. At the moment of defeat, the dead rose from their graves "and courageously repulsed the enemy, thus saving their descendants."

21. Grandma Henry's Love Story

My mother's father, whom I called Granddaddy, was hard working and rather taciturn. He spoke little, except when he was laughing and talking in Pennsylvania Dutch with his insurance customers. My mother's mother, whom I called Grandma, talked in a constant stream in English, considering herself to be emancipated from Pennsylvania Dutch. My grandparents did not speak overly much to each other.

One day Grandma told me the following story. Decades after their wedding day, their three children grown, grandchildren already born, Granddaddy told Grandma, "You were the most beautiful girl in the whole town!" At this point, Grandma paused in her telling of the story. Then she said, "Why didn't he ever tell me that before? I never knew I was beautiful!"

22. Mother's Love Story

My mother once told me, "I was the adored first child."

My mother wrote to her mother, my Grandma Henry, every single week from the time she went away to Bucknell College to the time (that same year) she married my father and they had their first three children before they turned twenty. She continued writing to her mother every week, regular as clockwork, for decades, until her mother, my Grandma Henry, died on August 29, 1987.

My mother's own dying was long and painful, involving diabetes and strokes. During the years of her extreme disablement, my father was her caretaker. Dr. Barbara Henry Long died on May 29, 2003, at 11:45 at night.

A couple of weeks after she died, in the midst of all the turmoil and arrangements, my father took out a framed photograph of my mother, taken when she was eighteen. "She gave me this picture after our first date," he told us. In the photograph, Barbara Jane Henry is young with a long and thinner face. Her brown hair curls softly around her face, and her eyes are shining with happiness.

23. Naming Names

The crime of Christoph Tanger, a German innkeeper, was stealing horses. He was tempted by the devil to associate with thieves. These are the facts reported in the printed account of his hanging, which took place on March 13, 1749, in Gemersheim, a town on the Rhine River in what is now southern Germany. The "leading out" of Christoph Tanger occupied four hours. The procession cheering him on to his execution sang "more than 20 of the finest Evangelical Lutheran hymns." Upon "entering the circle" it was intoned, "Now we are praying to the Holy Spirit." Christoph Tanger himself thanked the Lord and, according to his pastor, "repeatedly recommended to me his wife and children, that the latter should be raised in his religion, which is so much a consolation to him. Whereupon under constant cheering up he died without much pain!"

Two years later Christoph's widow, Anna, and their children arrived in Pennsylvania. Their German became Pennsylvania German, their Dutch became Pennsylvania Dutch. I am here because of the broken love between Christoph and Anna. I am here because of their son Andreas, witness at age six to his father's broken neck. I am here because of the love between Andreas Tanger and Catherine Lottman, married in 1768. I am here because of their children and their children's children, ending with my mother. They are the vessel from which my genes were poured. They are the ancestors who gave me this world. They are the lovers who put me into this blue dawn, watching and listening. . . .

Rolling Stone

James Bamford delves deep into the crossfire of the war of information and imagery to expose the work of the most secretive—and effective—tacticians of the endless Iraqi conflict. "The Man Who Sold the War," a massive reporting effort that includes a rare interview with General John Rendon, provides a glimpse into covert trading of rumors and information in order to foment war.

James Bamford

The Man Who Sold the War

There was a reason Judith Miller bought into the lies about Iraq—they were part of a $100 million PR campaign hatched by a shadowy Beltway consulting firm. Meet John Rendon, Bush's general in the propaganda war.

·   ·   ·

The road to war in Iraq led through many unlikely places. One of them was a chic hotel nestled among the strip bars and brothels that cater to foreigners in the town of Pattaya, on the Gulf of Thailand.

On December 17, 2001, in a small room within the sound of the crashing tide, a CIA officer attached metal electrodes to the ring and index fingers of a man sitting pensively in a padded chair. The officer then stretched a black rubber tube, pleated like an accordion, around the man's chest and another across his abdomen. Finally, he slipped a thick cuff over the man's brachial artery, on the inside of his upper arm.

Strapped to the polygraph machine was Adnan Ihsan Saeed al-Haideri, a forty-three-year-old Iraqi who had fled his homeland in Kurdistan and was now determined to bring down Saddam Hussein. For hours, as thin mechanical styluses traced black lines on rolling graph paper, al-Haideri laid out an explosive tale. Answering yes and no to a series of questions, he insisted repeatedly that he was a civil engineer who had helped Saddam's men to secretly bury tons of biological, chemical, and nuclear weapons. The illegal arms, according to al-Haideri, were buried in subterranean wells, hidden in private villas, even stashed beneath the Saddam Hussein Hospital, the largest medical facility in Baghdad.

It was damning stuff—just the kind of evidence the Bush administration was looking for. If the charges were true, they would offer the White House a compelling reason to invade Iraq and depose Saddam. That's why the Pentagon had flown a CIA polygraph expert to Pattaya: to question al-Haideri and confirm, once and for all, that Saddam was secretly stockpiling weapons of mass destruction.

There was only one problem: It was all a lie. After a review of the sharp peaks and deep valleys on the polygraph chart, the intelligence officer concluded that al-Haideri had made up the entire story, apparently in the hopes of securing a visa.

The fabrication might have ended there, the tale of another political refugee trying to scheme his way to a better life. But just because the story wasn't true didn't mean it couldn't be put to good use. Al-Haideri, in fact, was the product of a clandestine operation—part espionage, part PR campaign—that had been set up and funded by the CIA and the Pentagon for the express purpose of selling the world a war. And the man who had long been in charge of the marketing was a secretive and mysterious creature of the Washington establishment named John Rendon.

Rendon is a man who fills a need that few people even know exists. Two months before al-Haideri took the lie-detector test, the Pentagon had secretly awarded him a $16 million contract to target Iraq and other adversaries with propaganda. One of the most powerful people in Washington, Rendon is a leader in the strategic field known as "perception management," manipulating information—and, by extension, the news media—to achieve the desired result. His firm, the Rendon Group, has made millions off government contracts since 1991, when it was hired by the CIA to help "create the conditions for the removal of Hussein from power." Working under this extraordinary transfer of secret authority, Rendon assembled a group of anti-Saddam militants, personally gave them their name—the Iraqi National Congress—and served as their media guru and "senior adviser" as they set out to engineer an uprising against Saddam.

It was as if President John F. Kennedy had outsourced the Bay of Pigs operation to the advertising and public-relations firm of J. Walter Thompson.

"They're very closemouthed about what they do," says Kevin McCauley, an editor of the industry trade publication *O'Dwyer's PR Daily.* "It's all cloak-and-dagger stuff."

Although Rendon denies any direct involvement with al-Haideri, the defector was the latest salvo in a secret media war set in motion by Rendon. In an operation directed by Ahmad Chalabi—the man Rendon helped install as leader of the INC—the defector had been brought to Thailand, where he huddled in a hotel room for days with the group's spokesman, Zaab Sethna. The INC routinely coached defectors on their stories, prepping them for polygraph exams, and Sethna was certainly up to the task—he got his training in the art of propaganda on the payroll of the Rendon Group. According to Francis Brooke, the INC's man in Washington and himself a former Rendon employee, the goal of the al-Haideri operation was simple: pressure the United States to attack Iraq and overthrow Saddam Hussein.

As the CIA official flew back to Washington with failed lie-detector charts in his briefcase, Chalabi and Sethna didn't hesitate. They picked up the phone, called two journalists who had a long history of helping the INC promote its cause and offered them an exclusive on Saddam's terrifying cache of WMDs.

For the worldwide broadcast rights, Sethna contacted Paul Moran, an Australian freelancer who frequently worked for the Australian Broadcasting Corp. "I think I've got something that you would be interested in," he told Moran, who was living in Bahrain. Sethna knew he could count on the trim, thirty-eight-year-old journalist: a former INC employee in the Middle East, Moran had also been on Rendon's payroll for years in "information operations," working with Sethna at the company's London office on Catherine Place, near Buckingham Palace.

"We were trying to help the Kurds and the Iraqis opposed to Saddam set up a television station," Sethna recalled in a rare interview broadcast on Australian television. "The Rendon Group came to us and said, 'We have a contract to kind of do anti-Saddam propaganda on behalf of the Iraqi opposition.' What we didn't know—what the Rendon Group didn't tell us—was in fact it was the CIA that had hired them to do this work."

The INC's choice for the worldwide print exclusive was equally easy: Chalabi contacted Judith Miller of the *New York Times*. Miller, who was close to I. Lewis Libby and other neoconservatives in the Bush administration, had been a trusted outlet for the INC's anti-Saddam propaganda for years. Not long after the CIA polygraph expert slipped the straps and electrodes off al-Haideri and declared him a liar, Miller flew to Bangkok to interview him under the watchful supervision of his INC handlers. Miller later made perfunctory calls to the CIA and Defense Intelligence Agency, but despite her vaunted intelligence sources, she claimed not to know about the results of al-Haideri's lie-detector test. Instead, she reported that unnamed "government experts" called his information "reliable and significant"— thus adding a veneer of truth to the lies.

Her front-page story, which hit the stands on December 20, 2001, was exactly the kind of exposure Rendon had been hired to provide. AN IRAQI DEFECTOR TELLS OF WORK ON AT LEAST 20 HIDDEN WEAPONS SITES, declared the headline. "An Iraqi defector who described himself as a civil engineer," Miller wrote, "said he personally worked on renovations of secret facilities for biological, chemical and nuclear weapons in underground wells, private villas, and under the Saddam Hussein Hospital in Baghdad as recently as a year ago." If verified, she noted, "his allegations would provide ammunition to officials within the Bush administration who have been arguing that Mr. Hussein should be driven from power partly because of his unwillingness to stop making weapons of mass destruction, despite his pledges to do so."

For months, hawks inside and outside the administration had been pressing for a preemptive attack on Iraq. Now, thanks to Miller's story, they could point to "proof" of Saddam's "nuclear threat." The story, reinforced by Moran's on-camera interview with al-Haideri on the giant Australian Broadcasting Corp., was soon being trumpeted by the White House and repeated by newspapers and television networks around the world. It was the first in a long line of hyped and fraudulent stories that would eventually propel the U.S. into a war with Iraq—the first war based almost entirely on a covert propaganda campaign targeting the media.

By law, the Bush administration is expressly prohibited from disseminating government propaganda at home. But in an age of global communications, there is nothing to stop it from planting a phony pro-war story overseas—knowing with certainty that it will reach American citizens almost instantly. A recent congressional report suggests that the Pentagon may be relying on "covert psychological operations affecting audiences within friendly nations." In a "secret amendment" to Pentagon policy, the report warns, "psyops funds might be used to publish stories favorable to American policies, or hire outside contractors without obvious ties to the Pentagon to organize rallies in support of administration policies." The report also concludes that military planners are shifting away from the Cold War view that power comes from superior weapons systems. Instead, the Pentagon now believes that "combat power can be enhanced by communications networks and technologies that control access to, and directly manipulate, information. As a result, information itself is now both a tool and a target of warfare."

It is a belief John Rendon encapsulated in a speech to cadets at the U.S. Air Force Academy in 1996. "I am not a national-security strategist or a military tactician," he declared. "I am a politician, a person who uses communication to meet public-policy or corporate-policy objectives. In fact, I am an information warrior and a perception manager." To explain his philosophy, Rendon paraphrased a journalist he knew from his days as a staffer on the presidential campaigns of George McGovern and Jimmy Carter: "This is probably best described in the words of Hunter S. Thompson, when he wrote, 'When things turn weird, the weird turn pro.'"

.   .   .

John Walter Rendon Jr. rises at 3 A.M. each morning after six hours of sleep, turns on his Apple computer and begins ingesting information—overnight news reports, e-mail messages, foreign and domestic newspapers, and an assortment of government documents, many of them available only to those with the highest security clearance. According to Pentagon documents obtained by *Rolling Stone*, the Rendon Group is authorized "to research and analyze information classified up to Top Secret/SCI/SI/TK/G/HCS"—an extraordinarily high level of clearance granted to only a handful of defense contractors. "SCI" stands for Sensitive Compartmented Information, data classified higher than Top Secret. "SI" is Special Intelligence, very secret communications intercepted by the National Security Agency. "TK" refers to Talent/Keyhole, code names for imagery from reconnaissance aircraft and spy satellites. "G" stands for Gamma (communications intercepts from extremely sensitive sources) and "HCS" means Humint Control System (information from a very sensitive human source). Taken together, the acronyms indicate that Rendon enjoys access to the most secret information from all three forms of intelligence collection: eavesdropping, imaging satellites and human spies.

Rendon lives in a multimillion-dollar home in Washington's exclusive Kalorama neighborhood. A few doors down from Rendon is the home of former defense secretary Robert S. McNamara; just around the corner lives current defense secretary Donald Rumsfeld. At fifty-six, Rendon wears owlish glasses and combs his thick mane of silver-gray hair to the side, Kennedy-style. He heads to work each morning clad in a custom-made shirt with his monogram on the right cuff and a sharply tailored blue blazer that hangs loose around his bulky frame. By the time he pulls up to the Rendon Group's headquarters near Dupont Circle, he has already racked up a handsome fee for the morning's work: according to federal records, Rendon charges the CIA and the Pentagon $311.26 an hour for his services.

Rendon is one of the most influential of the private contractors in Washington who are increasingly taking over jobs long reserved for highly trained CIA employees. In recent years, spies-for-hire have begun to replace regional desk officers, who control clandestine operations around the world; watch officers at the agency's twenty-four-hour crisis center; analysts, who sift through reams of intelligence data; and even counterintelligence officers in the field, who oversee meetings between agents and their recruited spies. According to one senior administration official involved in intelligence-budget decisions, half of the CIA's work is now performed by private contractors—people completely unaccountable to Congress. Another senior budget official acknowledges privately that lawmakers have no idea how many rent-a-spies the CIA currently employs—or how much unchecked power they enjoy.

Unlike many newcomers to the field, however, Rendon is a battle-tested veteran who has been secretly involved in nearly every American shooting conflict in the past two decades. In the first interview he has granted in decades, Rendon offered a peek through the keyhole of this seldom-seen world of corporate spooks—a rarefied but growing profession. Over a dinner of lamb chops and a bottle of Châteauneuf du Pape at a private Washington club, Rendon was guarded about the details of his clandestine work—but he boasted openly of the sweep and importance of his firm's efforts as a for-profit spy. "We've worked in ninety-one countries," he said. "Going all the way back to Panama, we've been involved in every war, with the exception of Somalia."

It is an unusual career twist for someone who entered politics as an opponent of the Vietnam War. The son of a stockbroker, Rendon grew up in New Jersey and stumped for McGovern before graduating from Northeastern University. "I was the youngest state coordinator," he recalls. "I had Maine. They told me that I understood politics—which was a stretch, being so young." Rendon, who went on to serve as executive director of the Democratic National Committee, quickly mastered the combination of political skullduggery and media manipulation that would become his hallmark. In 1980, as the manager of Jimmy Carter's troops at the national convention in New York, he was sitting alone in the bleachers at Madison Square Garden when a reporter for ABC News approached him. "They actually did a little piece about the man behind the curtain," Rendon says. "A Wizard of Oz thing." It was a role he would end up playing for the rest of his life.

After Carter lost the election and the hard-right Reagan revolutionaries came to power in 1981, Rendon went into business with his younger brother Rick. "Everybody started consulting," he recalls. "We started consulting." They helped elect John Kerry to the Senate in 1984 and worked for the AFL-CIO to mobilize the union vote for Walter Mondale's presidential campaign. Among the items Rendon produced was a training manual for union organizers to operate as political activists on behalf of Mondale. To keep the operation quiet, Rendon stamped CONFIDENTIAL on the cover of each of the blue plastic notebooks. It was a penchant for secrecy that would soon pervade all of his consulting deals.

To a large degree, the Rendon Group is a family affair. Rendon's wife, Sandra Libby, handles the books as chief financial officer and "senior communications strategist." Rendon's brother Rick serves as senior partner and runs the company's Boston office, producing public-service announcements for the Whale Conservation Institute and coordinating Empower Peace, a campaign that brings young people in the Middle East in contact with American kids through video-conferencing technology. But the bulk of the company's business is decidedly less liberal and peace oriented. Rendon's first experience in the intelligence world, in fact, came courtesy of the Republicans. "Panama," he says, "brought us into the national-security environment."

In 1989, shortly after his election, President George H. W. Bush signed a highly secret "finding" authorizing the CIA to funnel $10 million to opposition forces in Panama to overthrow Gen. Manuel Noriega. Reluctant to involve agency personnel directly, the CIA turned to the Rendon Group. Rendon's job was to work behind the scenes, using a variety of campaign and psychological techniques to put the CIA's choice, Guillermo Endara, into the presidential palace. Cash from the agency, laundered through various bank accounts and front organizations, would end up in Endara's hands, who would then pay Rendon.

A heavyset, fifty-three-year-old corporate attorney with little political experience, Endara was running against Noriega's hand-picked choice, Carlos Duque. With Rendon's help, Endara beat Duque decisively at the polls—but Noriega simply named himself "Maximum Leader" and declared the election null and void. The Bush administration then decided to remove Noriega by force—and Rendon's job shifted from generating local support for a national election to building international support for regime change. Within days he had found the ultimate propaganda tool.

At the end of a rally in support of Endara, a band of Noriega's Dignity Battalion—nicknamed "Dig Bats" and called "Doberman thugs" by Bush—attacked the crowd with wooden planks, metal pipes, and guns. Gang members grabbed the bodyguard of Guillermo Ford, one of Endara's vice-presidential candidates, pushed him against a car, shoved a gun in his mouth and pulled the trigger. With cameras snapping, the Dig Bats turned on Ford, batting his head with a spike-tipped metal rod and pounding him with heavy clubs, turning his white guayabera bright red with blood—his own, and that of his dead bodyguard.

Within hours, Rendon made sure the photos reached every newsroom in the world. The next week an image of the violence made the cover of *Time* magazine with the caption POLITICS PANAMA STYLE: NORIEGA BLUDGEONS HIS OPPOSITION, AND THE U.S. TURNS UP THE HEAT. To further boost international support for Endara, Rendon escorted Ford on a tour of Europe to meet British prime minister Margaret Thatcher, the Italian prime minister, and even the pope. In December 1989, when Bush decided to invade Panama, Rendon and several of his employees were on one of the first military jets headed to Panama City.

"I arrived fifteen minutes before it started," Rendon recalls. "My first impression is having the pilot in the plane turn around and say, 'Excuse me, sir, but if you look off to the left you'll see the attack aircraft circling before they land.' Then I remember this major saying, 'Excuse me, sir, but do you know what the air-defense capability of Panama is at the moment?' I leaned into the cockpit and said, 'Look, major, I hope by now that's no longer an issue.'"

Moments later, Rendon's plane landed at Howard Air Force Base in Panama. "I needed to get to Fort Clayton, which was where the president was," he says. "I was choppered over—and we took some rounds on the way." There, on a U.S. military base surrounded by 24,000 U.S. troops, heavy tanks, and Combat Talon AC-130 gunships, Rendon's client, Endara, was at last sworn in as president of Panama.

•   •   •

Rendon's involvement in the campaign to oust Saddam Hussein began seven months later, in July 1990. Rendon had taken time out for a vacation—a long train ride across Scotland—when he received an urgent call. "Soldiers are massing at the border outside of Kuwait," he was told. At the airport, he watched the beginning of the Iraqi invasion on television. Winging toward Washington in the first-class cabin of a Pan Am 747, Rendon spent the entire flight scratching an outline of his ideas in longhand on a yellow legal pad.

"I wrote a memo about what the Kuwaitis were going to face, and I based it on our experience in Panama and the experience of the Free French operation in World War II," Rendon says. "This was something that they needed to see and hear, and that was my whole intent. Go over, tell the Kuwaitis, 'Here's what you've got—here's some observations, here's some recommendations, live long and prosper.'"

Back in Washington, Rendon immediately called Hamilton Jordan, the former chief of staff to President Carter and an old friend from his Democratic Party days. "He put me in touch with the Saudis, the Saudis put me in touch with the Kuwaitis, and then I went over and had a meeting with the Kuwaitis," Rendon recalls. "And by the time I landed back in the United States, I got a phone call saying, 'Can you come back? We want you to do what's in the memo.'"

What the Kuwaitis wanted was help in selling a war of liberation to the American government—and the American public. Rendon proposed a massive "perception management" campaign designed to convince the world of the need to join forces to rescue Kuwait. Working through an organization called Citizens for a Free Kuwait, the Kuwaiti government in exile agreed to pay Rendon $100,000 a month for his assistance.

To coordinate the operation, Rendon opened an office in London. Once the Gulf War began, he remained extremely busy trying to prevent the American press from reporting on the dark side of the Kuwaiti government, an autocratic oil-tocracy ruled by a family of wealthy sheiks. When newspapers began reporting that many Kuwaitis were actually living it up in nightclubs in Cairo as Americans were dying in the Kuwaiti sand, the Rendon Group quickly counterattacked. Almost instantly, a wave of articles began appearing telling the story of grateful Kuwaitis mailing 20,000 personally signed valentines to American troops on the front lines, all arranged by Rendon.

Rendon also set up an elaborate television and radio network, and developed programming that was beamed into Kuwait from Taif, Saudi Arabia. "It was important that the Kuwaitis in occupied Kuwait understood that the rest of the world was doing something," he says. Each night, Rendon's troops in London produced a script and sent it via microwave to Taif, ensuring that the "news" beamed into Kuwait reflected a sufficiently pro-American line.

When it comes to staging a war, few things are left to chance. After Iraq withdrew from Kuwait, it was Rendon's responsibility to make the victory march look like the flag-waving liberation of France after World War II. "Did you ever stop to wonder," he later remarked, "how the people of Kuwait City, after being held hostage for seven long and painful months, were able to get hand-held American—and, for that matter, the flags of other coalition countries?" After a pause, he added, "Well, you now know the answer. That was one of my jobs then."

•　　•　　•

Although his work is highly secret, Rendon insists he deals only in "timely, truthful and accurate information." His job, he says, is to counter false perceptions that the news media perpetuate because they consider it "more important to be first than to be right." In modern warfare, he believes, the outcome depends largely on the public's perception of the war—whether it is winnable, whether it is worth the cost. "We are being haunted and stalked by the difference between perception and reality," he says. "Because the lines are divergent, this difference between perception and reality is one of the greatest strategic communications challenges of war."

By the time the Gulf War came to a close in 1991, the Rendon Group was firmly established as Washington's leading salesman for regime change. But Rendon's new assignment went beyond simply manipulating the media. After the war ended, the Top Secret order signed by President Bush to oust Hussein included a rare "lethal finding"—meaning deadly action could be taken if necessary. Under contract to the CIA, Rendon was charged with helping to create a dissident force with the avowed purpose of violently overthrowing the entire Iraqi government. It is an undertaking that Rendon still considers too classified to discuss. "That's where we're wandering into places I'm not going to talk about," he says. "If you take an oath, it should mean something."

Thomas Twetten, the CIA's former deputy of operations, credits Rendon with virtually creating the INC. "The INC was clueless," he once observed. "They needed a lot of help and didn't know where to start. That is why Rendon was brought in." Acting as the group's senior adviser and aided by truckloads of CIA dollars, Rendon pulled together a wide spectrum of Iraqi dissidents and sponsored a conference in Vienna to organize them into an umbrella organization, which he dubbed the Iraqi National Congress. Then, as in Panama, his assignment was to help oust a brutal dictator and replace him with someone chosen by the CIA. "The reason they got the contract was because of what they had done in Panama—so they were known," recalls Whitley Bruner, former chief of the CIA's station in Baghdad. This time the target was Iraqi president Saddam Hussein and the agency's successor of choice was Ahmad Chalabi, a crafty, avuncular Iraqi exile beloved by Washington's neoconservatives.

Chalabi was a curious choice to lead a rebellion. In 1992, he was convicted in Jordan of making false statements and embezzling $230 million from his own bank, for which he was sentenced in absentia to twenty-two years of hard labor. But the only credential that mattered was his politics. "From day one," Rendon says, "Chalabi was very clear that his biggest interest was to rid Iraq of Saddam." Bruner, who dealt with Chalabi and Rendon in London in 1991, puts it even more bluntly. "Chalabi's primary focus," he said later, "was to drag us into a war."

The key element of Rendon's INC operation was a worldwide media blitz designed to turn Hussein, a once dangerous but now contained regional leader, into the greatest threat to world peace. Each month, $326,000 was passed from the CIA to the Rendon Group and the INC via various front organizations. Rendon profited handsomely, receiving a "management fee" of ten percent above what it spent on the project. According to some reports, the company made nearly $100 million on the contract during the five years following the Gulf War.

Rendon made considerable headway with the INC, but following the group's failed coup attempt against Saddam in 1996, the CIA lost confidence in Chalabi and cut off his monthly paycheck. But Chalabi and Rendon simply switched sides, moving over to the Pentagon, and the money continued to flow. "The Rendon Group is not in great odor in Langley these days," notes Bruner. "Their contracts are much more with the Defense Department."

Rendon's influence rose considerably in Washington after the terrorist attacks of September 11. In a single stroke, Osama bin Laden altered the world's perception of reality—and in an age of nonstop information, whoever controls perception wins. What Bush needed to fight the War on Terror was a skilled information warrior—and Rendon was widely acknowledged as the best. "The events of 11 September 2001 changed everything, not least of which was the administration's outlook concerning strategic influence," notes one Army report. "Faced with direct evidence that many people around the world actively hated the United States, Bush began taking action to more effectively explain U.S. policy overseas. Initially the White House and DoD turned to the Rendon Group."

Three weeks after the September 11 attacks, according to documents obtained from defense sources, the Pentagon awarded a large contract to the Rendon Group. Around the same time, Pentagon officials also set up a highly secret organization called the Office of Strategic Influence. Part of the OSI's mission was to conduct covert disinformation and deception operations—planting false news items in the media and hiding their origins. "It's sometimes valuable from a military standpoint to be able to engage in deception with respect to future anticipated plans," Vice President Dick Cheney said in explaining the operation. Even the military's top brass found the clandestine unit unnerving. "When I get their briefings, it's scary," a senior official said at the time.

In February 2002, the *New York Times* reported that the Pentagon had hired Rendon "to help the new office," a charge Rendon denies. "We had nothing to do with that," he says. "We were not in their reporting chain. We were reporting directly to the J-3"—the head of operations at the Joint Chiefs of Staff. Following the leak, Rumsfeld was forced to shut down the organization. But much of the office's operations were apparently shifted to another unit, deeper in the Pentagon's bureaucracy, called the Information Operations Task Force, and Rendon was closely connected to this group. "Greg Newbold was the J-3 at the time, and we reported to him through the IOTF," Rendon says.

According to the Pentagon documents, the Rendon Group played a major role in the IOTF. The company was charged with creating an "Information War Room" to monitor worldwide news reports at lightning speed and respond almost instantly with counterpropaganda. A key weapon, according to the documents, was Rendon's "proprietary state-of-the-art news-wire collection system called 'Livewire,' which takes real-time news-wire reports, as they are filed, before they are on the Internet, before CNN can read them on the air and twenty-four hours before they appear in the morning newspapers, and sorts them by keyword. The system provides the most current real-time access to news and information available to private or public organizations."

$\bullet$ $\bullet$ $\bullet$

The top target that the Pentagon assigned to Rendon was the Al-Jazeera television network. The contract called for the Rendon Group to undertake a massive "media mapping" campaign against the news organization, which the Pentagon considered "critical to U.S. objectives in the War on Terrorism." According to the contract, Rendon would provide a "detailed content analysis of the station's daily broadcast . . . [and] identify the biases of specific journalists and potentially obtain an understanding of their allegiances, including the possibility of specific relationships and sponsorships."

The secret targeting of foreign journalists may have had a sinister purpose. Among the missions proposed for the Pentagon's Office of Strategic Influence was one to "coerce" foreign journalists and plant false information overseas. Secret briefing papers also said the office should find ways to "punish" those who convey the "wrong message." One senior officer told CNN that the plan would "formalize government deception, dishonesty and misinformation."

According to the Pentagon documents, Rendon would use his media analysis to conduct a worldwide propaganda campaign, deploying teams of information warriors to allied nations to assist them "in developing and delivering specific messages to the local population, combatants, front-line states, the media and the international community." Among the places Rendon's info-war teams would be sent were Jakarta, Indonesia; Islamabad, Pakistan; Riyadh, Saudi Arabia; Cairo; Ankara, Turkey; and Tashkent, Uzbekistan. The teams would produce and script television news segments "built around themes and story lines supportive of U.S. policy objectives."

Rendon was also charged with engaging in "military deception" online—an activity once assigned to the OSI. The company was contracted to monitor Internet chat rooms in both English and Arabic—and "participate in these chat rooms when/if tasked." Rendon would also create a Web site "with regular news summaries and feature articles. Targeted at the global public, in English and at least four (4) additional languages, this activity also will include an extensive e-mail push operation." These techniques are commonly used to plant a variety of propaganda, including false information.

Still another newly formed propaganda operation in which Rendon played a major part was the Office of Global Communications, which operated out of the White House and was charged with spreading the administration's message on the War in Iraq. Every morning at 9:30, Rendon took part in the White House OGC conference call, where officials would discuss the theme of the day and who would deliver it. The office also worked closely with the White House Iraq Group, whose high-level members, including recently indicted Cheney chief of staff Lewis Libby, were responsible for selling the war to the American public.

Never before in history had such an extensive secret network been established to shape the entire world's perception of a war. "It was not just bad intelligence—it was an orchestrated effort," says Sam Gardner, a retired Air Force colonel who has taught strategy and military operations at the National War College. "It began before the war, was a major effort during the war and continues as post-conflict distortions."

In the first weeks following the September 11 attacks, Rendon operated at a frantic pitch. "In the early stages it was fielding every ground ball that was coming, because nobody was sure if we were ever going to be attacked again," he says. "It was 'What do you know about this, what do you know about that, what else can you get, can you talk to somebody over here?' We functioned twenty-four hours a day. We maintained situational awareness, in military terms, on all things related to terrorism. We were doing 195 newspapers and forty-three countries in fourteen or fifteen languages. If you do this correctly, I can tell you what's on the evening news tonight in a country before it happens. I can give you, as a policymaker, a six-hour break on how you can affect what's going to be on the news. They'll take that in a heartbeat."

The Bush administration took everything Rendon had to offer. Between 2000 and 2004, Pentagon documents show, the Rendon Group received at least thirty-five contracts with the Defense Department, worth a total of $50 million to $100 million.

. . .

The mourners genuflected, made the sign of the cross and took their seats along the hard, shiny pews of Our Lady of Victories Catholic Church. It was April 2, 2003—the start of fall in the small Australian town of Glenelg, an aging beach resort of white Victorian homes and soft, blond sand on Holdback Bay. Rendon had flown halfway around the world to join nearly 600 friends and family who were gathered to say farewell to a local son and amateur football champ, Paul Moran. Three days into the invasion of Iraq, the freelance journalist and Rendon employee had become the first member of the media to be killed in the war—a war he had covertly helped to start.

Moran had lived a double life, filing reports for the Australian Broadcasting Corp. and other news organizations, while at other times operating as a clandestine agent for Rendon, enjoying what his family calls his "James Bond lifestyle." Moran had trained Iraqi opposition forces in photographic espionage, showing them how to covertly document Iraqi military activities, and had produced pro-war announcements for the Pentagon. "He worked for the Rendon Group in London," says his mother, Kathleen. "They just send people all over the world—where there are wars."

Moran was covering the Iraq invasion for ABC, filming at a Kurdish-controlled checkpoint in the city of Sulaymaniyah, when a car driven by a suicide bomber blew up next to him. "I saw the car in a kind of slow-motion disintegrate," recalls Eric Campbell, a correspondent who was filming with Moran. "A soldier handed me a passport, which was charred. That's when I knew Paul was dead."

As the mass ended and Moran's Australian-flag-draped coffin passed by the mourners, Rendon lifted his right arm and saluted. He refused to discuss Moran's role in the company, saying only that "Paul worked for us on a number of projects." But on the long flight back to Washington, across more than a dozen time zones, Rendon outlined his feelings in an e-mail: "The day did begin with dark and ominous clouds much befitting the emotions we all felt—sadness and anger at the senseless violence that claimed our comrade Paul Moran ten short days ago and many decades of emotion ago."

The Rendon Group also organized a memorial service in London, where Moran first went to work for the company in 1990. Held at Home House, a private club in Portman Square where Moran often stayed while visiting the city, the event was set among photographs of Moran in various locations around the Middle East. Zaab Sethna, who organized the al-Haideri media exclusive in Thailand for Moran and Judith Miller, gave a touching tribute to his former colleague. "I think that on both a personal and professional level Paul was deeply admired and loved by the people at the Rendon Group," Sethna later said.

Although Moran was gone, the falsified story about weapons of mass destruction that he and Sethna had broadcast around the world lived on. Seven months earlier, as President Bush was about to argue his case for war before the U.N., the White House had given prominent billing to al-Haideri's fabricated charges. In a report ironically titled "Iraq: Denial and Deception," the administration referred to al-Haideri by name and detailed his allegations—even though the CIA had already determined them to be lies. The report was placed on the White House Web site on September 12, 2002, and remains there today. One version of the report even credits Miller's article for the information.

Miller also continued to promote al-Haideri's tale of Saddam's villainy. In January 2003, more than a year after her first article appeared, Miller again reported that Pentagon "intelligence officials" were telling her that "some of the most valuable information has come from Adnan Ihsan Saeed al-Haideri." His interviews with the Defense Intelligence Agency, Miller added, "ultimately resulted in dozens of highly credible reports on Iraqi weapons-related activity and purchases, officials said."

Finally, in early 2004, more than two years after he made the dramatic allegations to Miller and Moran about Saddam's weapons of mass destruction, al-Haideri was taken back to Iraq by the CIA's Iraq Survey Group. On a wide-ranging trip through Baghdad and other key locations, al-Haideri was given the opportunity to point out exactly where Saddam's stockpiles were hidden, confirming the charges that had helped to start a war.

In the end, he could not identify a single site where illegal weapons were buried.

•　　　•　　　•

As the war in Iraq has spiraled out of control, the Bush administration's covert propaganda campaign has intensified. According to a secret Pentagon report personally approved by Rumsfeld in October 2003 and obtained by *Rolling Stone*, the Strategic Command is authorized to engage in "military deception"—defined as "presenting false information, images or statements." The seventy-four-page document, titled "Information Operations Roadmap," also calls for psychological operations to be launched over radio, television, cell phones and "emerging technologies" such as the Internet. In addition to being classified secret, the road map is also stamped NOFORN, meaning it cannot be shared even with our allies.

As the acknowledged general of such propaganda warfare, Rendon insists that the work he does is for the good of all Americans. "For us, it's a question of patriotism," he says. "It's not a question of politics, and that's an important distinction. I feel very strongly about that personally. If brave men and women are going to be put in harm's way, they deserve support." But in Iraq, American troops and Iraqi civilians were put in harm's way, in large part, by the false information spread by Rendon and the men he trained in information warfare. And given the rapid growth of what is known as the "security-intelligence complex" in Washington, covert perception managers are likely to play an increasingly influential role in the wars of the future.

Indeed, Rendon is already thinking ahead. Last year, he attended a conference on information operations in London, where he offered an assessment on the Pentagon's efforts to manipulate the media. According to those present, Rendon applauded the practice of embedding journalists with American forces. "He said the embedded idea was great," says an Air Force colonel who attended the talk. "It worked as they had found in the test. It was the war version of reality television, and for the most part they did not lose control of the story." But Rendon also cautioned that individual news organizations were often able to "take control of the story," shaping the news before the Pentagon asserted its spin on the day's events.

"We lost control of the context," Rendon warned. "That has to be fixed for the next war."

The Atlantic Monthly

FINALIST—PROFILE WRITING

"Host," by David Foster Wallace, gives readers an every-angle view of conservative talk-radio personality John Ziegler, who broadcasts a stream of humor-laced invective every weeknight. In this wittily blown-out take on the traditional profile, Wallace explores Ziegler's hectic, lonely world and the peculiar cultural moment that has turned one man's cynicism and misery into radio magic.

David Foster Wallace

Host

(1)

Mr. John Ziegler, thirty-seven, late of Louisville's WHAS, is now on the air, "Live and Local," from 10:00 P.M. to 1:00 A.M. every weeknight on southern California's KFI, a 50,000-watt megastation whose hourly ID and Sweeper, designed by the station's

---

FCC regulations require a station ID to be broadcast every hour. This ID comprises a station's call letters, band, and frequency, and the radio market it's licensed to serve. Just about every serious commercial station (which KFI very much is) appends to its ID a Sweeper, which is the little tag line by which the station wishes to be known. KABC, the other giant AM talk station in Los Angeles, deploys the entendrerich "Where America Comes First." KFI's own main Sweeper is "More *Stimulating* Talk Radio," but it's also got secondary Sweepers that it uses to intro the half-hour news, traffic updates at seventeen and forty-six past the hour, and station promos. "Southern California's Newsroom," "The Radio Home of Fox News," and "When You See News Break, Don't Try to Fix It Yourself— Leave That to Professionals" are the big three that KFI's running this spring. The content and sound of all IDs, Sweepers, and promos are the responsibility of the station's Imaging department, apparently so named because they involve KFI's image in the LA market. Imaging is sort of the radio version of branding—the Sweepers let KFI communicate its special personality and 'tude in a compressed way.

> There are also separate, subsidiary tag lines that KFI develops specially for its local programs. The main two it's using for the *John Ziegler Show* so far are "Live and Local" and "Hot, Fresh Talk Served Nightly."

The whisperer turns out to be one Chris Corley, a voiceover actor best known for movie trailers. Corley's C2 productions is based in Fort Myers FL.

Imaging department and featuring a gravelly basso whisper against licks from Ratt's 1984 metal classic "Round and Round," is "KFI AM-640, Los Angeles—More *Stimulating Talk Radio*." This is either the eighth or ninth host job that Mr. Ziegler's had in his talk-radio career, and far and away the biggest. He moved out here to LA over Christmas—alone, towing a U-Haul—and found an apartment not far from KFI's studios, which are in an old part of the Koreatown district, near Wilshire Center.

The *John Ziegler Show* is the first local, nonsyndicated late-night program that KFI has aired in a long time. It's something of a gamble for everyone involved. Ten o'clock to one qualifies as late at night in southern California, where hardly anything reputable's open after nine.

It is currently right near the end of the program's second segment on the evening of May 11, 2004, shortly after Nicholas Berg's taped beheading by an al-Qaeda splinter in Iraq. Dressed, as is his custom, for golf, and wearing a white-billed cap w/ corporate logo, Mr. Ziegler is seated by himself in the on-air studio, surrounded by monitors and sheaves of Internet downloads. He

(By the standards of the U.S. radio industry this makes him almost movie-star gorgeous.)

is trim, clean-shaven, and handsome in the somewhat bland way that top golfers and local TV newsmen tend to be. His eyes, which off-air are usually flat and unhappy, are alight now with passionate conviction. Only some of the studio's monitors concern Mr. Z.'s own program; the ones up near the ceiling take muted, closed-caption feeds from Fox News, MSNBC, and what might be C-SPAN. To his big desk's upper left is a wall-mounted digital clock that counts down seconds. His computer monitors' displays also show the exact time.

Across the soundproof glass of the opposite wall, another monitor in the Airmix room is running an episode of *The Simpsons*, also muted, which both the board op and the call screener are watching with half an eye.

Pendent in front of John Ziegler's face, attached to the same type of hinged, flexible stand as certain student desk lamps, is a Shure-brand broadcast microphone that is sheathed in a gray foam filtration sock to soften popped p's and hissed sibilants. It is into this microphone that the host speaks:

"And I'll tell you why—it's because we're *better* than they are."

A Georgetown B.A. in government and philosophy, scratch golfer, former TV sportscaster, possible world-class authority on the O.J. Simpson trial, and sometime contributor to MSNBC's *Scarborough Country*, Mr. Ziegler is referring here to America versus what he terms "the Arab world." It's near the end of his "churn," which is the industry term for a host's opening monologue, whose purpose is both to introduce a show's nightly topics and to get listeners emotionally stimulated enough that they're drawn into the program and don't switch away. More than any other mass medium, radio enjoys a captive audience—if only because so many of the listeners are driving—but in a major market there are dozens of AM stations to listen to, plus of course FM and satellite radio, and even a very seductive and successful station rarely gets more than a five or six percent audience share.

"We're not perfect, we suck a lot of the time, but we are *better* as a people, as a culture, and as a society than they are, and we need to recognize that, so that we can possibly even *begin* to deal with the evil that we are facing."

When Mr. Z.'s impassioned, his voice rises and his arms wave around (which obviously only those in the Airmix room can see). He also fidgets, bobs slightly up and down in his executive desk chair, and weaves. Although he must stay seated and can't pace around the room, the host does not have to keep his mouth any set distance from the microphone, since the board op, 'Mondo Hernandez, can adjust his levels on the mixing board's channel 7 so that Mr. Z.'s volume always stays in range and never peaks or fades. 'Mondo, whose price for letting outside parties hang around Airmix is one large bag of cool-ranch Doritos per evening, is an immense twenty-one-year-old man with a ponytail, stony Meso-

'Mondo's lay explanation of what peaking is consists of pointing at the red area to the right of the two volumeters' bobbing needles on the mixing board: "It's when the needles go into the red." The overall mission, apparently, is to keep the volume and resonance of a host's voice high enough to be stimulating but not so high that they exceed the capacities of an AM analog signal or basic radio receiver. One reason why callers' voices sound so much less rich and authoritative than hosts' voices on talk radio is that it is harder to keep telephone voices from peaking.

Another reason is mike processing, which evens and fills out the host's voice, removing raspy or metallic tones, and occurs automatically in Airmix. There's no such processing for the callers' voices.

american features, and the placid, grandmotherly eyes common to giant mammals everywhere. Keeping the studio signal from peaking is one of 'Mondo's prime directives, along with making sure that each of the program's scheduled commercial spots is loaded into Prophet and run at just the right time, whereupon he must confirm that the ad has run as scheduled in the special Airmix log he signs each page of, so that the station can bill advertisers for their spots. 'Mondo, who started out two years ago as an unpaid intern and now earns ten dollars an hour, works 7:00–1:00 on weeknights and also board-ops KFI's special cooking show on Sundays. As long as he's kept under forty hours a week, which he somehow always just barely is, the station is not obliged to provide 'Mondo with employee benefits.

Prophet is the special OS for KFI's computer system—"like Windows for a radio station," according to Mr. Ziegler's producer.

The Nick Berg beheading and its Internet video compose what is known around KFI as a "Monster," meaning a story that has both high news value and tremendous emotional voltage. As is SOP in political talk radio, the emotions most readily accessed are anger, outrage, indignation, fear, despair, disgust, contempt, and a certain kind of apocalyptic glee, all of which the Nick Berg

Here is a sample bit of "What the *John Ziegler Show* is All About," a long editorial intro to the program that Mr. Ziegler delivered snippets of over his first several nights in January:

The underlying premise of the *John Ziegler Show* is that, thanks to its socialistic leanings, incompetent media, eroding moral foundation, aging demographics, and undereducated masses, the United States, as we know it, is doomed. In my view, we don't know how much longer we still have to enjoy it, so we shouldn't waste precious moments constantly worrying or complaining about it. However, because not everyone in this country is yet convinced of this seemingly obvious reality, the show does see merit in pointing out or documenting the demise of our nation and will take great pains to do so. And because most everyone can agree that there is value in attempting to delay the sinking of the *Titanic* as long as possible, whenever feasible the *John Ziegler Show* will attempt to do its part to plug whatever holes in the ship it can. With that said, the show realizes that, no matter how successful it (or anyone else) may be in slowing the downfall of our society, the final outcome is still pretty much inevitable, so we might as well have a good time watching the place fall to pieces.

Be advised that the intro's stilted, term-paperish language, which looks kind of awful in print, is a great deal more effective when the spiel is delivered out loud—the stiffness gives it a slight air of self-mockery that keeps you from being totally sure just how seriously John Ziegler takes what he's saying. Meaning he gets to have it both ways. This half-pretend pretension, which is ingenious in all sorts of ways, was pioneered in talk radio by Rush Limbaugh, although with Limbaugh the semi–self-mockery is more tonal than syntactic.

thing's got in spades. Mr. Ziegler, whose program is in only its fourth month at KFI, has been fortunate in that 2004 has already been chock-full of Monsters—Saddam's detention, the Abu Ghraib scandal, the Scott Peterson murder trial, the Greg Haidl gang-rape trial, and preliminary hearings in the rape trial of Kobe Bryant. But tonight is the most angry, indignant, disgusted, and impassioned that Mr. Z.'s gotten on-air so far, and the consensus in Airmix is that it's resulting in some absolutely first-rate talk radio.

John Ziegler, who is a talk-radio host of unflagging industry, broad general knowledge, mordant wit, and extreme conviction, makes a particular specialty of media criticism. One object of his disgust and contempt in the churn so far has been the U.S. networks' spineless, patronizing decision not to air the Berg videotape and thus to deny Americans "a true and accurate view of the barbarity, the utter *depravity*, of these people." Even more outrageous, to Mr. Z., is the mainstream media's lack of outrage about Berg's taped murder versus all that same media's hand-wringing and invective over the recent photos of alleged prisoner abuse at Abu Ghraib prison, which he views as a clear indication of the deluded, blame-America-first mentality of the U.S. press. It is an associated contrast between Americans' mortified response to the Abu Ghraib photos and reports of the Arab world's phlegmatic reaction to the Berg video that leads to his churn's climax, which is that we are plainly, unambiguously better than the Arab world—whereupon John Ziegler invites listeners to respond if they are so moved, repeats the special mnemonic KFI call-in number, and breaks for the :30 news and ads, on time to the second, as 'Mondo takes ISDN feed from Airwatch and the program's associate producer and call screener, Vince Nicholas—twenty-six and hiply bald—pushes back from his console and raises both arms in congratulation, through the glass.

> ISDN, in which the D stands for "Digital," is basically a phone line of very high quality and expense. ISDN is the main way that stations take feed for syndicated programs from companies like Infinity Broadcasting, premiere Radio Networks, etc. KFI has its own News department and traffic reporters, but on nights and weekends it subscribes to an independent service called Airwatch that provides off-hour news and traffic for stations in the LA area. When, at :17 and :46 every hour, Mr. Z. intros a report from "Alan La-Green in the KFI Traffic Center," it's really Alan LaGreen of Airwatch, who's doing ISDN traffic reports for different stations at different times all hour and has to be very careful to give the right call letters for the Traffic Center he's supposedly reporting from.

·　　·　　·

It goes without saying that there are all different kinds of stimulation. Depending on one's politics, sensitivities, and tastes in argumentation, it is not hard to think of objections to John Ziegler's climactic claim, or at least of some urgent requests for clarification. Like: Exactly what and whom does "the Arab world" refer to? And why are a few editorials and man-on-the-street interviews sufficient to represent the attitude and character of a whole diverse region? And why is al-Jazeera's showing of the Berg video so awful if Mr. Z. has just castigated the U.S. networks for *not* showing it? Plus, of course, what is "better" supposed to mean here? More moral? More diffident about our immorality? Is it not, in our own history, pretty easy to name some Berg-level atrocities committed by U.S. nationals, or agencies, or even governments, and approved by much of our populace? Or perhaps this: Leaving aside whether John Ziegler's assertions are true or coherent, is it even remotely helpful or productive to make huge, sweeping claims about some other region's/culture's inferiority to us? What possible effect can such remarks have except to incite hatred? Aren't they sort of irresponsible?

It is true that no one on either side of the studio's thick window expresses or even alludes to any of these objections. But this is not because Mr. Z.'s support staff is stupid, or hateful, or even necessarily on board with sweeping jingoistic claims. It is because they understand the particular codes and imperatives of large-market talk radio. The fact of the matter is that it is not John Ziegler's job to be responsible, or nuanced, or to think about whether his on-air comments are productive or dangerous, or cogent, or even defensible. That is not to say that the host would not defend his "we're better"—strenuously—or that he does not believe it's true. It is to say that he has exactly one on-air job, and that is to be stimulating. An obvious point, but it's one that's

KFI management's explanation of "stimulating" is apposite, if a bit slippery. Following is an excerpted transcript of a May 25 Q & A with Ms. Robin Bertolucci, the station's intelligent, highly successful, and sort of hypnotically intimidating Program Director. (The haphazard start is because the interviewing skills behind the Q parts are marginal; the excerpt gets more interesting as it goes along.)

Q: Is there some compact way to describe KFI's programming philosophy?

A: "What we call ourselves is 'More Stimulating Talk Radio.' "

Q: Pretty much got that part already.

A: "That is the slogan that we try to express every minute on the air. Of being stimulating. Being informative, being entertaining, being energetic, being dynamic ... The way we do it is a marriage of information and stimulating entertainment."

> Q: What exactly is it that makes informa-
> tion entertaining?
> A: "It's attitudinal, it's emotional."
> Q: Can you explain this attitudinal com-
> ponent?
> A: "I think 'stimulating' really sums it up.
> It's what we really try to do."
> Q: [strangled frustration noises]
> A: "Look, our station logo is in orange
> and black, and white—it's a stark, ag-
> gressive look. I think that typifies it.
> The attitude. A little in-your-face.
> We're not . . . stodgy."

> See, e.g., Mr. John Kobylt, of KFI's top-rated af-
> ternoon *John & Ken Show*, in a recent *LA Times*
> profile: "The truth is, we do everything for rat-
> ings. Yes, that's our job. I can show you the
> contract . . . This is not *Meet the Press*. It's not
> *The Jim Lehrer News Hour*."

> Or you could call it atavistic, a throwback. The
> truth is that what we think of as objectivity in
> journalism has been a standard since only the
> 1900s, and mainly in the United States. Have a
> look at some European dailies sometime.

often overlooked by people who complain about propaganda, misinformation, and irresponsibility in commercial talk radio. Whatever else they are, the above-type objections to "We're better than the Arab world" are calls to accountability. They are the sort of criticisms one might make of, say, a journalist, someone whose job description includes being responsible about what he says in public. And KFI's John Ziegler is not a journalist—he is an entertainer. Or maybe it's better to say that he is part of a peculiar, modern, and very popular type of news industry, one that manages to enjoy the authority and influence of journalism without the stodgy constraints of fairness, objectivity, and responsibility that make trying to tell the truth such a drag for everyone involved. It is a frightening industry, though not for any of the simple reasons most critics give.

·   ·   ·

> KFI has large billboards at
> traffic nodes all over metro
> Los Angeles with the same
> general look and feel, al-

Distributed over two walls of KFI's broadcast studio, behind the monitors and clocks, are a dozen promotional KFI posters, all in the station's eye-catching Halloween colors against the Sweeper's bright white. On each poster, the word "stimulating" is both italicized and underscored. Except for the door and sound-proof window, the entire studio is lined in acoustic tile with strange Pollockian patterns of tiny holes. Much of the tile is grayed and decaying, and the carpet's no color at all; KFI has been in this facility for nearly thirty years

though the billboards often carry both the Sweeper and extra tag phrases—"Raving Infomaniacs," "The Death of Ignorance," "The Straight Poop," and (against a military-camouflage background) "Intelligence Briefings."

and will soon be moving out. Both the studio and Airmix are kept chilly because of all the electronics. The overhead lights are old inset fluorescents, the kind with the slight flutter to them; nothing casts any sort of shadow. On one of the studio walls is also pinned the special set of playing cards distributed for the invasion of Iraq, these with hand-drawn Xs over the faces of those Baathists captured or killed so far. The great L-shaped table that Mr. Z. sits at nearly fills the lit-

The Airmix room's analogue to the cards is a bumper sticker next to the producer's station: WHO WOULD THE FRENCH VOTE FOR?— AMERICANS FOR BUSH

tle room; it's got so many coats of brown paint on it that the table-top looks slightly humped. At the L's base is another Shure microphone, used by Ken Chiampou of 3:00–7:00's *John & Ken*, its hinged stand now partly folded up so that the mike hangs like a wilted flower. The oddest thing about the studio is a strong scent of decaying bananas, as if many peels or even whole bananas were rotting in the room's wastebaskets, none of which look to have been emptied anytime recently. Mr. Ziegler, who has his ascetic side, drinks only bottled water in the studio, and certainly never snacks, so there is no way he is the source of the banana smell.

(He never leaves his chair during breaks, for example, not even to use the restroom.)

•   •   •

It is worth considering the strange media landscape in which political talk radio is a salient. Never before have there been so many different national news sources—different now in terms of both medium and ideology. Major newspapers from anywhere are available online; there are the broadcast networks plus public TV, cable's CNN, Fox News, CNBC, et al., print and Web magazines, Internet bulletin boards, *The Daily Show*, e-mail newsletters, blogs. All this is well known; it's part of the Media Environment we live in. But there are prices and ironies here. One is that the increasing control of U.S. mass media by a mere handful of corporations has—rather counterintuitively—created a situation of extreme fragmentation, a kaleidoscope of information options. Another is that the ever increasing number of ideological news outlets creates precisely the kind of relativism that cultural conservatives decry, a kind of epistemic free-for-all in which "the truth" is wholly a matter of perspective and agenda. In some respects all this variety is probably good, productive of difference and dialogue and so on. But it can also be confusing and stressful for the average citizen. Short of signing on to a particular mass ideology and patronizing only those partisan news sources that ratify what you want to believe, it is increasingly hard to determine which sources to pay attention to and how exactly to distinguish real information from spin.

EDITORIAL ASIDE It's hard to understand Fox News tags like "Fair and Balanced," "No-Spin Zone," and "We Report, You Decide" as anything but dark jokes, ones that delight the channel's conservative audience precisely because their claims to objectivity so totally enrage liberals, whose own literal interpretation of the tag lines makes the left seem dim, humorless, and stodgy.

EDITORIAL ASIDE Of course, this is assuming one believes that information and spin are different things—and one of the dangers of partisan news's metastasis is the way it enables the conviction that the two aren't really distinct at all. Such a conviction, if it becomes endemic, alters democratic discourse from a "battle of ideas" to a battle of sales pitches for ideas (assuming, again, that one chooses to distinguish ideas from pitches, or actual guilt/innocence from lawyers' arguments, or binding commitments from the mere words "I promise," and so on and so forth).

This fragmentation and confusion have helped give rise to what's variously called the "meta-media" or "explaining industry." Under most classifications, this category includes media critics for news dailies, certain high-end magazines, panel shows like CNN's *Reliable Sources*, media-watch blogs like instapundit.com and talkingpointsmemo.com, and a large percentage of political talk radio. It is no accident that one of the signature lines Mr. Ziegler likes to deliver over his opening bumper music at :06 is ". . . the show where we take a look at the news of the day, we provide you the facts, and then we give you the truth." For this is how much of contemporary political talk radio understands its function: to explore the day's news in a depth and detail that other media do not, and to interpret, analyze, and explain that news.

Which all sounds great, except of course "explaining" the news really means editorializing, infusing the actual events of the day with the host's own opinions. And here is where the real controversy starts, because these opinions are, as just one person's opinions, exempt from strict journalistic standards of truthfulness, probity, etc., and yet they are often delivered by the talk-radio host not as opinions but as revealed truths, truths intentionally ignored or suppressed by a "mainstream press" that's "biased" in favor of liberal interests. This is, at any rate, the rhetorical template for Rush Limbaugh's program, on which most syndicated and large-market political talk radio is modeled, from ABC's Sean Hannity and Talk Radio Network's Laura Ingraham to

> PURELY INFORMATIVE It's true that there are, in some large markets and even syndication, a few political talk-radio hosts who identify as moderate or liberal. The best known of these are probably Ed Schultz, Thom Hartmann, and Doug Stephan. But only a few—and only Stephan has anything close to a national audience. (whose show is really only semi-political) And the tribulations of Franken et al.'s Air America venture are well known. The point is that it is neither inaccurate nor unfair to say that today's political talk radio is, in general, overwhelmingly conservative.

Quick sample intros: Mike Gallagher, a regular Fox News contributor whose program is syndicated by Salem Radio Network, has an upcoming book called *Surrounded by Idiots: Fighting Liberal Lunacy in America*. Neal Boortz, who's carried by Cox Radio Syndication and JRN, bills himself as "High Priest of the Church of the Painful Truth," and his recent ads in trade publications feature the quotation "How can we take airport security seriously until ethnic profiling is not only permitted, but *encouraged*?"

5c. Mr. Z. identifies himself as a Libertarian, though he's not a registered member of the Libertarian party, because he feels they "can't get their act together," which he does not seem to intend as a witticism.

"Spot load" is the industry term for the number of minutes per hour given over to commercials. The point of the main-text sentence is that a certain percentage of the spots that run on KFI from 9:00 to noon are Rush/PRN commercials, and they are the ones who get paid by the advertisers. The exact percentages and distributions of local vs. syndicator's commercials are determined by what's called the "Clock," which is represented by a pie-shaped distribution chart that Ms. Bertolucci has on file but will show only a very quick glimpse of, since the spot-load apportionments for syndicated shows in major markets involve complex negotiations between the station and the syndicator, and KFI regards its syndicated Clocks as proprietary info—it doesn't want other stations to know what deals have been cut with PRN.

G. G. Liddy, Rusty Humphries, Michael Medved, Mike Gallagher, Neal Boortz, Dennis Prager, and, in many respects, Mr. John Ziegler.

KFI AM-640 carries Rush Limbaugh every weekday, 9:00 A.M. to noon, via live ISDN feed from Premiere Radio Networks, which is one of the dozen syndication networks that own talk-radio shows so popular that it's worth it for local stations to air them even though it costs the stations a portion of their spot load. The same goes for Dr. Laura Schlessinger, who's based in southern California and used to broadcast her syndicated show from KFI until the mid-nineties, when Premiere built its own LA facility and was able to offer Schlessinger more-sumptuous digs. Dr. Laura airs M–F from noon to 3:00 on KFI, though her shows are canned and there's no live feed. Besides 7:00–10:00 P.M.'s Phil Hendrie (another KFI host

---

In White Star productions' *History of Talk Radio* video, available at better libraries everywhere, there is footage of Dr. Laura doing her show right here at KFI, although she's at a mike in what's now the Airmix room—which, according to 'Mondo, used to be the studio, with what's now the studio serving as Airmix. (Why they switched rooms is unclear, but transferring all the gear must have been a serious hassle.) In the video, the little gray digital clock propped up counting seconds on Dr. Laura's desk is the same one that now counts seconds on the wall to Mr. Ziegler's upper left in the studio—i.e., it's the very same clock—which not only is strangely thrilling but also further testifies to KFI's thriftiness about capital expenses.

whose show went into national syndication, and who now has his own private dressing room and studio over at Premiere), the only other weekday syndication KFI uses is *Coast to Coast With George Noory*, which covers and analyzes news of the paranormal throughout the wee hours.

.　　　.　　　.

Whatever the social effects of talk radio or the partisan agendas of certain hosts, it is a fallacy that political talk radio is motivated by ideology. It is not. Political talk radio is a business, and it is motivated by revenue. The conservatism that dominates today's AM airwaves does so because it generates high Arbitron ratings, high ad rates, and maximum profits.

Radio has become a more lucrative business than most people know. Throughout most of the past decade, the industry's revenues have increased by more than 10 percent a year. The average cash-flow margin for major radio companies is 40 percent, compared with more like 15 percent for large TV networks; and the mean price paid for a radio station has gone from eight to more than thirteen times cash flow. Some of this extreme profitability, and thus the structure of the industry, is due to the 1996 Telecommunications Act, which allows radio companies to acquire up to eight stations in a given market and to control as much as 35 percent of a market's total ad revenues. The emergence of huge, dominant radio conglomerates like Clear Channel and Infinity is a direct consequence of the '96 Act (which the FCC, aided by the very conservative D.C. Court of Appeals, has lately tried to make even more permissive). And these radio conglomerates enjoy not just substantial economies of scale but almost unprecedented degrees of business integration.

Clear Channel bought KFI—or rather the radio company that owned KFI—sometime around 2000. It's all a little fuzzy, because it appears that Clear Channel actually bought, or absorbed, the radio company that had just bought KFI from another radio company, or something like that.

Example: Clear Channel Communications Inc. now owns KFI AM-640, plus two other AM stations and five FMs in the Los Angeles market. It also owns

It turns out that one of the reasons its old Koreatown studios are such a latrine is that KFI's getting ready to move very soon to a gleaming new complex in Burbank that will house five of Clear Channel's stations and allow them to share a lot of cutting-edge technical equipment and software. Some of the reasons for the consolidation involve AM radio's complex, incremental move from analog to digital broadcast, a move that's a lot more economical if stations can be made to share equipment. The Burbank hub facility will also feature a new and improved mega-Prophet OS that all five stations can use and share files on, which for KFI means convenient real-time access to all sorts of new preloaded bumper music and sound effects and bites.

As the board op, 'Mondo Hernandez is also responsible for downloading and cueing up the sections of popular songs that intro the *John Ziegler Show* and background Mr. Z.'s voice when a new segment starts. Bumper music is, of course, a talk-radio convention: Rush Limbaugh has a franchise on the Pretenders, and Sean Hannity always uses that horrific Martina McBride "Let freedom ring / Let the guilty pay" song. Mr. Z. favors a whole rotating set of classic rock hooks, but his current favorites are Van Halen's "Right Now" and a certain jaunty part of the theme to *Pirates of the Caribbean*, because, according to 'Mondo, "they get John pumped."

N.B. Mr. Z. usually refers to himself as either "Zig" or "the Zigmeister," and has made a determined effort to get everybody at KFI to call him Zig, with only limited success so far.

Premiere Radio Networks. It also owns the Airwatch subscription news/traffic service. And it designs and manufactures Prophet, KFI's operating system, which is state-of-the-art and much too expensive for most independent stations.

(Which means that the negotiations between KFI and PRN over the terms of syndication for Rush, Dr. Laura, et al. are actually negotiations between two parts of the same company, which either helps explain or renders even more mysterious KFI's reticence about detailing the Clocks for its PRN shows.)

All told, Clear Channel currently owns some 1,200 radio stations nationwide, one of which happens to be Louisville, Kentucky's WHAS, the AM talk station from which John Ziegler was fired, amid spectacular gossip and controversy, in August of 2003. Which means that Mr. Ziegler now works in Los Angeles for the same company that just fired him in Louisville, such that his firing now appears—in retrospect, and considering the relative sizes of the Louisville and LA markets—to have been a promotion. All of which turns out to be a strange and revealing story about what a talk-radio host's life is like.

(2)

For obvious reasons, critics of political talk radio concern themselves mainly with the programs' content. Talk station management, on the other hand, tends to think of content as a subset of personality, of how stimulating a given host is. As for the hosts—ask Mr. Ziegler off-air what makes him good at his job, and he'll shrug glumly and say, "I'm not really all that talented. I've got passion, and I work really hard." Taken so for granted that nobody in the busi-

"Passion" is a big word in the industry, and John Ziegler uses the word in connection with himself a lot. It appears to mean roughly the same as what Ms. Bertolucci calls "edginess" or "attitude."

ness seems aware of it is something that an outsider, sitting in Airmix and watching John Ziegler at the microphone, will notice right away. Hosting talk radio is an exotic, high-pressure gig that not many people are fit for, and being truly good at it requires skills so specialized that many of them don't have names.

To appreciate these skills and some of the difficulties involved, you might wish to do an experiment. Try sitting alone in a room with a clock, turning on a tape recorder, and starting to speak into it. Speak about anything you want—with the proviso that your topic, and your opinions on it, must be of interest to some group of strangers who you imagine will be listening to the tape. Naturally, in order to be even minimally interesting, your remarks should be intelligible and their reasoning sequential—a listener will have to be able to follow the logic of what you're saying—which means that you will have to know enough about your topic to organize your statements in a coherent way. (But you cannot do much of this organizing beforehand; it has to occur at the same time you're speaking.) Plus, ideally, what you're saying should be not just comprehensible and interesting but compelling, stimulating, which means that your remarks have to provoke and sustain some kind of emotional reaction in the listeners, which in turn will require you to construct some kind of identifiable persona for yourself—your comments will need to strike the listener as coming from an actual human being, some-

> Part of the answer to why conservative talk radio works so well might be that extreme conservatism provides a neat, clear, univocal template with which to organize one's opinions and responses to the world. The current term of approbation for this kind of template is "moral clarity."

> It is, of course, much less difficult to arouse genuine anger, indignation, and outrage in people than it is real joy, satisfaction, fellow feeling, etc. The latter are fragile and complex, and what excites them varies a great deal from person to person, whereas anger et al. are more primal, universal, and easy to stimulate (as implied by expressions like "He really pushes my buttons").

> This, too: Consider the special intimacy of talk radio. It's usually listened to solo—radio is the most solitary of broadcast media. And half-an-ear background-listening

is much more common with music formats than with talk. This is a human being speaking to you, with a pro-caliber voice, eloquently and with passion, in what feels like a one-to-one; it doesn't take long before you start to feel you know him. Which is

(as the industry is at pains to remind advertisers)

why it's often such a shock when you see a real host, his face—you discover you've had a picture of this person in your head without knowing it, and it's always wrong. This dissonant shock is one reason why Rush and Dr. Laura, even with their huge built-in audiences, did not fare well on TV.

one with a real personality and real feelings about whatever it is you're discussing. And it gets even trickier: You're trying to communicate in real time with someone you cannot see or hear responses from; and though you're communicating in speech, your remarks cannot have any of the fragmentary, repetitive, garbled qualities of real interhuman speech, or speech's ticcy unconscious "umm"s or "you know"s, or false starts or stutters or long pauses while you try to think of how to phrase what you want to say next. You're also, of course, denied the physical inflections that are so much a part of spoken English—the facial expressions, changes in posture, and symphony of little gestures that accompany and buttress real talking. Everything unspoken about you, your topic, and how you feel about it has to be conveyed through pitch, volume, tone, and pacing. The pacing is especially important: it can't be too slow, since that's low-energy and dull, but it can't be too rushed or it will sound like babbling. And so you have somehow to keep all these different imperatives and structures in mind at the same time, while also filling exactly, say, eleven minutes, with no dead air and no going over, such that at 10:46 you have wound things up neatly and are in a position to say, "KFI is the station

The exact-timing thing is actually a little less urgent for a host who's got the resources of Clear Channel behind him. This is because in KFI's Airmix room, nestled third from the bottom in one of the two eight-foot stacks of processing gear to the left of 'Mondo's mixing board, is an Akai DD1000 Magneto Optical Disk Recorder, known less formally as a "Cashbox." What this is is a sound compressor, which exploits the fact that even a live studio program is—because of the FCC-mandated seven-second delay—taped. Here is how 'Mondo, in exchange for certain vending-machine comestibles, explains the Cashbox: "All the shows are supposed to start at six past. But if they put more spots in the log, or say, like, if traffic goes long, now we're all of a sudden starting at seven past or something. The Cashbox can take a twenty-minute segment and turn it into a nineteen." It does this by using computerized sound-processing to eliminate pauses and periodically accelerate Mr. Z.'s delivery just a bit. The trick is that the Cashbox can compress sound so artfully that you don't hear the speed-up, at least not in a nineteen-for-twenty exchange ("You get down to eighteen it's risky, or down around seventeen you can definitely hear it"). So if things are running a little over, 'Mondo has to use the Cashbox—very deftly, via controls that look really complicated— in order to make sure that the Clock's adhered to and Airwatch breaks, promos, and ad spots all run as specified. A gathering suspicion as to why the Akai DD1000 is called the Cashbox occasions a *Q:* Does the station ever press 'Mondo or other board ops to use the Cashbox and compress shows in order to make room for additional ads? *A:* "Not really. What they'll do is just put an extra spot or two in the log, and then I've just got to do the best I can."

with the most frequent traffic reports. Alan LaGreen is in the KFI Traffic Center" (which, to be honest, Mr. Z. sometimes leaves himself only three or even two seconds for and has to say extremely fast, which he can always do without a flub). So then, ready: go.

> The only elocutionary problem Mr. Z. ever exhibits is a habit of confusing the words "censure" and "censor."

It's no joke. See for example the *John Ziegler Show*'s producer, Emiliano Limon, who broke in at KFI as a weekend overnight host before moving across the glass:

"What's amazing is that when you get new people who think that they can do a talk-radio program, you watch them for the first time. By three minutes into it, they have that look on their face like, 'Oh my God, I've got ten minutes left. What am I going to say?' And that's what happened to me a lot. So you end up talking about yourself [which, for complex philosophical reasons, the producer disapproves of], or you end up yammering." Emiliano is a large, very calm and competent man in his mid-thirties who either wears the same black *LA Times* T-shirt every day or owns a whole closetful of them. He was pulled off other duties to help launch KFI's experimental Live and Local evening show, an assignment that obviously involves working closely with Mr. Z., which Emiliano seems to accept as his karmic punishment for being so unflappable and easy to get along with. He laughs more than everyone else at KFI put together.

"I remember one time, I just broke after five minutes, I was just done, and they were going, 'Hey, what are you doing, you have another ten minutes!' And I was like, 'I don't know what else to say!' And that's what happens. For those people who think 'Oh, I could do talk radio,' well, there's more to it. A lot of people can't take it once they get that taste of, you know, 'Geez, I gotta fill all this time *and* sound interesting?'

"Then, as you keep on doing it over the days, there's something that becomes absolutely clear to you. You're not really acting on the radio. It's *you*. If no one really responds and the ratings aren't good, it means they don't like *you*." Which is worth keeping very much in mind.

. . .

An abiding question: Who exactly listens to political talk radio? Arbitron Inc. and some of its satellites can help measure how many are listening for how long and when, and they provide some rough age data and demographic specs. A lot of the rest is guesswork, and Program Directors don't like to talk about it.

From outside, though, one of the best clues to how a radio station understands its audience is spots. Which commercials it runs, and when, indicate how the station is pitching its listeners' tastes and receptivities to sponsors. In how often particular spots

For instance, one has only to listen to *Coast to Coast With George Noory*'s ads for gold as a hedge against hyperinflation, special emergency radios you can hand-crank in case of extended power failure, miracle weight-loss formulas, online dating services,

(ad-wise, a lucrative triad indeed)	etc., to understand that KFI and the syndicator regard this show's audience as basically frightened, credulous, and desperate.

are repeated lie clues to the length of time the station thinks people are listening, how attentive it thinks they are, etc. Specific example: Just from its spot load, we can deduce that KFI trusts its audience to sit still for an extraordinary amount of advertising. An average hour of the *John Ziegler Show* consists of four program segments: :06–:17, :23–:30, :37–:46, and :53–:00, or thirty-four minutes of Mr. Z. actually talking. Since KFI's newscasts are never more than ninety seconds, and since quarterly traffic reports are always bracketed by "live-read" spots for Traffic Center

A live read is when a host or newsperson reads the ad copy himself on-air. They're sort of a radio tradition, but the degree to which KFI weaves live reads into its programming is a great leap forward for broadcast marketing. Live-read spots are more expensive for advertisers, especially the longer, more detailed ones read by the programs' hosts, since these ads (a) can sound at first like an actual talk segment and (b) draw on the personal appeal and credibility of the host. And the spots themselves are often clearly set up to exploit these features—see for instance John Kobylt's live read for LA's Cunning Dental Group during afternoons' *John & Ken*: "Have you noticed how bad the teeth are of all the contestants in these reality shows? I saw some of this the other day. Discolored, chipped, misshaped, misaligned, rotted-out teeth, missing teeth, not to mention the bleeding, oozing, pus-y gums. You go to Cunning Dental

	Group, they will take all your gross teeth and in one
(It's unclear how one spells the adjectival form of "pus," though it sounds okay on-air.)	or two visits fix them and give you a bright shiny smile." Even more expensive than live reads are what's called "endorsements," which are when a host describes, in ecstatically favorable terms, his own personal experience with a product or service. Examples here include Phil Hendrie's weight loss on Cortislim, Kobylt's "better than 20-20" laser-surgery
Handel, whose KFI show is an LA institution in morning drive, describes his program as "in-your-face, informational, with a lot of racial humor."	outcome with Saddleback Eye Center, and Mr. Bill Handel's frustrations with dial-up ISPs before discovering DSL extreme. These ads, which are KFI's most powerful device for exploiting the intimacy and trust of the listener-host relationship, also result in special "endorsement fees" paid directly to the host.

sponsors, that makes each hour at least 40 percent ads; the percentage is higher if you count Sweepers for the station and promos for other KFI shows. And this is the load just on a local program, one for which the Clock doesn't have to be split with a syndicator.

It's not that KFI's unaware of the dangers here. Station management reads its mail, and as Emiliano Limon puts it, "If there's one complaint listeners always have, it's the spot load." But the only important issue is whether all the complaints translate into actual listener behavior. KFI's spot load is an instance of the kind of multivariable maximization problem that M.B.A. programs thrive on. It is obviously in the station's financial interest to carry just as high a volume of ads as it can without hurting ratings—the moment listeners begin turning away from KFI because of too many commercials, the Arbitron numbers go down, the rates charged for ads have to be reduced, and profitability suffers. But anything more specific is, again, guesswork. When asked about management's thinking here, or whether there's any particular formula KFI uses to figure out how high a spot load the market will bear, Ms. Bertolucci will only smile and shrug as if pleasantly stumped: "We have

> It's a little more complicated than that, really, because excessive spots can also affect ratings in less direct ways—mainly by lowering the quality of the programming. Industry analyst Michael Harrison, of *Talkers* magazine, complains that "The commercial breaks are so long today that it is hard for hosts to build upon where they left off. The whole audience could have changed. There is the tendency to go back to the beginning and re–set up the premise. It makes it very difficult to do what long-form programming is supposed to do."

SEMI-EDITORIAL Even in formal, on-record, and very PR-savvy interviews, the language of KFI management is filled with little unconscious bits of jargon—"inventory" for the total number of ad minutes available, "product" for a given program, or (a favorite) "to monetize," which means to extract ad revenue from a given show—that let one know exactly where KFI's priorities lie. Granted, the station is a business, and broadcasting is not charity work. But given how intimate and relationship-driven talk radio is, it's disheartening when management's only term for KFI's listeners, again and again, is "market."

more commercials than we've ever had, and our ratings are the best they've ever been."

How often a particular spot can run over and over before listeners just can't stand it anymore is something else no one will talk about, but the evidence suggests that KFI sees its audience as either very patient and tolerant or almost catatonically inattentive. Canned ads for local sponsors like Robbins Bros. Jewelers, Sit 'n Sleep Mattress, and the Power Auto Group play every couple hours, 24/7, until one knows every hitch and nuance. National saturation campaigns for products like Cortislim vary things somewhat by using both endorsements and canned spots. Pitches for caveat emptor–type nostrums like Avacor (for hair loss), Enzyte ("For natural male enhancement!"), and Altovis ("Helps fight daily fatigue!") often repeat once an hour through the night. As of spring '04, though, the most frequent and concussive ads on KFI are for mortgage and home-

CONSUMER ADVISORY As it happens, these two are products of Berkeley Premium Nutraceuticals, an Ohio company with annual sales of more than $100 million, as well as over 3,000 complaints to the BBB and the Attorney General's Office in its home state alone. Here's why. The radio ads say you can get a thirty-day free trial of Enzyte by calling a certain toll-free number. If you call, it turns out there's a $4.90 S&H charge for the free month's supply, which the lady on the phone wants you to put on your credit card. If you acquiesce, the company then starts shipping you more Enzyte every month and auto-billing your card for at least $35 each time, because it turns out that by taking the thirty-day trial you've somehow signed up for Berkeley's automatic-purchase program—which the operator neglected to mention. And calling Berkeley Nutraceuticals to get the automatic shipments and billings stopped doesn't much help; often they'll stop only if some kind of consumer agency sends a letter. It's

FYI: Enzyte, which bills itself as a natural libido and virility enhancer (it also has all those "Smiling Bob & Grateful Wife" commercials on cable TV), contains tribulis terrestris, panax ginseng, ginko biloba, and a half dozen other innocuous herbal ingredients. The product costs Berkeley, in one pharmacologist's words, "nothing to make." But it's de facto legal to charge hundreds of dollars a year for it, and to advertise it as an OTC Viagra. The FDA doesn't regulate herbal meds unless people are actually falling over from taking them, and the Federal Trade Commission doesn't have anything like the staff to keep up with the advertising claims, so it's all basically an unregulated market.

refi companies—Green Light Financial, HMS Capital, Home Field Financial, Benchmark Lending. Over and over. Pacific Home Financial, U.S. Mortgage Capital, Crestline Funding, Advantix Lending. Reverse mortgages, negative amortization, adjustable rates, APR, FICO . . . where did all these firms come from? What were these guys doing five years ago? Why is KFI's audience seen as so especially ripe and ready for refi? Betterloans.com, lendingtree.com, Union Bank of California, on and on and on.

the same with Altovis and its own "free trial." In short, the whole thing is one of those irksome, hassle-laden marketing schemes, and KFI runs dozens of spots per day for Berkeley products. The degree to which the station is legally responsible for an advertiser's business practices is, by FTC and FCC rules, nil. But it's hard not to see KFI's relationship with Berkeley as another indication of the station's true regard for its listeners.

(Calls to KFI's Sales department re consumers' amply documented problems with Enzyte and Altovis were, as the journalists say, not returned.)

· · ·

Emiliano Limon's "It's *you*" seems true to an extent. But there is also the issue of persona, meaning the on-air personality that a host adopts in order to heighten the sense of a real person behind the mike. It is, after all,

(somewhat paradoxically)

unlikely that Rush Limbaugh always feels as jaunty and confident as he seems on the air, or that Howard Stern really is deeply fascinated by porn starlets every waking minute of the day. But a host's persona is not the same as outright acting. For the most part, it's probably more like the way we are all slightly different with some people than we are with others.

In some cases, though, the personas are more contrived and extreme. In the slot preceding Mr. Z.'s on KFI, for instance, is the *Phil Hendrie Show*, which is actually a cruel and complicated kind of meta–talk radio. What happens every night on this program is that Phil Hendrie brings on some wildly offensive guest—a man who's leaving his wife because she's had a mastectomy, a Little League coach who advocates corporal punishment of players, a retired colonel who claims that females' only proper place in the military is as domestics and concubines for the officers—and first-time or casual listeners will call in and argue with the guests and (not surprisingly) get very angry and upset. Except the whole thing's a put-on. The guests are fake, their different voices done by Hendrie with the aid of mike processing and a first-rate board op, and the show's real entertainment is the callers, who don't know it's all a gag—Hendrie's real audience, which is in on the joke, enjoys hearing these callers get more and more outraged and sputtery as the "guests" yank their chain. It's all a bit like the old *Candid Camera* if the joke perpetrated over and over on that show were convincing somebody that a loved one had just died. So obviously Hendrie—whose show now draws an estimated one million listeners a week—lies on the outer frontier of radio persona.

> (who really is a gifted mimic)

> Apparently, one reason why Hendrie's show was perfect for national syndication was that the wider dissemination gave Hendrie a much larger pool of uninitiated listeners to call in and entertain the initiated listeners.

A big part of John Ziegler's on-air persona, on the other hand, is that he doesn't have one. This may be just a function of all the time he's spent in the abattoir of small-market radio, but in Los Angeles it plays as a canny and sophisticated meta-radio move. Part of his January introduction to himself and his program is "The key to the *John Ziegler Show* is that I am almost completely real. Nearly every show begins with the credo 'This is the show where the host says what he believes and believes what he says.' I do not make up my opinions or exaggerate my stories simply to stir the best debate on that particular broadcast."

Though Mr. Z. won't ever quite say so directly, his explicit I-have-no-persona persona helps to establish a contrast with weekday afternoons' John Kobylt, whose on-air voice is similar to

Ziegler's in pitch and timbre. Kobylt and his sidekick Ken Chiampou have a hugely popular show based around finding stories and causes that will make white, middle-class Californians feel angry and disgusted, and then hammering away at these stories/causes day after day. Their personas are what the *LA Times* calls "brash" and Chiampou himself calls "rabid dogs," which latter KFI has developed into the promo line "The Junkyard Dogs of Talk Radio." What John & Ken really are is professional oiks. Their show is credited with helping jump-start the '03 campaign to recall Governor Gray Davis, although they were equally disgusted by most of the candidates who wanted to replace him (q.v. Kobylt: "If there's anything I don't like more than politicians,

National talk-radio hosts like Limbaugh, Prager, Hendrie, Gallagher, et al. tend to have rich baritone radio voices that rarely peak, whereas today's KFI has opted for a local-host sound that's more like a slightly adenoidal second tenor. The voices of Kobylt, Bill Handel, Ken Chiampou, weekend host Wayne Resnick, and John Ziegler all share not only this tenor pitch but also a certain quality that is hard to describe except as sounding stressed, aggrieved, Type A: the Little Guy Who's Had It Up To Here. Kobylt's voice in particular has a consistently snarling, dyspeptic, fed-up quality—a perfect aural analogue to the way drivers' faces look in jammed traffic— whereas Mr. Ziegler's tends to rise and fall more, often hitting extreme upper registers of outraged disbelief.

Off-air, Mr. Z.'s speaking voice is nearly an octave lower than it sounds on his program, which is a bit mysterious, since 'Mondo denies doing anything special to the on-air voice except setting the default volume on the board's channel 7 a bit low because "John sort of likes to yell a lot." And Mr. Ziegler bristles at the suggestion that he, Kobylt, or Handel has anything like a high voice on the air: "It's just that we're passionate. Rush doesn't get all that passionate. You try being passionate and having a low voice."

(as in if you listen to an upset person say "I can't be*lieve* it!")

CONTAINS EDITORIAL ELEMENTS It should be conceded that there is at least one real and refreshing journalistic advantage that bloggers, fringe-cable newsmen, and most talk-radio hosts have over the mainstream media: they are neither the friends nor the peers of the public officials they cover. Why this is an advantage involves an issue that tends to get obscured by the endless fight over whether there's actually a "liberal bias" in the "elite" mainstream press. Whether one buys the bias thing or not, it is clear that leading media figures are part of a very different social and economic class than most of their audiences. See, e.g., a snippet of Eric Alterman's recent *What Liberal Media?*:

> No longer the working-class heroes of *The Front Page/His Gal Friday* lore, elite journalists in Washington and New York [and LA] are rock-solid members of the political and financial establishment about whom they write. They dine at the same restaurants and take their vacations on the same Caribbean islands . . . What's more, like the politicians, their jobs are not subject to export to China or Bangladesh.

This is why the really potent partisan label for the *NYT/Time/*network–level press is not "liberal media" but "elite media"—because the label's true. And talk radio is very deliberately not part of this elite media. With the exception of Limbaugh and maybe Hannity, these hosts are not stars, or millionaires, or sophisticates. And a large part of their on-air persona is that they are of and for their audience—the Little Guy—and against corrupt, incompetent pols and their "spokesholes," against smooth-talking lawyers and PC whiners and idiot bureaucrats, against illegal aliens clogging our highways and emergency rooms, paroled sex offenders living among us, punitive vehicle taxes, and stupid, self-righteous, agenda-laden laws against public smoking, SUV emissions, gun ownership, the right to watch the Nick Berg decapitation video over and over in slow motion, etc. In other words, the talk host's persona and appeal are deeply, totally populist, and if it's all somewhat fake—if John Kobylt can shift a little too easily from the apoplectic Little Guy of his segments to the smooth corporate shill of his live reads—then that's just life in the big city.

(Except some of your more slippery right-wing commentators use "elit*ist* media," which sounds similar but is really a far more loaded term.)

it's those wormy little nerds who act as campaign handlers and staff . . . We just happened to on our own decide that Davis was a rotting stool that ought to be flushed"). In '02, they organized a parade of SUVs in Sacramento to protest stricter vehicle-emissions laws; this year they spend at least an hour a day attacking various government officials and their spokesholes for failing to enforce immigration laws and trying to bullshit the citizens about it; and so on. But the *John & Ken Show*'s real specialty is gruesome, high-profile California trials, which they often cover on-site, Kobylt eschewing all PC pussyfooting and legal niceties to speak his mind about defendants like 2002's David Westerfield and the current Scott Peterson, both "scumbags that are guilty as sin." The point is that John Kobylt broadcasts in an almost perpetual state of affronted rage; and, as more than one KFI staffer has ventured to observe off the record, it's unlikely that

> Besides legendary stunts like tossing broccoli at "vegetable-head" jurors for taking too long to find Westerfield guilty, Kobylt is maybe best known for shouting, "Come out, Scott! No one believes you! You can't hide!" at a window's silhouette as the *J & K Show* broadcast live from in front of Peterson's house, which scene got re-created in at least one recent TV movie about the Scott & Laci case.

any middle-aged man could really go around this upset all the time and not drop dead. It's a persona, in other words, not exactly fabricated but certainly exaggerated . . . and of course it's also demagoguery of the most classic and unabashed sort.

But it makes for stimulating and profitable talk radio. As of Arbitron's winter '04 Book, KFI AM-640 has become the No. 1 talk station in the country, beating out New York's WABC in both Cume and AQH for the coveted 25–54 audience. KFI also now has the second highest market share of any radio station in Los Angeles, trailing only hip-hop giant KPWR. In just one year, KFI has gone from being the eighteenth to the seventh top-billing station in the country, which is part of why it

> The *John & Ken Show* pulls higher ratings in southern California than the syndicated Rush and Dr. Laura, which is pretty much unheard of.

> These are measurement categories in Arbitron Inc.'s Radio Market Reports, which reports come out four times a year and are known in the industry as "Books." In essence, Cume is the total measure of all listeners, and AQH (for "Average Quarter Hour") represents the mean number of listeners in any given fifteen-minute period.

received the 2003 News/Talk Station of the Year Award from *Radio and Records* magazine. Much of this recent success is attributed to Ms. Robin Bertolucci, the Program Director brought in from Denver shortly after Clear Channel acquired KFI, whom Mr. Z. describes as "a real superstar in the business right now." From all reports, Ms. Bertolucci has done everything from redesigning the station's ID and Sweeper and sound and overall in-your-face vibe to helping established hosts fine-tune their personas and create a distinctively KFI-ish style and 'tude for their shows.

Every Wednesday afternoon, Ms. Bertolucci meets with John Ziegler to review the previous week and chat about how the show's going. The Program Director's large private office is located just off the KFI prep room (where Mr. Z.'s own office is a small computer table with a homemade THIS AREA RESERVED FOR JOHN ZIEGLER taped to it). Ms. B. is soft-spoken, polite, unpretentious, and almost completely devoid of moving parts. Here is her on-record explanation of the Program Director's role w/r/t the *John Ziegler Show*:

"It's John's show. He's flying the airplane, a big 747. What I am, I'm the little person in the control tower. I have a different perspective—"

"I *have* no perspective!" Mr. Z. interrupts, with a loud laugh, from his seat before her desk.

"—which might be of value. Like, 'You may want to pull up because you're heading for a mountain.' " They both laugh. It's an outrageous bit of understatement: nine months ago John Ziegler's career was rubble, and Ms. B. is the only reason he's here, and she's every inch his boss, and he's nervous around her—

(On the other hand, he omits to wear his golf cap in her office, and his hair shows evidence of recent combing.)

which you can tell by the way he puts his long legs out and leans back in his chair with his hands in his slacks' pockets and yawns a lot and tries to look exaggeratedly relaxed.

The use of some esoteric technical slang occasions a brief Q & A on how exactly Arbitron works, while Mr. Z. joggles his sneaker impatiently.

In truth, just about everyone at KFI except Ms. B. refers to Arbitron as "Arbitraryon." This is because it's 100 percent diary-based, and diary surveys are notoriously iffy, since a lot of subjects neglect to fill out their diaries in real time (especially when they're listening as they drive), tending instead to wait till the night before they're

> due and then trying to do them from memory. Plus it's widely held that certain ethnic minorities are chronically mis- or over-represented in metro LA's Books, evidently because Arbitron has a hard time recruiting these minorities as subjects, and when it lands a few it tends to stick with them week after week.

Then they go over the past week. Ms. B. gently chides the new host for not hitting the Greg Haidl trial harder, and for usually discussing the case in his show's second hour instead of the first. Her thrust: "It's a big story for us. It's got sex, it's got police, class issues, kids running amok, video, the courts, and who gets away with what. And it's in Orange County." When Mr. Ziegler (whose off-air method of showing annoyance or frustration is to sort of hang his head way over to one side) protests that both Bill Handel and John & Ken have already covered the story six ways from Sunday every day and there is no way for him to do anything fresh or stimulating with it, Ms. B. nods slowly and responds: "If we were KIIS-FM, and we had a new Christina Aguilera song, and they played it heavy on the morning show and the afternoon show, wouldn't you still play it on the evening show?" At which Mr. Z. sort of lolls his head from side to side several times—"All right. I see your point. All right"—and on tonight's (i.e., May 19's) program he does lead with and spend much of the first hour on the latest Haidl developments.

By way of post-meeting analysis, it is worth noting that a certain assumption behind Ms. B.'s Christina Aguilera analogy—namely, that a criminal trial is every bit as much an entertainment product as a Top 40 song—was not questioned or even blinked at by either participant. This is doubtless one reason for KFI's ratings éclat—the near total conflation of news and entertainment. It also explains

> FOR THOSE OUTSIDE SOUTHERN CA Haidl, the teenage son of an Orange County Asst. Sheriff, is accused, together with some chums, of gang-raping an unconscious girl at a party two or three years ago. Rocket scientists all, the perps had videotaped the whole thing and then managed to lose the tape, which eventually found its way to the police.

why KFI's twice-hourly newscasts (which are always extremely short, and densely interwoven with station promos and live-read ads) concentrate so heavily on lurid, tabloidish stories. Post–Nick Berg, the station's newscasts in May and early June tend to lead with child-molestation charges against local clerics and teachers, revelations in the Peterson and Haidl trials, and developments in the Kobe Bryant and Michael Jackson cases. With respect to Ms. Bertolucci's on-record description of KFI's typical listener—"An information-seeking person that wants to know what's going on in the world and wants to be communicated to in an interesting, entertaining, stimulating sort of way"—it seems fair to observe that KFI provides a peculiar and very selective view of what's going on in the world.

Ms. B.'s description turns out to be loaded in a number of ways. The role of news and information versus personal and persona-driven stuff on the *John Ziegler Show,* for example, is a matter that Mr. Z. and his producer see very differently. Emiliano Limon, who's worked at the station for over a decade and believes he knows its audience, sees "two distinct eras at KFI. The first was the opinion-driven, personal, here's-my-take-on-things era. The second is the era we're in right now, putting the information first." Emiliano refers to polls he's seen indicating that most people in southern California get their news from local TV newscasts and Jay Leno's monologue on the *Tonight* show. "We go on the presumption that the average driver, average listener, isn't reading the news the way we are. We read *everything*." In fact, this voracious news-reading is a big part of Emiliano's job. He is, like most talk-radio producers, a virtuoso on the Internet, and he combs through a daily list of sixty national papers, 'zines, and blogs, and he believes that his and KFI's

[meaning for the station in its current talk format, which started sometime in the eighties. KFI itself has been on the air since 1922—the "FI" actually stands for "Farm Information."]

main function is to provide "a kind of executive news summary" for busy listeners. In a separate Q & A, though, Mr. Ziegler's take on the idea of his show's providing news is wholly different: "We're trying to get away from that, actually. The original thought was that this would be mostly an informational show, and now we're trying to get a little more toward personality" . . . which, since Mr. Z. makes a point of not having a special on-air persona, means more stuff about himself, John Ziegler—his experiences, his résumé, his political and cultural outlook and overall philosophy of life.

(3)

If we're willing to disregard the complicating precedents of Joe Pyne and Alan Burke, then the origins of contemporary political talk radio can be traced to three phenomena of the 1980s. The first of these involved AM music stations' getting absolutely murdered by FM, which could broadcast music in stereo

Again, this sort of claim seems a little tough to reconcile with the actual news that KFI concentrates on, but—as Mr. Z. himself once pointedly observed during a Q & A—interviewing somebody is not the same as arguing with him over every last little thing.

(with whom Emiliano, from all indications, does not enjoy a very chummy or simpatico relationship, although he's always a master of tact and circumspection on the subject of Mr. Z.)

The upshot here is that there's a sort of triangular dissonance about the *John Ziegler Show* and how best to stimulate LA listeners. From all available evidence, Robin Bertolucci wants the program to be mainly info-driven (according to KFI's particular definition of info), but she wants the information heavily editorialized and infused with 'tude and in-your-face energy. Mr. Ziegler interprets this as the P.D.'s endorsing his talking a lot about himself, which Emiliano Limon views as an antiquated, small-market approach that is not going to be very interesting to people in Los Angeles, who tend to get more than their share of colorful personality and idiosyncratic opinion just in the course of their normal day. If Emiliano is right, then Mr. Z. may simply be too old-school and self-involved for KFI, or at least not yet aware of how different the appetites of a New York or LA market are from those of a Louisville or Raleigh.

(famous "confrontational" talk hosts of the sixties)

and allowed for much better fidelity on high and low notes. The human voice, on the other hand, is mid-range and doesn't require high fidelity. The eighties' proliferation of talk formats on the AM band also provided new careers for some music deejays—e.g., Don Imus, Morton Downey Jr.—whose chatty personas didn't fit well with FM's all-about-the-music ethos.

The second big factor was the repeal, late in Ronald Reagan's second term, of what was known as the Fairness Doctrine. This was a 1949 FCC rule designed to minimize any possible restrictions on free speech caused by limited access to broadcasting outlets. The idea was that, as one of the conditions for receiving an FCC broadcast license, a station had to "devote reasonable attention to the coverage of controversial issues of public importance," and consequently had to provide "reasonable, although not necessarily equal" opportunities for opposing sides to express their views. Because of the Fairness Doctrine, talk stations had to hire and program symmetrically: if you had a three-hour program whose host's politics were on one side of the ideological spectrum, you had to have another long-form program whose host more or less spoke for the other side. Weirdly enough, up through the mid-eighties it was usually the U.S. right that benefited most from the Doctrine. Pioneer talk syndicator Ed McLaughlin, who managed San Francisco's KGO in the 1960s, recalls that "I had more liberals on the air than I had conservatives or even moderates for that matter, and I had a hell of a time finding the other voice."

> KGO happens to be the station where Ms. Robin Bertolucci, fresh out of Cal-Berkeley, first broke into talk radio.

The Fairness Doctrine's repeal was part of the sweeping deregulations of the Reagan era, which aimed to liberate all sorts of industries from government interference and allow them to compete freely in the marketplace. The old, Rooseveltian logic of the Doctrine had been that since the airwaves belonged to everyone, a license to profit from those airwaves conferred on the broadcast industry some special obligation to serve the public interest. Commercial radio broadcasting was not, in other words, originally conceived as just another for-profit industry; it was supposed to meet a higher standard of social responsibility. After 1987, though, just another industry is pretty much what radio became, and its only real responsibility now is to attract and retain listeners in order to generate revenue. In other words, the sort of distinction explicitly drawn by FCC Chairman Newton Minow in the 1960s—namely, that between "the public interest" and "merely what interests the public"—no longer exists.

> (except, obviously, for some restrictions on naughty language)

CONTAINS WHAT MIGHT BE PERCEIVED AS EDITORIAL ELEMENTS It seems only fair and balanced to observe, from the imagined perspective of a Neal Boortz or John Ziegler, that Minow's old distinction reflected exactly the sort of controlling, condescending, nanny-state liberal attitude that makes government regulation such a bad idea. For how and why does a federal bureaucrat like Newton Minow get to decide what "the public interest" is? Why not respect the American people enough to let the public itself decide what interests it? Of course, this sort of objection depends on precisely the collapse of "the public interest" into "what happens to interest the public" that liberals object to. For the distinction between these two is *itself* liberal, as is the idea of a free press's and broadcast media's special responsibilities—"liberal" in the sense of being rooted in a concern for the common good over and above the preferences of individual citizens. The point is that the debate over things like the Fairness Doctrine and the proper responsibility of broadcasters quickly hits ideological bedrock on both sides.

DITTO (Which does indeed entail government's arrogating the power to decide what that common good is, it's true. On the other hand, the idea is that at least government officials are elected, or appointed by elected representatives, and thus are somewhat accountable to the public they're deciding for. What appears to drive liberals most crazy about the right's conflation of "common good" / "public interest" with "what wins in the market" is the conviction that it's all a scam, that what the deregulation of industries like broadcasting, health care, and energy really amounts to is the subordination of the public's interests to the financial interests of large corporations. Which is, of course, all part of a very deep, serious national argument about the role and duties of government that America's having with itself right now. It is an argument that's not being plumbed at much depth on political talk radio, though—at least not the more legitimate, non-wacko claims of some on the left [a neglect that then strengthens liberal suspicions that all these conservative talk hosts are just spokesholes for their corporate masters . . . and around and around it all goes].)

The crucial connection with the F.D.'s repeal was not Rush's show but that show's syndicatability. A station could now purchase and air three daily hours of Limbaugh without being committed to programming another three hours of Sierra Club or Urban League or something.

EFM Media, named for Edward F. McLaughlin, was a sort of Old Testament patriarch of modern syndication, although Mr. McL. tended to charge subscribing stations cash instead of splitting the Clock, because he wanted a low spot load that would give Rush maximum air time to build his audience.

More or less on the heels of the Fairness Doctrine's repeal came the West Coast and then national syndication of *The Rush Limbaugh Show* through Mr. McLaughlin's EFM Media. Limbaugh is the third great progenitor of today's political talk radio partly because he's a host of extraordinary, once-in-a-generation talent and charisma—bright, loquacious, witty, complexly authoritative—whose show's blend of news, entertainment, and partisan analysis became the model for legions of imitators. But he was also the first great promulgator of the Mainstream Media's Liberal Bias idea. This turned out to be a brilliantly effective rhetorical move, since the MMLB concept functioned simultaneously as a standard around which Rush's audience could rally, as an articulation of the need for right-wing (i.e., unbiased) media, and as a mechanism by which any criticism or refutation of conservative ideas could be dismissed (either as biased or as the product of indoctrination by biased media). Boiled way down, the MMLB thesis is able both to exploit and to perpetuate many conservatives' dissatisfaction with extant media sources—and it's this dis-

In truth, Rush's disdain for the "liberal press" somewhat recalls good old Spiro Agnew's attacks on the Washington press corps (as in "nattering nabobs," "hopeless, hysterical hypochondriacs," etc.), with the crucial difference being that Agnew's charges always came off as thuggish and pathetic *in that "liberal press,"* which at the time was the only vector for their transmission. Because of his own talent and the popularity of his show, Rush was able to move partisan distrust for the mainstream "liberal media" into the mainstream itself.

satisfaction that cements political talk radio's large and loyal audience.

•   •   •

In the best Rush Limbaugh tradition, Mr. Ziegler takes pride in his on-air sense of humor. His media criticism

> JUST CLEAR-EYED, DISPASSIONATE REASON Notwithstanding all sorts of interesting other explanations, the single biggest reason why left-wing talk-radio experiments like Air America or the Ed Schultz program are not likely to succeed, at least not on a national level, is that their potential audience is just not dissatisfied enough with today's mainstream news sources to feel that it has to patronize a special type of media to get the unbiased truth.

is often laced with wisecracks, and he likes to leaven his show's political and cultural analyses with timely ad-lib gags, such as "It's maybe a good thing that Catholics and Muslims don't tend to marry. If they had a kid, he'd grow up and then, what, abuse some child and then blow him up?" And he has a penchant for comic maxims ("Fifty percent of all marriages are confirmed failures, while the other fifty percent end in divorce"; "The female figure is the greatest known evidence that there might be a God, but the female psyche is an indication that this God has a very sick sense of humor") that he uses on the air and then catalogues as "Zieglerisms" on his KFI Web site.

Mr. Z. can also, when time and the demands of prep permit, go long-form. In his program's final hour for May 22, he delivers a mock commencement address to the Class of 2004, a piece of prepared sit-down comedy that is worth excerpting, verbatim, as a sort of keyhole into the professional psyche of Mr. John Ziegler:

> Class of 2004, congratulations on graduation . . . I wish to let you in on a few secrets that those of you who are not completely brain-dead will eventually figure out on your own, but, if you listen to me, will save a lot of time and frustration. First

> > Again, this is all better, and arguably funnier, when delivered aloud in Mr. Z.'s distinctive way.

of all, most of what you have been taught in your academic career is not true. I am not just talking about the details of history that have been distorted to promote the liberal agenda of academia. I am also referring to the big-picture lessons of life as well. The sad truth is that, contrary to what most of you have been told, you *cannot* do or be anything you want. The vast majority of you ... will be absolutely miserable in whatever career you choose or are forced to endure. You will most likely hate your boss because they will most likely be dumber than you think you are, and they will inevitably screw you at every chance they get ... The boss will not be the only stupid person you encounter in life. The vast majority of people are *much, much* dumber than you have ever been led to believe. Never forget this. And just like people are far dumber than you have been led to believe, they are also *far* more dishonest than anyone is seemingly willing to admit to you. If you have any doubt as to whether someone is telling you the truth, it is a safe bet to assume that they are lying to you ... Do not trust anyone unless you have some sort of significant leverage over him or her and they *know* that you have that leverage over them. Unless this condition exists, anyone—and I mean *anyone*—can and probably will stab you in the back.

> EDITORIAL QUIBBLE It's unclear just when in college Mr. Z. thinks students are taught that they can do or be anything. A good part of what he considers academia's leftist agenda, after all, consists in teaching kids about social and economic stratification, inequalities, uneven playing fields—all the U.S. realities that actually limit possibilities for some people.
>
> (if conservatively disposed, please substitute "allegedly")

That is about one sixth of the address, and for the most part it speaks for itself.

One of many intriguing things about Mr. Ziegler, though, is the contrast between his deep cynicism about backstabbing and the naked, seemingly self-destructive candor with which he'll discuss his life and career. This candor becomes almost paradoxical in Q & As with an outside correspondent, a stranger whom Mr. Z. has no particular reason to trust at those times when he winces after saying something and asks that it be struck from

The best guess re Mr. Z.'s brutal on-record frankness is that either (a) the host's on- and off-air personas really are identical, or (b) he regards speaking to a magazine correspondent as just one more part of his job, which is to express himself in a maximally stimulating way (there was a tape recorder out, after all).

(for a magazine, moreover, that pretty much everyone around KFI regards as a chattering-class organ of the most elitist liberal kind)

the record. As it happens, however, nearly all of what follows is from an autobiographical time-line volunteered by John Ziegler in late May '04 over a very large medium-rare steak. Especially interesting is the time-line's mixture of raw historical fact and passionate

(while both eating and watching a Lakers play-off game on a large-screen high-def TV, which latter was the only condition he placed on the interview)

editorial opinion, which Mr. Z. blends so seamlessly that one really can believe he discerns no difference between them.

1967–1989: Mr. John Ziegler grows up in suburban Philadelphia, the elder son of a financial manager and a homemaker. All kinds of unsummarizable evidence indicates that Mr. Z. and his mother are very close. In 1984, he is named High School Golfer of the Year by the *Bucks County Courier Times*. He's also a three-year golf letterman at Georgetown, where his liberal arts studies turn out to be "a great way to prepare for a life of being unemployed, which I've done quite a bit of."

1989–1995: Mr. Z.'s original career is in local TV sports. He works for stations in and around Washington DC, in Steubenville OH, and finally in Raleigh NC. Though sports

(especially the one at Raleigh's WLFL Fox 22—"My boss there was the worst boss in the history of bosses")

news is what he's wanted to do ever since he was a little boy, he hates the jobs: "The whole world of sports and local news is so disgusting . . . local TV news is half a step above prostitution."

1994–1995: Both personally and professionally, this period constitutes a dark night of the soul for John Ziegler. Summer '94: O.J. Simpson's ex-wife is brutally murdered. Fall '94: Mr. Ziegler's mother is killed in a car crash. Winter '95: During his sportscast, Mr. Z. makes "an incredibly tame joke about O.J. Simpson's lack of innocence" w/r/t his wife's murder, which draws some protest from Raleigh's black community. John Ziegler is eventually fired from WLFL because the station "caved in to Political Correctness." The whole nasty incident marks the start of (a) Mr. Z.'s deep, complex hatred for all things PC, and (b) "my history with O.J." He falls into a deep funk, decides to give up sports broadcasting, "pretty much gave up on life, actually." Mr. Z. spends his days watching the O.J. Simpson trial on cable television, often sitting through repeat broadcasts of the coverage late at night; and when O.J. is finally acquitted, "I was nearly suicidal." Two psychiatrist golf buddies talk him into going on antidepressants, but much of the time O.J. is still all Mr. Ziegler can think and talk about. "It got so bad—you'll find this funny—at one point I was so depressed that it was my goal, assuming that he'd be acquitted and that [O.J.'s] Riviera Country Club wouldn't have the guts to kick him out, that I was going to become a caddy at Riviera, knock him off, and see whether or not [a certain lawyer Mr. Z. also played golf with, whose name is here omitted] could get me off on jury nullification. That's how obsessed I was." The lawyer/golfer/friend's reaction to this plan is not described.

?!

Late 1995: Mr. Z. decides to give life and broadcasting another shot. Figuring that "maybe my controversial nature would work better on talk radio," he takes a job as a week-end fill-in host for a station in Fuquay-Varina NC—"the worst talk-radio station on the planet . . . to call the station owner a redneck was insulting to rednecks"—only to be abruptly fired when the station switches to an automated Christian-music format.

Early 1996: "I bought, actually *bought*, time on a Raleigh talk-radio station" in order to start "putting together a Tape," although Mr. Z. is good enough on the air that they soon put him on as a paid host. What happens, though, is that this station uses a certain programming con-sultant, whose name is being omitted—"a pretty big name in the industry, who [however] is a *snake*, and, I believe, extremely overrated—and he at first really took a shine to me, and then told

> A Tape is sort of the radio/TV equivalent of an artist's portfolio.

> As Mr. Z. explains it, consultants work as freelance advisers to different sta-tions' Program Directors—"They sort of give the P.D. a cover if he hires somebody and it doesn't work out."

me, *told me*, to do a show on how I got fired from the TV job, and I did the show," which evidently involves retelling the original tame O.J. joke, after which the herpetic consultant stands idly by as the station informs Mr. Z. that " 'We're done with you, no thank you,' which was another blow."

1996–1997: Another radio consultant recommends Mr. Z. for a job at WWTN, a Nashville talk station, where he hosts an evening show that makes good Book and is largely hassle-free for several months. Of his brief career at WWTN, the host now feels that "I kind of self-destructed there, actually, in retrospect. I got frustrated with man-agement. I was right, but I was stupid as well." The trouble starts when Tiger Woods wins the 1997 Masters. As part of his commen-tary on the tournament, Mr. Z.

> (the whole story of which is very involved and takes up almost half a microcassette)

> (whom the host reveres—a standing gag on his KFI program is that Mr. Z. is a deacon in the First Church of Tiger Woods)

posits on-air that Tiger constitutes living proof of the fact that "not all white people are racists." His supporting argument is that "no white person would ever think of Tiger as a nigger," because whites draw a mental distinction "between people who just happen to be black and people who act like niggers." His reason for broadcasting the actual word "nigger"? "This all goes back to O.J. I hated the fact that the media treated viewers and listeners like children by saying 'Mark Fuhrman used the N-word.' I despised that, and I think it gives the word too much power. Plus there's the whole hypocrisy of how black people can use it and white people can't. I was young and naive and thought I could stand on principle." As part of that principled stand, Mr. Z. soon redeploys the argument and the word in a discussion of boxer Mike Tyson, whereupon he is fired, "even though there was very little listener reaction." As Mr. Z. understands it, the reason for his dismissal is that "a single black employee complained," and WWTN's parent, "a lily-white company," feared that it was "very vulnerable" to a discrimination lawsuit.

1998–1999: Mr. Z. works briefly as a morning fill-in at Nashville's WLAC, whose studios are right across the street from the station that just fired him. From there, he is hired to do overnights at WWDB, an FM talk station in Philadelphia, his home town. There are again auspicious beginnings . . . "except my boss, [the P.D. who hired him], is completely unstable and ends up punching out a consultant, and gets fired. At that point I'm totally screwed—I have nobody who's got my back, and everybody's out to get me." Mr. Z. is suddenly fired to make room for syndicated raunchmeister Tom Leykis, then is quickly rehired when listener complaints get Leykis's program taken off the air . . . then is refired a week later

> For those unfamiliar with Tom Leykis: Imagine Howard Stern without the cleverness.

when the station juggles its schedule again. Mr. Z. on his time at WWDB: "I should have sued those bastards."

Q: So what exactly is the point of a host's having a contract if the station can evidently just up and fire you whenever they feel like it?

A: "The only thing a contract's worth in radio is how much they're going to pay you when they fire you. And if they fire you 'For Cause,' then they don't have to pay you anything."

2000: John Ziegler moves over to WIP, a famous Philadelphia sports-talk station. "I hated it, but I did pretty well. I can do sports, obviously, and it was also a big political year." But there is both a general problem and a specific problem. The general problem is that "The boss there, [name omitted], is an evil, evil, evil, *evil* man. If God said, 'John, you get one person to kill for free,' this would be the man I would kill. And I would make it brutally painful." The specific problem arises when "Mike Tyson holds a press conference, and calls himself a nigger. And I can't resist—I mean, here I've gotten fired in the past for using the word in relation to a person who calls *himself* that now. I mean, my God. So I tell the story [of having used the word and gotten fired for it] on the air, but I do not use the N-word—I *spell* the N-word, every single time, to cover my ass, and to also make a point of the absurdity of the whole thing. And we get one, *one*, postcard, from a total lunatic black person—misspellings, just clearly a lunatic. And [Mr. Z.'s boss at WIP] calls me in and says, 'John, I think you're a racist.' Now, first of all, *this guy* is a racist, I mean he is a *real* racist. I am anything but a racist, but to be

> In the Q & A itself, Mr. Z. goes back and forth between actually using the N-word and merely referring to it as "the N-word," without apparent pattern or design.

EDITORIAL OPINION This is obviously a high-voltage area to get into, but for what it's worth, John Ziegler does not appear to be a racist as "racist" is generally understood. What he is is more like very, very insensitive—although Mr. Z. himself would despise that description, if only because "insensitive" is now such a PC shibboleth. Actually, though, it is in the very passion of his objection to terms like "insensitive," "racist," and "the N-word" that his real problem lies. Like many other post-Limbaugh hosts, John Ziegler seems unable to differentiate between (1) cowardly, hypocritical acquiescence to the tyranny of Political Correctness and (2) judicious, compassionate caution about using words that cause pain to large groups of human beings, especially when there are several less upsetting words that can be used. Even though there is plenty of stuff for reasonable people to dislike about Political Correctness as a dogma, there is also something creepy about the brutal, self-righteous glee with which Mr. Z. and other conservative hosts defy all PC conventions. If it causes you real pain to hear or see something, and I make it a point to inflict that thing on you merely because I object to your reasons for finding it painful, then there's something wrong with my sense of proportion, or my recognition of your basic humanity, or both.

(just one person's opinion . . .)

THIS, TOO (And let's be real: spelling out a painful word is no improvement. In some ways, it's worse than using the word outright, since spelling it could easily be seen as implying that the people who are upset by the word are also too dumb to spell it. What's puzzling here is that Mr. Ziegler seems much too bright and self-aware not to understand this.)

called that by *him* just made my blood boil. I mean, life's too short to be working overnights for this fucking bastard." A day or two later Mr. Z. is fired, For Cause, for spelling the N-word on-air.

Q: It sounds like you've got serious personal reasons for disliking Political Correctness.

A: "Oh my God, yes. My whole life has been ruined by it. I've lost relationships, I can't get married, I can't have kids, all because of Political Correctness. I can't put anybody else through the crap I've been through. I can't do it."

Mr. Z. explains that he's referring here to the constant moving around and apartment-hunting and public controversy caused by the firings. His sense of grievance and loss seems genuine. But one should also keep in mind how vital, for political talk hosts in general, is this sense of embattled persecution—by the leftist mainstream press, by slick Democratic operatives, by liberal lunatics and identity politics and PC and rampant cynical pandering. All of which provides the constant conflict required for good narrative and stimulating radio. Not, in John Ziegler's case, that any of his anger and self-pity is contrived— but they can be totally real and still function as parts of the skill set he brings to his job.

A corollary possibility: The reason why the world as interpreted by many hosts is one of such thoroughgoing selfishness and cynicism and fear is that these are qualities of the talk-radio industry they are part of, and they (like professionals everywhere) tend to see their industry as a reflection of the real world.

2001: While writing freelance columns for the *Philadelphia Inquirer* and *Philadelphia Daily News*, Mr. Ziegler also gets work at a small twenty-four-hour Comcast cable-TV network in Philly, where he's a writer and commentator on a prime-time issues-related talk show. Although Comcast is "an evil, evil, evil company, [which] created that network for the sole purpose of giving blowjobs to politicians who vote on Comcast legislation," Mr. Z. discovers that "I'm actually really good at talk TV. I was the best thing that ever happened to this show. I actually ended up winning an Emmy, which is ironic." There are, however, serious and irresolvable problems with a female producer on the show, the full story of which you are going to be spared (mainly because of legal worries).

2002: John Ziegler is hired as the mid-morning host at Clear Channel's WHAS in Louisville, which Arbitron lists as the fifty-fifth largest radio market in the U.S. According to a local paper, the host's "stormy, thirteen-month tenure in Louisville was punctuated by intrigue, outrage, controversy and litigation." According to John Ziegler, "The whole story would make a great movie—in fact, my whole life would make a great movie, but this in particular would make a great movie." Densely compressed synopsis: For several quarters, Mr. Z.'s program is a great success in Louisville.

"I'm doing huge numbers—in one Book I got a fifteen share, which is ridiculous." He is also involved in a very public romance with one Darcie Divita, a former LA Lakers cheerleader who is part of a morning news show on the local Fox TV affiliate. The relationship is apparently Louisville's version of Ben & J.Lo, and its end is not amicable. In August '03, prompted by callers' questions on his regular "Ask John Anything" feature, Mr. Z. makes certain on-air comments about Ms. Divita's breasts, underwear, genital grooming, and libido. Part of the enduring controversy over John Ziegler's firing, which occurs a few days later, is exactly how much those comments and/or subsequent complaints from listeners and the Louisville media had to do with it. Mr. Z. has a long list of reasons for believing that his P.D. was really just looking for an excuse to can him. As for all the complaints, Mr. Z. remains bitter and perplexed: (1) "The comments I made about Darcie's physical attributes were extremely positive in nature"; (2) "Darcie had, in the past, *volunteered* information about her cleavage on my program"; (3) "I've gone much further with other public figures without incident . . . I mocked [Kentucky Governor] Paul Patton for his inability to bring Tina Conner to orgasm, [and] no one from management ever even mentioned it to me."

> Here, some of John Ziegler's specific remarks about Darcie Divita are being excised at his request. It turns out that Ms. Divita is suing both the host and WHAS —Mr. Z.'s deposition is scheduled for summer '04.

John Ziegler on why he thinks he was hired for the Live and Local job by KFI: "They needed somebody 'available.'" And on

> (after what Ms. Bertolucci characterizes as "a really big search around the country")

> Mr. Z. explains the scare quotes around "available" as meaning that the experimental gig didn't offer the sort of compensation that could lure a large-market host away from another station. He describes his current KFI salary as "in the low six figures."

the corporate logic behind his hiring: "It's among the most bizarre things I've ever been involved in. To simultaneously be fired by Clear Channel and negotiate termination in a market where I had immense value and be courted by the same company in a market where I had no current value is beyond explicable."

Mr. Z. on talk radio as a career: "This is a terrible business. I'd love to quit this business." On why, then, he accepted KFI's offer: "My current contract would be by far the toughest for them to fire me of anyplace I've been."

•   •   •

Compared with many talk-radio hosts, John Ziegler is unusually polite to on-air callers. Which is to say that he doesn't yell at them, call them names, or hang up while they're speaking, although he does get frustrated with some calls. But there are good and bad kinds of frustration, stimulation-wise. Hence the delicate art of call screening. The screener's little switchboard and computer console are here in the Airmix room, right up next to the studio window.

JZS Producer Emiliano Limon: "There are two types of callers. You've got your hard-core talk-radio callers, who just like hearing themselves on-air"—these listeners will sometimes vary the first names and home cities they give the screener, trying to disguise the fact that they've been calling in night after night—"and then there are the ones who just, for whatever reason, respond to the topic." Of these latter a certain percentage are wackos, but some wackos actually make good on-air callers. Assoc. prod. and screener Vince Nicholas: "The trick is knowing what kooks to get rid of and what to let through. People that are kooky on a particular issue—some of these Zig likes; he can bust on them and have fun with them. He likes it."

> Vince (who is either a deep professional admirer or a titanic suck-up) states several times that John Ziegler is excellent with callers, dutifully referring to him each time as "Zig."

Vince isn't rude or brusque with the callers he screens out; he simply becomes more and more laconic and stoned-sounding over the headset as the person rants on, and finally says, "Whoa, gotta go." Especially obnoxious and persistent callers can be placed on Hold at the screener's switchboard, locking up their phones until Vince decides to let them go. Those whom the screener lets through enter a different, computerized Hold system in which eight callers at a time can be kept queued up and waiting, each designated on Mr. Z.'s monitor by a different colored box displaying a first name, city, one-sentence summary of the caller's thesis, and the total time waiting. The host chooses, cafeteria-style, from this array.

> 'Mondo Hernandez confirms on-record that Vince's screener voice sounds like someone talking around a huge bong hit.

In his selections, Mr. Z. has an observable preference for female callers. Emiliano's explanation: "Since political talk radio is so white male–driven, it's good to get female voices in there." It turns out that this is an industry convention; the roughly 50–50 gender mix of callers one hears on most talk radio is because screeners admit a much higher percentage of female callers to the system.

One of the last things that Emiliano Limon always does before airtime is to use the station's NexGen Audio Editing System to load various recorded sound bites from the day's broadcast news onto a Prophet file that goes with the Cut Sheet. This is a numbered list of bites available for tonight's *John Ziegler Show*, of which both Mr. Z. and 'Mondo get a copy. Each bite must be pre-

> NexGen (a Clear Channel product) displays a Richter-ish-looking sound wave, of which all different sizes of individual bits can be highlighted and erased in order to tighten the pacing and compress the sound bite. It's different from 'Mondo's Cashbox, which tightens things automatically according to pre-set specs; using NexGen requires true artistry. Emiliano knows the distinctive vocal wave patterns of George W. Bush, Bill O'Reilly, Sean Hannity, and certain others well enough that he can recognize them on the screen without any sound or ID. He is so good at using NexGen that he manages to make the whole high-stress Cut Sheet thing look dull.

cisely timed. It is an intricate, exacting process of editing and compilation, during which Mr. Z. often drums his fingers and looks pointedly at his watch as the producer ignores him and always very slowly and placidly edits and compresses and loads and has the Cut Sheet ready at the very last second. Emiliano is the sort of extremely chilled-out person who can seem to be leaning back at his station with his feet up on the Airmix table even when he isn't leaning back at all. He's wearing the *LA Times* shirt again. His own view on listener calls is that they are "overrated in talk radio," that they're rarely all that cogent or stimulating, but that hosts tend to be "overconcerned with taking calls and whether people are calling. Consider: This is the only type of live performance with absolutely no feedback from the audience. It's natural for the host to key in on the only real-time response he can get, which is the calls. It takes a long time with a host to get him to forget about the calls, to realize the calls have very little to do with the wider audience."

Vince, meanwhile, is busy at the screener's station. A lady with a heavy accent keeps calling in to say that she has vital information: a Czech newspaper has revealed that John Kerry is actually a Jew, that his grandfather changed his distinctively Jewish surname, and that this fact is being suppressed in the U.S. media and must be exposed. Vince finally tries putting her on punitive Hold, but her line's light goes out, which signifies that the lady has a cell phone and has disengaged by simply turning it off. Meaning that she can call back again as much as she likes, and that Vince is going to have to get actively rude. 'Mondo's great mild eyes rise from the board: "Puto, man, what's that about?" Vince, very flat and bored: "Kerry's a Jew." Emiliano: "Another big advent is the cell phone. Before cells you got mostly homebound invalids calling in.

'Mondo and Vince clearly enjoy each other, exchanging "*puto*" and "*chilango*" with brotherly ease. When Vince takes a couple days off, it becomes difficult to get 'Mondo to say anything about anything, Doritos or no.

Q: (based on seeing some awfully high minute-counts in some people's colored boxes on Vince's display): How long will callers wait to get on the air? *Emiliano Limon:* "We get some who'll wait for the whole show. [Laughs] If they're driving, what else do they have to do?" Q: If a drunk driver calls in, do you have to notify the police or something? A: "Well, this is why screening is tricky. You'll get, say, somebody calling in saying they're going to commit suicide—sometimes you have to refer the call. But sometimes you're getting pranked. Keep in mind, we're in an area with a lot of actors and actresses anxious to practice their craft. [Now his feet really are up on the table.] I remember we had Ross Perot call in one time, it sounded just like him, and actually he really was due to be on the show but not for an hour, and now he's calling saying he needs to be on right now because of a schedule change. Very convincing, sounded just like him, and I had to go, 'Uh, Mr. Perot, what's the name of your assistant press liaison?' Because I'd just talked to her a couple days prior. And he's [doing vocal impression]: 'Listen here, you all going to put me on the air or not?' And I'm: 'Umm, Mr. Perot, if you understand the question, please answer the question.' And he hangs up. [Laughs] But you would have *sworn* this was Ross Perot."

Some of his personal reasons for this have been made clear. But the Simpson case also rings a lot of professional cherries for Mr. Ziegler as a host: sports, celebrity, race, racism, PC and the "race card," the legal profession, the U.S. justice system, sex, misogyny, miscegenation, and a lack of shame and personal accountability that Mr. Z. sees as just plain evil.

[Laughs] Now you get the driving invalid."

(4)

Historically, the two greatest ratings periods ever for KFI AM-640 have been the Gray Davis gubernatorial recall and the O.J. Simpson trial. Now, in early June '04, the tenth anniversary of the Ron Goldman/Nicole Brown Simpson murders is approaching, and O.J. starts to pop up once again on the cultural radar. And Mr. John Ziegler happens to be more passionate about the O.J. Simpson thing than maybe any other single issue, and feels that he "know[s] more about the case than anyone not directly involved," and is able to be almost unbearably stimulating about O.J. Simpson and the utter indubitability of his guilt. And the confluence of the murders' anniversary, the case's tabloid importance to the nation and business impor-

tance to KFI, and its deep personal resonance for Mr. Z. helps produce what at first looks like the absolute Monster talk-radio story of the month.

On June 3, in the third segment of the *John Ziegler Show*'s second hour, after lengthy discussions of the O.J. anniversary and the Michael Jackson case, Mr. Z. takes a phone call from one "Daryl in Temecula," an African American gentleman who is "absolutely astounded they let a Klansman on the radio this time of night." The call, which lasts seven minutes and eighteen seconds and runs well over the :46 break, ends with John Ziegler's telling the audience, "That's as angry as I've ever gotten in the history of my career." And Vince Nicholas, looking awed and spent at his screener's station, pronounces the whole thing "some of the best talk radio I ever heard."

> This annoys Alan LaGreen of Airwatch enough to cause him to snap at 'Mondo on an off-air channel (mainly because Alan La-Green now ends up having to be the KFI Traffic Center during an interval in which he's supposed to be the Traffic Center for some country station); plus it pushes 'Mondo's skills with the Cashbox right to their limit in the hour's segment four.

Some portions of the call are untranscribable because they consist mainly of Daryl and Mr. Z. trying to talk over each other. Daryl's core points appear to be (1) that Mr. Z. seems to spend all his time talking about black men like Kobe and O.J. and Michael Jackson—"Don't white people commit crimes?"—and (2) that O.J. was, after all, found innocent in a court of law, and yet Mr. Z. keeps "going on about 'He's guilty, he's guilty—' "

"He *is*," the host inserts.

Daryl: "He was acquitted, wasn't he?"

"That makes no difference as to whether or not he did it."

> It turns out to be impossible, off the air, to Q & A Mr. Ziegler about his certainty re O.J.'s guilt. Bring up anything that might sound like reservations, and Mr. Z won't say a word—he'll angle his head way over to the side and look at you as if he can't tell whether you're trying to jerk him around or you're simply out of your mind.

> It's different if you ask about O. J. Simpson *l' homme*, or about specific details of his psyche and marriage and lifestyle and golf game and horrible crimes. For instance, John Ziegler has a detailed and fairly plausible-sounding theory about O.J.'s motive for the murders, which boils down to Simpson's jealous rage over his ex-wife's having slept with Mr. Marcus Allen, a former Heisman Trophy winner and current (as of '94) NFL star. Mr. Z. can defend this theory with an unreproduce-

ably long index of facts, names, and media citations, all of which you can ask him about if you keep your face and tone neutral and simply write down what he says without appearing to quibble or object or in any way question the host's authority on the subject.

(For instance, you cannot ask something like whether Ms. Simpson's liaison with Marcus Allen is a documented fact or just part of Mr. Z.'s theory —this will immediately terminate the Q & A.)

"O.J., Kobe: You just thrive on these black guys."

It is here that Mr. Z. begins to pick up steam. "Oh yeah, Daryl, right, I'm a racist. As a matter of fact, I often say, 'You know what? I just wish another black guy would commit a crime, because I hate black people so much.'"

Daryl: "I think you do have more to talk about on black guys. I think that's more '*news*' " . . . which actually would be kind of an interesting point to explore, or at least address; but Mr. Z. is now stimulated.

"As a matter of fact, Daryl, oftentimes when we go through who's committed the crimes, there are times when the white people who control the media, we get together and go, 'Oh, we can't talk about that one, because that was a white guy.' This is all a big conspiracy, Daryl. Except, to be serious for a second, Daryl, what really upsets me, assuming you're a black guy, is that you ought to be *ten* times more pissed off at O.J. Simpson than I am, because you know why?"

Daryl: "You can't tell me how I should feel. As a forty-year-old black man, I've seen racism for forty years."

Mr. Z. is starting to move his upper body back and forth excitedly in his chair. "I bet you have. I bet you have. And here's why you ought to be pissed off: Because, out of all the black guys who *deserved* to get a benefit of the doubt because of the history of racism which is real in this country, and which is insidious, the one guy—*the one guy*—who gets the benefit of all of that pain and suffering over a hundred years of history in this country is the one guy who deserves it less than anybody else, who sold his race out, who tried to talk white, who only had white friends, who had his ass kissed all over the place because he decided he wasn't really a black guy, who was the first person in the history of this country ever accepted by white America, who was actually able to do commercial endorsements because he pretended to be white, and *that's the guy? That's the guy? That's the guy* who gets the benefit of that history, and that doesn't piss you off, *that doesn't piss you off?*" And then an abrupt decrescendo: "Daryl, I can assure you that the last thing I am is racist on this. This is the last guy who should benefit."

In case memories of the trial have dimmed, Mr. Z. is referring here to the defense team's famous playing of the race card, the suggestion that the LAPD wanted to frame O.J. because he was a miscegenating black, etc.

TINY EDITORIAL CORRECTION Umm, four hundred?

John Ziegler is now screeching—except that's not quite the right word. Pitch and volume have both risen ('Mondo's at the channel 7 controls trying to forestall peaking), but his tone is meant to connote a mix of incredulity and outrage, with the same ragged edge to the stressed syllables as—no kidding—Jackson's and Sharpton's. Daryl of Temecula, meantime, has been silenced by the sheer passion of the host's soliloquy . . . and we should note that Daryl really has stopped speaking; it's not that Mr. Z. has turned off the volume on the caller's line (which is within his power, and which some talk-radio hosts do a lot, but Mr. Z. does not treat callers this way).

(Mr. Z. means the first *black* person—he's now so impassioned he's skipping words. [It never once sounds like babbling, though.])

(voice breaking a bit here)

EDITORIAL OPINION Again, it's nothing so simple as that he doth protest too much; but it would be less discomfiting if Mr. Z. didn't feel he could so totally *assure* Daryl of this—i.e., if Mr. Z. weren't so certain that his views are untainted by racism. Not to mention that the assurance resonates strangely against all the host's vented spleen about a black

Is it wimpy or white-guiltish to believe that we're all at least a little bit racist in some of our attitudes or beliefs, or at any rate that it's not impossible that we are?

man's "selling out his race" by "pretending to be white." Not, again, that Mr. Z. wears a pointy hood—but he seems weirdly unconscious of the fact that Simpson's ostensible betrayal of his race is something that only a member of that race really has the right to get angry about. No? If a white person gets angry about a black person's "pretending to be white," doesn't the anger come off far less as sympathy with the person's betrayed race than as antipathy for somebody who's trying to crash a party he doesn't belong at? (Or is Mr. Z. actually to be admired here for not giving a damn about how his anger comes off, for not buying into any of that it's-okay-for-a-black-person-to-say-it-but-not-okay-for-a-white-person stuff? And if so, why is it that his "selling out" complaints seem creepy and obtuse instead of admirable [although, of course, how his complaints "seem" might simply depend on the politics and sensitivities of the individual listener (such that the whole thing becomes not so much stimulating as exhausting)]?)

> (Better than "the right" here might be "the rhetorical authority.")

. . .

And then June 4, the night following the Daryl interchange, turns out to be a climactic whirlwind of production challenges, logistical brinksmanship, meta-media outrage, Simpsonian minutiae, and Monster-grade stimulation. As is SOP, it starts around 7:00 p.m. in KFI's large central prep room, which is where all the local hosts and their producers come in to prepare for their shows.

The prep room, which station management sometimes refers to as the production office, is more or less the nerve center of KFI, a large, complexly shaped space perimetered with battered little canted desks and hutches and two-drawer file cabinets supporting tabletops of composite planking. There are beat-up computers and pieces of sound equipment and funny Scotch-

> The standard of professionalism in talk radio is one hour of prep for each hour on the air. But Mr. Ziegler, whose specialty in media criticism entails extra-massive daily consumption of Internet and cable news, professes to be "pretty much always prepping," at least during the times he's not asleep (3:00–10:00 A.M.) or playing golf (which since he's moved to LA he does just about every day, quite possibly by himself—all he'll say about it is "I have no life here").

taped bits of office humor (e.g., pictures with staffers' heads Photoshopped onto tabloid celebrities' bodies). Like the studio and Airmix, the prep room is also a D.P.H.-grade mess: half the overhead fluorescents are either out or flickering nauseously, and the gray carpet crunches underfoot, and the wastebaskets are all towering fire hazards, and many of the tabletops are piled with old books and newspapers. One window, which is hot to the touch, overlooks KFI's gated parking lot and security booth and the office of a Korean podiatrist across the street.

> There is also another large TV in the prep room, this one wired to a TiVo digital recording system so that anything from the day's cable news can be tagged, copied, and loaded into NexGen and prophet. The TV gets only one channel at a time, but apparently certain cable stuff can also be accessed on one of the prep-room computers by a producer who knows what he's doing.

> Examples of volumes pulled at random from the tabletops' clutter: Dwight Nichols's *God's Plans for Your Finances*, the Hoover Institution's *Education and Capitalism: How Overcoming Our Fear of Markets and Economics Can Improve America's Schools*, and Louis Barajas's *The Latino Journey to Financial Greatness*.

Overall, the layout and myriad tactical functions of the prep room are too complicated to try to describe this late in the game. At one end, it gives on to the KFI newsroom, which is a whole galaxy unto itself. At the other, comparatively uncluttered end is a set of thick, distinguished-looking doors leading off into the offices of the Station Manager, Director of Marketing & Promotions, Program Director, and so on, with also a semi-attached former closet for the P.D.'s assistant, a very kindly and eccentric lady who's been at KFI for over twenty years and wears a high-tech headset that one begins, only over time, to suspect isn't really connected to anything.

> (who's usually long gone by the time the *JZS* staff starts prepping)

There are three main challenges facing tonight's *John Ziegler Show*. One is that Emiliano Limon is off on certain personal business that he doesn't want described, and therefore Mr. Vince Nicholas is soloing as producer for the very first time. Another is that last night's on-air exchange with Daryl of Temecula is the type of intensely stimulating talk-radio event that cries out for repetition and commentary; Mr. Z. wants to rerun certain snippets of the call in a very precise order so that he can use them as jumping-off points for detailing his own "history with O.J." and explaining why he's so incandescently passionate about the case.

The third difficulty is that Simpson's big anniversary Q & A with Ms. Katie Couric is airing tonight on NBC's *Dateline*, and the cuts and discussions of the Daryl call are going to have to be interwoven with excerpts from what Mr. Z. refers to several times as "Katie's blowjob interview." An additional complication is that *Dateline* airs in Los Angeles from 8:00 to 10:00 P.M., and it has also now run teases for stories on the health hazards of the Atkins diet and the dangerously lax security in U.S. hotels. Assuming that *Dateline* waits and does the O.J. interview last (which it is clearly in the program's interests to do), then the interview's highlights will have to be recorded off TiVo, edited on NexGen, loaded onto Prophet, and queued up for the Cut Sheet all very quickly, since Mr. Z.'s opening segment starts at 10:06 and it's hard to fiddle with logistics once his show's under way.

"You're going to need to kick some ass tonight, bud," Mr. Z. tells Vince as he highlights bites in a transcript of Daryl's call, eliciting something very close to a salute.

Thus Vince spends 7:00–8:00 working two side-by-side computers, trying simultaneously to assemble the cuts from last night's call, load an MSNBC interview with Nicole Brown Simpson's sister directly into NexGen, and track down a Web transcript of tonight's *Dateline* (which on the East Coast has already aired) so that he and Mr. Z. can choose and record bites from the Couric thing in real time. 'Mondo, who is back boardopping the ISDN feed of 7:00–10:00's *Phil Hendrie Show*, nevertheless comes in from Airmix several times to stand behind Vince at the terminals, ostensibly to see what's going on but really to lend moral support. 'Mondo's shadow takes up almost half the room's east wall.

John Ziegler, who is understandably quite keyed up, spends some of the pre-*Dateline* time standing around with an extremely pretty News-department intern named Kyra, watching the MSNBC exchange with half an eye while doing his trademark stress-relieving thing of holding two golf balls and trying to align the dimples so that one ball stays balanced atop the other. He is wearing a horizontally striped green-and-white golf shirt, neatly pressed black shorts, and gleaming New Balance sneakers. He keeps saying that he cannot be*lieve* they're even giving Simpson air time. No one points out that his shock seems a bit naive given the business realities of network TV news, realities about which John Ziegler is normally very savvy and cynical. Kyra does venture to observe, quietly, that the Simpson thing draws even bigger ratings than today's Scott Peterson, who—

> Nobody ever ribs Mr. Z. about the manual golf-ball thing vis-à-vis, say, Captain Queeg's famous ball bearings. It is not that he wouldn't get the allusion; Mr. Z. is just not the sort of person one kids around with this way. After one mid-May appearance on *Scarborough Country*, re some San Diego schoolteachers getting suspended for showing the Nick Berg decapitation video in class, a certain unnamed person had tried joshing around with him, in an offhand and lighthearted way, about a supposed very small facial tic that had kept appearing unbeknownst to John Ziegler whenever he'd used the phrase "wussification of America" on-camera; and Mr. Z. was, let's just say, unamused, and gave the person a look that chilled him to the marrow.

"Don't even compare the two," Mr. Z. cuts her off. "O.J.'s just in his own world in terms of arrogance."

The designated *JZS* intern, meanwhile, is at the prep room's *John & Ken Show* computer, working (in Vince's stead) on a comic review feature called "What Have We Learned This Week?," which is normally a Friday standard but which there may or may not be time for tonight. At 7:45 P.M. it is still 90° out, and smoggy. The windows' light makes people look greenish in the areas where the room's fluorescents are low. A large spread of takeout chicken sits

(negotiated ahead of time with Vince as the price for letting a mute, unobtrusive outside party observe tonight's prep)

> 'Mondo eventually starts taking plates of food back into Airmix with him.

> (a UC-Irvine undergrad, name omitted)

uneaten and expensively congealing. Mr. Z.'s intern spends nearly an hour composing a mock poem to Ms. Amber Frey, the mistress to whom Scott Peterson evidently read romantic verse over the phone. The poem's final version, which is "Roses are red / Violets are blue / If I find out you're pregnant / I'll drown your ass too," takes such a long time because of confusions about the right conjugation of "to drown."

"And to top it off," Mr. Z. is telling Kyra as her smile becomes brittle and she starts trying to edge away, "to top it off, he leaves Nicole's body in a place where the most likely people to find it are his *children*. It's just a fluke that couple found her. I don't know if

> (meaning the Bundy Drive crime scene, which Mr. Z. has evidently walked every inch of)

you've ever walked by there, but it's really dark at night, and they were in a, like [gesturing, one golf ball in each hand], cave formation out at the front."

Sure enough, *Dateline* runs the anti-Atkins story first. For reasons involving laser printers and a special editing room off the on-air news cubicle, there's suddenly a lot of running back and forth.

In Airmix, 'Mondo is eating Koo Koo Roo's chicken while watching Punk'd, an MTV show where friends of young celebrities collude with the producers to make the celebrities think

> 'Mondo can neither confirm nor deny that these supposedly outraged uninitiated callers are maybe themselves fakes, just more disembodied voices that Hendrie and his staff are creating, and that maybe the real dupes are us, the initiated audience, for believing that the callers are genuine dupes. 'Mondo has not, he confesses, ever considered this possibility, but he agrees that it would constitute "a serious mind-fuck" for KFI listeners.

they're in terrible legal trouble. 'Mondo is very careful about eating anywhere near the mixing board. It's always around 60° in this room. On the board's channel 6 and the overhead speakers, Phil Hendrie is pretending to mediate between apoplectic callers and a man who's filing sexual-harassment charges against female co-workers who've gotten breast implants. For unknown reasons, a waist-high pile of disconnected computer keyboards has appeared in the Airmix room's north corner, just across the wall from KFI's Imaging studio, whose door is always double-locked.

It is only right that John Ziegler gets the spot directly in front of the prep room's TV, with everyone else's office chairs sort of fanned out to either side behind him. Seated back on his tailbone with his legs out and ankles crossed, Mr. Z. is able simultaneously to watch *Dateline*'s are-you-in-danger-at-luxury-hotels segment, to hear and help rearrange Vince's cuts from the MSNBC exchange, and to highlight those parts of the O.J.–Katie Couric transcript that he wants to make absolutely sure to have Vince load from TiVo into Prophet when the greedy bastards at *Dateline* finally air the interview. It must be said, too, that Vince is an impressive surprise as a

> (which Vince was able to find online, but which had to be specially reconfigured and printed in order to restore the original line breaks and transcript format of, this being one cause of all the running around between 8:00 and 8:30, as well as another reason why it took the *JZS* intern so long to finish his quatrain, which he is even now fidgeting in his chair and trying to decide on just the right moment to show to Mr. Z.)

producer. He's a veritable blur of all-business competence and technical savvy. There are none of Emiliano's stoic shrugs, *sotto* wisecracks, or passive-aggressive languor. Nor, tonight, is Vince's own slackerish stoner persona anywhere in view. It is the same type of change as when you put a fish back in the water and it seems to turn electric in your hand. Watching Vince and the host work so well as a team induces the night's first strange premonitory jolt: Emiliano's days are numbered.

The broadcast studio is strange when no one's in here. Through the soundproof window, 'Mondo's head looks small and far away as he inclines over the spot log. It seems like

> Sure enough, within just weeks Emiliano Limon will have left KFI for a job at New York's WCBS.

a lonely, cloistered place in which to be passionate about the world. Mr. Z.'s padded host chair is old and lists slightly to port; it's the same chair that John Kobylt sits in, and morning drive's Bill Handel, and maybe even Dr. Laura back in the day. The studio wastebaskets have been emptied, but the banana scent still lingers. It might simply be that John and/or Ken eats a lot of bananas during afternoon drive. All the studio's monitors are on, though none is tuned to NBC. On the Fox News monitor up over the digital clock, Sean Hannity and Susan Estrich are rerunning the Iowa Caucuses clip of Howard Dean screaming at the start of his concession speech. They play the scream over and over. Ms. Estrich is evidently filling in on *Hannity and Colmes.* "They have hatred for George W. Bush, but they don't have ideas," Sean Hannity says. "Where are the ideas on the left? Where is the thinking liberal?" Susan Estrich says, "I don't know. I don't have a full-time job on TV, so I can't tell you."

> It is a medical commonplace that bananas are good for ulcers.

All multi-tasking ends when *Dateline*, after two teases and an extra-long spot break, finally commences the interview segment. It is Katie Couric and O.J. Simpson and Simpson's attorney in a living room that may or may not be real. One tends to forget how unusually, screen-fillingly large O.J.'s head is. Mr. Ziegler is now angled forward with his elbows on his knees and his fingers steepled just under his nose. Although he does, every so often, let loose with a "Katie Couric sucks!" or "Katie Couric should be fucking *shot!*," for the most part a person seated on the host's far flank has to watch his upper face—his right eye's and nostril's dilations—to discern when Mr. Z.'s reacting strongly or thinking about how he'll respond to some specific bit of Simpson's "sociopathic BS" when it's his turn to talk.

> Vince's broad back is now to the TV and everyone around it as he uploads real-time TiVo feed into NexGen and edits per his host's written specs.

It's odd: if you've spent some time watching Mr. Z. perform in the studio, you can predict just what he'll look like, how his head and arms will move and eyes fill with life as he says certain things that it's all but sure he'll say on-air tonight, such as "I have some very, very strong opinions about how this interview was conducted," and "Katie Couric is a disgrace to journalism everywhere," and that O.J.'s self-presentation was "delusional and arrogant beyond all belief," and that the original trial jury was "a collection of absolute nimrods," and that to believe in Simpson's innocence, as Ms. Couric says a poll shows some 70 percent of African Americans still do, "you have to be either crazy, deluded, or stupid—there are no other explanations."

All of this John Ziegler will and does say on his program—although what no one in the prep room can know is that a second-hour Airwatch flash on the imminent death of Ronald W. Reagan will cut short Mr. Z.'s analysis and require a total, on-the-fly change of both subject and mood.

(who is in so many ways the efficient cause, ideologically and statutorily, of today's partisan media, and whose passing will turn out to be June's true Monster . . .)

To be fair, though, there truly are some dubious, unsettling things about the *Dateline* interview, such as for instance that NBC has acceded to O.J. Simpson's "no editing" condition for appearing, which used to be an utter taboo for serious news organizations. Or that O.J. gets to sit there looking cheery and unguarded even though he has his lawyer almost in his lap; or that most of Katie Couric's questions turn out to be Larry King–size fluffballs; or that O.J.

The only bit of genuine fun is during the interview's first commercial break, when the opening ad is for Hertz—*Hertz*, of old O. J.-running-through-airports-spots fame—and Mr. Z. throws his head back and asks if he's really seeing what he's seeing. Even Vince turns around in his chair to look. Hertz's placement of an ad here is a brilliant, disgusting, unforgettable piece of meta-meta-media marketing. It's impossible not to laugh . . . and yet Mr. Z. doesn't. (Neither do the room's two interns, though that's only because they're too young to get the meta-reference.)

Simpson responds to one of her few substantive questions—about 1994's eerie, slow-motion Bronco chase and its bearing on how O.J.'s case is still perceived—by harping on the fact that the chase "never ever, in three trials that I had, it never came up," as if

EDITORIALIZING, OR JUST STATING THE OBVIOUS? Plus there's the creepy question of why O.J. Simpson is doing a murder-anniversary TV interview at all. What on earth does he stand to gain from sitting there on-camera and letting tens of millions of people search his big face for guilt or remorse? Why subject himself to America's ghoulish fascination? And make no mistake: it is fascinating. The interview and face are riveting television entertainment. It's almost impossible to look away, or not to feel that special kind of guilty excitement in the worst, most greedy and indecent parts of yourself. You can really feel it—this is why drivers slow down to gape at accidents, why reporters put mikes in the faces of bereaved relatives, why the Haidl gang-rape trial is a hit single that merits heavy play, why the cruelest forms of reality TV and tabloid news and talk radio generate such numbers. But that doesn't mean the fascination is good, or even feels good. Aren't there parts of ourselves that are just better left unfed? If it's true that there are, and that we sometimes choose what we wish we wouldn't, then there is a very serious unanswered question at the heart of KFI's Sweeper: "More *Stimulating*" of what?

For instance, it's troubling that her delivery is that of someone who's choosing her words with great care, when clearly the words have already been chosen, the question scripted. Which would seem to mean she's acting.

(It goes without saying that this is just one person's opinion.)

that had anything to do with whatever his behavior in the Bronco really signified (and at which non-answer, and Ms. Couric's failure to press or follow up, Mr. Z. moans and smears his hand up and down over his face). Or that O.J.'s cheerful expression never changes when Katie Couric, leaning forward and speaking with a delicacy that's either decent or obscene, inquires whether his children ever ask him about the crime. And when someone in the arc of chairs around John Ziegler says, almost to himself, that the one pure thing to hope for here is that Simpson's kids believe he's innocent, Mr. Z. gives a snort of reply and states, very flatly, "They know, and he knows they know, that he did it." To which, in KFI's prep room, the best response would probably be compassion, empathy. Because one can almost feel it: what a bleak and merciless world this host lives in—believes, nay, knows for an absolute *fact* he lives in. I'll take doubt.

Los Angeles Magazine

FINALIST—PROFILE WRITING

What would drive someone to join today's Army, perhaps to die for a cause that may never be won? In "The Recruit," writer Jesse Katz bears witness to the circumstances that turn an introspective college dropout into an Army private. Katz paints a painstakingly detailed picture of the military's power to seduce, and captures the final days of a boy's civilian life.

Jesse Katz

The Recruit

He is affluent and educated, a suburban kid who has grown up weighing options, not chasing last resorts. now he wants to fight for us in Iraq. what made him become a soldier?

I, Matt Ludwig . . .

He is a white boy, slender and pasty, with wide blue eyes, dirty blond sideburns, a translucent mustache, and a tangled goatee. He wears a limp, day-old T-shirt and saggy, nylon cargo pants. For the occasion he has removed his knit Billabong beanie, which normally clings like a burglar's tuque to the top of his brow, and his twin cubic-zirconia earrings, which the girl he likes had goaded him into acquiring just a couple weeks before.

do solemnly swear . . .

His right arm is raised. His left is tucked behind the small of his back. He rocks, ever so slightly, on the balls of his feet, reciting his oath in suite 1039, the Ceremony Room, a red-carpeted, wood-paneled chamber within the Los Angeles station of the United States Military Entrance Processing Command. It is one of those monumental yet invisible rituals of the city—thousands of recruits, from every branch of the service, herded each year through a concrete bunker on the fringes of Crenshaw, pledging to fight and, if necessary, die to protect what the lieutenant on the dais calls "our way of life." On this October afternoon, the fifth session of the day, there are fifteen young men and women taking that plunge, some already shorn and fit, others looking too squeamish or too thuggish to have even considered it. Matt stands near the front, itching for a cigarette. He is unassuming yet overcaffeinated, somewhere between geeky and cool, a mix of Tom Petty and David Spade, with a touch of Shaggy from *Scooby-Doo*.

to support and defend . . .

He is here from Simi Valley, the embodiment of neat suburbia, a community perpetually ranked among the safest in the nation. He is halfway through a bachelor's degree at California Lutheran University, a $29,000-a-year investment. His parents are affluent professionals, liberals turned evangelicals who have taken pains to shelter Matt from the excesses of their generation. He reacts to news with an "Oh, my goodness!" or a "How crazy is that?" He is twenty but has never voted.

the Constitution . . .

Eleven days earlier, Matt was at work, ringing up a Grand Slam Slugger. He had just clocked in, another morning shift at Denny's, practicing the niceties of cashier and host. Handing him the check was a sergeant first class, tall and chiseled and stiff. He wore a creased olive uniform. There were stripes on his epaulets and medals on his chest. Matt was nearly a foot shorter, his emerald uniform billowing from a spidery waist. Pinned to his breast, there was a name tag: WE WILL PUT OUR CUSTOMERS FIRST. Matt asked the soldier how everything was. "You ever thought about the army?" the soldier asked Matt.

of the United States . . .

America needs Matt Ludwig. Without him, without the quarter of a million other volunteers who join the armed forces every year, we face the specter of a draft, of anyone's son or daughter being shipped off to combat. Yet there is something awkward and cheerless about watching it happen, about witnessing a kid—caught between adolescence and adulthood, undaunted but inexperienced, whom we do not even trust with a beer—take such a giant leap. Matt is not driven by desperation. He is not fanatical or blustery or reckless. He does not have to do this, and if a few things about his life were different, he probably would not be swearing it away. But things are not different, which is why Matt finds himself here, seeking, asking—who he is, what he believes in, how he wants to be remembered. They are the epic questions of any life, questions that do not always come with satisfactory answers. If this freshly minted private wants to fight for us, if he is willing to die for us in Iraq, should we salute him as a hero? Or pray he comes to his senses? "Nothing's ever felt so right," Matt says.

so help me God.

The first oath of Matt's life was anything but voluntary. Standing before his first-grade class at the Capital Christian Center, he was instructed to accept Jesus as his savior.

Capital Christian had been his parents' idea, a fundamentalist megachurch that towers over Highway 50 on the outskirts of Sacramento. Matt was raised in nearby Cameron Park, on the western slope of gold country. It is a landscape more rustic, less invented, than Southern California's, but after a childhood of religious study, of pursuing "excellence in Christ," Matt was choking on graces and airs. "Everything's basically forced down your throat," he says. "I saw so many people put up a front, like, 'Oh, I'm such a great Christian,' because that's what everybody wanted to hear." As a teenager he had to take a vow of sexual chastity until marriage. To guard against temptation, the school banned all dancing, hosting a banquet instead of a prom. In 2002, the year Matt graduated, Capital Christian made headlines for expelling a kindergartner—the child's mother had refused to give up her job as a stripper. "They always played it up like we needed to be protected against the evils of the world, but in order to defend against that you need to know what's going on in the world, and they don't teach that," Matt says. "There's no life preparation."

Without any faith to lose, Matt headed south, to Cal Lutheran, the secluded 3,000-student liberal arts university in Thousand Oaks that, by comparison, scarcely qualified as religious. In his first year he slew all the taboos of home: smoke, drink, sex. It was eye-opening, just not in the way he expected. No longer bound by a moralistic code, Matt found he was still in a place consumed by appearances, by rigid rules of status and class. He was surrounded, at last, by an abundance of female possibilities, but having never played the game—acquired the requisite brands, mastered the appropriate styles—he felt himself harshly judged. He came to a bitter and self-defeating conclusion. "There's a lot of cute girls," he says, "but they're all uptight bitches." Matt grew isolated, skipping classes and winging tests. He is possessed by a peculiar blend of intelligence and spaciness, the kind of student who can ace a final without cracking a book, then flub the one exam he tries to pass. He fixated on chess, waging fervid matches against his cell phone. His brain is wired that way, for games of logic and strategy, to the exclusion sometimes of a wider cultural awareness. One semester he signed up for modern dance; to his disappointment and embarrassment, it did not prove to be a course in hip-hop technique. He declared himself a criminal justice major, then lost interest in school altogether. Before classes resumed last September, he requested a leave of absence. There had to be something else. "I don't care what I have to do," Matt says, "I'm not going back home."

He started at Denny's for $7.50 an hour. It was enough to move out of the dorms and into a rooming house on the Mexican side of Simi, not far from the Metrolink tracks. He slept on the floor, next to a pile of *Maxim* magazines and Carl's Jr. wrappers, sharing a bathroom with half a dozen other renters. "I feel so different from the main people I am supposed to be with, like middle-class, upper-class white," he says. "It's like I just got sick of them. They treat you like shit. I like real people who don't put up a front."

Denny's is just a mile from the army's Simi Valley recruiting station, one of 55 in the Los Angeles Recruiting Battalion and more than 1,685 worldwide, which together are responsible for procuring nearly 100,000 new soldiers a year. That is not a target. It is an order. Every recruiter has a quota—usually two enlistees per month—which means endless days of trolling for prospects, suggesting, enticing, inspiring, cajoling, an army of salesmen unleashed on the civilian world. The recruiting doctrine, a thirteen-page primer known as Pamphlet 350-7, is straight out of the Zig Ziglar school: "The army is a product which can be sold. . . . We are salesmen in every sense of the word. . . . You are the best advertisement for the army. . . . Stand tall, look sharp, and assume an attitude that says to your community, 'Here I am, your army recruiter. Focus on me.'" On that October morning at Denny's, Matt may have seen a soldier grabbing breakfast. But the soldier, Timothy J. Waud, was at work. "You've got to win their hearts and minds," says Waud, his shirttails pulled taut by stays running down to his socks. "You've got to act like you care about these kids—for real. Not just because you're paid to."

The army's Los Angeles battalion, which covers an immense swath of Southern California, from the Central Valley to the Orange County line, has struggled to accomplish its mission. It was called on to enlist 3,615 soldiers last year; it managed 1,968. A sixteen-year veteran, the last five as a recruiter, Waud approaches the job like a Green Beret, eating little, sleeping less, setting his clocks fifteen minutes fast to keep ahead of the action. As chief of the Thousand Oaks station for most of 2004, he came closer than any other commander in the battalion to making his numbers—delivering thirty-two of the thirty-seven enlistees he was supposed to drum up. That he succeeded in an upscale community, thought to be above the army's typical inducements, sent his stock even higher. A week before dropping in at Denny's, he was assigned to turn around the Simi Valley station, one of the region's worst performers last year. Matt suddenly had the king of L.A. recruiters in his backyard. "I'm not going from number one to the bottom," Waud had vowed. "Ain't gonna happen."

Like most young adults of the post-9/11 age, Matt had been subjected to the military's overtures, one more urgent than the last, ever since high school. The marines came calling first; he shrugged them off. Later it was the navy; not a second thought. He was neither a bleeding heart nor a flag-waving patriot. "I question everything," Matt says. "Politically, I'm kind of in between. I play devil's advocate on all sorts of stuff. I have no faith, but I'm not an atheist. I dunno, is there a term for that?" Now his suitor was the army, the largest and perhaps least glamorous of the services, a recruiter once again sizing him up—and at a time that could hardly have been less auspicious. The previous month, the U.S. death toll in Iraq had topped 1,000, an artificial milestone perhaps, but a test nonetheless of America's stomach for a war with no end in sight. The list so far had included 127 from California, more than any other state in the nation. Among the mourned, three from right here: in January, a Simi Valley High School graduate; in March, a Moorpark High graduate; in April, another Simi graduate. "Pretty much everything I've learned, I've learned from myself—trial and error," Matt says. "Fortunately there haven't been many errors. I wouldn't be this far. I just make good judgments, I guess."

·　　·　　·

When Matt's parents were his age, Vietnam was raging and the draft was in full swing, their own politics to the left. They would not be the only two '60s Democrats to reinvent themselves as '80s Republicans, but the arc of their pendulum was so dizzying, it continues to roil their lives. "They've just flip-flopped all over the place," Matt says. "After hearing their histories, it still makes no sense to me."

His mother, Michelle, shares a lineage and a maiden name with Beat icon Jack Kerouac. At Carondelet, a private all-girls school in San Francisco's East Bay, she was suspended for handing out pamphlets at the behest of the Weather Underground. "They had kind of come up to me: 'Will you distribute these flyers about our antiwar rally on campus?' " she says. "When you're that young, you're so idealistic and so vulnerable." Matt's dad, Mark, also grew up a peacenik. He walked precincts for McGovern in high school. Later he studied prelaw at UC Davis but dropped out to backpack across Europe. "In my family, we hated the military," he says. "I never would have thought about joining. It would have been the last thing, a disgusting thing, for me to do."

They met at a Sacramento life insurance company, two young executives-in-training seeking stability, a newlywed couple slowly waxing conservative. Michelle nudged Mark about church. "We weren't Christians when we got married," she says. Mark promised to give it a try, once they had kids. Matt, the eldest of their four, was born in '83, at the height of the Reagan revolution. "I still wanted to play racquetball on Sunday mornings with my buddies," Mark says. "Michelle kept saying, 'Remember what we said.' I started going, but I didn't want to be there. It took months to sink in." By the time Matt was ready for kindergarten, his father had given himself over to Capital Christian, a 6,000-member Assemblies of God congregation. The Ludwigs continued that way for much of the next two decades, classes, sermons, seminars, socials, everything for Cap Christian—"our church family," says

Mark. Then one day Michelle stopped going. The church, she decided, had grown too impersonal, the doctrine too extreme. "It's a very narrow, ultraconservative viewpoint that's presented," she says, "and there wasn't much freedom of discussion to argue that viewpoint, either at church or in our home." Matt had just left for Cal Lutheran, a step his mother endorsed but that his father derided as an expensive lark. In rapid succession, Michelle moved out, met a man, filed for divorce, and got married—last September 11, at the Aladdin in Las Vegas. Nothing has been the same.

"I don't understand what's happened to her," Mark says. "Here we are, we believe the Bible is the word of God, and it's clear—*clear*—and we go along, raising our family, believing that, and all of a sudden you say, 'I don't believe that anymore, I'm going to divorce you.' I can't stress how astounding this behavior is in the context of the way our family has lived our lives."

. . .

Clutching his phone and cigarettes, Matt walks through the tinted-glass doors of the Simi Valley recruiting center, forty-eight hours after he first met Waud. The station is in a shopping plaza, off the Tapo Canyon exit of the 118 freeway, next to a Fatburger, a Dairy Queen, and a Curves for Women. Sometimes it seems as if Simi is all name-brand chains and fabricated environments—babbling fountains and piped-in music and private security. Matt calls it Pleasantville. "So perfect," he says. "So bland."

Conscious of being courted, Matt looks both anxious and aloof, unsure if he should be making a good impression or feigning nonchalance. His snowboarder's cap, the color of cream gravy, is pulled low, affording him a touch more swagger than he might have sported at the restaurant. His fingers are threaded around an I ♥ MEXICO key chain. "My girlfriend's Hispanic," Matt explains.

Before the pitch can begin, he will need to take a test, a short multiple-choice exam to gauge his eligibility. The popular conception of the military may be that it preys on the wayward and dim, but any number of shortcomings—including the failure to graduate high school—can disqualify an otherwise eager candidate. Matt parks himself in front of a laptop computer. The questions on the screen range from the vexing (What is the solution for x, if $8x - 2 - 5x = 8$?) to the bellicose (What is the meaning of *maim*? Of *ravage*? Of *obliterate*?). Time runs out before he can finish. He still scores in the eighties. "Obviously," says Waud, welcoming Matt into his office, "you're not a dumb guy."

Matt's chair is set up to the side of Waud's desk, so that they face each other, elbow to elbow. On the wall is a framed *Sports Illustrated* cover devoted to Pat Tillman, the former NFL star who was killed last year, by friendly fire, in Afghanistan. A radio is tuned to classic rock, the volume a little too high. A member of Rotary, Waud has been trained to establish rapport, to ask open-ended questions, to zero in on his prospect's DBM, or dominant buying motive. He gets Matt talking about speed, about the thrill of hitching himself to a turbocharged machine. In high school Matt owned a Toyota Supra, voted the best car of his senior class. Until the engine gave out, he blazed through quarter-mile drags, regularly topping 120. In the process he got to know more than a few cops. "In a good way?" Waud asks. "Yeah, well, sometimes," Matt says. He has been looking into the California Highway Patrol, sort of an if-you-can't-beat-'em-join-'em approach. But the CHP, pinched by the state's budget crisis, has been in no rush to hire.

"What got you interested in being a cop in the first place?" Waud asks.

"Kind of the war," Matt says. "I don't really know."

"What is it about the war that triggered something in you," Waud asks, "whereas it made other people go, '*Waa-haa*, I'm scared'?"

"I'm sick of the status quo, like just doing the same thing day after day. It's nice to be part of history."

"You sound like a guy that wants to go out there and blow shit up."

"My purpose for going into the military is, like, I'd *want* to go fight," Matt says. "I hear other people: 'Oh, I don't want to go over.' I dunno, you're a soldier. Why not fight? That's your job."

"Right," Waud says.

They talk about the jobs the army offers, 212 in all, from cook to mechanic to pilot to sniper. With Matt's score, he could probably qualify for anything. None offers a guarantee of combat, just as none comes with an assurance of nondeployment. It would all depend on his specialty, his unit, world events, and luck. Waud pulls out a three-ring binder, each page held in a laminated sleeve. He shows Matt pictures of rifles. Of tanks. Of missiles. Of choppers. "I used to play war games, like Risk, Axis and Allies, Stratego," Matt says. "Does that lead into anything?" Waud tells him about military intelligence, his own job before becoming a recruiter. "It was a blast," Waud says, "like playing a big ol' board game." Matt strokes the tuft on his chin. He has spent less than an hour in the presence of Waud, and yet Waud already senses Matt is ripe. He leans forward. "If we could find you a job out of 200 and some odd jobs that fit what you're looking to do, maybe get you a little incentive, maybe a little extra money in your pocket, do a little traveling or something like that," he says, "do you think this is something that you'd look into?" Then Waud sinks back in his chair, cocks an eyebrow, and waits.

It might be that Matt is caught up in the moment, that he is focused on the excitement and adventure being sold, not the sacrifice. It might be that he is responding to Waud's authority, to a confident and imposing adult figure who has deemed him worthy of attention. Or it might be that the army just means cash for a new car. Matt never asks for time to think.

"Definitely," he says. "Oh yes, definitely."

"Congratulations," says Waud, shaking Matt's hand. "That's all *I* can offer. Nothing in any recruiting station will put you in the army."

He explains the next step, taking the full three-hour exam known as the ASVAB, short for armed services vocational aptitude battery. It will require a formal appointment and a trip to Los Angeles. "If you want," Waud says, "I could run you down there Friday afternoon, take the test, and—boom!—have you back by dinner."

"Can I get a shirt?" asks Matt, eyeing the ARMY OF ONE freebies scattered around the office.

"You show back up," Waud says, "you get a shirt."

· · ·

Matt has more than thirty numbers programmed into his cell, each with a distinct tone. Most are snippets of streetwise bravado—50 Cent, Lil' Kim, Chingy, DMX—except for his mother's number, which rings to the *Ghostbusters* theme, and his father's, which is from *Batman*. Neither of them had known he was going to meet with a recruiter. "They haven't really known me for two and a half years," Matt says. "I'm a completely different person than when I left."

He breaks the news first to his mom. She is a human resources analyst for Cooperative Personnel Services, a recruiter in her own right who screens and hires employees for county governments in Northern California. "She kind of flipped out," Matt says. "She was like, 'What? *No!* Do you know how many people are dying over there?' " Then he calls his dad. He is the director of underwriting for Health Net of California, one of the country's largest managed care providers. "I think he's living vicariously through me," Matt says. "He was happier about it than I was."

· · ·

Taking the ASVAB means journeying into another acronym, MEPS, the military entrance processing station. The country has sixty-five of them—their motto, "Freedom's Front Door"—through which all recruits must pass. Southern California's is in the African American heart of southwestern L.A., where La Brea Avenue meets Baldwin Hills. For a Simi Valley recruit, the drive there can be like a trip through the looking glass, an hour or two in thick traffic, from the 118 to the 405 to the 10, making the transition from suburban exile (Waud's office is a few blocks from the courthouse that rendered the Rodney King verdicts) to urban core (MEPS was torched during the ensuing riots).

Even though he arrived in Ventura County more than two years ago, Matt has hardly set foot in L.A. Entering the city, he cranes his neck, staring at people, studying graffiti, absorbing a panorama scrubbed clean by the autumn rains. The young inhabit a naive universe, their restless energy at least partly a function of their innocence. But Matt's blind spots, for a kid so bright, can be mystifying. As the car veers onto the Santa Monica Freeway, away from the Westside, he points to the hills. "Is that the real one?" Matt asks. There is silence, none of his escorts too sure of the question. Matt is undeterred. "The real Hollywood sign?" he asks again.

Down La Brea, across Jefferson, over the railroad tracks, and into a parking lot behind the Rancho Cienega Sports Complex, the car finally pulls to a stop. Matt's driver, Staff Sergeant Sean Donahue, leads him through a chain-link security gate, into the rear of MEPS, past an armed guard and a metal detector. He instructs Matt not to leave the facility for any reason—the neighborhood being too dangerous, according to the military, even to step out for a smoke. At the front desk they are stopped by a soldier in battle fatigues. He nods at Matt's beanie. "Sir, can you take off your hat for us?" Matt looks at Donahue. "It's a military thing," Donahue says. Two hours later Matt is done, early this time. His score is even better than before, a ninety-six, which puts him in the top 4 percent of the nearly half a million applicants who take the ASVAB every year.

"That's pretty good, right?" Matt asks.

"That's excellent," Donahue says.

"There's only one question I didn't know," Matt says. "What does *acquiescence* mean?"

.   .   .

As promised, Matt receives his T-shirt. It is XXL. He asks if there is anything smaller. "Unfortunately," Waud says, "it's one size fits all." Matt puts himself at five feet seven, 120 pounds. He is two months shy of his twenty-first birthday yet has the build of a junior high scrub. For as long as he can remember, size has been his bane, a barrier to sports, to romance, to commanding the respect of teachers and bosses. Waud tries to empathize. "The thing I always had going for me, I was the tall guy," he says. "Girls love tall guys," Matt says. "That was my *only* game," Waud tells him. Matt has dreamed of getting a tattoo across the top of his back. If he survives boot camp, he will do it. He already knows what it will say: too much to prove. "It's not that I have a Napoleon complex," Matt says. "I'm not out to prove that I'm better than other people. It's just to prove that I'm average, that I can keep up with everyone. I've had to prove myself—what I know, what I am—to other people my whole life." Instead of a tattoo Matt has a decal. It is stuck across the rear window of his car, now a Hyundai, the cheapest, barest-boned model available. In neat white letters it says: TRUST NO BITCH.

If Matt had a girlfriend—and that is a term he uses warily—her name would be Olga Hernandez. She entered Cal Lutheran the same year he did, a working-class Mexican American girl from San Fernando who shares his outsider's perspective on phoniness and wealth. Olga had been a softball star in high school; she has hips and curves and enough muscle to work as an undercover security guard at the JC Penney in the Thousand

Oaks mall. She once took Matt home, to see her old neighborhood and meet her Spanish-speaking parents, the first boy she had ever invited. "Basically we have a relationship, just not spoken," Matt says. "We can lie together on the bed and cuddle for hours. But it's a something-we-never-act-on type of thing." He is sitting outside, at one of the several Starbucks he frequents in Simi Valley, smoking Marlboros and sipping his usual, an iced grande vanilla latte, which he orders at least two or three times a day, no matter the weather. He has begun to shiver. His teeth are chattering. His neck is twitching. He often ends up this way, chilled, underdressed, nerves jangling from tobacco and caffeine. It somehow makes him look smaller, to be so clenched. He is anxious to see Olga, to tell her about the army. "She doesn't know yet," Matt says. "She'll probably pass out."

He drives the Hyundai to Cal Lutheran. There is only one parking spot near Olga's dorm. He starts to back in. It is spacious, wide enough to accommodate a Hummer. Before he can straighten out, Matt's rear tire bangs into the curb. He cranks the wheel, then tries again. Forward and back, cutting and braking—three, four, five times before he finally gets himself parallel. Street racing was Matt's equalizer, the antidote to being slight. Maybe the army is, too, a force so much larger and more powerful than he, with all the weaponry he needs to impose his will on an adversary. Matt shrugs. "I can drive like a maniac," he says, "but I can't park worth a shit."

.   .   .

The army wants to know everything about Matt.

"Have you registered for the selective service?" Waud asks him.

"What's that?" Matt says.

"Have you ever been a conscientious objector?" Waud asks.

"What's a conscientious objector?" Matt replies.

"Are you allergic to wool?" Waud continues. "Are you missing a testicle?" Asthma? Jaundice? Collapsed lung? Sleepwalking? Bed-wetting? Night blindness? Periods of unconsciousness?

Matt shakes his head.

"Have you ever been treated for alcohol dependence?" Waud asks.

"Well," Matt deadpans, "I was a college student for two years."

The interrogation, which requires *X*s and initials on every answer, signals Matt's graduation from prospect to full-fledged recruit. The scope is so vast, the details so difficult to verify, he is having a hard time taking it seriously. Then something hits home. Waud asks about prescription drugs. It leads to a story about childhood, to the roots of Matt's self-image. When he was eleven or twelve, his indifference to school already causing him trouble, Matt was treated for attention deficit disorder. He took Ritalin, then Adderall, but stopped once he got to college. In truth, he never believed in the syndrome or accepted that he was among its sufferers. His mother, however, thought it explained a lot. She became a champion of ADD education, even serving as chairperson of the Cameron Park chapter of CHADD, the nation's leading support group. "It's like, all of a sudden my mom got interested in it," Matt says, "and then all of a sudden, all her kids had it."

"It's so weird," Waud says. "I know I would have been an attention-deficit kid if I was growing up in a big city like this or in this era. Fortunately I was on two and a half acres of country yard, and my parents were like, 'Go outside and kick the ball against the wall, go run with the dogs. . . .'"

"It's just kind of like being a kid," Matt says.

"Most of the time, the ones that are quote-unquote *hyper* and not paying attention—it's mostly because they're advanced," Waud says.

"And bored," Matt says. "They're creative, and they want to do other stuff that's actually stimulating."

"I think that's one of the worst things that's happened to society," Waud says. " 'I can't control my kids—give 'em drugs.' "

For Matt there was another, unforeseen consequence of taking this medication, much of which was amphetamine based. Throughout puberty, while other kids were sprouting, Matt had no appetite. "You're never hungry," he says. "I blame my being small on that."

· · ·

He would have given anything for Olga to be awed by his mettle, humbled by his selflessness. But her reaction is neither adulatory nor weepy. "Why do you want to do that bullshit?" she snaps at Matt." Especially now?" Olga wants to be an FBI agent or, maybe, the first female owner of the Dodgers. Her dorm room is decorated with posters of Ken Griffey Jr. and the rap trio G-Unit. A bullet casing and a pair of miniature handcuffs hang from the rearview mirror of her Jeep Laredo. There is nothing fragile about Olga; there is, she worries, about Matt. "I won't say I baby him or that I, like, have pity on him," she says. "He's a smart boy. But he's, like, naive in certain things. He says, 'Sometimes, you act like my mom.' Well, sometimes he acts like a little kid."

In the lexicon of recruiting, Olga is known as a COI, or center of influence. It applies to anyone in the community, friend, relative, coach, pastor, whose perspective on the military, pro or con, might sway a potential enlistee. Olga's politics are shaped by the personal—a friend from high school, now a marine, is on his second tour of Iraq. "The first time, he loved it," Olga says. "He was all gung ho, like, 'Let's go out there and kick some ass.' The next time, he called me and he was crying on the phone. I guess he saw his sergeant blow up and a bunch of his friends—three of them died, plus the sergeant—and he was crying, saying, 'This is crazy. I don't want to be here. You know, we've killed so many innocent people.' He goes, 'It's funny, but a lot of soldiers are talking about killing themselves.' It's so sad. I mean, this is a guy who was just, like, totally hard-core."

Olga does not want to see Matt hurt. She does not want to be the one hurting him. "Every day I try to figure out why he's really doing this," she says. "I just don't think it's him."

. . .

On a drizzly Wednesday afternoon, a week after his first interview with Waud, Matt is summoned to physical training, or PT, as he comes to know it. To get through boot camp, Matt will need to do forty-two push-ups in two minutes, fifty-three sit-ups in two minutes, and a two-mile run in less than sixteen minutes and thirty seconds. The strength portion does not especially worry him—he would be glad to bulk up—but running at such a speed strikes Matt as an alarming stunt. He has been smoking since he entered Cal Lutheran, three-quarters of a pack a day now. He started because of a girl; they experimented together while dating, she lost interest in him, he kept the habit. All day long Matt has been smoking. On his way to PT he smokes again.

For the next hour, as the weather grows worse, Waud plays drill sergeant, barking commands at the young recruits, seven or eight of them, Matt gasping and wincing, the occasional passerby with an umbrella staring at their choreographed exertion. It is a rare sight, these soldiers-to-be stomping around in the muck of a city park, forming columns, turning in unison, practicing thirty-inch steps, then trotting, jogging, and breaking into a steady run. As they loop around the playground, Waud prods them with cadence, the call-and-response chants that are a staple of army life.

"I wanna be an airborne ranger," he cries.

"I wanna be an airborne ranger," replies Matt, his voice rising above the chorus.

"Live a life of death and danger," Waud sings.

"Live a life of death and danger," Matt sings.

"Airborne ranger," they repeat. "Death and danger."

Back at the car, Matt lights up. He is fretting over the necessity of going cold turkey once he gets to basic training, but he seems energized by the camaraderie of this early initiation rite, by what the army calls the "soldierization" process. Societies have engaged in such rituals since the beginning of time, culling their young males, subjecting them to hardship, and ultimately transforming them into that culture's notion of what it means to be a man. In the postindustrial age, manhood tends to be measured in economic terms, a reflection of salary and career. The army remains one of those primal tests, a chance to earn entry into a group as mighty as any on this planet—to be sworn and reborn, transcending civilian life. "You kind of leave that world behind," Matt says, inhaling deeply. "Even when you come back, you're still not quite part of it."

Matt's favorite movie is *Tombstone*, the 1993 take on the Wyatt Earp–Doc Holliday story. He has watched it maybe thirty times. "They both know there's really good odds they're going to die," Matt says. "But at least they'll die fighting for something. It's like taking a risk to prove a point." That same notion, of the underdog outmaneuvering a superior foe, even if it means going down in a blaze of glory, permeates the rest of Matt's interests. He admires Confederate general Robert E. Lee and Nazi field marshal Erwin Rommel, both of whom became renowned for their tactical brilliance despite fighting for a doomed and discredited cause. He has read Sun Tzu's *Art of War* four or five times, each in a different translation. In high school, he lost days engaged in MMORPGs, or massive multiplayer online role-playing games, sort of Internet-based versions of Dungeons and Dragons. "I just like the idea of pulling off unbelievable things," Matt says, "of beating someone with your mind."

Until the army, the closest Matt had come to applying those lessons was at Chevron, his employer before Denny's. While working an all-nighter in 2003, he was robbed by a man with a snub-nosed revolver and "the craziest, piercing eyes." The gun was stuck inches from Matt's face. Matt played it cool, reaching into the register and scooping out the cash. Afterward, his manager wanted him to take some time off, maybe see a psychologist. Matt reported for his next shift. "It seems like an experience that might alter other people's lives, like, 'Oh, I love life,' but it didn't change me in the least," Matt says. "Didn't even faze me. I've never really cared about death. It's not that, 'Oh, I'm invincible.' I know that I'm mortal. It's just that—it's kind of bad to say, I know people look down on this, but I don't really care—it's just that, What is there to live for in this life?"

●　　●　　●

The morning after PT, Matt is back at Denny's, behind the register, an apron hanging from his hips. It is three days before Halloween, and the restaurant is decked out in graveyard decor, a mock tombstone chattering at customers. Matt is at the front, greeting and seating, his banter practiced and polite: "How many? . . . Wherever you like . . . Have a good one . . . " A couple of middle-aged regulars, Tammy and Richard, walk in, oddball sweethearts who are something of a handful. They used to visit Matt when he worked at Chevron. Now they look for him at Denny's. Among the staff they are known, not so affectionately, as "the Simples." "You guys need anything?" Matt asks. "No, we're just here to pester," Tammy says.

Matt has a brother, Ben, who is eighteen and consigned to a group home. Severely autistic and afflicted with Tourette's syndrome, he alternates between sullen withdrawal and violent fits. Matt, more than anyone, has learned to reach Ben, to calm his rages and brighten his mood. "I was always the one to protect him," Matt says. "I'm the only one he really listens to." Tammy presses her face against a toy-crane machine by the front door. She slips in some quarters and begins rocking the joystick, skimming over the trove of stuffed animals with the game's mechanical claw. "This thing is hopeless—totally, pathetically hopeless," she announces. Matt steps out from behind the counter, a fistful of quarters to the rescue. He takes aim at a pumpkin-shaped bear. "I'll win him," Matt says. "I don't put anything past Matt—if he puts his mind to it, he can do it," Richard says. Matt lowers the crane. The claw closes in on the bear's head. As he raises it, the animal lurches, then drops back to the pile. "So dang close," says Tammy. Matt tries again. "Right there—grab it, grab it, grab it!" Tammy shouts. The bear slips again. "Nooooooo!" she wails. Matt feeds the machine one more time. "If I had the money, believe me, I'd do it for you," Tammy says. Matt snares the orange-bellied animal. It tumbles out the chute. Tammy clutches her prize. "Oh, thank you!" she cries, dancing across the foyer.

Matt's manager glares at them. She tells Matt to clean the pie carousel. He begins spraying, wiping the glass, removing expired desserts. Then she tells him to wait tables. He begins taking orders, serving drinks, running back and forth to the kitchen. A line has formed up front. She tells him to get back to the register. A laminated poster—the Denny's "Declaration of Hospitality"—hangs behind him. To Matt it is just another front, a pledge without substance. By now, customers are complaining. The manager snaps at Matt again. Matt tears off his Denny's shirt. The lunch rush is on, the restaurant in limbo. There is not much principle at stake; Matt will be gone soon, anyway. But there is drama. The army has given him a once-in-a-lifetime chance to play Johnny Paycheck, an excuse not to be nice. "Bye," he says, dropping his uniform on the counter. "I quit."

·   ·   ·

Matt's mom fears the army will take the best years of her son's life. She knows, from her own work, how hard it is for veterans to reenter the job force with marketable skills, how easily they can return home damaged, even broken, by what they have experienced. "Matt thinks my objections are just that I'm an overprotective mom, that I'm afraid he's going to get killed in Iraq," Michelle says. "But there's a side of him that's not adult, that doesn't know the reality of it."

Matt's dad hopes the army will redeem the best years of his son's life. He is sure that a military environment—"a place where there's character and discipline and integrity"—will straighten him out, especially compared with the indulgences of a fancy Southern California college. "It's perfect for him, really," Mark says. "Once he gets adjusted to it, I think he'll just thrive."

When the marriage began to crumble, Matt sided with his mom. She is the realist of the family, grounded, analytical, and flexible enough to let him smoke and drink under her roof. With Matt's encouragement, Michelle tried to pull the youngest two children out of Capital Christian. "Me, personally, I would never send my kids there," Matt says. Mark obtained a court order, keeping them enrolled. The legal battle now centers on Ben. Mark is challenging Michelle for custodianship; in Matt's eyes his father could commit no greater hypocrisy. "Everything to my dad is public appearance—what other people think," he says. "Having a kid like that, who will embarrass him in public, he never accepted it. He never wanted to deal with it. He kind of treated him like he wasn't even his son." It is not hard to see the army as Matt's refuge from this turmoil, an organization that—good or bad—is at least *real*: demanding, messy, hands-on, but without pretense. As a soldier, he might not be free, but he will be unavailable, transported to a world beyond his parents' reach.

The irony, of course, is that his father—the figure Matt is trying to distance himself from—sees in this parting the seeds of a homecoming, a necessary step before reconciliation. When Michelle left, she handed Mark a list of his faults. Among them was his obsession with military history. He has a library full of World War II books. He has turned European vacations into tours of bunkers and shrines. Mark wonders if her displeasure over

Matt's interest in the army is not really about something else, about the son becoming the father. "God says in his Bible, 'The word will not return void,'" Mark says. "Matt knows the truth and has been taught the truth. Somewhere along the way, I am confident, he will grab that truth and take it as his own."

.   .   .

His enlistment comes on his mom's birthday. Matt needs to be at MEPS before dawn. Waud offers to drive him down the night before and put him up at the Westin Los Angeles Airport, another of those invisible intersections between the military and civilian worlds. The hotel is a MEPS way station, the official lodging of recruits on the eve of signing up or shipping out. The third floor hosts a MEPS office, where newcomers are checked in every evening, and a MEPS lounge, where they can watch movies or send e-mails. Waud goes over the rules: no room service, no minibar, no pay-per-view TV, no wandering after the 10 P.M. curfew. "Get some sleep," he tells Matt. "I can tell you, tomorrow you're going to be tired." Matt spends most of the night smoking, reclined by the swimming pool, which is drained and cordoned off with police tape. Jets roar overhead. Palms sway in the damp coastal haze. L.A. feels distant, a shimmering dreamscape, less important than it has ever been. Matt goes to his room. He has brought nothing but the clothes on his back. He watches *Law & Order* and *CSI*. Then he goes out to smoke again. "I'm not in a friendly mood today," he says. "Everyone's getting ready for the tough front they'll have to put on tomorrow."

The wake-up call comes automatically, a 3 A.M. reveille. By 3:30, Matt is downstairs, in front of the lobby, already lighting a smoke. A breakfast buffet has been laid out. He can stomach only a few bites. A Westin courtesy shuttle is idling at the curb. Matt smokes another, his last for the next dozen hours. At a quarter to four, he is on the bus. It is dark, stuffy, tight, a payload of thirty or forty bleary kids, none too sure of the right posture or vocabulary—sarcasm, formality, indifference—for such a portentous occasion. Matt clutches his paperwork, a manila envelope stamped with his name and social security number. Another fifteen minutes go by. "Hurry up and wait," somebody in the back whispers. The driver, at last, pulls onto Century Boulevard, rumbling through Inglewood, then up and over the hills. At MEPS, the doors are locked. The recruits line up outside and wait again. "Okay, single-file line, back it up," booms a sergeant in camouflage wear. "Everyone sitting down, stand up. Face me. All right. Good morning." He goes over the rules of MEPS: no hats, no backpacks, no sunglasses, no piercings, no cell phones, no smoking, no sleeping, no sagging pants. Matt hikes his up. The corridors are labyrinthine, with colored arrows—blue, red, yellow, green—leading to each phase of induction. Glossies of President Bush and Donald Rumsfeld hang on the walls. In one corner, there is an arcade, with toy guns strafing the screens of Police 911 and Dark Silhouette.

For the next several hours Matt is poked and prodded, weighed and measured, fingerprinted, vision tested, drug tested, HIV tested, and directed to bend and spread. As the morning drags on, the time-honored intramural rivalries of the military can already be seen taking shape. A couple of would-be marines taunt Matt, insisting that the army is always far behind them, at the rear of any attack. "Oh yeah?" Matt shoots back. "Well, we've got more combat deaths in Iraq than you." A marathon of *Rocky* movies play back-to-back in the waiting room. Matt buys some TGI Friday's potato skins from a vending machine; unsure of the rules, he sneaks them, one at a time, from the pouch of his sweatshirt.

Nobody joins the military—indeed, nobody leaves MEPS—without a trip to the counseling office. Recruiters can make all the promises in the world, but only a guidance counselor can put an offer on the table, turn the recruiter's pitch into reality. It is possible to spend an anxious night at the Westin, get on that fiendishly early bus, endure hours of intrusive examination, then hours more of boredom, only to discover that the job that had sounded so perfect has already been filled. Recruiters sometimes get a bad rap, as if they were the ones playing bait and switch. But they operate in the dark, too. "We cross our fingers, hold our breath, pray on the little Buddha belly," says Waud, who is barred from mingling with Matt until a contract has been signed. Basically, MEPS is to recruiting what the sales manager's office is to buying a car. Everyone who enters these doors is essentially a captive, deliberately worn down and conveniently unaware of what products are actually in stock. There is still no obligation to join. But it would take an uncommonly resolute kid to withstand such a grind, then walk away if the job being offered did not sound quite right. By the time he is introduced to his counselor, Matt is so frazzled, he looks ready to take anything. "I'm gonna get drunk tonight," he says. "Well, no, not drunk. Yeah . . . *drunk*."

The counselor is a former army ranger, Sergeant First Class David Gardner. Bald and plump, he is sitting at a computer, the screen set to an American flag. "Okay, what are you looking at doing, bro?" he asks Matt.

"Um, my main ones I want, like the top-of-the-list ones are, like, intelligence and counterintelligence," Matt says.

"Let's talk about it real quick. I want to make sure you understand what you're getting into. A lot of people look at it and think, 'I'm 007.' It's not like that."

"But there's fieldwork?" Matt asks. "It's not just a desk job?"

"Oh yeah," Gardner says. "There's no safe job from going to Iraq."

"Oh no—see, I'd want to go," Matt says. "I just don't know, with all the training, if I'd make it in time."

"I don't know, either," Gardner says. "But I would imagine the war on terror's not just going to be wrapped around Iraq. That's my prediction. There's other countries on the hit list out there."

As it turns out, counterintelligence is not available, but intelligence analyst is. "Happy?" Gardner asks. "I'm good," Matt says. He will become known as a 96-Bravo. His enlistment period will be four years of active duty plus another four in the reserves. The army wants him to do nine weeks of basic training at Fort Leonard Wood, Missouri, followed by seventeen weeks of specialized training at Fort Huachuca, Arizona. If he can leave as soon as November 24, the day before Thanksgiving, he will receive a $6,000 "seasonal" bonus. He will get another $8,000 as a reward for his college background. It is a $14,000 jackpot, the first half of which will be payable in mid-2005, once he gets to his duty station. Where that might be is anyone's guess. "Shit, they're giving me fourteen grand to join!" Matt says. "It kind of means someone wants you, if they're willing to pay you that much."

As if on cue, Waud appears. Matt is Private Ludwig now. "Congratulations, once again, young man," Waud tells him. Outside, Matt fumbles for a smoke. It is 4 P.M., Friday traffic, a long stop-and-go slog back to Simi Valley. "I like this song," Matt says. Waud turns up the radio. Social Distortion is on KROQ:

Reach for the sky
'Cause tomorrow may never come

Depleted, overwhelmed, Matt finally gives in to the rhythms of the drive. His chin drops to his chest. He slumps forward, bobbing against his seat belt. He sleeps until Waud cuts the engine.

·   ·   ·

Tuesday is Election Day. It is the first presidential race of Matt's adult life. He declares himself a Bush supporter but has never bothered to register. "Who'd you vote for?" He is talking into his cell. "You would. . . . That's 'cause you believe in propaganda. . . . He's full of crap, Olga. . . . Anyways, Miss Political, I'm not the one who likes *Fahrenheit 9/11*. . . . Yeah, right. . . . Michael Moore's so minority and all. . . . Shut up, fat girl. . . . Don't even try to talk shit. . . ." Then Matt's battery dies. "She's going to be freakin' pissed," he groans.

Matt's relationship with Olga is like a chess match. All positioning and leverage, angles and gambits. Olga is accustomed to guys falling for her. Matt has seen them, tongues wagging, done before they even get a chance. He does not want to be among them. "I'd sleep with her, just because I'm a guy," Matt says. "But I'm one of her few friends that's resisted for so long. She's used to everybody worshiping her, running back to kiss her ass." If their relationship were intimate, it seems safe to say, Matt probably would not be seeking his future in the army. Sex has come too sporadically for him to just walk away, especially from a prize as coveted as Olga. It is not as if the choice, though, has belonged only to him. "I don't want to sound mean," Olga says, "but I could kick his ass, and I don't want to be with a guy whose ass I can kick."

Now there are only three weeks left, perhaps the last three weeks they will share together. Matt is planning their final night. Olga sends him text messages, saying they need to talk. Matt calls but gets no response. "She seems like she has something she wants to tell me," he says. "Lately," says Olga, "he's been acting different, like he wants to tell me something."

·　　·　　·

In the end there is no party, no tears. Matt piles everything he owns into the back of his car—dirty clothes mostly, two pillows, a basketball—and heads north, up the 5, to leave it all with his parents. He flies back down. They do not follow. He crashes in the Cal Lutheran dorms, only thirty-five dollars to his name. Olga tries to reach him again. Matt is no longer playing along. "She needs someone to teach her a lesson," Matt says. "I want her to have regrets." Matt had taken out his earrings for his trip to

MEPS; by the time he remembers to put them back in, the skin has already closed.

He spends his last night with an old flame, the same girl who turned him into a smoker. He takes her to the Spearmint Rhino, in Oxnard, for a gaze at the all-nude gyration. Whatever Matt thinks he is going to get out of this encounter, the arrival of cops, weapons drawn, storming the joint, cannot be good. There has been a report, apparently, of a couple with a gun. They zero in on Matt first. He scoops up his $1 bills from the table. They pat him down, quiz him, run his ID. "I'm leaving for boot camp tomorrow," Matt pleads. By the time they let him go, his date is interested in nothing more than a hug. "I'm more of boyfriend material," Matt says later, "than a hit-it-and-quit-it guy." The next morning he pulls out his wallet. He is at Starbucks with some Cal Lutheran friends. They had bet him—ten bucks—he would not be able to score.

One of them, Micah Kapono Naruo, is a shrewd chess player, Matt's nemesis on the board. "He's usually more defensive," Micah says. "I usually do more attacking." Sergeant Waud is expected any minute. Matt's farewell is a hasty match, one he knows he has no chance of winning.

"Matt!" Micah scolds, sliding his bishop into an undefended rook.

"Damn it," Matt says. "I forgot about that guy."

"Check," Micah says.

"I hate it when you do that shit," Matt says.

"Check," Micah says.

"Hmm," Matt says. "Now I'm just trying to delay the game."

Before he can fly out, Matt needs to return to MEPS for a final check-up, which means two more nights at the Westin. It occurs to him, between the sleeplessness and the drudgery, that he is being subjected to more rules and regulations than he has been at any time since leaving Capital Christian. He is about to embark on a cross-country odyssey, be entrusted with multimillion-dollar equipment, perhaps risk his life on a far-off battlefield, and yet he is being treated like a child—no smoking, no drinking, no girls, no leaving campus. The army is supposed to be the final act of Matt's desheltering, his entry into a world of grit and guts. Yet it also shares much with the church: the hierarchy, the vestments, the leaps of faith, the commandments not meant to be questioned. Matt will be doing big things but within a narrow structure.

Matt's file, from his examination at MEPS, lists him at five feet four, 110 pounds. It is hard to know what to make of these new figures—the measurements, essentially, of a jockey. Matt is sure they are wrong, which is possible. Bureaucracies can be careless. But it is just as possible, maybe more so, that they are accurate. Neither explanation is welcome: The army has sold him short, or he has overestimated himself.

On his last night at the hotel, Matt decides to shave. First he does his goatee. Then he returns to the sink and wipes away his mustache. His head was already cropped; before they parted, his dad had bought an electric trimmer. Now Matt is decidedly impish, four or five years taken off with the fuzz. He looks to be regressing—a version of Dorian Gray, growing younger as he turns into a soldier. "Damn, my face feels weird," he says, stroking his naked chin.

.   .   .

As always, the wake-up call comes at 3. Breakfast at 3:30. Bus at 4. Only this time, as it idles in the predawn chill, Matt cannot be found. He is scheduled to travel with seven other privates, all headed to Fort Leonard Wood. They do not yet know who he is or what he looks like, but they recognize that a comrade is missing. One of them calls Matt's room. Another searches the restaurant. A third climbs up the steps of the bus. "Is there a Matt Ludwig on board?" he shouts into the darkness, getting only coughs and snickers in response.

For the last six weeks, Matt's identity has hinged on this day. Joining the army was less a decision than an intuition, a moment of clarity, a burst of autonomy. Now that the time has arrived, how could he be missing it? What could he possibly be thinking? Finally, Matt stumbles out of the Westin's elevators, dazed and sheepish. "I never heard the phone," he mumbles, peeved at himself for bungling such a simple task, and so soon into his new life. He gets on the bus. "It's okay," someone from the back drawls, "we still love you." The last on, Matt's group is the first off at LAX: Southwest, flight 2719, bound for St. Louis. It is the busiest travel day of the year.

At the gate he finds a Starbucks. The usual, iced grande vanilla latte. But this time, no place to smoke. He has just enough battery left in his cell phone to check for messages. He powers it on. Nobody has called. At 6:45, a tangerine glow creeps across the tarmac. Matt takes his place in line. On his boarding pass, they have gotten his name wrong: Lidwig. The forecast calls for rain, turning to snow by the time he arrives.

Vanity Fair

WINNER—ESSAYS

"What would I do if I suddenly found I had a short time to live?" asks writer Marjorie Williams, for whom this hypothetical question becomes sadly real. After learning that, at forty-three, she has incurable liver cancer, Williams describes a journey from diagnosis to discovery. Living on borrowed time with her husband and two young children, she affirms the importance of savoring every moment, even while facing the issues brought on by her imminent death. This dramatic and analytic account of her ordeal was published posthumously.

Marjorie Williams

A Matter of
Life and Death

I t was cancer—a brutally sudden death sentence: the doctors
told the author she had probably less than six months. For a
woman with two young children and a full life, that prognosis was devastating, but also, in some ways, oddly liberating. And
so began more than three years of horror, hope, and grace, as she
learned to live, and even laugh, on borrowed time

. . .

The beast first showed its face benignly, in the late-June warmth
of a California swimming pool, and it would take me more than
a year to know it for what it was. Willie and I were lolling happily
in the sunny shallow end of my in-laws' pool when he—then only
seven—said, "Mommy, you're getting thinner."

It was true, I realized with some pleasure. Those intractable ten
or fifteen pounds that had settled in over the course of two preg-
nancies: hadn't they seemed, lately, to be melting away? I had
never gained enough weight to think about trying very hard to
lose it, except for sporadic, failed commitments to the health club.
But I'd carried—for so many years I hardly noticed it—an unpleasant sensation of being more cushiony than I wanted to be.
And now, without trying, I'd lost at least five pounds, perhaps
even eight.

I suppose I fell into the smug assumption that I had magically restored the lucky metabolism of my twenties and thirties, when it had been easy for me to carry between 110 and 120 pounds on a frame of five feet six inches. True, in the months before Willie's observation, I'd been working harder, and more happily, than I had in years—burning more fuel through later nights and busier days. I'd also been smoking, an old habit I'd fallen into again two years earlier, bouncing back and forth between quitting and succumbing, working up to something like eight cigarettes a day.

Of course Willie noticed it first, I now think: children major in the study of their mothers, and Willie has the elder child's umbilical awareness of me. But how is it that I didn't even question a weight loss striking enough for a child to speak up about? I was too happy enjoying this unexpected gift to question it even briefly: the American woman's yearning for thinness is so deeply a part of me that it never crossed my mind that a weight loss could herald something other than good fortune.

·　　·　　·

As it happened, I took up running about a month later, in concert with quitting smoking for good. By the end of the summer I was running about four miles a day, at least five days a week. And with all that exercise I found I could eat pretty much anything I wanted without worrying about my weight. So more weight melted away, and the steady weight loss that might have warned me something was going badly wrong disguised itself instead as the reward for all those pounding steps I was taking through the chill of early fall, the sting of winter, the beauty of spring's beginning. I went from around 126 pounds, in the spring of 2000, to about 109 a year later.

Somewhere in there my period became irregular—first it was late, then it stopped altogether. Well, I'd heard of this: women who exercise heavily sometimes do become amenorrheic. I discussed it with my gynecologist in January, and he agreed it was no real cause for alarm. He checked my hormone levels and found I definitely hadn't hit perimenopause, but what I most remember about that visit is the amazed approval with which he commented on the good shape I was in.

Around that time—I can't pinpoint exactly when—I began to have hot flashes, almost unnoticeable at first, gradually increasing in intensity. Well, I said to myself, I must be perimenopausal after all; a gynecologist friend told me that hormone levels can fluctuate so much that the test my doctor had done wasn't necessarily the last word on the subject.

Then one day in April I was lying on my back, talking idly on the telephone (strangely, I don't remember to whom), and running my hand up and down my now deliciously scrawny stomach. And just like that I felt it: a mass, about the size of a small apricot, on the lower right side of my abdomen. My mind swung sharply into focus: Have I ever felt this thing before, this lump? Well, who knows, maybe this is a part of my anatomy I was just never aware of before—I had always had a little layer of fat between my skin and the mysteries of the innards. Maybe there was some part of the intestine that felt that way, and I had just never been thin enough to notice it before.

You know how you've always wondered about it: Would you notice if you had a sudden lump? Would you be sensible enough to do something about it? How would your mind react? For all of us, those wonderings have a luxuriantly melodramatic quality. Because surely that isn't really how it works; you don't just stumble onto the fact that you have a lethal cancer while you're gabbing on the phone like a teenager. Surely you can't have a death sentence so close to the surface, just resting there, without your being in some other way aware of it.

I thought about calling my doctor, but then remembered that I had a full checkup scheduled in about three weeks anyway; I would bring it up then. In the intervening weeks I often reached down to find this odd bump: sometimes it wasn't there, and at other times it was. Once, I even thought it had moved—could I possibly be feeling it three inches up and two inches to the left, nearly underneath my belly button? Surely not. This must be just another sign that I was imagining things.

Checkup day came. I had been seeing the same doctor for at least a decade. I'd chosen him casually, foolishly, at a time in my life when having a general practitioner didn't seem like a very important decision. For most of the past decade almost all my healthcare issues had taken me to the office of my obstetrician, the man who delivered my two babies. To him I felt infinitely bonded. And because he had tested my health so diligently—and appropriately for a mother who had her first baby at thirty-five— I hadn't really seen the need, for years, for a general checkup.

So this doctor I was seeing now had never had to see me through anything serious. But he had always handled what little I brought to him with sympathy and dispatch; I had a mild liking for him.

To begin the checkup, he ushered me into his office, fully clothed, to talk. I told him about all of it: the stopped periods, the hot flashes, the fact that I could intermittently feel a mass in my belly. But I also told him what seemed most true to me: that over-all I felt healthier than I'd been in years.

Right off the bat, Dr. Generalist advised me to press the matter of hot flashes, and of the vanished period, with my gynecologist. No Hormones Handled Here. Then he ushered me into his examining room next door, with the standard instruction to dress in a flimsy robe while he stepped out of the room. He inspected me in all the typical ways, then told me to get back in my clothes and step back into his office. I had to remind him that I had reported a strange lump in my abdomen. So he had me lie back down, and felt all around that area. No mass. He got me to feel there, too; it was one of those times when I couldn't feel it.

"I would think," he said, "that what you're feeling is stool that's moving through your bowel. What you're feeling is a loop of intestine or something where the stool is stuck for a while. That's why sometimes it's there and sometimes it's not. The bad things don't come and go; the bad things only come and stay." He could send me off for a lot of tests, he said, but there really wasn't any point in going to that trouble and expense, because I was so obviously a perfectly healthy patient. He repeated all the same information in a letter mailed to me the following week after my blood tests came back: Healthy healthy healthy.

Looking back, I know I was uneasy even after I got this clean bill of health. Sometimes I sensed what seemed like a flicker of movement in my belly, and got the oddest feeling that I might be pregnant. (At one point, I even bought a home pregnancy test and furtively took it in a stall in the ladies' room in the little mall that housed the pharmacy.) Every now and then, the mass in my abdomen actually stuck out when I lay on my back; once, I looked down to see my stomach distinctly tilted—high on the right side, much lower on the left. I was at some pains never to point this out to my husband, Tim.

·   ·   ·

Finally, on the last Friday night in June 2001, I had a huge hot flash while my husband was tickling my back, in bed. Suddenly I was drenched; I could feel that his fingers could no longer slide easily along the skin of my back. He turned to me, astonished: "What *is* this?" he asked. "You're *covered* in sweat."

It was as if someone had at last given me permission to notice fully what was happening inside me. I made an appointment with my gynecologist—the earliest one I could get was the next week, on Thursday, July 5—and began deliberately noticing how overwhelming the hot flashes had gotten. Now that I was paying close attention, I realized they were coming fifteen or twenty times a day, sweeping over and through me and leaving me sheathed in a layer of sweat. They came when I ran, making my joyous morning run a tedious slog that must be gotten through; they came when I sat still. They exceeded anything that had been described to me as the gradual coming of menopause. This was more like walking into a wall. On both Monday and Tuesday of that week, I remember, I stopped about two miles into my morning run, simply stopped, despite the freshness of the morning and the beauty of the path I usually cut through the gardened streets of Takoma Park. Any runner knows the feeling of having to push past the body's observation that it might be more fun to walk slowly home and pop open a beer (just keep putting one foot in front of the other), but this was something different, like an override system I could no longer ignore. It said: Stop. It said: This is a body that can no longer afford to run.

·   ·   ·

My gynecologist's office is way, way out in the long exurban belt stretching westward from D.C. Pat was running late that afternoon, so it was probably after five when he finally called me into his office. I told him about the hot flashes, and about the lump I was feeling in my abdomen. "Yup, you're in menopause," he said somewhat brusquely. "We can start giving you hormones, but first let's check out that lump you say you're feeling."

We went into the examining room, where he keeps his ultrasound equipment. He'd given me dozens of quick exams with it over my childbearing years. I hopped up on the table, and he slapped on some of the chilly goo they apply to your belly, to make the ultrasound mouse slide over your skin, and almost immediately he stopped: "There," he said. "Yeah, there's something here." He looked at it a bit more, very briefly, then started snapping off his gloves. His face looked as neutral as he could possibly make it, which alarmed me instantly. "Just so you know," he said quickly, "it's probably fibroids. I'm not thinking cancer, but I am thinking surgery. So get dressed and come on back to my office, and I'll explain."

We sat back down on opposite sides of his desk. But before we talked, he called out to his receptionist, who was just packing up for the evening. "Before you go," he said, "I need you to book her an ultrasound and a CT scan. Tomorrow, if possible."

I told Pat he was scaring me: what was all this speed about if he wasn't thinking cancer?

"Well," he said, "I'm pretty sure it's not—I'll explain why in a minute—but I hate to have something like this hanging over a weekend. I want to know for sure what we're dealing with."

He went on to explain that he'd seen what looked like a fairly large growth on my ovary, but that it didn't look like ovarian cancer; its consistency was different. (Here, he drew me a picture on the back of a piece of scrap paper.) He explained that fibroids can sometimes be removed with surgery but that very often they grew back, even worse than before. His own typical recommendation, for a woman who was done having babies, he said, was a hysterectomy.

"Does this have anything to do with my hot flashes?" I asked.

"No, not a thing, in all probability. You just happen to be starting menopause, too."

I felt on the verge of tears. When I left, I sat in the car to collect myself, boggling at the thought of losing my uterus at the age of forty-three. I didn't even call my husband on my cell phone. I just wanted to calm down and get home and then seek the sanctuary of his sympathy.

The next morning, Pat's office called to say they had scored a formal ultrasound examination at three in the afternoon, in a D.C. radiology practice I'd visited from time to time before. When I got there, Pat's nurse told me, they would give me an appointment— probably early the next week—to come back for a CT scan.

I told my husband I didn't need him to come to the sonogram: it would probably only give a clearer picture of what Pat's ultrasound had already told us, I assumed. There's nothing painful or difficult about a sonogram, and I didn't want to haul Tim out of work twice; I knew I'd want him with me for the CT scan later.

That was a bad decision.

I remember waiting endlessly at the desk for the receptionist to finish a peckish, convoluted phone conversation with the manager of the garage downstairs, about why she'd been billed wrong for that month's parking. She talked on and on ("Yes, I *know* that's what I owe for each month, but I already paid you for both June and July"), with zero self-consciousness about keeping a patient standing there at the desk. There was a sign that instructed one to sign in and then take a seat, but, of course, I needed to talk to her about scheduling the CT scan after the sonogram. She kept flicking her hand at me and trying to shoo me toward a chair, then pointing at the sign. I just waited.

Finally I told her why I was standing there: "Um, CAT scan . . . The doctor's office told me . . . as soon as possible. . . . "

"What are you?" she said. A puzzled silence. "I mean, what *kind* are you?"

"Well, um, they're looking at something in my pelvis—"

"Oh, body," she said, her scowl regathering. "We are really, really booked on bodies." She started to flip through her appointment book. I stood there, trying to radiate as palatable a combination of charm and distress as I could manage. "Well, I'll talk to the doctor," she finally mumbled. "Ask me again when your sonogram's done. We might be able to do Monday morning, eleven o'clock."

· · ·

When my father was under treatment for cancer, which put him in and out of various hospitals for five years, I used to roll my eyes at the way he ingratiated himself with all the staff. You could walk into intensive care and he'd be there, his face wan against the pillow, but with his usual charming, modest smile ready for everyone. He would introduce his nurse and tell you where she was born, and how her sister wrote romance novels, and that her brother was on a track-and-field scholarship at the State University of New York.

Part and parcel, I thought, of his lifelong campaign to be loved by everyone he met. He had always put more energy into captivating strangers than anyone else I knew.

But I learned right away, when I went for this very first test, how wrong I'd been. As a patient, you come to feel that you need everyone—from the chairman of the oncology service at a major cancer center down to the least-paid clerk in the admissions department—to like you. Some of them may have the power to save your life. Others have the power to make you comfortable in the middle of the night, or to steer away from you the nurse-in-training who is still just learning to insert IVs, or to squeeze you in for a test you might otherwise wait days for.

I was discovering this truth on my back, while the ultrasound technician guided her wand through the chilly gel she had squeezed onto my belly. She was a friendly young woman with a Spanish accent of some kind, and her job was to get an accurate picture of what was going on in my pelvis while divulging the least information possible to the anxious patient. My job was to find out as much as I could, as quickly as I could.

So there I am: "Gosh, Friday afternoon . . . Have you had a long week? . . . How long have you been working in ultrasound? . . . Oh! Is that my ovary there, really? . . . Ah, so you're taking pictures now . . . Uh-huh . . . Gee, that must be the growth my gynecologist was talking about."

Under this onslaught of niceness, the technician begins to think aloud a bit. Yes, she is seeing a growth. But usually fibroids, which grow from the outside of the uterus, move in concert with it: poke the uterus and the growth will move too. This growth seemed to be independent of the uterus.

Is it a mild chill I'm feeling, or a mild thrill? I am still reeling at the thought that I might have a hysterectomy at forty-three; perhaps I am thinking it would at least be fun to have something more interesting than a fibroid?

But if there is a tinge of that interest, it vanishes when she speaks again: "Huh. Here's another one." And another. Suddenly, we are seeing three strange round plants that yield to a mild shove, but don't behave like anything she's ever seen before. She is doubly skeptical now about the fibroid theory. My gynecologist had examined me in detail the previous January, so much of what we're looking at has to have grown within six months. Fibroids, she says, don't grow nearly that fast.

I am surprised that she is so forthcoming, but soon see that it is of little use to me: she is looking at something she's never seen before. She summons the doctor—the chief radiologist in the practice—who in turn summons a younger colleague she is training. They all crowd around the machine in fascination.

Again, we do the poking-the-uterus exercise. We try the transvaginal sonography wand. Their mystification has begun to make me seriously frightened. I begin to question the doctor very directly. She is quite kind. She really can't say what she's seeing, she tells me.

It almost seems an afterthought—the indulgence of a hunch—when the doctor turns to the technician and says, "Try moving up, yes, to the navel or so." I can still remember the feel of the equipment casually gliding up toward my navel, and then a sudden, palpable tension in the air. For, immediately, another large growth—one even bigger than the three below—looms into view.

. . . .

This is the moment when I know for certain that I have cancer. Without anyone's even looking very hard, this exam has been turning up mysterious blobs in every quarter. I go very still as the doctor begins directing the technician to turn here, look there.

Her voice has dropped almost to a whisper, and I don't want to distract her with my anxious questions: I can hold them long enough for her to find out what I need to know.

But then I hear one of them mumble to the other, "You see there? There is some ascites . . . ," and I feel panic wash through me. Along with my sisters, I nursed my mother through her death from a liver illness, and I know that ascites is the fluid that collects around the liver when it is badly diseased.

"Are you finding something on my liver too?" I croak.

"Yes, something, we're not sure what," says the doctor, pressing a sympathetic hand to my shoulder. And then suddenly I'm aware that they've made a decision to stop this exam. What's the point in finding more? They've found out enough to know that they need the more subtle diagnostic view of a CT scan.

"Is there a case to be made against my freaking out now?" I ask.

Well, yes, replies the doctor. There's a lot we don't know; there's a lot we need to find out; it could be a great range of different things, some of which would be better than others.

"But then let me ask you this way," I press. "Do you know of anything other than cancer that could give rise to the number of growths we just saw? Could it be anything benign?"

"Well, no," she says. "Not that I'm aware of. But we'll be sure to work you in Monday morning for a CT scan, and then we'll know a lot more. I'm going to call your doctor now, and then I assume you'd like to talk to him after me?"

She shows me to a private office to wait; she will let me know when I should pick up the phone there. In the meantime, I choose a free phone line and dial my husband's cell phone. I have caught him somewhere on the street. There is a huge noise behind him; he can barely hear me.

"I need you—" I begin, barely in control of my voice. "I need you to get in a cab and come to the Foxhall medical building."

This is what he says: "O.K." He doesn't say, "What's wrong?" He doesn't ask, "What did the test show?" It is my first glimpse of the miraculous generosity that will help me get through everything that is about to happen. He can tell how tenuous my control is; he can tell that I need him; he has agreed without speech to hold the anxiety of knowing nothing more for the twenty minutes it will take him to get here.

After this, I talk briefly with my gynecologist on the phone. Pat's first words are "What time's your CT scan? I'm going to cancel all my Monday-morning appointments and come to your scan." I have never heard of a doctor coming to a CAT scan before this. It foretells the huge seams of good fortune that will run through the black rock of the next three years. There is nothing like having a doctor who really cares about you—who can speed up the inhuman pace of medical time, which usually leaves patients begging to hear their test results, waiting too many days for an appointment, at a loss until the conveyor belt brings along the next hurried intervention. Pat is one of the doctors who are willing to break the rules: Here is my cell-phone number—call me anytime this weekend. We will figure out together what to do on Monday.

Somehow, my husband and I stagger through the weekend. Every hour or so one of us steals away to a computer to re- or misdiagnose for the fourteenth time. The truth is we know for sure I have some kind of cancer, and that any cancer that has metastasized is bad, and that that is all we will know for a few more days.

.   .   .

Finally, Monday comes. After the CT scan, Pat takes me directly to the hospital to get prodded by his favorite surgeon, whom I'll call Dr. Goodguy. ("The surgeon I'd take my own family to," Pat says.) In the examining room, Dr. Goodguy frowns over my films, palpates my abdomen, interviews me, and schedules me for both an M.R.I. that afternoon and a biopsy two days later. I think to ask how big all these growths are. *Several oranges and even one grapefruit,* Dr. Goodguy says, my first inkling that citrus metaphor is essential to cancer treatment.

Being a patient requires that you master the Zen of living in hospital time, tuning out as much as possible while also demanding a constant vigilance, because some people really will screw up your treatment if you're not paying strict attention. When I go for my M.R.I., the technician—a lovely, smiling man with a very uncertain command of English—seems very vague about what, exactly, he's supposed to be examining. I insist that he call Dr. Goodguy's office.

Pat and Dr. Goodguy have been scratching their heads. What could possibly grow so fast, and so widely? Probably—maybe—lymphoma. They keep telling me this, which would be the good news, because lymphomas are increasingly treatable. My gynecologist friend, Laura, has told me the same thing over the weekend. My psychotherapist nods at the wisdom of this off-the-cuff prognosis. I find myself on the point of hysterical laughter. How many more people, I wonder, are going to tell me, Congratulations! You've got lymphoma!!

By Thursday afternoon this is no longer funny. I've had a biopsy the previous day, and Dr. Goodguy calls about three P.M. He has a Very Serious Doctor Voice on, and jumps right in: "Well, this isn't good. It's not lymphoma. Your pathology report shows that your tumor is consistent with hepatoma, which is, uh, which is liver cancer." Already I am struggling: does "consistent with" mean they think that but they don't really know it? No, those are just scientific weasel words they use in pathology reports. (A pathologist, I will learn, would look at your nose and report that it is consistent with a breathing apparatus.)

I know this diagnosis is very, very bad. Liver cancer is one of the possibilities I researched in my compulsive tours of the Internet over the weekend, so I already know it's one of the worst things you can have. Still, I say to the doctor, "Well, how bad is that?"

"I won't avoid it. It's very serious."

"And it would presumably be bad news that it's already created other tumors around my body?"

"Yes. Yes, that is a bad sign."

A lovely man, who's doing a hard job with a patient he just met three days before. There are at least five large metastases of the cancer in my pelvis and abdomen, and the mother ship—a tumor the size of a navel orange—straddles the channel where the major blood vessels run into and out of the liver. Tumors so widespread automatically "stage" my cancer at IV(b). There is no V, and there is no (c).

When I hang up the phone I call Tim and tell him. We make it as clinical a conversation as possible, because otherwise there will be so much feeling it might stand in the way of acting. He is on his way home, right away.

I call my friend Liz and tell her. I tell her some of the statistics— that, as I read the data, I may be dead by Christmas. Liz almost always says the perfect thing, from the heart, and now she says the two things I most need to hear. The first is "I want you to know that, whatever happens, I will be with you the whole way."

The second is "And you know that all of us—but this is my promise—we will all work to keep you alive in your children's minds." Now tears are pouring down my cheeks, and they feel good.

•　　•　　•

The drama of discovery and diagnosis happened so long ago, and has been followed by so many drastic plot twists, that it feels to me like ancient history. But I've noticed that almost everyone I talk to is very curious to know those details. Whenever the whim of disease takes me into the view of a new doctor or nurse, we fall into the standard, boring rhythm of summarizing history and condition (when diagnosed; at what stage; what treatments have been administered since, with what results). If the person I'm talking to is young and relatively inexperienced, I may find myself more schooled in this procedure even than she or he is. But there always comes a moment when their professionalism suddenly drops, their clipboards drift to their sides, and they say, "Uhn, how—do you mind if I ask you how you happened to find out you had cancer?" I realize at these times that they are asking as fellow humans, not too much younger than I am, and their fascination is the same as everyone else's: Could this happen to me? How would I know? What would that feel like?

We have all indulged this curiosity, haven't we? What would I do if I suddenly found I had a short time to live . . . What would it be like to sit in a doctor's office and hear a death sentence? I had entertained those fantasies just like the next person. So when it actually happened, I felt weirdly like an actor in a melodrama. I had—and still sometimes have—the feeling that I was doing, or had done, something faintly self-dramatizing, something a bit too attention-getting. (I was raised by people who had a horror of melodrama, but that's another part of the story.)

In two months I will mark the finish of year 3 B.T.—my third year of Borrowed Time. (Or, as I think of it on my best days, Bonus Time.) When I was diagnosed with Stage IV(b) liver cancer in early July of 2001, every doctor was at great pains to make clear to me that this was a death sentence. Unless you find liver cancer early enough to have a surgeon cut out the primary tumor before it spreads, you have little chance of parole. The five-year survival rate for those who can't have surgery is less than 1 percent; my cancer had spread so widely that I was facing a prognosis somewhere between three and six months. I was forty-three; my children were five and eight.

Liver cancer is so untreatable because chemotherapy has little effect. There are other, localized treatments that can slow the growth of the main tumor, or tumors, in the liver. (They pump chemo through an artery directly into the tumors and block the exits; they ablate them with radio-frequency waves; they freeze them; or they install localized chemo pumps to blast them.) But if the cancer has spread, the medical textbooks say, there is no therapy that can stop it, or even slow it down much. Chemo has about a 25 to 30 percent chance of having any impact, and even then it will almost always be a small and transient one: a slight and temporary shrinkage, a short pause in the cancer's growth, a check on further metastases that can add to the patient's pain.

But for some reasons I know and others I don't, my body—with the help of six hospitals, dozens of drugs, a teeming multitude of smart doctors and nurses, and a heroically stubborn husband—has mounted a miraculous resistance. As seriously fucked cancer patients go, I am an astonishingly healthy woman.

I live at least two different lives. In the background, usually, is the knowledge that, for all my good fortune so far, I will still die of this disease. This is where I wage the physical fight, which is, to say the least, a deeply unpleasant process. And beyond the concrete challenges of needles and mouth sores and barf basins and barium, it has thrown me on a roller coaster that sometimes clatters up a hill, giving me a more hopeful, more distant view than I'd expected, and at other times plunges faster and farther than I think I can endure. Even when you know the plunge is coming—it's in the nature of a roller coaster, after all, and you know that you disembark on the bottom and not the top—even then, it comes with some element of fresh despair.

I've hated roller coasters all my life.

·   ·   ·

But in the foreground is regular existence: love the kids, buy them new shoes, enjoy their burgeoning wit, get some writing done, plan vacations with Tim, have coffee with my friends. Having found myself faced with that old bull-session question (What would you do if you found out you had a year to live?), I learned that a woman with children has the privilege or duty of bypassing the existential. What you do, if you have little kids, is lead as normal a life as possible, only with more pancakes.

This is the realm of life in which I make intensely practical decisions—almost, these three years on, without thinking about it. When we bought a new car last fall, I chose it, bargained for it, and paid for it with the last of an old retirement account my father had left me. And then I registered it only in my husband's name—because who needs the hassles over title if he decides to sell it later? When an old crown at the back of my lower right jaw began to disintegrate last summer, I looked at my dentist, whose fastidiousness I have relied on for almost twenty years, and said, Jeff, look: I'm doing O.K. right now, but I've got every reason to think it would be foolish to sink $4,000 into, um, infrastructure at this point. Is there anything sort of half-assed and inexpensive we could do, just to get by?

Sometimes I feel immortal: whatever happens to me now, I've earned the knowledge some people never gain, that my span is finite, and I still have the chance to rise, and rise, to life's generosity. But at other times I feel trapped, cursed by my specific awareness of the guillotine blade poised above my neck. At those times I resent you—or the seven other people at dinner with me, or my husband, deep in sleep beside me—for the fact that you may never even catch sight of the blade assigned to you.

Sometimes I simply feel horror, that most elementary thing. The irreducible fear, for me, is the fantasy that I will by some mistake be imprisoned in my body after dying. As a child I never enjoyed a minute of any campfire stories of the buried-alive genre. And even without that unwelcome and vivid fear in my mind, I can't find any way around the horror of being left alone down there in the dark, picked apart by processes about which I'm a little bit squeamish even when they're just fertilizing my daylilies. Intellectually, I know it won't matter to me in the slightest. But my most primal fear is that somehow my consciousness will be carelessly left behind among my remains.

But, of course, I am already being killed, by one of nature's most common blunders. And these blunt fears are easily deconstructed as a form of denial: if I'm stuck alive in my coffin, well, that will in some sense override the final fact of my death, no? I can see these dread-filled fantasies as the wishes they are: that I really can stay in this body I love; that my consciousness really will run on past my death; that I won't just . . . die.

．　　　．　　　．

There are a million lesser fears. The largest category concerns my children, and weighs both the trivial and the serious. I fear that my Alice will never really learn to wear tights. (You'd think, from watching my husband try to help her into them on the rare occasion when he's asked, that he'd been asked to perform a breech birth of twin colts at the peak of a blizzard). That no one will ever really brush her fine, long hair all the way through, and that she will display a perpetual bird's nest at the back of her neck. (And— what? People will say her slatternly mother should have drummed better Hair Care into her family's minds before selfishly dying of cancer?) That no one will ever put up curtains in my dining room, the way I've been meaning to for the last three years.

Deeper: Who will talk to my darling girl when she gets her period? Will my son sustain that sweet enthusiasm he seems to beam most often at me? There are days I can't look at them—literally, not a single time—without wondering what it will do to them to grow up without a mother. What if they can't remember what I was like? What if they remember, and grieve, all the time?

What if they don't?

But even this obvious stuff, the dread and sorrow, make up a falsely simple picture. Sometimes, early on, death was a great dark lozenge that sat bittersweet on my tongue for hours at a time, and I savored the things I'd avoid forever. I'll never have to pay taxes, I thought, or go to the Department of Motor Vehicles. I won't have to see my children through the worst parts of adolescence. I won't have to be human, in fact, with all the error and loss and love and inadequacy that come with the job.

I won't have to get old.

It says a lot about the power of denial that I could so automatically seek (and find!) the silver lining that might come with dying of cancer in my forties. For good and ill, I no longer think that way. The passage of time has brought me the unlikely ability to work, simultaneously, at facing my death and loving my life.

Often it is lonely work. And I have nothing happy to impart about the likelihood that I will have to take chemotherapy for the rest of my life—nothing, except that I should be so lucky. But I am now, after a long struggle, surprisingly happy in the crooked, sturdy little shelter I've built in the wastes of Cancerland. Here, my family has lovingly adapted to our awful tumble in fortune. And here, I nurture a garden of eleven or twelve different varieties of hope, including the cramped, faint, strangely apologetic hope that, having already done the impossible, I will somehow attain the unattainable cure.

.   .   .

Our first stop, after I received my diagnosis, was the office of my G.P., the one who missed all the signs and symptoms of my disease. We were not feeling especially confident in his skills, but we thought he might have ideas about treatment, and could at least perform the service of doing a full set of blood tests.

As we were driving over to Dr. Generalist, Tim turned to me at a stoplight and said, "I just want you to know: I'm going to be a total prick." What he meant by this was that there was no log he wouldn't roll, no connection he wouldn't tap, no pull he wouldn't use. Tim, a fellow journalist, is a man who would rather swallow gravel than use a job title to get a good table at a restaurant. But within an hour of hearing the bad news, he had scored me an appointment early the next Monday at Memorial Sloan-Kettering Cancer Center, in New York City, one of the country's most eminent cancer-treatment centers. Tim had done this by the simple expedient of calling Harold Varmus, president and chief executive officer of M.S.K.C.C., with whom we'd formed a warm but very tangential friendship when Harold was in Washington running the National Institutes for Health during the Clinton administration. These are the kinds of appointments, I was to learn, that some people wait weeks or even months for. I say that not in the spirit of a boast, only as a reminder that in this way, as in most others, medicine is unfair—rationed in fundamentally irrational ways. But when your own time comes, you will pull pretty much every string available to get what you need.

By the next morning—it was still only the day after my diagnosis—I had a noon appointment with the topmost G.I. oncologist available at Johns Hopkins University Medical Center, which is in Baltimore, a little less than an hour from our house. This conquest of the appointment book was the doing of another friend, one of my bosses. We also got an appointment at the National Cancer Institute for later the following week.

So I had all the appointments I needed, and a husband who did yeoman legwork running from place to place getting copies of M.R.I.'s and CT scans and pathologists' reports and blood tests. If speed was needed in my case, I was well on my way to a record pace.

Just one problem: all this moving and shaking, driving to Baltimore and flying to New York, took us to the very same brick wall. In strode the doctor (usually trailing a retinue of students) to meet me, ask me a little about the onset of my disease. Out he went with my films under his arm, to look at them in privacy. In he came, quietly, his pace slowed and his face grim. He said some version of what the oncologist at Hopkins had said: "I couldn't believe—I just told my colleague, 'There is no way she looks sick enough to have this degree of disease. Someone blew this diagnosis.' Then I looked at this M.R.I."

It fell to the man at Hopkins to be the first to tell us just how bad my situation was. But they all said more or less the same thing: The Hopkins doc did it while focusing intently on the shape of his cuticles, turning his fingers in and then splaying them forward like a bride showing off her new rock. Another did it while holding my hand and looking sweetly into my face. "My dear," this one said, "you're in desperate trouble." One did it in the midst of a completely impenetrable lecture on the chemistry of chemotherapy. One did it with a look of panic on his face.

What it boiled down to was: We have nothing to do for you. You can't have surgery, because there's so much disease outside the liver. You're not a good candidate for any of the newer interventional strategies, and we can't do radiation, because we'd destroy too much viable liver tissue. All we can do is chemotherapy, and to be honest, we really don't expect much in the way of results.

The first time we heard this lecture, at Hopkins, we stepped blinking into the sunshine of a hot July day. "I need to take a walk," I told my husband, and we set off in the direction of Baltimore's Fell's Point neighborhood. Before long, I wanted to sit and talk. The only place we could find to sit was the concrete staircase of a public library. We sat there to absorb what we'd just heard.

"Maybe," said Tim, "the doctors at Sloan-Kettering will have something different to say."

"I doubt it," I said, out of the certainty of my Internet travels and the doctor's unambiguous pessimism. This pretty much set the pattern Tim and I would follow for the coming months: he took care of the hope, and I took care of getting ready to die.

·　　·　　·

The days fractured into lurching, indelible moments and odd details that stuck. The way the Sloan-Kettering waiting room—lush with Rockefeller-funded orchids and a plashing water sculpture—had nice rows of seats whose armrests were attached with Velcro so you could tear them away when you needed to sit and sob in your husband's arms. The black-and-white bumper sticker on the glass door of an East Side coffee shop we stopped into while killing time before an appointment: THIS IS REALLY HAPPENING, it said, in what felt like a message nailed there just for my eyes.

For the first ten days or so, I had a necessary composure. I got to and through all those appointments. I went to my desk and put together a filing system for all the names and information that were flooding into our life. I knew I wanted to keep it together while we decided what we were going to tell the children.

But after our discouraging visit to Sloan-Kettering, I could feel the waters at the dam getting close to overflowing. We decided to stay in New York an extra night or two to take advantage of the hospital's offer of a PET scan, which might identify new tumors, or spot the regression of old ones, more quickly than a CT scan.

As we sat in that plush waiting room making this decision, it came to me that I couldn't bear to continue staying with the old friends who had put us up the night before. They were contemporaries of my parents' and very dear to me, but I couldn't face talking to anyone about this latest news, or having to be in the least bit socially adept.

Tim, who knows me so well, put his arm around me and said, "Let's not think about money. Where do you want to go?" I brightened for a moment. There might not be any treatments out there that would work for me, but, by God, New York had some fine hotels. "Mmmm . . . the Peninsula?" So off we went to the land of high thread counts and long baths with a TV screen just above the taps.

It's amazing how you can distract yourself in the midst of such a dramatic experience—because you can't believe such awful news twenty-four hours a day. So I surrendered to the pleasures of a great hotel for about a day. I had my hair washed and blow-dried, and received a pedicure in the Peninsula salon. (I still remember sitting there staring, staring at all the colors of polish I could pick from. It took on the crazy proportions of an important decision: A docile sort of peach? A very feminine light pink, which might acknowledge surrender? Hell no: I chose a violent red, brighter than fire engines, bright as lollipops.)

Then, feeling beautiful, I actually danced around the room when Tim was out, my CD headphones blasting Carly Simon in my ears. When I was done I looked out the window of our room on the eighth floor, down all those hard surfaces to the tarmac of Fifth Avenue, and wondered what it would feel like just to jump. Would it be better or worse than what I was stepping into?

That night, finally, the dam broke. I was lying in bed with Tim when I realized it was all true: I was dying. Soon I would be dead. No one else would be in it with me.

I would be the one on the bed, and when the hospice nurse stopped by, my dearest loves would retreat to the hallway and swap impressions—separated from me already. Even while still alive, I would leave their party. I lay under those wonderful sheets and felt cold to the bone. I began to cry, loud, then louder. I shouted my terror. I sobbed with my entire rib cage. Tim held me while I heaved it out this way, a titanic purging. I was so loud that I wondered why no one called the police to say there was a woman getting murdered across the hall. It felt good to let go, but that feeling was little. It was dwarfed by the recognition I had just allowed in.

· · ·

We have come to think of my cancer not just as a disease but also as a locale. Cancerland is the place where at least one of us is often depressed: it is as if my husband and I hand the job back and forth without comment, the way most couples deal with child-minding or being the Saturday chauffeur.

I try to remember that I'm one of the luckiest cancer patients in America, by dint of good medical insurance, great contacts who gained me access to the best of the best among doctors, an amazing support system of friends and family, and the brains and drive to be a smart and demanding medical consumer, which is one of the very hardest things I've ever done. I'm quite sure that if I were among the 43 million of my fellow Americans who have no health insurance—let alone really good insurance—I'd be dead already. As it is, I never see a hospital bill that hasn't already been paid. And there is no co-payment on the many medications I've taken. Which is fortunate: one of them—the Neupogen with which I inject myself every day for a week after chemo to boost my bone marrow's production of white cells—costs about $20,000 a year.

For me, time is the only currency that truly counts anymore. I have weathered days of chemo-induced wretchedness and pain without a whimper, only to come unglued when some little glitch suddenly turns up to meddle with the way I had planned to use some unit of time: that this half-hour, and the contents I had planned to pour into it, are now lost to me forever seems an insupportable unfairness. Because of course any old unit of time can suddenly morph into a bloated metaphor for the rest of your time on earth, for how little you may have and how little you may control it.

Most of the time, for the past three years, even my good days have given me energy to do only one Big Thing: lunch with a friend, writing a column, a movie with the kids. Choose, choose, choose. I find myself on the phone with someone I'd love to see, and then I look at my calendar and find that, realistically, my next episode of unscheduled Free Play is five weeks off, on the far side of my next treatment, and even then there will really only be a total of about seven hours I can assign before the treatment after that. I am forced to admit that, in this cramped context, I don't actually want to spend two of these hours with the person I'm talking to. These forced choices make up one of the biggest losses of sickness.

But on the other side of this coin is a gift. I think cancer brings to most people a new freedom to act on the understanding that their time is important. My editor at the *Washington Post* told me, when I first got sick, that after his mother recovered from cancer his parents literally never went anywhere they didn't want to. If you have ever told yourself, breezily, that life is too short to spend any of it with your childhood neighbor's annoying husband, those words now take on the gleeful raiment of simple fact. The knowledge that time's expenditure is important, that it is up to you, is one of the headiest freedoms you will ever feel.

Some of my choices surprise me. One afternoon—a blowy day in early spring, the first day when the sun actually seemed to out-power the wind—I ducked a meeting people were counting on me to come to, and I didn't lie or apologize for my reasons, be-cause the most pressing thing I could possibly do that afternoon was plant something purple in that little spot next to the garden gate, the one I'd been thinking about for two years.

Time, I now understand, used to be a shallow concept to me. There was the time you occupied, sometimes anxiously, in the present (a deadline in three hours, a dentist's appointment for which you were ten minutes late); and there was your inarticulate sense of time's grander passage, and the way it changes with age.

Now time has levels and levels of meaning. For example, I have clung for a year and a half to a friend's observation that young children experience time in a different way from adults. Since a month can seem an eternity to a child, then every month I man-age to live might later teem with meaning and memory for my children. This totem is all I need during times when my pockets are otherwise empty of wisdom or strength.

Since I was diagnosed, I have had an eternity of time—at least six times as much as I was supposed to have—and sometimes I think that all of that time has been gilded with my knowledge of its value. At other moments, I think sadly of how much of the past three years has been wasted by the boredom and exhaustion and enforced stillness of treatment.

•   •   •

Not long after my diagnosis, in the pleasant offices of one of my new doctors, a liver specialist, we finally had the obligatory conversation about how I could have gotten this cancer. "You've got no cirrhosis," he said wonderingly, ticking off the potential causes on his fingers. "You've got no hepatitis. It's wild that you look so healthy."

So how do you think I got it? I asked.

"Lady," he said, "you got hit by lightning."

My biggest fear in those early days was that death would snatch me right away. An oncologist at Sloan-Kettering had mentioned, parenthetically, that the tumor in my vena cava could give birth at any time to a blood clot, causing a fast death by way of pulmonary embolism. The tumor was too close to the heart for them to consider installing a filter that would prevent this. It would be "rational," he said, in answer to our questions, to make it a policy for me not to drive anywhere with the children in the car.

I knew, too, that the disease outside my liver had grown with incredible speed. Only a couple of weeks after diagnosis, I began having symptoms—including stomach pain bad enough to hospitalize me for two days. After watching my father's five-year battle with cancer, I was aware that a cascade of side effects could begin at any time, some of them fatal.

I wasn't ready, I said to friends. Not in the way I could be ready in, oh, three or four months. Perhaps I was kidding myself in imagining that I could compose myself if only I had a little time. But I think not entirely. I had watched my parents die three years earlier, seven weeks apart—my mother, ironically, of liver disease, and my father of an invasive cancer of unknown origin. I had a pretty good idea, I thought, of what was coming.

But from almost the first instant, my terror and grief were tinged with an odd relief. I was so lucky, I thought, that this was happening to me as late as forty-three, not in my thirties or my twenties. If I died soon there would be some things I'd regret not having done, and I would feel fathomless anguish at leaving my children so young. But I had a powerful sense that, for my own part, I had had every chance to flourish. I had a loving marriage.

I'd known the sweet, rock-breaking, irreplaceable labor of parenthood, and would leave two marvelous beings in my place. I had known rapture, and adventure, and rest. I knew what it was to love my work. I had deep, hard-won friendships, and diverse, widespread friendships of less intensity.

I was surrounded by love.

All this knowledge brought a certain calm. I knew, intuitively, that I would have felt more panicked, more frantic, in the years when I was still growing into my adulthood. For I had had the chance to become the person it was in me to be. Nor did I waste any time wondering why. Why me? It was obvious that this was no more or less than a piece of horrible bad luck. Until then my life had been, in the big ways, one long run of good luck. Only a moral idiot could feel entitled, in the midst of such a life, to a complete exemption from bad fortune.

•   •   •

So now my death—as a given—dominated my relationships with all of those close to me: With my two dear, dear older sisters, to whom I was doubly bonded by the shared ordeal of helping my mother die, and with my stepmother—a contemporary of mine, who had seen my father through his five ferocious years of survival. With my best friends—who spoiled and cosseted and fed and sat with me, rounding up great brigades of clucking acquaintances to bring us dinners, saying just the right thing, and never turning aside my need to talk: especially my need to talk about when, not if. My friend Liz even went out to look over the local residential hospice, to help me work through my practical concerns about whether, with children so young, I was entitled to die at home.

Above all, of course, death saturated my life with my children—Willie, then eight, and Alice, then five. I don't think death (as opposed to illness) dominated their view of me, but it certainly barged its cackling way into my heart and mind during even the simplest of family interchanges. After talking to friends and reading several books, Tim and I had decided to handle the matter openly with them: We told them that I had cancer, and what kind. We told them about chemotherapy, and how it would make me seem even sicker than I looked then. We emphasized that they couldn't catch cancer and had nothing to do with causing it.

Beyond that, we would answer with honesty any question they asked, but wouldn't step ahead of them in forcing their knowledge of just how bad things were. When the timing of my death revealed itself, then we would have to tell them. Above all, I wanted to spare them the loss of their childhood to a constant vigilance: if they knew we would talk to them honestly, they wouldn't have to put all their energy into figuring out at every turn what new distress was agitating the air around them. Neither of them, at first, chose to ask the $64,000 question. But I couldn't lay eyes on them without seeing them swallowed by the shadow of devastation to come.

· · ·

Notice, though, that I don't include my husband among those to whom my death was an imminent fact. From the moment of diagnosis, Tim rolled up his sleeves and went to work. In this way, we divided the work of assimilating our nightmare: I addressed myself to death; he held a practical insistence on life. It was the best possible thing he could have done for me, although it often separated us at the time. It could make me crazy, lying awake on the left side of the bed, wanting to talk about death, while Tim lay awake on the right side, trying to figure out the next five moves he had to make to keep me alive, and then, beyond that, to find the magic bullet in which I did not believe.

But I never thought of refusing treatment. For one thing, it was obvious that I owed my children any shot at reprieve, no matter how improbable. Also, my doctors said that even the slim prospect of mitigation was worth a try. And so, Tim and I drifted into a tacit, provisional agreement to act as if . . . As if, while I began chemotherapy, I were in some genuine suspense about the outcome.

Yet it made me furious anytime someone tried to cheer me up by reciting the happy tale of a sister-in-law's cousin who had liver cancer but now he's eighty and he hasn't been troubled by it in forty years. I wanted to scream, *Don't you know how sick I am?* I knew how narcissistic and self-dramatizing this sounded. Still, it enraged me when anyone said, *Aaanh, what do doctors know? They don't know everything.* I was working so hard to accept my death: I felt abandoned, evaded, when someone insisted that I would live.

That was a deeper anger than the irritation I felt at the people—some of them important figures in my life—who had memorably inappropriate reactions. I can't count the times I've been asked what psychological affliction made me invite this cancer. My favorite *New Yorker* cartoon, now taped above my desk, shows two ducks talking in a pond. One of them is telling the other: "Maybe you should ask yourself why you're inviting all this duck hunting into your life right now."

One woman sent me a card to "congratulate" me on my "cancer journey," and quoted Joseph Campbell to the effect that in order to achieve the life you deserved you had to give up the life you had planned. Screw you, I thought. *You* give up the life *you* had planned.

Common wisdom insists, in answer to the awkward feelings that always accompany sickness and death, that there's really no wrong thing to say. This is entirely false. Around the same time I started treatment, my friend Mike revealed to all his friends that he had been dealing for some years with Parkinson's disease. We began a competition, by e-mail, to see who could compile the most appalling reactions.

I found my best ones in hospitals, among doctors and nurses who seemed unacquainted with—or terrified of—fear and death, who were constantly holding up the garlic of their difference from me, to ward me off even as they pretended to minister to me. There was the nurse who hissed at me, with inexplicable ire, "You have a very bad disease, you know." There was the nurse's aide at Georgetown University Hospital who trudged into my room one morning, heaved a great sigh, and said, "I tell you, I hate working the oncology floor. It's so depressing." Her aunt had died of cancer, she said, and, "boy, is that an awful disease."

At least her oddball gloom was right out there on the surface. Perhaps worst of all was the nurse in the chemo-infusion ward, with whom I fell into conversation to while away my seventh hour of chemotherapy on a gray day in late December. We talked idly about vacations we'd like to take someday. "Oh well," she said, putting down my chart and stretching kittenishly on her way out the door, "I have all the time in the world."

I had bought deeply into the pessimism of the doctors treating me. We think our culture lauds the stubborn survivor, the one who says, "I will beat this cancer," and then promptly wins the Tour de France. But the truth is that there is a staggering vulnerability in asserting one's right to hope. Even most of the doctors who have from time to time promoted my optimism tend to wash their hands of it as soon as some procedure or potion fails to pan out. So I have carried what hope I have as a furtive prize.

This attitude was driven, too, by what I brought to the fight. I grew up in a house where there was a premium on being wised up to impending disapproval or disappointment, and there was punishment by contempt for any blatant display of innocence or hopeful desire. It was all too easy for me to feel shamed in the blast of medicine's certainty. If I carried hope from the start, I did it in secret, hiding it like an illegitimate child of a century past. I hid it even from myself.

It is in my personality, anyway, to linger on the dark side, sniffing under every rock, determined to know the worst that may happen. Not to be caught by surprise. I was raised in a family full of lies—a rich, entertaining, well-elaborated fivesome that flashed with competition and triangles and changing alliances. If your sister was becoming anorexic, no one mentioned it. When your father's ubiquitous assistant came along on family vacations year after year, and sat at picnics with him thigh-to-thigh, no one named the strangeness of it. That my parents divided me and my sisters up between themselves and schooled us in scorn for the other team: that was certainly never acknowledged. But it married me for life to the inconvenient argument, the longing to know what was real.

.   .   .

Hence, even when my prospects for recovery or remission have looked best, there has always been one face of my being that was turned toward the likelihood of death—keeping in touch with it, convinced that denying it any entry would weaken me in ways I couldn't afford. Forced into a corner, I'll choose truth over hope any day.

I worried, of course, that I was dooming myself. Americans are so steeped in the message that we are what we think, and that a positive attitude can banish disease. (You'd be amazed how many people need to believe that only losers die of cancer.) Was my realism going to shoot down any possibility of help? Superstitiously, I wondered.

But it turns out that hope is a more supple blessing than I had imagined. From the start, even as my brain was wrestling with death, my body enacted some innate hope that I have learned is simply a part of my being. Chemotherapy would knock me into a passive misery for days. And then—depending on which formula I was taking at the time—a day would come when I would wake up feeling energetic and happy and very much like a normal person. Whether the bad time I had just had lasted five days or five weeks, some inner voice eventually said—and still says—*Never mind*. Today is a ravishing day, and I will put on a short skirt and high heels and see how much of the future I can inhale.

·　　·　　·

Three weeks after my diagnosis, on the morning of my first chemotherapy, my liver specialist dictated notes that closed with this fragmentary, misspelled sentence: "It is to be hoped . . . , unlikel that we will get a second chance."

Two chemo cycles later, I had a CT scan that showed dramatic shrinkage in all my tumors—shrinkage by as much as half. Dr. Liver actually hugged me, and hinted that it was not impossible I might be a "complete responder." The first thing you learn when you get cancer is that the disease you've always thought of as ninety or one hundred precise conditions is in fact hundreds of different diseases, which shade into each other all along the spectrum. And I turned out to have some mysterious fluke, a bit of biological filigree in the makeup of my tumors, that rendered them far better targets than I'd had any right to expect.

I went right out and bought four bottles of champagne and invited our eight dearest friends to the house for a party. It was a beautiful September night and we all ate pizza on the front porch. The kids were thrilled by the energy of it all, without quite understanding it. (After all, I still had cancer, didn't I? And they hadn't known how firmly I had felt sealed in my coffin before now.) It was as if a door far across a dark room had opened a small crack, admitting brilliant light from a hallway: it was still a long, long shot, I knew, but now at least I had something to drive toward. A possible opening, where before there had been none.

I became a professional patient. And all my doctors learned my name.

—May 2004

Marjorie Williams was a Vanity Fair *contributing editor and a writer for the* Washington Post. *She died of cancer in January 2005 at the age of forty-seven. A collection of her writing, entitled* The Woman at the Washington Zoo *(Public Affairs), was published in the fall of 2005.*

The New Yorker

**WINNER—
COLUMNS AND
COMMENTARY**

Rising above the cacophony of competing voices in the punditry-industrial-complex, Hendrik Hertzberg's "Talk of the Town" essays provide a perspective that too few social commentators offer nowadays. Hertzberg makes sense of bewildering and often unnerving topics with insight, fair-mindedness, and authority.

Hendrik Hertzberg

Mired

How did we—not just Americans but human beings in general—come to be? Opinions differ, but for most of recorded history the consensus view was that people were made out of mud. Also, that the mud was originally turned into people by a being or beings who themselves resembled people, only bigger, more powerful, and longer-lived, often immortal. The early Chinese theorized that a lonely goddess, pining for company, used yellow mud to fashion the first humans. According to the ancient Greeks, Prometheus sculpted the first man from mud, after which Athena breathed life into him. Mud is the man-making material in the creation stories of Mesopotamian city-states, African tribes, and American Indian nations.

The mud theory is still dominant in the United States, in the form of the Book of Genesis, whose version of the origin of our species, according to a recent Gallup poll, is deemed true by 45 percent of the American public. Chapter 2, in verses 6 and 7, puts it this way:

But there went up a mist from the earth, and watered the whole face of the ground.

And the Lord God formed man of the dust of the ground, and breathed into his nostrils the breath of life; and man became a living soul.

Mud is not mentioned by name, but you'd have to be a pretty strict biblical literalist not to infer that mud is what you get when you add water to dust.

A competing theory is that people, along with the rest of the earth's animals and plants, evolved over billions of years, beginning as extremely simple organisms and, via the accumulation of the tiny fraction of random mutations that turn out to be useful, developing into more complex ones. This view has gained many adherents since it was conceived, a century and a half ago, by Charles Darwin. It commands solid majorities in most of the developed world, and, thanks to the overwhelming evidence for its validity, has the near-unanimous support of scientists everywhere. Here in the United States, according to Gallup, it is subscribed to by about one-third of the populace—still running second to mud, but too large a market share to ignore altogether, especially in some of the battleground states.

On the one hand this, on the other hand that. George W. Bush is not normally the type to endorse shilly-shallying, but this time he went for it. At a "round table" with Texas reporters, the president was asked to comment on "what seems to be a growing debate over evolution versus intelligent design" and whether "both should be taught in public schools."

> *The president:* I think—as I said, harking back to my days as my governor—both you and Herman are doing a fine job of dragging me back to the past. (Laughter.) Then, I said that, first of all, that decision should be made to local school districts, but I felt like both sides ought to be properly taught.
>
> *Q:* Both sides should be properly taught?
>
> *The president:* Yes, people—so people can understand what the debate is about.
>
> *Q:* So the answer accepts the validity of intelligent design as an alternative to evolution?

> *The President:* I think that part of education is to expose
> people to different schools of thought, and I'm not sug-
> gesting—you're asking me whether or not people ought
> to be exposed to different ideas, and the answer is yes.

Looked at one way, this colloquy is an occasion for national
shame, albeit with a whiff of the risible: here is our country's
leader, the champion-in-chief of educational standards, blandly
equating natural science and supernatural supposition as "different schools of thought." Looked at another way, it represents
progress of a sort. Twenty-five years ago, Ronald Reagan, then the
Republican candidate for president, endorsed the teaching of
"creationism"; five years ago, George W. Bush did the same. "Creationism" holds that dinosaurs and people coexisted and that the
fossil record is a product of Noah's flood. Next to that, "intelligent
design" represents a scientific advance, or a tactical retreat, or
maybe just the evolutionary process at work. I.D. recognizes that
the age of the universe is measured in billions, not thousands, of
years; that fossils are evidence, not divine tricks to test believers'
faith; and that organisms change over time, sometimes via natural selection. This is tantamount to an admission that the Genesis story is poetry, not history; allegory, not fact.

But I.D.—whose central (and easily refuted) talking point is
that certain structures of living things are too intricate to have
evolved without the intervention of an "intelligent designer" (and
You know who You are)—enjoys virtually no scientific support. It
is not even a theory, in the scientific sense, because it is untestable
and unsupportable by empirical evidence. It is a last-ditch skir-
mish in a misguided war against reason that cannot be won and,
for religion's sake as well as science's, should not be fought. If the
president's musings on it were an isolated crotchet, they would
hardly be worth noting, let alone getting exercised about. But
they're not. They reflect an attitude toward science that has in-
fected every corner of his administration. From the beginning,

the Bush White House has treated science as a nuisance and scientists as an interest group—one that, because it lies outside the governing conservative coalition, need not be indulged. That's why the White House—sometimes in the service of political Christianity or ideological fetishism, more often in obeisance to baser interests like the petroleum, pharmaceutical, and defense industries—has altered, suppressed, or overriden scientific findings on global warming; missile defense; H.I.V./AIDS; pollution from industrial farming and oil drilling; forest management and endangered species; environmental health, including lead and mercury poisoning in children and safety standards for drinking water; and non-abstinence methods of birth control and sexually transmitted–disease prevention. It has grossly misled the public on the number of stem-cell lines available for research. It has appointed unqualified ideologues to scientific advisory committees and has forced out scientists who persist in pointing out inconvenient facts. All this and more has been amply documented in reports from congressional Democrats and the Union of Concerned Scientists, in such leading scientific publications as *Nature*, *Scientific American*, *Science*, and *The Lancet*, and in a new book, *The Republican War on Science*, by the science journalist Chris Mooney.

Mooney's book is more judicious than its move-product title, which, as he acknowledges in an opening chapter, is not meant to apply to moderate Republicans past (such as Dwight D. Eisenhower) or present (such as John McCain). Anyway, a few small fissures are beginning to appear in the stone wall. Bill Frist, M.D., the Senate majority leader, has broken with the White House on stem-cell research. The White House science adviser, John H. Marburger III, evidently embarrassed by his boss's evolutionary equivocations, told the *Times* that "intelligent design is not a scientific concept." And the cover story in the current *National Journal*, a well-informed and relentlessly nonpartisan Washington weekly, reports that growing numbers of Republican politicians and corporate chieftains "who once dismissed as unproven the idea that the burning of fossil fuels is causing a harmful rise in Earth's temperature have now concluded that global warming is real—and very dangerous." As a result, the magazine says, "Advocates of muscular governmental efforts to slow or reverse global warming predict that the United States will eventually take strong action—but they doubt that such action will come on Bush's watch." In this White House, science's name is mud. And, unlike those intelligent designers in the sky, all this crowd knows how to do is sling it.

Virginia Quarterly Review

FINALIST—
REVIEWS AND CRITICISM

Sven Birkerts's essay on a book that changed his life is as much memoir as criticism. In every achingly personal paragraph, Birkerts deftly weaves his own soul-searching journey as a reader with that of the book's protagonists. The result is journalism that is profoundly intimate and universal.

Sven Birkerts

Humboldt's Gift

Whenever someone asks me to name my favorite novel, I find myself putting on a ridiculous but revealing little performance, pretending to a natural consternation—after all, who can narrow a lifetime's evolving preferences down to a single title?—but in fact using the consternation as a cover for the real calculation, which is whether I have the interest or energy to explain my choice. For in fact I do have a favorite novel—*Humboldt's Gift* by Saul Bellow—but I know it to be an eccentric work, one that a number of reputable critics had problems with when it was published, and that many intelligent readers I know have shaken their heads over. How much easier to cite *Middlemarch*, or *Portrait of a Lady*, or *Ulysses*, or *To the Lighthouse*, all works that I admire without reservation. But the question was *favorite* novel, which I take to mean the novel that I visit most often in my thoughts, that I know most intimately down to the cell-structure of its cadences, that fills me with the greatest covetousness *and* inspires me to emulation. Most simply: When I think of *Humboldt's Gift* I immediately want to write.

They say that love is blind, but I don't buy it. Love is often well aware of the flaws of the beloved—but love is love because it overrules the fault-finding impulse altogether in the name of . . . In the name of some flow of higher sympathy that feels like an end in itself. I love *Humboldt's Gift*—much as anyone can be said to love a book—and my love is unperturbed by all that my judging intellect whispers as I read—that it is structurally lopsided, over-wrought in its Rudolph Steiner–inspired meditations, improbable in its *deus ex machina* resolutions. I grant that there are problems and shortcomings, but they do not ruffle my devotion at all. And this fascinates me.

I remember my first reading of *Humboldt's Gift* with an almost exaggerated vividness, though I can't recall how the book itself came into my possession. I mention this because I know that my copy was a new hardcover—cover price a round $10—and because this was a period in my life when I was routinely counting the change spread out on the dresser top. I would never have paid full price in a bookstore. Was it a birthday gift? That makes sense, because my birthday is in late September, and I read the novel first in October of 1975 in a single great gulp. And this I remember because it was the most desperate season in my life so far and for a long time after I credited Bellow with helping to save me from a descent into utter hopelessness.

That story is outwardly simple enough. The previous August I had ended a relationship with the woman I had believed was the love of my life. I had left our life in Maine and returned broke and empty-handed to my old haunts in Ann Arbor, where I had gone to college a few years before. I had been back for some weeks, and whatever plan I had for rebuilding my life was not working. Though I had a small room I rented and a job in a bookstore, these were not support enough. I would wake up each day wondering how I would make it through to the next. The sadness was overwhelming. I had no one except my sister to confide in, and nothing at all to hold against my thoughts of "never again." One afternoon I snapped. I made the impulsive (and ultimately foolish) decision to borrow money from a friend and fly to Boston the next morning. There I would board the first bus north. I had no idea of what I might do, or even of what I was after; but once I'd decided there was no other choice. There was only the rest of the day and the night to get through.

In my room, a shabby attic box high up among the tree tops—it felt that way—I paced and kneaded my hands, Raskolnikov in every sense but the criminal. I was beside myself, twitching in my skin. I had no idea how I would pass the time. And then—I can't remember why—from among the handful of books I had stacked up on my dresser, I took down *Humboldt's Gift* and, miracle of miracles, read. I turned the pages through the late afternoon and the evening, and then on through the night. I read like I'd never read anything before, with a lock-on fury that pushed the world and my extraordinary anxiety aside. At first it was to get away from my situation, and then at some point that shifted and I was reading to get further and further in. Did I finish? I don't think so, not entirely. But I entered so deeply into the narrative of Charlie Citrine's fate that I awakened, by reader's proxy—that sympathetic magic that is part of what can happen between book and author—my own sense of fatedness, and it was there in me at every moment in the next days as I walked up and down the roads outside Kennebunkport and blundered through the finale of what had been the finest friendship of my life.

About that night I remember several things. I remember the narrow spring-shot bed that was part of the Calvary of that room, that season, and how I arranged myself there, propped up in a corner, scarcely minding the discomfort, mainly glad that I was able to rig the desk lamp on the chair to get the right illumination. And, contents aside—for of course Bellow's narration impressed itself on me with a once-in-a-lifetime clarity—I remember the physical book, the cover and the feel of the pages, pulpier than any paper I'd felt before in a trade hardcover, an anomaly which somehow became linked in my mind with the eccentric novelty of Bellow's plot, underscoring for me the feeling that this was not just another novel, was in fact an advance posting of imminent changes in the literary life of our times.

We never know, do we, if the future is just more of the present pushed forward, or whether the look and feel—not to mention the core essence—of life might not be changing? Isn't this part of the galvanizing horror—and thrill—of great disasters: the possibility that the great change might have at last begun? For my part, I subscribed for a long time to the idea that artists and writers were, *pace* Pound, our antennae, and that if news of transformation were to come, it would be through the channels they created. And when I read *Humboldt's Gift*, keyed-up, white-knuckling through my own inner torment, I felt that something very new and important was being delivered. Bellow had done it. He had gotten to that level of seeing where lives could be viewed without derision as destinies; he had given me a glimpse of a larger system of meaning that I could use directly in my life. And he had done it in a way that felt of the moment, contemporary.

I did not recognize all of this directly, of course. I experienced it as I experience much of what I read—as atmosphere, as tone, as an agitation of suppositions and surmises, as a kind of extended daydream. But the correcting gaze of hindsight now tells me that it was there from the start, drawn—all of it—like electricity through the circuit system of the opening passage:

> The book of ballads published by Von Humboldt Fleisher in the Thirties was an immediate hit. Humboldt was just what everyone had been waiting for. Out in the Midwest I had certainly been waiting eagerly, I can tell you that. An avant-garde writer, the first of a new generation, he was handsome, fair, large, serious, witty, he was learned. The guy had it all. All the papers reviewed his book. His picture appeared in *Time* without insult and in *Newsweek* with praise. I read *Harlequin Ballads* enthusiastically. I was a student at the University of Wisconsin and thought about literature day and night. Humboldt revealed to me a new way of doing things. I was ecstatic. I envied his luck, his talent, and his fame, and I went east in May to have a look at him—perhaps to get next to him. The Greyhound bus, taking the Scranton route, made the trip in about fifty hours. That didn't matter.

The bus windows were open. I had never seen real mountains before. Trees were budding. It was like Beethoven's *Pastorale*. I felt showered by the green within. I felt showered by the green, within. Manhattan was fine, too. I took a room for three bucks a week and found a job selling Fuller Brushes door to door. And I was wildly excited about everything. Having written Humboldt a long fan letter, I was invited to Greenwich Village to discuss literature and ideas. He lived on Bedford Street, near Chumley's. First he gave me black coffee, and then poured gin in the same cup. "Well, you're a nice-enough looking fellow, Charlie," he said to me. "Aren't you a bit sly, maybe? I think you're headed for early baldness. And such large emotional handsome eyes. But you certainly do love literature and that's the main thing. You have sensibility," he said. He was a pioneer in the use of this word. Sensibility later made it big. Humboldt was very kind. He introduced me to people in the Village and got me books to review. I always loved him.   (1)

The pull was irresistible. I loved the velocity, the declarative forthrightness, the apparent ease with which Bellow nailed the urgency of literary adoration, a vice to which I was highly susceptible back in my middle twenties, and which I have only very slowly outgrown. But beyond the adoration was something more potent still—the narrator's certainty that this business of poetry and writing and publishing mattered, that it was the sovereign real thing.

Humboldt's Gift is a baggy, talky book, crammed with episodic set-pieces—comic as well as elegiac interludes—but the gist of the narration is as follows. Charlie Citrine, the man pegged early on as having 'sensibility,' is in Chicago fumbling through what is thankfully never called a 'midlife crisis,' but which bears all of the now clichéd markings of that disorder. A successful thinker and man of letters (he has two Pulitzers under his belt), Charlie finds himself in his mid-fifties assailed from all sides as well as from within. His ex-wife, Denise, has her cut-throat lawyers after him for a fat divorce settlement; his sensuously manipulative younger girlfriend, Renata, is trying to get him to go with her to Madrid, with some idea that she will reconnect with her long-lost father and marry Charlie. Moreover, his beloved Mercedes has just been pulverized by a bat-wielding hood named Rinaldo Cantabile, who claims that Charlie welched on paying a poker debt and who now insists on restitution.

At the same time, more centrally, Charlie, an amateur student of the anthroposophy of Rudolph Steiner (premised on the possibility of the attainment of ever-higher states of spiritual consciousness), has begun to experience vivid memories of the eponymous Humboldt, the great friend of his young manhood, the poet—supposedly based on the poet Delmore Schwartz—who went down to pills, alcohol, and dementia in his own middle years, and who Charlie now feels he abandoned to his demons.

The novel becomes a self-accounting on every level, its diverse plot strands drawn together, its elements put into play, by the revelation that a legacy of sorts left by Humboldt has turned up. How Bellow manages to orchestrate everything is hard to discover, even when the pieces are all lined up for study, but then this has always been Bellow's particular art—creating a narrative voice so rich and suggestive, so fluid in its movements between past and present, that the plod of sequential development is avoided altogether. There is the feeling when reading this novel that a tightly rolled sultan's carpet has splashed open before our eyes with a single prompting nudge of the foot.

I have read *Humboldt's Gift* four or five times now and each time it tunes me up differently, not to the point where I would say it's a new novel—for the sense of deep familiarity remains for me one of its magnetic attractions—but in terms of offering me vital new information. That's the kind of book it is, and don't we all have them—books we reread not for any purpose of overt self-betterment, not to add to our trophy bag, but because they nourish us with clues about the nature of life as we try to solve it for ourselves?

When I lay in that ramshackle bed in that tiny upstairs room in Ann Arbor, threading the sentences end to end as if my life depended on it, I took two major kinds of solace from my reading. The first, as I already suggested, was the solace of literature mattering, this in spite of the fact that literature—writing—does not in the end save either Humboldt, who for all his literary wisdom went down in flames, ultimately consumed by the very demons that originally drove him to write, or Charlie, who never does make headway on his great projected study of boredom. Even so, the intoxication Bellow creates in the opening sections is so powerful, so triumphantly idealized, that it is enough—and here I crib from Joseph Brodsky's "Roman Elegies"—"enough to last the whole blackout." Page after page we are lifted by a mighty swell as Bellow does what he does best of all: summoning the passion of the mind for ideas and the being for expressions of beauty. He does it by main force of enthusiasm, with lists, little symphonic surges of reference, evoking through his rhythms the very excitement he is bent on conveying.

But Bellow does not just rely on the cumulative power of the catalogue. He creates the surrounding atmosphere—the *mise en scene*—and invites us into the life of the moment, sharpening our sense of the pressure of intellect and sensibility on these characters.

In one of his early Chicago reveries (he is hiding from the world for the morning, meditating on Humboldt), Charlie recalls a visit he paid to the poet and his wife Kathleen when they lived in rural New Jersey. He gets the manic chaos of the drive out, leaving New York with Humboldt at the wheel of his old Buick. "Steering, he was humped huge over the wheel, he had small-boy tremors of the hands and feet, and he kept the cigarette holder between his teeth. He was agitated, talking away, entertaining, provoking, informing, and snowing me" (21). And: "We were off: he discussed machinery, luxury, command, capitalism, technology,

Mammon, Orpheus and poetry, the riches of the human heart, America, world civilization. His task was to put all of this, and more, together. The car went snoring and squealing through the tunnel and came out in bright sunlight" (22).

Then they arrive: "Briars lashed the Roadmaster as we swayed on huge springs through rubbishy fields where white boulders sat. The busted muffler was so loud that though the car filled the lane there was no need to honk. You could hear us coming. Humboldt yelled, 'Here's our place!' and swerved. We rolled over a hummock or earth-wave. The front of the Buick rose and then dived into the weeds" (22).

And so it goes, the most vividly deployed scene-making setting us up for the cataracting conversation, which I excerpt midflow lest the pages-long hammering overwhelm everything else:

About Eliot he seemed to know strange facts no one else had ever heard. He was

> filled with gossip and hallucination as well as literary theory. Distortion was inherent, yes, in all poetry. But which came first? And this rained down on me, part privilege, part pain, with illustrations from the classics and the sayings of Einstein and Zsa Zsa Gabor, with references to Polish socialism and the football tactics of George Halas and the secret motives of Arnold Toynbee, and (somehow) the used-car business. Rich boys, poor boys, jewboys, chorus girls, prostitution and religion, old money, new money, gentleman's clubs, Back Bay, Newport, Washington Square, Henry Adams, Henry James, Henry Ford, Saint John of the Cross, Dante, Ezra Pound, Dostoevski, Marilyn Monroe and Joe DiMaggio, Gertrude Stein and Alice, Freud and Ferenczi.
>
> (31)

The early pages of *Humboldt's Gift* offer a supercharged saturation of such heady referential narrative. Remembering his great doomed friend, Charlie recreates in the rhythm of his thoughts a sense of the very mania that brought Humboldt down. To me, a confused, intellectually ambitious twenty-four-year-old, it was an elixir. Even in the state I was in, my reading brought me to a pitch of wanting. This was it. This was the life of the mind; this had to be what brilliance felt like. These were not the isolated facts and concepts—the slow contents of the books I studied. This was the pay-off, this was how a powerful mind took hold of the world, turning the rough givens of circumstance into intense comprehension. This was how the world was remade into meaning, and I believed then that there was no higher use to which the responsive psyche could be put.

I'd had my own glimpses of this fever, but at a much lower level. I'd put in my seasons working in bookstores, falling now and then into associative fugues in which every page I scanned somehow related to something else I'd just been reading. Night after night I'd made my way home from the store with stacks of borrowed books in bags, frustrated that I could only follow one path at a time, wishing for some Faustian pill that would confer on me the mastery I craved, even at the price of ———. Well, I had nothing much to offer up in trade.

Bellow's Humboldt passages lit all of this up in me, that night as later, removing me from the immediate burn of my romantic obsession, in part through my absorption in the writing, but also by drawing the energies of one obsession temporarily into another. From the exalted vantage offered by Humboldt's intellect—a vantage comprehending history, poetry, politics—my lovelorn condition seemed consolingly small-potatoes. The problem with these easily acquired perspectives is that they don't last long once the book is closed.

Then there was the balm of commiseration, the great gift of the later chapters. Here I could join Bellow's narrative to my own. Heartache was the link. In the novel, Charlie has gone with Renata to Europe. He has not done the right thing, has not offered to make her an honest woman. And now, suddenly—to him, shockingly—Renata has disappeared. She has stranded Charlie in Madrid with her elderly mother, the scheming Senora, and her young son. And Charlie is stunned, bereft. "Good-by, good-by to those wonderful sensations," he thinks. "Mine at least had been the real thing. And if hers were not, she had at least been a true and understanding pal. In her percale bed. In her heaven of piled pillows. All that was probably over" (417).

The news arrives while Charlie is still in Madrid. Renata has married his rival, the mortuary king Flonzaley. Charlie goes into a precipitous decline. At one point, he imagines how he must look to others in the *pensione* he has retired to: "His brown eyes were red from weeping, he dressed with high elegance although the kitchen smells made his clothing noticeably rancid, he tried with persistent vanity to comb his thin and graying hair over the bald middle of his head and was always disheartened when he realized that in the lamplight his scalp was glistening" (437).

Oh the sadness and indignity of life! And what a bond I felt, pushing through the later pages of the novel in the early morning hours after a night of turning pages. In Charlie's abandonment I saw my own, even though technically speaking I had been the one who went away. No matter. The absence he felt touched the absence I felt, and between fiction and life there passed a sense of the Virgilian 'tears of things' that accomplished the paradoxical miracle of art—it fortified me, allowed me to admit my grief and at the same time to hold it as in a frame. And when I finally finished, a day later, seeing Charlie through to his hard-won acceptance, to his redemptive moment of laying his ghosts to rest and pushing on, I felt subtly altered.

I find this whole transaction fascinating, how in reading I experience the emotional situations created by the author, the way these scenarios play upon my own susceptible nature, sometimes so intensely that I experience a full-blown physical agitation, a kind of shortness of breath of the whole being. How much of this,

I wonder, is the result of the author's art, the formal tension of scene-making and the sentence by sentence evocation of feeling-states in the characters, and how much has to do with the intensity of my own projected emotions? To what degree was I filling in Charlie's sense of loss with my own? My guess now, after my most recent rereading, is that it was quite a bit. Moved as I was, I was not devastated this time through. But then, I was reading a novel that has become familiar; I knew in advance that Charlie would get past his grief. My focus—this time as in earlier rereadings—was on other things.

At some point after this first encounter, *Humboldt's Gift* took on a somewhat different significance for me. It became, along with everything else, a literary model, a work I nearly fetishized for its voice and narrative energy, for its human reach. Bellow, I thought, had cracked the code. Almost alone among contemporary novelists, he had found a way to show the complexity of our way of living without losing the contemplative register or sacrificing the full emotional spectrum. He could be, as the situation required, philosophical, comedic, descriptively evocative, elegiac, dramatic—and he could get in close to the endless psychological push-pull of relationships, the tenderness and leveraging manipulation of lovers, the *odi et amo* of embattled friendships . . . I fell in love with Bellow's scenes and, even more specifically, his prose. So many moments spoke to me *exactly*. Whole sequences of his sentences lit me up but also filled me with the despairing thought that I could never write as well, though of course it is the hubris of every young writer to imagine that all obstacles to greatness will be overcome in the indeterminate future.

I'll let a single passage showcase the prose for me. Here is Charlie, set to meet Cantabile at the old Russian Bathhouse, describing the clientele:

> These Division Street steam-bathers don't look like the trim
> proud people downtown. Even old Feldstein pumping his

Exercycle in the Downtown Club at the age of eighty would be out of place on Division Street. Forty years ago Feldstein was a swinger, a high roller, a good-time Charlie on Rush Street. In spite of his age he is a man of today, whereas the patrons of the Russian Bath are cast in an antique form. They have swelling buttocks and fatty breasts as yellow as buttermilk. They stand on thick pillar legs affected with a sort of creeping verdigris or blue-cheese mottling of the ankles. After steaming, these old fellows eat enormous snacks of bread and salt herring or large ovals of salami and dripping skirt-steak and they drink schnapps. They could knock down walls with their hard stout old-fashioned bellies. Things are very elementary here. You feel that these people are almost conscious of obsolescence, of a line of evolution abandoned by nature and culture. So down in the superheated subcellars all these Slavonic cavemen and wood demons with hanging laps of fat and legs of stone and lichen boil themselves and splash ice water on their heads by the bucket. Upstairs, on the television screen in the locker room, little dudes and grinning broads make smart talk and leap up and down. They are unheeded. Micket who keeps the food concession fries slabs of meat and potato pancakes, and, with enormous knives, he hacks up cabbages for coleslaw and he quarters grapefruits (to be eaten by hand). The stout old men mounting in their bedsheets from the blasting heat have a strong appetite.　　　(78)

This is more than just a bravura description. Any good sense-attuned writer could have put together the details. What makes the passage stand out for me is the deep, almost primal regard—the love, the awe—Bellow transmits. We feel, through Charlie, that we are spying on history itself—our ancestors' ancestors caught in full-flesh. How does he manage everything at once, the grotesque excess, the atmosphere, the analogies? There is always a mystery with great writing, how one thing is brought to combine with another. How do I account for the sense I get while reading that this is not just a scene, an evocation of people in a place, but something almost closer to a philosophy? That Charlie's particular regard is in some deep way also a reflection on the ontological fitness of what Irving Howe called "the world of our fathers"? These staggering old troglodytes are, in Charlie's vision of things—a vision we have by this point become immersed in—set against the new, the young, the modern ("Upstairs, on the television screen in the locker room, little dudes and grinning broads make smart talk or leap up and down") and if they are a physical shambles with their fatty old breasts, they are yet a force of superior denomination. They are—so I read it—closer to fundamental *being*.

And then there is the voice, Charlie's wonderful—and nearly simultaneous—command of registers, how he can swerve from the wise-guy voice ("dudes" and "broads") to the reflective ("these people are almost conscious of obsolescence"), to the overtly literary-descriptive ("They stand on thick pillar legs affected with a sort of creeping verdigris") and pull it off.

Though I envy more than a few writers, coveting this one's fluency, that one's exactitude, I am seldom provoked to outright emulation. *The Catcher in the Rye* had that effect, I remember, and *Lolita*, but no novel got to me in the way that *Humboldt's Gift* did, especially in my younger years. The mere contemplation of the Bellovian sweep would set me thinking along parallel tracks. I wanted badly to write a novel of equal range and texture, alive down to its least bit character, able to transmit the drama of the inner life even as it staged episodes from the human comedy and registered in its least inflection the tone of our times. I sat long hours straining to dream up the perfect opening, the sentence that would seem as electric and inevitable as Bellow's beautifully simple: "The book of ballads published by Von Humboldt Fleisher in the Thirties was an immediate hit." It was not to be. I did not understand that the perfect sentence is not a happy accident but something more like a consummation, an announcement that everything—the whole work—is in place, ready.

. . .

I want to stay near this business of voice, the particular spanning of outer and inner that Bellow has fashioned to such a high art. For the voice was a big part of what so affected me in my most recent reading of the novel. Indeed, this time through I was less caught up in the tragedy of Humboldt, or the comedic Chicago set-pieces, or even the romantic travails which were so piercing to me the first time. I was, this time, most taken up with Bellow's rendering of Charlie as a man aswim in time, a man in search of the larger synthesis.

In my earlier readings of the novel I somehow missed the importance of the fact that Charlie was a middle-aged man not just living his life, but even more significantly reliving it. But this is—dare I say *mercifully*—the blindness of youth. Young, we cut the cloth of the world to our own feelings and understandings. To me, back then, Charlie was just an adult of indeterminate adult status. I had no way of grasping him otherwise. I hadn't, certainly when I was first reading *Humboldt*, experienced the wonderful and terrible ways in which at a certain point the film of our own lives doubles over on itself, returning us to things we had thought safely buried, recirculating old poisons, throwing the glare of hindsight down onto choices made. . . . Well, now I know. And this time in my reading I got it. I grasped—felt—the extent to which the work is—and I don't think the comparison is that far-fetched—Bellow's *Inferno*. Charlie is nothing if not a man awakening to himself in the middle of a dark wood and finding that the straight way has become lost. Of course, where Dante is allegorical, Bellow is often hammy and oblique, full of comic and ironic impulses. But the overall feeling of the work is nonetheless one of often sorrowful retrospection. And the ultimate thrust is transformational—the point is to show us a man who goes into his darkness to wrestle his devils, and who finally comes through.

The core confrontation is, of course, with memories of his younger self, more particularly of his friendship with Humboldt and what he must face there: his own egotism, his fear of the decline and failure Humboldt represented, and the fact that he deserted the poet in his time of need. Of course the relationship is complex, and Humboldt from his side acted unpardonably toward Charlie, using him as a pawn in his paranoid schemes, taking advantage of his loyalty, and later, when Charlie found success as a playwright, trying to sabotage him. That Humboldt drifted in and out of delusion only partially exonerates him. Charlie had good reasons for pulling away from his friend in the end.

But these kinds of reasons and explanations only satisfy on what we might call the psychological plane. Charlie in middle age is determined to break through to a higher spiritual apprehension of things, and from his new vantage—when he can attain it—he sees the past very differently. Tormenting and manipulative as his friend was, he was also, over and above that, a radiant spirit, a man of soul dreaming his way toward the original world: "Ah Humboldt had been great," thinks Charlie, "handsome, high-spirited, buoyant, ingenious, electric, noble. To be with him made you feel the sweetness of life. We used to discuss the loftiest things—what Diotima said to Socrates about love, what Spinoza meant by *amor dei intellectualis*. To talk to him was sustaining, nourishing" (162). And in the light of this recognition, Charlie has come up seriously short in his self-accounting. When, toward the end of the poet's life, Charlie spotted him standing in shambles on a streetcorner, eating a "dusty" pretzel, he turned away. For this he cannot forgive himself.

It is the intensity of his remorse, perhaps, that lets Charlie stage the scenes of their early friendship with such piercing clarity. The memories of Humboldt carry the first part of the book. At the same time, they establish the vibrant inwardness of Charlie in middle age and make plausible his aspirations toward—as the title of his master Rudolph Steiner's book would have it—"knowledge of the higher worlds and its attainment."

Charlie's (and Bellow's) insistent mysticism, the repeated invocation of Steiner, his teachings and spiritual exercises, confounded critics and reviewers when the book first appeared. The novel was seen to be full of crackpot excess and distended metaphysical passages. I disagree. Plucking from one of these almost at random, I find:

> For in spirit, says Steiner, a man can step out of himself and let things speak to him about themselves, to speak about what has meaning not for him alone but also for them. Thus the sun the moon the stars will speak to nonastronomers in spite of their ignorance of science. In fact it's high time that this happened. Ignorance of science should not keep one imprisoned in the lowest and weariest sector of being, prohibited from entering into independent relations with creation as a whole. The educated speak of the disenchanted (a boring) world. But it is not the world, it is my own head that is disenchanted. The world cannot be disenchanted. (203)

It's true, some of Charlie's anthroposophical riffs go on too long, straining the already loosely carpentered structure of the novel. But for whatever reason—and I am no Steinerite—I don't mind.

That last sentence is somewhat dishonest, or at least misleading. I say "for whatever reason," making it seem that I am in the dark about my own predilections, as if to say more would be to risk exposure. The truth is that I spend much of my life egging myself closer to the ledge—to some more open recognition of forces beyond what we usually credit in our ordinary day. I torment myself with the possibility that there might indeed be planes of higher meaning, available syntheses. Part of the enormous appeal of this novel for me is that a writer as gifted and intelligent as Bellow shows himself unapologetically interested in this very thing. What a man to have on the team. What a ratification!

This appetite is not new. When I was much younger it pulled me toward Whitman (briefly), or, differently, Lawrence; later there was Rilke. Even so, I remember in my early readings of the novel being impatient, wanting to get past these pages to get to scenes and more sensory passages. But this time I lingered, savoring. For if middle age has taught me about the undertow power of memory, it has also made me very keen to learn how the outer man can in all the situations of life draw on his inwardness, not just in the interest of greater understanding, or for solace, but because I do believe that contact with our deeper intuitions actually repositions us in whatever situation we are in *and* thus changes the situation—the Heisenberg principle borrowed from scientific experiment and applied to living itself. Changed awareness affects the way things happen.

Obviously there is no way to argue this coherently, certainly no way to prove it, but I will say that of all of the novel's many features, the most striking for me this time through was the sense Bellow conveyed of experience unfolding with larger thematic inflection. He could only achieve this rare effect because he had created in Charlie Citrine a character deeply attuned to these thematic surges. And indeed, in a sense the whole point of the novel, at one level, is Charlie's recognition of this movement of meaning and his eventual giving over to it. When he does—when he gives up the Renata struggle in Madrid, and accepts his character, and his responsibility for all that has happened to him, I experienced a great sense of lifting free. Charlie has come through—he has come to terms with the demons of his own character—and if he does not look up at the end to glimpse, as did Dante, the stars, he does make the decision to rebury his old friend Humboldt (literally and figuratively) and on leaving the cemetery pauses to identify a budding crocus under last autumn's leaves.

I won't pretend that I have tapped fully the wisdoms of Bellow's book or brought them into my life, but time has done its steady work and I do feel, more than ever before, that I can recognize how these understandings and intuitions have a place in my life. It's too early, yet—for me, as indeed for Charlie—to claim with any certainty that there are in fact higher worlds to be entered. None of us may ever know for sure. But I will say that the reading of the novel, the imaginative projection that it asks, filled the days with a thematic resonance that seemed to be my own life—and past—vibrating in direct sympathy with the life on the page. *Humboldt's Gift* is my "favorite" book because it keeps renewing itself for me as I get older, outpacing me in a way that makes me speed my step.

Harper's Magazine

FINALIST—REPORTING

"Death of a Mountain," by Erik Reece, provides an intricate and intimate examination of the environmental destruction wrought by a radical new form of strip-mining called "mountain removal"—the systematic leveling of a mountain—and the corruption prevalent in the Appalachian mining industry.

Erik Reece

Death of a Mountain

Radical Strip Mining and the Leveling of Appalachia

September 13, 2003, Lost Mountain

Look hard and you can find Lost Mountain in grid 71, coordinate B-10 of the *Kentucky Atlas and Gazetteer*. According to that topological map, the summit rises 1,847 feet above Lost Creek, whose headwaters come to life on the mountain's north face. This morning I left the bluegrass region of central Kentucky, where I live, and drove east along the Mountain Parkway, where the last of the rolling grasslands, dotted with black tobacco barns, finally gives way to the Cumberland Plateau, the foothills of which may be the oldest mountain range in the world, the Appalachians. From there, a narrow two-lane road follows the meanderings of Lost Creek, so named because hunters frequently lost their bearings when they ventured too far from the stream itself. When the blacktop ends, I navigate an old logging road that winds up and around Lost Mountain, ending at its peak. I set the parking brake on my truck and get out to take a look around.

I notice that a fire tower standing here a year ago has been blown or torn from its foundation and sent crashing down the ridge side. But even without the tower's perspective, looking off to the north I can see thousands of acres—former summits—that have been flattened by mountaintop mining. Where once there were jagged, forested ridgelines, now there is only a series of plateaus, staggered gray shelves where grass struggles to grow in crushed rock and shale. When visitors to eastern Kentucky first see the effects of this kind of mining, they often say the landscape looks like the Southwest—a harsh tableland interrupted by steep mesas. I, too, have traveled through Arizona and New Mexico in the late spring when ocotillo and Indian paintbrush are in bloom, and I understand the allure of that harsh landscape. But this is not the desert Southwest; it is an eastern broadleaf forest. At least it should be.

There was a time in this region when union miners would have extracted the coal that lies beneath Lost Mountain with hand picks and shovels in deep underground shafts. But twenty-six years after Jimmy Carter signed into law the Surface Mining Control and Reclamation Act (SMCRA), the coal industry has developed much more expedient and much more destructive methods of mining. Instead of excavating the contour of a ridge side, as strip miners did throughout the 1960s and '70s, now entire mountaintops are blasted off, and almost everything that isn't coal is pushed down into the valleys below. As a result, the Environmental Protection Agency estimates that more than 700 miles of healthy streams have been buried by mountaintop removal—some say the number is twice that—and hundreds more have been damaged. Blasting on the mine sites has cracked the foundations of nearby homes and polluted hundreds of family wells. Creeks run orange with sulfuric acid and heavy metals. Wildlife populations have been summarily dispersed. An entire ecosystem has been dismantled.

I have come to Lost Mountain because in February Leslie Resources Inc. was granted a state permit to mine this ridgeline. I came here to see what an eastern mountain looks like before, during, and after its transformation into a western desert.

October 25, 2003, Lost Mountain

Before mining starts on Lost Mountain, I hike up the old logging road that winds to the summit. At one muddy wheel rut, I stop to sketch the tracks of a deer, a fox, a raccoon, and a wild turkey. Then I drop down into the forest proper, the watershed that feeds Lost Creek. After extricating myself from a blackberry thicket, I climb noisily over a barricade of fallen tree limbs. A crow warns a white-tailed deer of my approach, and the doe hoofs it up over the ridgetop. When she is gone, I find myself standing beneath an austere canopy of tulip poplars. This is Kentucky's state tree, and it grows as straight as a flagpole. Daniel Boone once hollowed out a sixty-foot canoe from a single tulip poplar and packed his family down the Ohio River in it. The tulip tree is also one of the first hardwoods to establish dominance after a deciduous forest has been cleared by fire, a blowdown, or, in this case, the chain saws that chewed through here about forty years ago. These poplars have already lost their leaves, and sunlight fills the understory of younger sassafrases, hickories, and sugar maples. The woods are quiet except for a pileated woodpecker; the songbirds are already vacationing in Belize and other points south.

Given time, one hundred years or so, oaks, beeches, and hickories would come to dominate this transitional forest. Three different communities of highly diverse trees would eventually agree on a silent charter about how best to inhabit these elevations. But that's not going to happen here.

I wander on down the ridge. Without thinking, I begin to follow the moist furrow of an intermittent stream. A lacework of tributaries feeds the lower creeks, but they flow only during wetter periods. I step around moss-covered cobble and maidenhair ferns that grow in the shape of delicate tiaras. Colonies of liverwort cover some of the rocks like small, green scallops. These modest-looking organisms carry on pretty fascinating sex lives: The liverwort needs rain to spawn. And its preferred habitat seems to be these rain-catching, intermittent streams. During a downpour, the male liverwort extends a tiny, umbrella-shaped antenna. When a drop of rain hits it, sperm explodes inside that raindrop and bounces a couple of feet, where with any luck a female liverwort has sent up a little umbrella of her own to catch the sperm-laden droplets.

In this way the unassuming liverwort dramatizes one of the issues at the heart of mountaintop removal. In response to the charge that such mining methods bury hundreds of central Appalachian streams, Bill Caylor, president of the Kentucky Coal Association, is quick to point out that an intermittent stream, such as this one, is not really a stream at all, because there are no fish in it. According to this line of thought, if something like the liverwort is of no immediate and obvious use to us, then it is of no use at all. That modest flora like liverwort help hold rich soil in place, purify water downstream, and provide habitat to other small animals such as salamanders—or that they even hold an intrinsic value beyond what we might understand today—is a logic to which *Homo sapiens americanus* seems curiously immune.

When I reach the mouth of the intermittent stream, I follow Lost Creek until I can see no signs of human intervention, not even the inevitable Bud Light can. I sit down on the bank, beneath the yellow glow of beeches and maples. Dark water glistens in the shallows below. Squirrels rustle through the leaves. Trees decay where they have fallen, providing shelter and food. A Carolina wren hops among the tangled branches. These days it is thought unfashionable, even backward, to talk about *laws of nature* or to read a philosophy, a *morality*, into the workings of the natural world. For 4,000 years, theologians and philosophers have debated whether an Intelligent Designer stands behind it all. I have nothing to contribute to that discussion. But this much seems clear: this *forest* certainly demonstrates an *intelligence*, one it has been honing for 290 million years. Its economy is a closed loop that transforms waste into food. In that alone it is superior to our human economy, where the end of the line is not nutrients but rather toxic industrial waste. Is there *design* behind this natural intelligence? I have no idea. But I will venture this: *The forest knows what it's doing.*

Compare the two economies: the forest's and ours. The sulfur dioxide that escapes from coal-burning power plants is responsible for acid rain, smog, respiratory infections, asthma, and lung disease. Due to acid rain and mine runoff, there is so much mercury in Kentucky streams that any pregnant woman who eats fish from them risks serious, lifelong harm to the fetus she carries. And this year, thanks in large part to coal burning, climatologists found record-high levels of climate-altering carbon dioxide in the atmosphere. A forest, by contrast, can store twenty times more carbon than croplands or pastures. Its leaf litter slows erosion and adds organic matter to the soil. Its dense vegetation stops flooding. Its headwater streams purify creeks below it. A contiguous forest ensures species diversity. A forest, in short, does all of the things that the mining and burning of coal cannot—that is its intelligence.

November 4, 2003, Lost Mountain

This morning I cast my vote for the Kentucky gubernatorial candidate who accepted the fewest contributions from the coal industry. Now, driving up the muddy switchbacks of Lost Mountain, I can see a thin column of gray smoke rising over the next ridge. As I round a bend near the summit, the forest falls away below my driver's-side window. I am not speaking figuratively. The trees that lined the left side of this road two weeks ago, and that held in place the southern slope of Lost Mountain, are gone. Stumps line the road. Down below, all of the ground cover and topsoil has been churned under—"grubbed"—by D-9 bulldozers. Nothing but mud, rock, and fallen trees remains.

I park my truck out of sight of the workers below and sit down on one of the stumps. This mountainside has been scalped; the trees that covered it now lie in massive piles all down the slope. A burning pyre lies at the bottom, and a haze of smoke fills this concave southern valley. One dozer, with its huge crescent blade, slowly pushes the other piles down into the fire. And although a sustainable, value-added timber industry is the region's most promising alternative to coal, this coal company, and many others, don't even bother to save the timber they do cut.

On the next ridge over, another dozer is pushing boulders out of the way to carve a haul road for the coal trucks. All around me there is nothing but rock, smoke, and ravaged soil. Then I see standing a few feet away a single green seedling, shooting out a dozen small branches. Somehow the dozer missed it, and now the entire emptiness of the slope gathers around this seedling like an unbearable presence, a ghost forest.

And not just any forest. What heightens the tragedy of surface mining in central Appalachia is that the chain saws and dozers are stripping away the oldest and most diverse forests in North America. A million years ago, the Pleistocene glaciers forced northern trees to migrate south. But the glaciers never reached this part of the Appalachians, and when the massive ice sheets finally retreated, they left in their wake a landscape that looked much like a modern strip mine. Consequently, over hundreds of thousands of years, the Appalachians were responsible for reforesting North America. But no other forest ever achieved its diversity of tree species. The forests of Appalachia are called "mixed mesophytic," because they inhabit a "middle" climate and because the canopy comprises an astonishing number of mature trees, with no one species dominating. They remain the continent's seedbed, its mother lode. Now the industrial equivalent of an ice age glacier will soon scour Lost Mountain, and the hopes of any kind of forest will be gone.

Back at home three hours later, I turn on the election results. My candidate has been soundly beaten.

.   .   .

In April 2000, the Martin County Coal Corporation asked the Army Corps of Engineers for a permit to create twenty-seven valley fills from surface mining near Inez, Kentucky. Although the fill would bury more than six miles of streams in the county, the Corps granted the permit request. The EPA immediately stepped in and urged the Corps to reconsider authorization. The EPA argued that "the discharges of fill material authorized for this project present an imminent danger of irreparable harm to wildlife and recreational areas." The Corps, however, refused to suspend MCCC's permit, and by the end of summer 2001 the valley fills had begun.

Then in August, Kentuckians for the Commonwealth filed a federal lawsuit against the Army Corps of Engineers, asking the court to suspend the permit. They argued that the Clean Water Act, which allows only for clean "fill," not "waste," prevented debris from mountaintop mining to be disposed of in U.S. waters. In May of 2002, with a decision in the lawsuit still pending, the Corps issued a new regulation under the Clean Water Act to define "fill" as any debris created by mining. U.S. District Judge Charles H. Haden immediately rejected that change, countering that "only the United States Congress can rewrite the Act to allow fills with no purpose or use but the deposit of waste." Haden also ruled that spoil from mountaintop mining was clearly waste, which could not be deposited in streams. Judge Haden's decision had the potential to shut down massive strip-mining operations throughout the coalfields of Appalachia, but by January 2003 the conservative U.S. Fourth Circuit Court had overturned Haden's decsision, and in May of that year, the Draft Programmatic Environmental Impact Statement (EIS) was released. Its findings and proposals have occasioned the latest round of arguments about coal and conservation.

The 5,000-page document admitted that mountaintop removal is bad, and for the usual reasons: it buries headwater streams, causes erosion and flooding, degrades water quality downstream, kills aquatic life, shakes the walls and cracks the foundations of nearby homes, and wipes away huge portions of an extremely diverse ecosystem. The solution? The Interior Department proposed streamlining the mine-permit process and doing away with the rule that requires a one-hundred-foot buffer zone between streams and mine sites. No limitations on mountaintop removal were proposed. Coal operators could still fill up to 250 acres of a watershed with the rubble that was once a mountaintop. Mine sites could still leach toxic acids into creeks where small valley communities once performed baptisms.

December 17, 2003, Lost Mountain

Over the years I've heard numerous stories about do-gooders and documentary filmmakers who set out to inspect a strip mine only to find themselves confronted with the blade of a D-9 dozer, raised to windshield level and bearing down fast upon them. I decided not to show my wife the article in this morning's paper about a state surface-mine inspector who died after being found beaten and unconscious in his home, his body mutilated by human bite marks. But I also can't quite shake that image, so I've decided to follow a less conspicuous road that leads around the backside of Lost Mountain, through a small community called Harveytown.

Christmas lights outline the trailers and small clapboard houses that are clustered tightly at the creek side, as if gravity itself had set them there. The western side of the mountain shows fewer scars from logging, and a series of sandstone outcrops stretches along the ridgeline, providing vital shelter to smaller animals, including the endangered wood rat. This unfortunately named rodent is actually quite handsome, with large eyes and long whiskers. Americans particularly should feel an affinity for this rapacious collector of baubles. If something shines—a piece of glass, aluminum foil, a shotgun shell—the wood rat takes it home. He piles the loot just outside his nest, which sits back in a narrow rock crevice. No one knows why. Perhaps he just wants a bigger midden pile than the wood rat living next door.

All through Appalachia, wood rats are on the decline. A parasitic roundworm has decimated much of the population, and the forest fragmentation caused by strip mining—the creation of smaller woodlots with an increased circumference—has made it much easier for foxes and bobcats to prey upon them. Strip mining is also a leading cause of species extinction. This Cumberland Plateau is one particular "hot spot" of ecological concern because two thirds of its bird population is also in decline.

Earlier in the fall, I climbed along this same ridgeline, going from one rock formation to another, looking for evidence of wood rats. Now, three months later, I'm climbing this ridge again, this time to get a decent, discreet look at the mining on the other side. I can already hear large equipment churning. At the ridgetop, I circle north and crouch under a stand of young trees. Two enormous backhoes are clawing away at the substrate directly beneath me. Slowly they cut a vertical rock wall all along the inside of this hollow to lay the wide road that coal trucks will need to maneuver the mountainside. Along with bulldozers and graders, they have already cut a quarter-mile road stretching down to the highway. Eventually the road will stretch up to the summit, providing access to the top three coal seams that lie beneath Lost Mountain. But here, at mid-elevation, the work has gotten tougher. The dozers are no longer shoving aside topsoil; now they are struggling with boulders. They carve away as much of an opening as they can while the backhoes load the loosened rock onto haul trucks. When those huge beds are full, the trucks begin creeping up a makeshift path to a flat bench near the top of the mountain. I watch through binoculars as they back to the edge of the bench. Slowly, a hydraulic lift raises the bed, sending eighty-five tons of brown sandstone and gray slate spilling down the mountainside.

·   ·   ·

There is no better place to understand the semiology of a strip mine than at Goose Pond, a five-acre "reclamation" area that sits in the middle of a massive mountaintop-removal project called the Starfire Mine, in Breathitt County. One might begin at the top, with the term "overburden." What is burdened in this case is the coal seam down below; overburden is the oak-pine forest, the topsoil, and 200 feet of sandstone that stand between the coal operator and the coal seam. When miners dislodge the overburden, it becomes "spoil." And according to the proposed rule change, the spoil that is dumped into the valleys below will not be "waste" but "fill." Streams are not buried; rather, valleys are filled.

"Reclamation," however, is the term that finally puts us squarely in the realm of Orwellian slipknots. Speaking plainly, to reclaim something is to get it back. The 1977 Surface Mining Control and Reclamation Act requires coal operators to restore the "approximate original contour" (AOC) of the land they have mined. According to the Kentucky Department of Natural Resources, "The condition of the land after the mining process must be equal to or better than pre-mining conditions." Scanning the reclaimed portions of the Starfire mine site, I can see hundreds of acres of rolling savanna, planted with an exotic lespedeza, one of the few grasses that will survive in this shale. But in what sense does a savanna "approximate" a summit? In what sense is a grassland monoculture "equal to or better than" a mixed mesophytic forest? The reality is that mountains pitched at a grade as steep as the Appalachians cannot be restored. Gravity and topography are working against you.

Perhaps sensing that the AOC stipulation would be a hard sell, lawmakers added this provision to SMCRA: coal operators could obtain an "AOC variance" if they could prove that the post-mined land would be put to "higher or better uses." In the beginning that meant commercial or residential development. A few housing complexes and even a prison were built on these sites (when the prison watchtowers started to lean due to subsidence, locals dubbed the facility Sink Sink). But there weren't nearly enough developers clamoring to fill these barren flats with strip malls or apartment complexes. And it was much cheaper to plant grass on an abandoned mine site and call it a "pasture" or, better yet, a "wildlife habitat."

That is what has happened at Goose Pond, where rock islands dot the still water and hardscrabble trees cling to the cobble. Above the pond stands a small wooden observation deck, replete with two of those mounted viewing stations you find at Niagara Falls. Looking only through these binoculars, one might indeed be fooled into thinking that this was some kind of wildlife sanctuary. But back away two steps and you will see a behemoth blue crane sitting in a deep pit behind the pond, swinging its massive arm back and forth like the fin of a mechanical shark. Attached to the crane is a dragline that rakes a house-sized maw across the coal seam, scooping up 100 tons of rock at a time. Down inside the pit sits an explosives truck. Its tank reads: THE POWER TO MOVE MOUNTAINS. Coal trucks rumble past on all sides of the pond. Highwalls frame the horizon. But none of that matters. A coal company has only to erect the flimsy trappings of a tourist stop and they have converted a wasteland into an area of "public use." Who wouldn't want to fish for trout in the shadow of a dragline?

Still, my favorite part of Goose Pond is a large sign that stands next to the observation deck. It is covered with pictures of pink lady's slipper, large-leaved magnolia, ruffed grouse, painted trillium, spotted salamander, and a wood rat, and it reads, "These are some of the other wildlife and plant species you may encounter during your visit." The word "other" adds a particular absurdity to what is already an outrageous lie. All of the species pictured are inhabitants of a deciduous forest, the likes of which this place won't be able to sustain for thousands of years.

· · ·

Coal operators are not an easily intimidated bunch. But there is probably no one in the state of Kentucky who rattles their cage like a forty-eight-year-old grandmother named Teri Blanton. A former chairperson of Kentuckians for the Commonwealth, the state's largest social-justice organization, Blanton has spent the last two decades helping coalfield residents fight the corporations that have turned so much of eastern Kentucky into what she calls a toxic dump.

One can get a real education in environmental corruption and smash-mouth class warfare by tracking the last twenty years of Blanton's life. She grew up in a small town called Dayhoit, in Harlan County, where four generations of her family had lived along White Star Hollow. It was the kind of community where neighbors shared their coal in the winter, and on a rare piece of flatland, one man, Millard Sutton, grew enough vegetables to feed nearly everyone in town. Families took turns helping out in his garden. Blanton moved to Michigan in the seventies to start a family, then moved back to Dayhoit in 1981 as a single mother of two. Her career as an activist started shortly afterward, when she phoned the highway department and asked for someone to clean up the large puddle of black water and coal sludge that stood in front of her trailer where her children caught the school bus. The highway department called the coal company that was mining around White Star Hollow, and the company responded by sending a coal truck to slowly circle Blanton's trailer all day. "That really burnt my ass," Blanton recalled, "that they thought they could shut me up by intimidation." That coal company, owned by two brothers, James and Aubra Dean, never did clean up the mess, and in the end, after Blanton's relentless badgering, the highway department built a new road up to her trailer.

Unfortunately, Blanton's problems were about to get much bigger than a slurry puddle. Since moving back to Dayhoit, Blanton's two children had been constantly sick. Sometimes, after bathing, they would break out in what their doctor called "a measle-like rash." But they didn't have the measles. The groundwater that fed their well had been poisoned with vinyl chloride, trichloroethylene, and a dozen other "volatile organic contaminants," or VOCs. On a three-acre plot a half-mile from Blanton's home, the McGraw Edison Company was rebuilding mining equipment. In the process they sprayed trichloroethylene-based degreasing solvents on transformers and capacitors. They piped PCB-laden transformer oil directly into Millard Sutton's large garden. They even sprayed it on the dirt roads of the next-door trailer park to, as they said, "help keep the dust down." They were just being good neighbors.

In the late eighties and early nineties Blanton, along with two other Dayhoit women, Joan Robinett and Monetta Gross, began pushing state and federal agencies to test their water. "In the media we were portrayed as these hysterical housewives who didn't know what we were talking about," Blanton recalled. Finally, after many of the wells were found to be contaminated by chemicals from the plant (which had since been sold and resold), the EPA declared Dayhoit a Superfund site in 1992 and put it on the National Priorities List of hot spots. "I moved back to Harlan County thinking I was bringing my children home to a safe place," Blanton said. "Instead I brought them back to a chemical wasteland."

The EPA excavated 5,000 tons of contaminated soil from around the plant, then trucked it to Alabama, where it was stored next to a poor, African American community. To extract the contaminated groundwater, a pump-and-treat system was installed on the site of the abandoned plant. This catalytic oxidation unit filtered out some of the VOCs and released the remaining elements, including carcinogens, into the air to be quickly dispersed. At least that was the plan. Blanton began researching pump-and-treat systems and found that they had been tested at sites where winds were high. But White Star Hollow was a different story. "It's like a bowl where the fog sits down on the river until the middle of the day," Blanton said. "And I lived right at the fog line, and as the crow flies not very far from the plant. In my mind, I knew they were going to poison me and my kids all over again."

Blanton loaded her trailer onto a flatbed, took her children, and left White Star Hollow.

On a bright cold day in November, I drove with Blanton back to Dayhoit. We passed the trailer park that sat next to the McGraw Edison plant, as well as the field that used to be Millard Sutton's garden. Blanton pointed to the yellow house next to it. "Everyone in that house died of cancer," she said. And she said it more than once as we traveled up the hollow.

The road followed Ewing Creek, running brown from recent rains. And then, as we followed it farther upstream, the water turned orange. Blanton pointed for me to pull off at a rusting cattle gate, where a sign read: MOUNTAIN SPUR COAL COMPANY. We got out and climbed the gravel road that led to an abandoned strip mine. A nasty orange syrup called acid mine water was pouring out of a pipe that drained an open mine pit. The sulfuric acid collected in a small pond, then spilled over into the creek below. Blanton lit a cigarette. "I grew up on this creek," she said. "I grew up walking these mountains, and I've watched them crumble before my very eyes. It just makes me angrier and angrier knowing that these people can operate in such a manner and get by with it."

For years the Dean brothers, along with a third partner, Carl McAfee, have been playing an elaborate shell game that keeps them in business and free from any responsibility to the land or local landowners. It works like this: the three men own several companies that remain in good standing with state regulators. Then they set up smaller companies with names like Limousine Coal, Master Blend, and Mountain Spur. These operations lease equipment from the "good" company and post a small bond that will supposedly cover the cost of reclamation should the company declare bankruptcy, which is exactly what they do. The shell company forfeits its bond, which is never enough to complete the reclamation, and local communities are left with cracked foundations, a contaminated creek, poisoned wells, and steep slopes that pour mud down when it rains because there is no vegetation to hold soil in place.

In October 2002, Blanton tried to block a permit from being issued to one of these shell companies, Shamrock Fuel. Before a hearing officer from the Office of Surface Mining, she laid out an extensive paper trail showing that at least one of the men, or his wife, was named as an "incorporator" or an officer in every one of the companies that had abandoned reclamation and declared bankruptcy. But, curiously, the OSM ruled that it could find no clear link between the companies. And the fight to penalize violators of SMCRA was made even harder by a puzzling 1999 verdict in the U.S. Court of Appeals for the District of Columbia. In *National Mining Association v. Department of the Interior*, the court ruled that permits could not be denied to companies for violations at mines they no longer controlled. So all coal operators like the Deans have to do is declare bankruptcy, start a new company, and move on to the next permit.[1]

Across the creek from where we stood, I could see the home of Blanton's childhood friend Debbie Williams. Before the mining started here, she spent $7,000 to have a new well dug. But as soon as the blasting began, her faucet was running as orange as the water now draining from this mine. The foundation of her house and her chimney have been cracked. But the Deans have not yet been forced to reimburse Williams, and it's likely they won't be. Just up the ridge, another one of their companies, Sandlick Coal, continues to strip away the trees and the coal.

[1] The Deans did not respond to repeated requests for comment on this article.

Before leaving Dayhoit, Blanton and I stopped at the White Star Cemetery, which sits in a small clearing. Some of the headstones were so old I could barely distinguish them from the large rocks that had rolled down the mountainside. "Hey, this is pretty," Blanton said. "I don't think I've ever been up here on a day I wasn't burying someone." Many of the newer tombs were set aboveground in cement vaults. Blanton pulled back some plastic flowers beside one of her cousin's markers. "She lived next to what we called the killer well," Blanton said. "Everyone who lived around that well died."

In the middle of the cemetery were buried two of Garnett Howard's three sons, the two who were born after he started working at the McGraw Edison plant. "They both developed non-Hodgkin's lymphoma before they were thirty and died," Blanton said. We stared in silence at the dates on the markers. "Almost nobody in Dayhoit lives past fifty-five," she went on. "At the meetings the people from the EPA would accuse us of being too emotional. I told them, 'Let all of your family members and friends die around you and see if you don't get emotional.' " She knelt beside the grave of a high school friend. On the headstone was a depiction of a father and son standing beside a stream. "He was a real redneck," Blanton said, breaking into a smile. "I loved him."

February 23, 2004, Lost Mountain

Forty years ago Lyndon Johnson came to eastern Kentucky, the poorest place in America, to declare his War on Poverty. His limousine maneuvered the pocked roads of Martin County, and, with Lady Bird at his side, the president stopped at some tar-papered shacks to assure a few families that he would bring them into his Great Society. At that time, Appalachia's poverty rate stood at 31 percent. Since then, nearly 2,300 miles of roads have been laid across the region and more than 800,000 families have gotten indoor plumbing. And today eastern Kentucky's poverty rate hovers around, well, 30 percent. If you look at a map of central Appalachia—in Kentucky, West Virginia, and Tennessee—the areas that the Appalachian Regional Commission deems "distressed" are almost without exception the ones that have seen the most strip mining.

Up on Lost Mountain, the ground is muddy and covered by a light snow. The dozers have erased almost all the logging roads, shoving aside topsoil and subsoil in search of the number 11 coal seam. Leslie Resources has now blocked off every dirt road leading up Lost Mountain with imposing iron gates. I don't take it personally. Eastern Kentuckians are as attached to their ATVs as urban Kentuckians are to their SUVs, and while both do their respective share of environmental damage, it's the former that Leslie is trying to keep off Lost Mountain. NO TRESPASSING signs hang on all the gates, but, since Leslie leases only the mineral rights to the property, I tell myself it has no jurisdiction to keep me off property it doesn't own. I duck under one gate on the eastern side of the mountain and start walking. Chain saws have mowed down most of the trees on this slope, and they all lie where they fell. Only the dead trees have been left standing, and woodpeckers move back and forth between them as if they can't believe their luck—nothing now stands between them and the carpenter ants that colonize diseased beech trees.

Higher up, where the hardwood trees still stand, I pass a sign tacked to one that reads: DANGER BLASTING. Almost on cue a siren sounds to signal a coming blast. I am still too far from the site to actually see the explosion, but two minutes later, when the blast sounds out over the hollow, I feel a slight trembling beneath my boots. After a few more minutes, a yellow plume moves through the trees, carrying with it the sharp smell of sulfur.

I drop down the ridge side to a lower logging road that leads directly to the source of the smoke. I can hear the constant beeping of haul trucks inching back to the edge of the hollow fill. A few months ago, I could follow this gravel road up to the mountaintop. Now I find it blocked by a row of impregnable boulders. Peering over them, I can see only the top of a truck as it raises its bed and sends another load of rubble down into the valley. I can, however, tell that what used to be a ridgeline leading west is now nowhere in sight.

I circle back around the mountain and begin climbing through the younger trees and wild roses that still cover the northern slope. The last obstacles are the capstones that mark the summit. I shimmy into a narrow crevice of rock, find a foothold, and haul myself up. At the crest, doubled over and gasping, I still see in the dirt the same traces of wild turkey, grouse, and raccoons that I saw months ago. The mountaintop is still here, still as it was. These obdurate boulders attest to it. It's not until I reach the other side of this summit and look down that I see what has changed.

The lower ridgeline is nearly gone. What was, last month, a gradual slope leading westward is now, right below me, a fifty-foot vertical drop that gives way to dark pits and gray ledges.

You can think of this mountain, or any mountain in Appalachia, as a geological layer cake with four- to eight-foot seams of coal separated by much thicker bands of sandstone, slate, and shale. The seams are numbered in descending order: the one nearest the summit is the Hazard 12 seam, and about three hundred feet below lies Hazard 9. The narrator of Merle Travis's famous folk song "Sixteen Tons" begins his lament with,

> I was born one mornin' when the sun didn't shine
> Picked up a shovel and I walked to the mine
> I hauled sixteen tons of number 9 coal
> And the straw-boss said, "Well, bless my soul."

That same number 9 coal seam lies beneath Lost Mountain, a few hundred feet below the summit, but no deep miners are trying to dig it out. Why bother? Why send hundreds of miners burrowing underground when a few men armed with explosives and bulldozers can blast right down to the seam? And whereas in the forties it took one miner all day to load sixteen tons of coal out of a deep mine, today one man behind the wheel of a loader can in five minutes fill a coal truck with sixty tons of this bituminous rock. What makes strip mining so cost-efficient is precisely what makes it so devastating.

Here on Lost Mountain, the crew goes straight for the highest three seams, where there is less earth to move and a more ready supply of coal. The dozers have pushed much of the vegetation and topsoil to the edge of this man-made plateau, called an area mine. The twisted trees and mounded dirt form a berm around the darker crater. Young maples and hickories stubbornly hold on at the edge of the mining, where so much of the topsoil has been upturned and compacted. What compounds the problems of mountaintop removal is that when the bedrock is disturbed, it increases in volume by 20 percent; that additional matter is called "swell" and will eventually be dumped down into the valley below.

Staying out of sight, I loop down to the edge of the mining and duck in behind three toppled pine trees. From here the whole scene is in front of me. At the far edge of the mine site, a white "powder tower" now stands, filled with explosive material. In front of it, dozers have shaved down to the number 10 seam. A loader scrapes the coal into mounds, then shovels them into the first coal trucks to climb Lost Mountain. Those trucks will take their loads five miles up highway 80 to Leslie Resource's coal tipple, which sits beside the north fork of the Kentucky River. There the coal will be processed and loaded onto railcars or barges.

The whistle blows at 4:30—quitting time. The workers grab their lunch coolers and jump down from the dozers, trucks, and loaders. I retrace my path down the backside of the mountain. My face and arms bear the scars of blackberry gauntlets, and my water bottle is empty. My thoughts have turned from the ravages of strip mining to the shelves of cold beer at the BP station down below. I am not looking ahead, not looking at anything really, when the huge silver maw of a bulldozer comes lunging over the ridge about twenty feet in front of me. The driver doesn't see me; he is cocked at too steep an angle. I leap back over several fallen trees and take cover. Whatever else bulldozers do, they do not move fast. This one backs down the hill, coughs another cloud of black smoke into the air, then lurches back into view, shoving topsoil to the side. The driver pauses each time to get his bearings, and each time I get another look at the huge, serrated blade. For the first time, I understand completely why Harry Caudill, author of *Night Comes to the Cumberlands*, described it as a "monstrous scimitar."

Once the driver has cleared a space to work, he sets about the real task—knocking down trees. I'm startled to see how easily a twenty-year-old maple succumbs to the dozer's blade. The dozer is graceless and resolute. Each time the driver backs down the hill to take a run at another tree, I scramble about fifty yards farther away. When I am finally far enough down the mountain to escape the driver's notice, I take a seat on a stump. It is almost dusk, and the mountain has darkened to a silhouette. I can no longer see the dozer. But from the stump, I watch as one tree after another falls against the violet light of the setting sun.

·　　·　　·

After the draft Environmental Impact Statement on mountaintop removal was released in 2003, several forums were held in Kentucky and West Virginia to allow for public comment on the study. This struck me as a rather cynical formality, but I drove down to the hearing at the Hal Rogers Center in Hazard, Kentucky, to hear what coalfield citizens had to say. There were about 150 people in the auditorium, mostly men. They wore Carhartt jackets and work boots; some still had on their hard hats. Up on stage the drafters of the EIS document sat at a long table. All the heavy hitters were there—the Environmental Protection Agency, the Army Corps of Engineers, the Department of the Interior's Office of Surface Mining, the Fish and Wildlife Service. They sat attentive, with pens poised, ready to take the public pulse.

Anyone who wished would have five minutes to speak his or her piece. The first speaker, Bill Caylor, president of the Kentucky Coal Association, began by complaining for thirty seconds that he had prepared a twelve-minute speech and why couldn't somebody do something about the time limit. Then Caylor, a man with thick white hair and a neat white mustache, asked for a show of hands of those who had come to support strip mining. If anyone besides me didn't raise a hand, it was hard to tell. Having sized up his audience, Caylor launched into a barrage of statistics: 120 million tons of coal were mined in Kentucky last year, placing the state third in extraction behind West Virginia and Wyoming; that coal fetches $3 billion annually; 80 percent of Kentucky coal is sold out of state; in the last fifteen years, coal-related employment has dropped 61 percent; at 4.1 cents per kilowatt hour, Kentucky coal is the cheapest energy source around. "We're like the Saudi Arabia of America," Caylor announced, meaning, I think, that Appalachia has a lot of fossil fuel, and not that the region's poor have been greatly oppressed by a wealthy minority that controls the fuel.

Still, I puzzled over his fact sheet. Coal jobs have dropped 61 percent precisely because strip mining requires far fewer men to operate much larger machinery. It seemed hardly an argument for decreasing regulation on mountaintop removal. And in what sense was it a good thing that 80 percent of Kentucky's coal is sold out of state? Why should Dayton and Detroit—or China, for that matter—get the coal but be held accountable for none of the environmental consequences of its extraction? And if everyone is doing so well, why is eastern Kentucky the nation's capital for Oxycontin abuse?

Caylor was followed by a long line of miners and mining engineers. One man read an exhaustive list of every Hazard business that had been built on flattened land. The crowd was generous with its applause. Several speakers drew attention to the deer, elk, and turkey that had returned to the region after mountaintop removal began. The wife of a miner pleaded for her husband's job, then asked, "What use are the mountains to us other than coal?"

Then up stepped a gray-haired man in a blue suit and a flamboyant purple tie. He said his name was Paul David Taulbee. His grandfather had helped log the mountains back in 1912, and had then worked as a deep miner from 1915 to 1952. His father worked in the mines for twenty-eight years. I suspect there were country preachers in the family as well, because it quickly became clear that Taulbee had come to deliver a sermon. He wasn't talking to the men and women up on stage; he was addressing the congregation.

He was tired—sick and tired—of outsiders coming into eastern Kentucky and telling its people what they *should* do. He hinted at a conspiracy afoot by the rest of the state to keep eastern Kentucky poor. He wanted the federal government and the Army Corps of Engineers and the Environmental Protection Agency to leave this region and its people *alone* to mine as they saw fit. "We want to be unbound and left alone so we can develop to the fullest extent," he stormed, one finger held high. Were that to happen, all of those native people who had followed the outward migration north for better jobs would come back home. Eastern Kentucky would finally thrive. Because, Taulbee intoned, what the outsiders should never forget is this: "The only way to *stay* in the mountains is to *mine* the mountains!" A standing ovation followed. The moderator called for a short break. Everyone went out to smoke.

It was gray and drizzling. I started up my fossil-fuel-burning truck and headed home. I replayed the hearing in my head. It's true that the contour mining of the seventies cut out shelves in these mountains and made room for the chain stores that followed an expanded highway. But anyone who has ever looked down on the strip jobs from a plane knows there is enough flatland in eastern

Kentucky to plop down 10,000 Wal-Marts. And most of that land is completely inaccessible. As for the return of game animals, deer populations have risen all over the eastern United States, not just around abandoned mines. The elk that do graze around the edges of reclaimed sites were reintroduced a few years ago from western states. Strip mining had nothing to do with it.

As for Paul David Taulbee, I could tell him that surface mining accounts for only 5,000 jobs in all thirty counties of eastern Kentucky, averaging out to 167 jobs per county. I could tell him that the old deep-mining jobs aren't coming back, and the people who left for Cincinnati and Cleveland might not want to either, especially if they were coming back to wasted mountains and dead streams. I could tell him that if coal hadn't brought prosperity to the mountains in the last ninety years, it probably isn't likely to do so.

But Taulbee isn't going to listen to me. I'm an *outsider*, as he had said, the worst kind of elitist, who thinks a mountain is more important than someone's job. The miner's wife had asked, "When are you going to start thinking about us instead of the environment?" But perhaps the harder question is this: When in Appalachia are we going to start thinking about both at once?

March 29, 2004, Lost Mountain

It's eighty degrees and sunny. I'm driving fast alongside Lost Creek, with the windows down and Neil Young wailing on an old cassette. Redbud and white dogwood are blooming along the steep slopes and up pristine gorges. Down below, junked cars and hot-water heaters are rusting on some grassless patches of land in front of sagging trailers. What is remarkable about the ugliness of Appalachian poverty is its closeness and contrast to the spectacular mountains rising around it.

If the day were not so nice, I might be chastened by the number of wooden crosses, each of which marks a spot where someone met a violent death. Take one of the poorest parts of the country, add to it alcohol and pills, hard curves and coal trucks, and what you get are a lot of little white crosses staggered along the roadside.

I set my parking break at the usual spot below Lost Mountain and hike to the top. On the bench right below me, a white truck carrying a large tank pulls into view. To get a better look, I shuffle about thirty feet down the ridge side and wedge myself between two boulders that I hope will provide decent cover when the blasting starts. "Flyrock" is the rather benign term for everything that scatters when the explosives are detonated. Regulators from the state Department of Natural Resources tell me they have cracked down on blasting violations in the last few years. People were getting hurt, chimneys and house foundations were cracking, dishes were shattering. I heard about an older couple in Knox County who were sitting beside their small pool one afternoon when a boulder came flying at them from a strip job behind their house. It landed in the pool and cracked the concrete bottom. This year eight off-site flyrock violations were reported in Kentucky; in one case, children were playing in their pool when debris started falling around them.

Down below, the driver of a blast-hole drill is slowly working his way around the perimeter of this bench, boring a sixty-foot-deep hole about every ten feet. With a long, vertical drill carriage attached to the chassis, the machine moves with the slow unsteadiness of a man carrying a long ladder. I can hear a low grinding sound as the hydraulic motor builds torque and the long drill bit tears away at the sandstone.

While the rock drill moves from hole to hole, two men step out of the truck that carries the explosives. A long tube that stretches over the top of the tank now swings to the side, where one of the men holds a narrow plastic bag up to the mouthpiece. A brownish substance fills the bag with a concoction known in the coal industry as AMFO. The acronym stands for ammonium nitrate and fuel oil. Timothy McVeigh detonated 4,000 pounds of it in Oklahoma City. The typical blast on a Kentucky strip mine is ten times that.

AMFO is too volatile to transport, so the ammonium is mixed with diesel fuel at the mine site. The two men drop the mixture down into one of the blast holes, then repeat the process around the edge of the bench. Finally, they pack blasting caps—detonators—into each hole and string them together with a long orange fuse. As their truck and the rock drill pull away from the bench, the warning siren sounds. Each permitted mining operation must follow something called the scaled distance equation, which calculates the amount of explosives that can be used relative to the nearest residential or commercial structure. Regulators make quarterly inspections of the mine sites and use seismographs to measure each blast. But the problem, coalfield residents will tell you, is that all of the inspections are announced, which makes it rather easy for a coal company to exceed the blasting limits as soon as the inspectors are gone.

When this particular blast finally goes off, it looks something like a Las Vegas fountain suddenly coming to life. Except it is spewing rock instead of water. All at once white plumes of debris shoot out of every hole, and then seem to hang for a moment at about thirty feet. Two seconds after the blast, the entire outer ledge falls away, as if it had been shaken by an earthquake, which of course it has. I duck and cover as smaller debris scatters in my direction. An acrid yellow smoke hangs in the air, and a fine gray powder settles over this section of the mine site. Slowly, the haul trucks and front-end loader move in to truck away all of the loosened rock. From this perspective it is easy to understand why Teri Blanton calls mountaintopping "bomb and bury." "Removal" is certainly too clinical, too surgical, a term. All of this rubble will be dumped down into the valley fill, and this same process will be repeated thousands of times across the mine site.

I climb back up to the crest, then drop down the backside of Lost Mountain. Here the ridgeline forms another large bowl, and all sides bear the crisscrossed scars of bulldozers that have leveled most of the trees. My T-shirt snags on the briars of young black locust trees. I pull myself up over a series of bald escarpments, where the sun has cast an almost lavender color over the sandstone. Abruptly, I stumble into a clearing, an artificial shelf carved out by a bulldozer. An uprooted maple puts out, for the last time, its long scarlet stamens. Other trees lean away, half unearthed. Above me rises a thirty-foot mound of debris. Loosened by blasting, then pushed aside, this rock-and-shale mound forms a rim around the entire mine site. I climb up over the boulders and buried tree limbs until I am crouching at the edge of this cratered landscape. It looks from here as if a meteor has hit this side of the mountain.

•   •   •

I first met Damon Morgan at one of the public hearings in Hazard. Both sides were sounding off about the Bush Administration's proposal to allow mining within one hundred feet of streams, a practice prohibited by the SMCRA. Several engineers from TECO Energy had been extolling the job growth that coal brought to the region. Then Morgan stepped to the podium, wearing denim overalls, a red flannel shirt, and a white straw cowboy hat. He looked to be in his seventies. "These people who talk about coal bringing jobs," he began, "why you wouldn't have no problem at all selling them a sky hook." I wasn't sure what a sky hook was, but I was pretty sure this was the genuine article—a self-made, free-thinking mountaineer, stepping right out of the past.

The engineers from TECO also had claimed that many headwater streams were actually dirtier before mining, when local people dumped their garbage in the hollows. To that Morgan replied, "You're right, they're not as dirty now. Because they're not there." He said the stream that ran beside his family's cabin is now buried under sixty feet of what used to be a mountaintop called Huckleberry Ridge. And all around him, Leslie Resources continues leveling mountains and burying streams. After the hearing, I asked if I could come down to take a look.

Sure enough, when I reached Morgan's modest log cabin that April morning, he and his wife were sitting on their porch, listening to the incessant beeping of haul trucks creeping along the ridgetops all around them.

Morgan was drafted right out of high school and sent to Okinawa and Iwo Jima. "When I was in the service, I thought a lot about this land," he says, "how I used to hunt on it as a kid, and how I used to come up here and sing. I decided to save up my money and buy this place when I got back." And he did. He payed $1,000 for 100 acres, which today is the only stretch along Bad Creek that hasn't been strip-mined.

We climbed on Morgan's ATV and followed gravel switchbacks up the mountain. Morgan pointed out a rare white chestnut tree. Down this ridge side, he has set out a row of chestnut saplings, which he imported from Virginia and hopes will survive the blight that wiped out the native chestnuts in the forties. Back then, as the oldest of twelve children, Morgan worked with his father on the family's scratch farm. "We'd take a hillside like this and grub it up and plant corn and beans," he said. "That's the way we made a living. We had forty or fifty head of hogs, and we turned them back up in here." Many other families did the same. The hogs would feast all summer on beechnuts.

It was a marginal economy even for marginal land, but it sustained a family of fourteen. Soon, though, the railroads that had been laid alongside the Cumberland and Kentucky rivers would signal the end of such sustenance living. An extractive economy had arrived. Once the major timber barons were through, there were no beech trees left and no beechnuts for the hogs.

Morgan cranked up the ATV and we ventured higher. He pointed to an outcrop hidden by taller trees. "The man I bought this land from," Morgan shouted over the eighteen-horsepower engine, "that's where he set his still. His wife had a bell down at the house and she'd ring it if any revenuers came around." We rode across the ridgeline that marked the boundary of Morgan's property. Everything from there down to his cabin belonged to him; everything over the ridge—at least the mineral rights—to one coal company or another.

We rode past the last stands of chestnut oak and mountain laurel. Then we made a hard right and suddenly were driving across the savanna landscape so typical of a post-reclamation mountaintop-removal job. Brown lespedeza waved like prairie grass. "This was reclaimed over thirty years ago," Morgan said, but it had only a few pines and scattered black locusts to show for it. When we reached the edge of this shelf, Morgan shut off the vehicle. Across the valley was another scene I was becoming used to. The same company that was mining Lost Mountain had reduced one more forested watershed to another dark wasteland.

"That used to be a big beautiful mountain," Morgan said. "Now look at it."

A black butte rose up from a series of staggered black plateaus that stretched out against the horizon. Narrow rivulets caused by erosion ran down the sides of the benches. The characteristic gray haul roads wound through it all. The ugly panorama dwarfed the line of dozers that sat below the nearest bench. And the only thing that was keeping those dozers off Morgan's property was a piece of legislation he had spent twenty years fighting to enact.

In the 1880s and '90s, a native Kentucky schoolteacher named John C. C. Mayo began riding through the eastern counties on horseback, offering gold dollars to farmers who would sell him their mineral rights. Since the farmers made their living off the surface of the land, selling what was underneath seemed like a good idea. Many signed a contract called the "broad form deed," so named because it gave the deed holders broad rights to extract the coal by any means they desired. The farmers obviously imagined that miners would tunnel under their land using picks and shovels, then haul the coal out with ponies. At the turn of the century, no one who sold their mineral rights could have imagined the industrial evolution that would lead to strip mining.

Mayo bought up thousands of mineral parcels, which he then sold or leased to coal companies. The companies themselves soon got into the game of buying mineral rights under the broad form deed. Near the turn of the century, Kentucky River Land and Coal Co. paid as little as a quarter an acre for the coal under Morgan's property. And when he bought these hundred acres back in the forties, the company still had every right to strip off every pound of topsoil to claim its coal.

This happened all over eastern Kentucky. Men who had learned to drive tanks during World War II had no problem climbing onto D-9 bulldozers and cutting benches along the side of a mountain. Then in 1961 the Tennessee Valley Authority, a major provider of hydroelectric power, decided to get into the coal business. The TVA signed contracts to buy 16.5 million tons of strip-mined coal.

Under the broad form deed, the mining was ruthless and the landowners were powerless. Mrs. Bige Ritchie, who lived on Sassafras Creek, watched a bulldozer plow through a family graveyard. It upended the coffin of her infant son and pushed it down the mountainside. "I like to lost my mind over it," she told Ben A. Franklin of the *New York Times*.

The conflict finally came to a head in 1965, when landowners took up their rifles and refused to let the bulldozers destroy their property. Citizen groups started forming to fight the broad form deed. Damon Morgan joined just about all of them and served as chairman of the Citizens Coal Council. Finally, in 1988, Kentuckians voted for a state constitutional amendment that required coal operators to get a landowner's permission before mining.

That law saved Morgan's home and land, but he still has to look out every day at the thousands of acres that have been destroyed all around him.

"I belong to a lot of peaceful organizations," he said as we stared down at the lifeless mine site. "We believe in dialogue. Well, I believe in dialogue, too. But sometimes. . . . " His voice trailed off. "We're fighting terrorism right now," he said, and he wasn't talking about Islamic militants. "If people are going to poison you to death, I think we should do whatever is necessary to put a stop to it. The state and federal government won't do nothing. I don't want to say take the law into your own hands. That's a big step. But . . . I don't know."

Morgan turned around in his seat to take in an as-yet-unscathed range just to the left of the strip mine. Color was coming back to the red maples. Cherry and serviceberry trees were blooming. "See how that holler zigzags in and out of those mountains," he said. "That's where Main Creek runs down into Greasy Creek. Sometimes I think I'll just take my gun and my dog, go walking down through there, and just keep going." For several moments, we watched his other, imaginary self disappear down into the valley, beyond the strip job, back into the past.

April 12, 2004, Lost Mountain

Franz Kafka's short story "Before the Law" begins like this: "Before the Law stands a doorkeeper. To this doorkeeper there comes a man from the country and prays for admittance to the Law. But the doorkeeper says that he cannot grant admittance at the moment." And behind this doorkeeper are many others, all guarding the Law. "These are difficulties the man from the country has not expected," writes Kafka; "the Law, he thinks, should surely be accessible at all times and to everyone." The man waits for days, which turn into years. At times he tries to bribe the doorkeeper, who accepts the money with this fateful remark: "I am only taking it to keep you from thinking you have omitted anything." In the end the man dies, and with finality the doorkeeper shuts the door.

Now, "Kafkaesque" is not a term I throw around lightly. But if you go to enough public hearings on surface-mining legislation, it soon becomes clear that what you are watching is a drama of grand futility straight out of Kafka's parables. And the actors know it. The officials from the Office of Surface Mining sit stoically, almost indifferently, at a table in the center of the stage. One after another coalfield citizens step to the podium to have their say about the effects of weakening regulations on strip mining, and one after another they announce to anyone naive enough to believe in participatory democracy that this is all a done deal anyway. Yet still they put themselves through this compulsory charade. The stenographer who sits at the side of the stage, taking it all down, is himself a character Kafka would have particularly loved—the man endlessly writing a report that no one will ever read.

Yet perhaps the most pitiful part of Kafka's allegory is the bribe that the man from the country offers the doorkeeper. Compared with the huge sums of money that corporations are allowed to give politicians, this one man's bribe is laughable. Over the last four years, the coal industry has contributed $8.5 million to Republicans; only 11 percent of its contributions have gone to Democrats. And over the last four years, the percentage of polluted waterways in Kentucky alone has risen by 12 percent; almost half of the state's streams are unfishable and unswimmable. What is the connection? Consider the case of Steven Griles.

It has been well documented that Griles worked as a lobbyist for the coal and oil industries before he was tapped to be George W. Bush's Deputy Secretary of the Interior. During each year of his term at Interior, Griles has received a $284,000 deferred-compensation package from his former employer, National Environmental Strategies (NES). The *Washington Post* reported that

Griles met at least three times with the National Mining Association (NMA), a former client of NES, while NMA was seeking looser standards on mountaintop removal. Which is exactly what NMA got. Since the 1977 Surface Mining Control and Reclamation Act states in rather plain language that mining permits can be granted only if "no damage will be done to natural watercourses," the Department of the Interior under Griles proposed in January 2004 a rule "*clarifying* [my italics] the circumstances in which mining activities . . . may be allowed within 100 feet of a perennial or intermittent stream." The "clarification" requires that "the mining operation has been designed, to the extent possible, to minimize impacts on hydrology, fish and wildlife . . . prior to allowing mining within 100 feet of a perennial or intermittent stream." It's the phrase "to the extent possible" and the word "prior" that could render the protection of SMCRA unenforceable.

With all this in mind, I decided it might be a good time to look for the headwaters of Lost Creek. I pull off the road beside a small house that sits closest to the mining on Lost Mountain. Chickens strut around a neat back yard, and behind the chickens I can hear the low voice of Lost Creek. I follow it up a narrow gorge, stepping over cobble and fallen tree limbs. Two days of rain have brought the stream to life. Chickweed and rue anemone bloom modestly along the creek side. Bent trillium is about to spread its maroon petals.

Halfway up the gorge, the trickling stream emerges beneath a large beech tree surrounded by rhododendron. I take a seat on a fallen branch to contemplate Lost Creek's modest beginning. There is something intrinsically rewarding about finding the source of any stream. What is not as rewarding is to hear machinery rumbling above its source. I climb up the creek bed until I can see a backhoe prying loose boulders and subsoil up at the head of the hollow. It is working in tandem with a dozer, slowly extending a bench along the back side of the mountain. The backhoe chips away at the rockface with its long mechanical arm, and the dozer pushes the debris aside. According to the mining maps for this job, none of the spoil is supposed to be deposited in this creek bed. But this month, under the Freedom of Information Act, I elicited fourteen single-spaced pages of violations by Leslie Resources. Since 1985, Leslie has racked up over 500 citations. Forty-seven of those violations pertain to water quality, and twenty-four are for illegal use of explosives. Leslie Resources, these documents show, is particularly lax about keeping sediment out of streams.[2]

To avoid the dozer and backhoe, I cut a wide tack around the back side of the mountain. Near the ridgetop, ground pine has begun to poke its bright green fronds up through matted leaves. This coniferous-looking fern tops out at seven inches, but its distant ancestor, *Lepidodendron*, grew to 150 feet as it breathed in vast amounts of carbon. That was more than 300 million years ago. These trees that looked like giant ferns often fell into oxygen-poor bogs, and so they never decayed. Instead, molten heat and geological pressure hardened them into compressed layers of the black, carbon-rich rock that is disappearing fast from the other side of this ridge.

When I reach the mountaintop, I discover how fast. The dirt road that led along the eastern ridge of Lost Mountain is gone, and so is the eastern ridge. What was once an arching razorback is now a sunken crater. An explosion goes off inside the deep pit, but I see only the tops of the gray blast plumes. The source of Lost Creek lies right below this pit, just over the ridge. What this blasting will do to the groundwater might not be fully understood for several years. What is known is that when underground pirite is oxidized through blasting, it releases sulfuric acid. And it is al-

[2]Leslie Resources has since been bought by International Coal Group, which did not respond to requests for comment on this article.

most certain that the blasting on Lost Mountain will create underground fissures through which mine acid will drain down into seeps that will leach out into this watershed.

The erosion caused by surface runoff also causes problems that can best be measured by driving about fifteen miles to the Falling Rock watershed in Robinson Forest. That watershed feeds one of the cleanest streams in Kentucky, Clemons Fork. Its level of conductivity—that is, dissolved ions—is usually between fifty and sixty. Its chlorides, magnesium, and sodium levels are all less than two milligrams per liter of water. But one has only to go a half-mile downstream to the confluence of Clemons Fork and Buckhorn Creek, which sits directly below a strip mine, to find that the conductivity has risen to 1,000, the magnesium and calcium to 25, and the sulfates from less than 10 to 300. Whereas Clemons Fork can sustain roughly one hundred species, water conditions at Buckhorn Creek have been so severely degraded that at most ten species can survive.

May 6, 2004, Lost Mountain

The photos of American torture at Abu Ghraib surfaced this week. I have often felt despondent about decisions that American presidents have made in my name, but this is the first time I have felt truly embarrassed to be an American. I am looking forward to seeing Lost Creek; I am remembering my favorite line from Thoreau: "He who hears the rippling of rivers in these degenerate days will not utterly despair." And when I pull off the main road north of Hazard, the creek is running clear and strong beneath the mixed mesophytic forest, now in full leaf. Families have set out their creekside gardens. Neat rows of early greens are almost a foot high.

I park my truck on the east side of the mountain and start up toward the headwaters of the creek. Canopy leaves have now closed over this gorge, turning the air cool and moist. They have also muffled the sound of the large machines over the next ridge.

As I step deliberately over the slick stones, an unannounced explosion makes the entire ridge side tremble. But it is the mental shock more than the physical tremor that knocks me off balance, and I fall against a patch of ferns. I right myself and start climbing up the left bank, toward a clearing that affords a profile of the mining. From that vantage point, at about 1,000 feet, the mountain looks like a hideous wedding cake, a series of black and gray ledges that lead up to the summit, now only a rocky knob. There, an abandoned cinder-block shack still stands like some ominous cake decoration, covered in graffiti that bears this promising sentiment: MIKE LOVES ME BITCH.

I drop down into the watershed, where all of the leaves are covered with the chalky gray residue of blasting, then I follow my usual climb up the back side of Lost Mountain. Near the peak chestnut oaks dominate the canopy. Sassafrases and redbuds fill in the understory, where a cool breeze is moving. I step around foamflowers and bright red catchflies, so called because their sticky stem slows down insects to guarantee a fair exchange of nectar for pollen.

Although this side of the forest is quiet, I notice a silent ovenbird eyeing me from a low twig about thirty feet away. He has a handsome brown head, similar to a wood thrush's, but his white breast is streaked with black instead of spotted like the thrush. This neotropical migrant has probably just returned to its breeding ground. The males reach the eastern forests about two weeks before the females to establish territory. He is usually an ardent suitor, his habits made famous by Robert Frost's poem "The Oven Bird":

> There is a singer everyone has heard
> Loud, a mid-summer and mid-wood bird,
> Who makes the solid tree trunks sound again.

Biologists speak of "indicator species," those that can tell us something important about an ecosystem. In Frost's poem the ovenbird is indicative of lateness—lateness of season and lateness of the human industrial age.

> He says thè early petal-fall is past,
> When pear and cherry bloom went down in showers
> On sunny days a moment overcast;
> And comes that other fall we name the fall.
> He says the highway dust is over all.

Frost slyly suggests that "that other fall" is both the natural season of dying and the human separation from a prelapsarian state of nature. And then the machine suddenly enters the garden, kicking up dust—in this particular case, the dust from coal trucks and AMFO blasts. Finally, Frost's ovenbird becomes an indicator in a final sense:

> The bird would cease and be as other birds
> But that he knows in singing not to sing.
> The question that he frames in all but words
> Is what to make of a diminished thing.

The overbird's song is a eulogy. In singing he knows there is less and less worth singing about. And so he poses the crucial question: *What to make of a diminished thing?* The answer, of course, lies just over this ridge.

From the summit, I ease down the southern slope around boulders and a stand of wild azaleas covered with nodding orange blooms. I take up a position behind the largest chestnut oak still standing on this side of the mountain. Two feet beyond it, a highwall drops about seventy feet straight down to the number 11 coal seam, which is now a flat black plateau, stretching out like a tarmac. At the EIS hearing, one man had stepped to the microphone and asked, "What are these mountains good for? They're all up and down." He would be pleased with what has transpired here on Lost Mountain, where a pilot could easily land a small prop plane on the wide level shelf below. As it is, two front-end loaders are filling the bucket of a coal truck from both sides. When they are finished, a long mechanical arm pulls a red, white, and blue tarp up over the coal. The truck pulls away and another takes its place. Since I started coming to Lost Mountain, the price of coal per ton has jumped from $34 to $55—coal prices usually follow oil prices—and the pace of its extraction has quickened.

One of the permit maps drawn up for this particular job shows the "pre-mining" contour of the mountain as a dotted line—something almost hypothetical, arbitrary. The "post-mining" contour is designated by two dark lines, flat as a dead man's EKG. When I first looked at that map, it seemed impossible. More than 200 feet lay between the dotted outline of the mountaintop and the flat line that indicated a reclaimed "pasture." Didn't the engineers know this was solid rock up here? Didn't they know this ridgeline had been standing longer than the Himalayas? Now, of course, I see they knew that perfectly well, and they knew exactly what they were doing. I had made the mistake of thinking in geological time. But as Rachel Carson wrote in *Silent Spring*, "In the modern world there is no time." It has been annihilated by explosives and fossil fuel and hydraulic rock drills.

The pit that had been blasted out of the eastern ridge last month is now a gigantic black gash that opens like a canyon onto the southern side of the mountain. Around on the western side all that's left is a pocked, deracinated landscape, strewn with boulders and absent of anything that could be mistaken for life. Off in the distance, I count nine pickup trucks. Nine men—that is all it takes to bring this mountain low.

When the 4:30 whistle blows and those pickups have disappeared down the mountain, I circle around to the nearest bench. From here, the highwall reaches forty feet up to the summit, where a clutch of pine trees hangs over the precipice. I climb over the rubble down on the western side, then follow the lower, longer highwall that sits above the number 10 seam. Because this land-scape shifts so quickly beneath the force of the explosives and dozers, a sense of vertigo sets in as I wander around these unnatural formations. Where last month I walked a ridgeline, this month, in exactly the same place, I'm standing on a black plateau, and it's hard to even remember what the original contour looked like. I know it was here, I know there were a few trees left. Now there's nothing. Everything that once stood here now lies a hundred feet away, down in the massive hollow fill. I stretch out my arms and slowly turn full circle. My throat tightens and my breath becomes suddenly short. I cannot see one living thing.

. . .

In October 2000 the largest environmental disaster east of the Mississippi occurred when a coal slurry impoundment pond broke through an underground mine shaft and spilled more than 300 million gallons of black toxic sludge into the headwaters of Coldwater and Wolf Creek in Inez, Kentucky—in the same county where Lyndon Johnson stood on a miner's porch and first announced his War on Poverty. When coal is cleaned, the resulting by-product is a gelatinous mixture called coal slurry. That is what flooded through Inez—black waves that moved with the speed and the consistency of volcanic lava, smothering everything in its path. Yards and gardens were buried; bridges were swept away. Basketball hoops looked like buoys in a black ocean. The only thing people on Coldwater Creek had to be thankful for was their lives. Unlike the 1972 Buffalo Creek pond break that killed 125 people, no one died that day in Martin County. But although the slurry spill was thirty times the size of the *Exxon-Valdez* disaster, the *New York Times* made no mention of it. One Martin County resident finally concluded, "We're just not quite as cute as those otters." In other words, the Prince William Sound was a pristine estuary; but the Appalachian mountains and its people were already damaged goods.

In 1972 a West Virginia governor's commission asked a twenty-three-year-old mining engineer named Jack Spadaro to investigate the Buffalo Creek disaster. That experience, along with Spadaro's feeling that the Buffalo Creek break could have been avoided, led him to spend the next thirty years studying impoundment dams, and in 1996 he joined the U.S. Mine Health and Safety Administration (MSHA) to ensure better regulation of existing slurry ponds and dams.

Two days after the Martin County spill, Spadaro was named the number-two man on a team sent to investigate the causes of the pond break. What the team found was disturbing. After a 1994 spill from that same impoundment pond had released 100 million gallons of slurry, an MSHA engineer made nine recommendations that needed to be addressed before the impoundment pond was used again. Martin County Coal Corporation, which was responsible for the pond break, followed none of the recommendations. Then Scott Ballard, a mining engineer who had worked as a consultant for Martin County Coal, reported to MSHA that after his own investigation of the pond following the 1994 spill, Martin County Coal had only fifteen feet of material instead of the required one hundred between the pond and the mine. "It was never intended to prevent a breakthrough in any form or fashion," Ballard told MSHA. "In fact, the question was asked during the review process, Will this prevent it? and the answer was emphatically, 'No.' There's no guarantees. There's nothing here that will prevent a breakthrough."

Who asked that question? Spadaro found that at least five Martin County Coal executives were aware of Ballard's findings, and the risk of another slurry flood, but did nothing. By the end of 2000, Spadaro and the other investigators thought they had collected enough evidence to charge Massey Energy of Richmond,

Virginia, the parent company of Martin County Coal, with willful and criminal negligence.[3]

And then George W. Bush was elected to his first term as president.

It is no secret, and no surprise, that Bush, along with Kentucky senator Mitch McConnell, received millions of dollars in campaign contributions from the coal industry. Massey Energy alone donated $100,000 to a Republican Senate campaign committee headed by McConnell. I mention the Kentucky senator because, aside from being the Senate's lead opponent of campaign finance reform, he is also the husband of Labor Secretary Elaine Chao—to whom MSHA answers.

Within days of Bush's inauguration, a new team leader, Tim Thompson, was named to the Martin County investigation. Thompson told Spadaro and the other investigators to wrap up their work immediately. The investigators wanted to cite Martin County Coal for eight violations, including willful negligence. Thompson and Dave Lauriski, MSHA's new assistant secretary, whittled that down to two menial charges. Spadaro refused to sign the report and resigned from the investigation team.

On June 4, 2003, Spadaro was placed on administrative leave. That day he was called to Washington, D.C., supposedly on MSHA business. While he was gone, federal officials searched his Beckley, West Virginia, office and changed the locks. As justification, Dave Lauriski and John Caylor, the agency's deputy assistant secretary, scraped together bogus charges that Spadaro had abused his authority while superintendent of the Mine Health Safety Academy.

MSHA's retaliatory treatment of Spadaro along with Scott Ballard's testimony about Martin County Coal's negligence after the 1994 pond break suggest a clear attempt on the part of someone in the Bush Administration to protect Massey Energy from crim-

---

[3]Massey Energy did not respond to requests for comment on this article.

inal prosecution, at the expense of hundreds of people who live below that impoundment pond in Inez, Kentucky. It's a neat pattern of corruption. Everyone has everyone else's back, and the one whistle-blower who tried to speak out for the public's interest is left spinning in the wind.

In October, Jack Spadaro left MSHA quietly rather than accept a demotion and a transfer far from his home in Hamlin, West Virginia. When I talked to him earlier in the year, he joked that as a regulator in the Bush administration, "the most dangerous thing you can do is do your job." He also told me he believed flash floods, mudslides, and rockslides caused by valley fills were as potentially dangerous as impoundment ponds. In August 2004 a boulder rolled down off a strip mine in Inman, Virginia, just across the Kentucky border, and crushed to death a sleeping three-year-old, Jeremy Davidson.

September 26, 2004, Lost Mountain

It was one year ago this month that I first came to Lost Mountain. When I look back at the pictures I took then, I see dense stands of trees and rolling ridgetops painted orange and yellow by autumn coolness. Now I see a long gray plateau piled with mounds of wasted rock and soil. It's drizzling as I start up the eastern slope. Today is a Sunday, as it was a year ago, and the rain has kept even the smaller weekend crews away. At about 1,400 feet, I begin walking along the top edge of a long highwall that marks the eastern boundary of the land permitted for mining. This cliff line drops about a hundred feet down to the number 10 coal seam, where several pyramids of coal stand ready to be loaded away.

I'm walking along a thin strip of soil here at the edge of the highwall that divides the strip mine from the forest. The oaks and maples descend down into the watershed on my right, and the highwall drops away abruptly to my left. The sharp contrast between these two landscapes, heightened by the fall color and the gray mine site, gives me the strange sensation that I am walking on the edge of Creation, on a thin membrane between the world and the not-world. Everything past this point is an abyss, a lifeless canvas, a preternatural void.

At the end of the highwall, I climb down onto the mine site. The wet coal crunches softly under my boots. I walk toward the former mountaintop, where I had parked my truck a year ago. Because all of this earth has been churned over many times, my boots sink easily into the orangish mud. It's slow going. I drop down into the woods, as a shortcut, cross a narrow ravine, then climb back up through the inevitable blackberry brambles and young sassafras trees.

Stepping over a final berm of spoil, I find myself standing where the capstones once sat. Now all of the vegetation has been shaved away. A long yellow fuse winds up to what once was the mountaintop but is now only an awful black knob. I follow the fuse to the edge of that small plateau, leveled off at the number 11 coal seam. The wasted summit is now a series of tall gray mounds of rock piled to my right. To my left, the entire eastern ridgeline has been carved up and hollowed out; now it is only one wide black crater. And down in front of me, a gray bench has been turned to concrete by the heavy trucks that, over and over, have backed to its edge, then methodically dumped this mountaintop down its side. I'm standing in the middle of a wasteland, a dead zone.

It won't always look this bad up here. Eventually all of this hardened spoil will be graded and hydroseeded with an exotic grass. This man-made desert will be "reclaimed" as a "pasture." But from now on, Lost Mountain will only exist as a icon on a map; the real thing is gone.

From here, I take in the entire panorama of this churned-under ridgeline, this eviscerated forest. I think for a moment that I might write a short poem, a eulogy to Lost Mountain. Nothing comes to mind. There is nothing here that seems the proper subject of poetry.

Not that I came to Lost Mountain for inspiration. Although I have been inspired by its songbirds, its watersheds, its wildflowers, I knew its fate a year ago when I started wandering the flanks that no longer exist. I climbed to its summit again and again to see what can't be observed from below—the systematic destruction of an entire biological community. In essence, I came to Lost Mountain looking for what Aldo Leopold called an ecological education. "One of the penalties of an ecological education," wrote Leopold, "is that one lives alone in a world of wounds." It's hard to find a better description for the situation of those, like Teri Blanton and Damon Morgan, who face the challenge of living in the desperate, poisoned world of the Appalachian coal country.

.   .   .

There is a stock metaphor among conservationists when the talk turns to logging or strip mining. It is the analogy of a forest as library: the rain forests and the mixed mesophytic forests of North America are like the great library of Alexandria. Burn off such a forest and you might as well have destroyed the last surviving copies of Aristotle and Maimonides. Consider that one in every ten plant species contains anticancer compounds. In a purely selfish sense, humans who care about the survival of their species should find the current rate of extinction (about one species every hour) rather alarming. I may think—I do think—that preserving species diversity enriches the very concept of life, but it also holds the secrets to the perpetuation of human life. In the end the natural world does not need conserving. The planet has survived five great extinctions; it can survive the one we are bringing on. And given time, it will grow back. No, it is we who need conserving. And if we are to survive, we must develop what Leopold called a "land ethic," which, if successful, would "change the role of *Homo sapiens* from conqueror of the land-community to plain member and citizen of it."

Standing on this sterile ledge, I am surrounded by the work of conquerors. No one who felt a responsibility to other citizens within a community would destroy its water, homes, wildlife, and woodlands. The difference between conquerors and community is the difference between the words "economy" and "ecology," both of which come from the same Greek root: *oikos*, or "home." But only ecology has remained true to its roots. A true case of home economics would, as Leopold said, make sure that the place called home maintains its health and stability. To create an environment where mudslides, flooding, and slurry spills are common will not ensure a community's health. To bulldoze and burn a renewable resource—trees—will not ensure its stability. To tear a nonrenewable resource from the ground to provide short-term economic gain for the few and long-term environmental destruction and disease for the many is undemocratic, unsustainable, and stupid.

We are, unfortunately, a nation that values technology and wealth much more than we value community, and the result is the wasted land that lies all around me. If our species is to make it through this century, the forces of science and technology must be tempered by two other forces—ethics and aesthetics. All ethical philosophies, from Aristotle on down, are based on this ecological principle as stated by Leopold: "The individual is a member of a community of interdependent parts." And as the cave art at Lascaux makes brilliantly clear, we are a species that has evolved to find beauty in the natural world. This trait serves—or should serve—an evolutionary purpose: we love what we find beautiful, and we do not destroy what we love. A strip job is more than a moral failure; it is a failure of the imagination. It is time we stopped thinking like those who conquer a mountain and started thinking like the mountain itself.

GQ

FINALIST—PROFILE WRITING

Facing a weary and reluctant subject, Chris Heath set out to write the definitive profile of country music's surviving bad man, Merle Haggard. "The Last Outlaw" is an examination of the raw and extraordinary life that produced some of country music's most enduring and canonical songs. As Merle himself says, Heath's piece "puts me on the shelf."

Chris Heath

The Last Outlaw

Waylon's gone, Cash has been laid to rest. But Merle Haggard stands as country's remaining black-hat rebel, the last man singing for the underdog. At sixty-eight, as he readies himself for a new record and a date with the Stones, he is still proud and pissed off.

·　　·　　·

Merle Haggard doesn't want to tell his story anymore. "They don't want to hear about the easy part, the good days that you did," he says. "They want to hear about the places they haven't been. The pain they haven't felt."

And if he should be persuaded to share himself one more time . . . well, in his sixty-eight years he has never been the kind of man to approach anything with half a heart. But it hurts. On the third morning I've made my way to the modest hillside house in the idyllic Northern California countryside near Lake Shasta, where he lives on 200 acres with his fifth wife, Theresa, and two teenage children, it turns out that he has tried to cancel my visit, but the message hasn't reached me. He invites me in anyway.

"This is why I don't do these things," he says. "It's like revisiting an old wound and pulling the bandage off and scraping the scab off. It's too emotional. When you ask about a man's leg and then you ask about his dick . . . it's like squeezing an orange."

"It gets highly emotional for him," Theresa explains.

"God, highly emotional is not the word," says Haggard. "It's something else besides emotional. It's deeper than that. . . . Fuck, yesterday evening when I got done, man, I felt like I'd fucking been in jail again."

•   •   •

This fall Merle Haggard will release a new album. I don't think anybody is quite sure how many have come before it; his first came out in 1965, and by 1974 he was already releasing the thirtieth (called, with delightful insouciance, *Merle Haggard Presents His 30th Album*). Within them, he has laid down one of the last great living catalogs of country-music songs. Most of the best he wrote himself, songs that did perhaps the hardest and most wonderful thing a song can do—join together a handful of simple, common-place words in a way that somehow makes them new and true and eternal, their wisdom and poetry hidden in plain sight.

Not all of his greatest songs dealt with troubles—he has written with majesty about love and dignity and gratitude and pride and standing up for what you believe in—but trouble and heartache certainly felt like his most natural neighborhoods: how life is hard, how hearts break easier than they mend, and how it sometimes seems as though everything but loneliness will abandon you, of anger looking for its rightful home, of wanting to stay but knowing there's something just as deep within a certain kind of man that forever tugs at him to leave.

When Haggard first became famous, in the '60s, he was best known as the man who sang songs about wanderers, fugitives, and the terminally luckless.

"I hate to be that easy to figure out," he says now when reminded of this. "But it's probably true. . . . I sometimes feel like

I'm standing up for the people that don't have the nerve to stand up for themselves. I just enjoyed winning for the loser. I'd never been around anything except losers my whole life."

I ask him whether he wrote so many sad and angry songs because he was sad and angry or because that's what he was good at.

"I had been sad and angry," he reflects, "and now I was composed and in a position to do good for the sad and angry."

.   .   .

As Merle Haggard sits there in his favorite rocking chair, facing a giant flat-screen TV silently showing the news, it is stirring to think how far he has traveled, not just through time but through history. When Merle Haggard's parents moved from Oklahoma to California in 1935, two years before his birth, they were part of the great Dust Bowl migration westward. They settled into a converted railroad boxcar on the outskirts of Bakersfield, and his father got a job on the Sante Fe railroad. The first thing of consequence Haggard remembers is going to choose a puppy for his third birthday—a fox terrier called Jack, who would live nineteen years and die while Haggard was in San Quentin prison. From early on, he liked music. He remembers noticing that his mother didn't approve of the people close to the family who played music. To her, entertainers were rebels and heathens. His father didn't approve of entertainers, either, on the surface, but in his expression young Merle sometimes detected another story: maybe that of a would-be musician and rebel who had been steered straight by a strong, sensible woman. "I think they were interesting to me because I'd seen that look in his eye," says Haggard. "I didn't know what it was about."

When he was nine, the life he knew and loved crumbled away. That Wednesday night, Merle had been to a prayer meeting with his mother. He was annoyed that his mother was with him, because he liked turning over garbage cans with his friends on the way home. Near the house, he went ahead of her, and so it was Merle who found his father in his big chair, tears on his cheeks, half paralyzed from a stroke. By June he was dead.

Haggard has always identified his father's death as the event that set him on a different path, the one that would first lead him to prison, but he says that only just recently did it strike him exactly how it has shaped his life since then. It came to him while he was watching a TV documentary about Kirk and Michael Douglas. "I think what I've always looked for in life is my father's approval," he says. "I think that was the biggest thing I was robbed of. And it took me down many paths. It motivates you to do what I did . . . whatever you have to do, looking for approval. Always making a new record, always writing another song. Who knows? It may have inspired everything."

●　　　●　　　●

On a shelf in Merle Haggard's living room is an Amtrak conductor's cap. On other flat surfaces are old model trains. Haggard spends a little time one morning discussing a boxed model train with his thirteen-year-old son, Ben, in technical terms that leave me behind in seconds. Trains have long been an obsession of Haggard's, in life and in song. In the '70s, he had a model train set reputed to be worth a quarter of a million, which still exists somewhere on this property. He even released an album in 1976 called *My Love Affair with Trains*, which included the song "No More Trains to Ride":

> Born the son of a railroad man
> Who rode 'em until he died
> I'd like to live like my daddy did
> But there's no more trains to ride.

It was the first sign that there was something within Haggard that would have to bust out. "I was eleven years old when I first hopped a freight train," he recalls. "Didn't go far. Went about a hundred miles, and they arrested me in Fresno." He soon was off again. "I grew up beside the railroad track," he says, "and the way to leave town was on a train. All we knew was that there was something out there that was intriguing about being on your own. And it was really calling to me at an early age. I had excuses—I could say, Well, my mother was left with me to raise—but that wasn't the reason. It was just some inner yearning, that I didn't really understand then and probably can't explain now, caused me to jump those freights in search of something."

The irony was that he was allowed to ride for free on the Santa Fe railroad after his father's death, but whenever the spirit took him to ride the rails, that never crossed his mind as an option. "I never really enjoyed those rides I took on the passenger train," he says. "They were just: So what? Ho hum. What I was after wasn't on those passenger trains."

· · ·

I met Merle Haggard for the first time this April, backstage at the Beacon Theatre in New York. He was on tour with Bob Dylan and had just played a sprightly set of old and new songs in the swinging country jazz style he now favors, spiced with banter, much of it alluding to the passing of time. "We've been on the road for forty years," he tells the audience. "We're the only band I know that uses nurses instead of roadies." (Such things are jokes and not jokes, too. His editorial page on merlehaggard.com has a spirited defense of the Dixie Chicks' freedom to say what they want, even if he doesn't agree with it, followed by a note of thanks to his dentist.)

Any chance I might have to speak properly with Haggard at the Beacon disappears when, thirty seconds after I have introduced myself, I am followed through the door by the eighty-nine-year-old guitarist Les Paul, who, understandably, takes preference. As Haggard picks at some raw vegetables and dip off a plastic plate, they talk about Oklahoma in the oldest of days. There's something greatly touching in the way Haggard, now the senior of nearly everyone he meets, defers to Les Paul as his elder. (He'll later describe this meeting as "like finally getting to meet one of your favorite uncles.") They huddle close, speaking quietly. Haggard nods, and the next thing I hear him say is, "By the time you get close to the answers, it's nearly all over."

      ·   ·   ·

When he was fourteen, a Texas lady introduced Merle to life at its fullest. He had hitched there with a friend. At a brothel in Amarillo, he was turned down because of his youth, until an older, more stately woman in an electric-pink dress stepped forward. She announced, "I'll babysit with him," and soon it was done.

"It's a fond memory, it is," he says. He reminisces how before he and his friend went to the brothel, they'd been shopping: "I went to a hockshop and bought some secondhand cowboy boots—figured if I'm in Texas, I'd better put on some boots. That was 1951, and I've been wearing cowboy boots ever since." (Today's are faded green ostrich. "The ostrich don't like it," he says, "but everybody else does.")

"It was an interesting day. A lot of people say, 'I can't remember anything anymore,' and really I can't, but there are certain things that you can't get out of your mind. I guess they're there because you want them there. Exquisite times."

I ask him whether he was a different person when he walked out of the brothel than he had been when he walked in.

He considers this a moment. "Not really," he decides. "I think the cowboy boots affected me more. I mean, the gal just affirmed what I already knew, but the cowboy boots made a new man out of me."

      ·   ·   ·

The way Merle Haggard has always told it, his rebelliousness and slippage into teenage criminality and the escalating punishments he received formed a kind of toxic spiral that dragged him deeper into trouble. He says that it was the correctional facilities he was sent to as a youth that really sent him in the wrong direction: "You start off with a truancy problem, and they send you to jail with big-time criminals. Pretty soon your idols become Jesse James and Bonnie Parker and John Dillinger, rather than Babe Ruth and Muhammad Ali." When he describes the horrors of these places in detail, I remark that it's surprising he's not more angry. "Oh, I'm pretty angry, Chris," he says. "I've always been angry."

Not long after the young Merle Haggard started being locked up, he started escaping. In total, he says, he would escape seventeen times from various institutions. At times he jumped fences, broke through doors, risked his life leaping farther than men should leap. But sometimes he simply picked a moment when he could just go. "I noticed early on that people looked right at you and didn't see you," he says. "If you just walked the right speed, you could almost walk right through them."

Perhaps that's how he imagined it could continue: mess up, be sent away for a bit, escape, be sent away for a bit longer, get out, repeat. But then, right before he reached twenty-one, after an incident where he drunkenly tried to break into a restaurant that was still open and the arresting officers also found a stolen check-printing machine in his car, after which he compounded everything by escaping from the local jail, he discovered that this time he had messed up badly enough to be sent to San Quentin.

His offense carried a sentence of between six months and fifteen years inside, but Haggard says that in those days they didn't tell you how long you would serve, and that was the worst thing of all. As he put it in his first autobiography: "God, that does something to a man's mind that never heals up right." He was there for three years. In the same book, he referred to witnessing "horrors too terrible to think about, much less talk about," though in his writings he has given enough detail—"I watched one man kill another over a simple insult"; "sometimes when I lay in my bunk I could hear men crying out in pain from being raped by other inmates"; "I saw a black man burned to death on a ladder. . . . The five-hundred-gallon vat of starch he was checking boiled over on him, burning his black skin completely white"—that you pray there was little more.

During his stay, he was sent to solitary for seven days when he was found drunk. Luckily, the guards didn't seem to realize that it was Haggard who had been brewing beer from oranges, sugar, and yeast and selling it around the prison for cigarettes. "We called it orange beer," he says, "and it tasted like orange beer."

Maybe his time in solitary, where a Bible offered itself as consolation by day and a pillow by night, was the saving of him, and maybe it wasn't. While he was in prison, he was given a chance to be smuggled out inside a desk that had been made by inmates for a judge's office in San Francisco. No one had slipped from San Quentin for many years, but the escape was a successful one. Haggard, though, had the sense not to go—the sense to know that this time, running might close down his options for good. When Haggard was released, it was with at least two ambitions: to make something of music, and to never go back to prison.

Many of his biggest early hits, like "Branded Man," "Sing Me Back Home," and "Mama Tried," alluded to a criminal past, but Haggard maintains that the real-life backdrop to these songs was unknown to the public until he appeared on Johnny Cash's TV show. Cash tried to convince him that people should know and would like him more if they did. Haggard wasn't sure. Cash at least had a good if hokey way of bringing up the subject. On camera he suggested to Haggard that he felt he had seen him before, and the conversation naturally led to the first time they had been under the same roof. When Cash had first played in San Quentin on January 1, 1959, Haggard had been in the audience.

Though Haggard would briefly go back to jail—for five days the press never found out about, in Sacramento in 1967, for driving without a license, which he remembers felt "like five years"—once the hits started, these were golden years. "All I had to do was pay attention, you know," he recalls. "Show up and sing. All the doors were open. Everyone had a smiling, agreeable attitude. Friends and thieves alike, you know." Then, in 1969, came the song that would become Haggard's biggest pop hit, "Okie from Muskogee," and that would change his career once more. "It probably set it back about forty years," he mutters.

There are, says Haggard, "about seventeen hundred ways to take that song," and over his career he has alternately endorsed and sidestepped most of them. In it, the narrator he was thinking of—*I'm proud to be an Okie from Muskogee*—was some version of his father. On the surface, and to some extent beneath it, the song was a celebration of traditional conservative American values at a time of great turbulence—of short-haired, drug-free Americans who believe in the flag, don't burn their draft cards, and are proud to be square if square is what they are.

But Haggard says he regretted the song almost immediately. He feels, with reason, that it pushed away a part of his audience and that it brought him attention he never wanted; the segregationist presidential candidate George Wallace, presumably sniffing a kindred spirit, made overtures to him, albeit ones that were rejected. If there were two paths his career could have taken from there, the one he had chosen was cemented by his next single. He had suggested a song called "Irma Jackson," a thoughtful tale of an interracial romance, but he was argued out of it. Instead, he released "The Fightin' Side of Me"—a wonderful, defiant roar of a song, but one that helped fix him in the public imagination as the champion of angry, proud conservatives who had had enough:

> When they're runnin' down our country, man,
> They're walkin' on the fightin' side of me.

These days, Haggard seems to reduce much of the fuss about "Okie from Muskogee" to its position on marijuana, perhaps because it is the part of the song his subsequent life most completely disavowed. *We don't smoke marijuana in Muskogee*, the song begins, and at the time, this was true for Haggard: He had smoked it neither there nor anywhere else. He didn't until he was forty-one, when he was advised to do so by a physician. "I didn't like the way it made me feel at first," he says, "so they coaxed me and showed me." Soon the cure took hold. "The only thing they didn't tell me," he says, "was how habit-forming it was."

· · ·

Often, returning for an encore on that recent tour, Bob Dylan would lean down to the microphone above his keyboard and sing these words:

> The warden led a prisoner
> Down the hallway to his doom . . .

The song, "Sing Me Back Home," is one of Haggard's—perhaps his finest. It draws on his time in San Quentin and his experience with death-row prisoners: a dark and beautiful hymn about the power of song to release you from even the most awful and unavoidable here and now. Haggard says that Dylan asked him before their first date together, "I've got it in my show—do you do it every night?"

"I said, 'I don't do it at all when Bob Dylan's doing it,'" says Haggard. "It's hard to sing, anyway. It's hard for me. It requires you to go there in your mind, to get there—and to be part of what you're singing about is somewhat painful. You've got to climb inside it all."

Haggard laughs wryly when I ask whether Dylan explained anything about why he had chosen the song. "Not only did he not tell me anything," says Haggard, "I don't know of anybody that's ever met him that he's ever said anything to. He does not let anybody see his hold cards. He has his hold cards close to his chest."

I tell Haggard that I read on the Internet how, on Haggard's birthday, Dylan walked into his celebration and handed him a present in a crinkled Whole Foods grocery bag. This, it turns out, is true.

"He said, 'Happy birthday,' placed it in my hands very carefully, and turned around and walked off. That was it."

Haggard's recollection of what was in the bag is that it was a fifth of Crown Royal whisky and something like a Bob Dylan T-shirt. "It was very nice, the gift," he says, "but the presentation was worth a million dollars. It was like Marlon Brando walking in and saying happy birthday."

Haggard shouts toward the kitchen to confirm the contents of the bag with Theresa. A good thing he does; her memory is somewhat different.

"He gave you a sheriff's badge," she says. "He gave you a lure about this big"—her fingers are far apart—"and a copy of his book, signed . . ."

"Wasn't there a T-shirt and a fifth of Crown Royal or something like that?"

"No."

"Who gave me that? Someone gave me that."

"I don't know. He signed the book, a really nice thing it says in there. A really great compliment. And that lure—I don't know if he knows anything about fishing, but it's about this big, for pike fishing."

"There's some connotation about that lure, I think," says Haggard.

"Oh, and then he gave you some cowboy chocolates," says Theresa. "It was original. Oh, and I know what else he gave you. He gave you two magazines. One for real old antique classic cars."

"I didn't remember what was in there," says Merle to Theresa. "Thank you for your mind." He turns to me, smiling, and says, mock-apologetically, "I may not know anything, Chris."

•   •   •

Merle Haggard remembers the '70s, in a fashion. "God," he sighs, "it went by like it was about two weeks long. . . . Then it was the '80s, and the '80s flew by. . . . "

When I ask him about partying too much along the way, he swiftly corrects me. "I never did party too much," he says. "There were periods of my life where I was in between wives, when there was a flamboyant lifestyle that was debatable as to whether anybody should have had that much fun. And you know, the Lord knows all about it, and I'm sure that I'll have to pay for it all. But there was a period of time that went by in my life that I doubt that there were many people on the face of the earth in any period of the past or in the future that enjoyed their life much more than I did."

That having been said, there were five months in 1983 when Haggard, as he puts it, "spun off pretty bad." He had been jilted by a woman who he thought loved him, and his response was to buy $2,000 of cocaine and retire hurt to his houseboat. "For about five months there, man, I had quite a party," he recalls. "And different famous people came in and out of that party and saw the condition of it, and I'm sure a lot of them figured I'd never survive." Haggard says he snapped out of it when he realized that he had been on his houseboat naked with some good-looking woman for five days and had yet to have sex with her, though that was what they were both there for. He says he never did cocaine again.

He mentions a few things he considers to be mistakes over the years. He thinks he shouldn't have walked out of rehearsals for *The Ed Sullivan Show* just because they kept making him dance through tulips and look gay. Maybe he shouldn't have turned down a series of six movies with Burt Reynolds, one of which was *Smokey and the Bandit*. He certainly shouldn't have accepted the advice he was given in the early '70s to sell the twenty-five burger franchises he owned from a chain expanding out of Ohio for the $265,000 he had paid for them; Wendy's ended up doing pretty well after that.

•   •   •

In the midmorning of the second day, members of his band start drifting into his living room, where they rehearse, forming a circle that curves outward from Haggard and his favorite chair. Haggard tells one of them that he had a cigar yesterday, his first tobacco in nearly fifteen years. He had been listening to *Coast to Coast AM*, where a guy was talking about the medical benefits of tobacco in a good cigar without pesticides. Haggard thought he and Theresa should test whether it was true. It tasted good and gave them both a little lift, and he's been hankering for it today. "It opened up a whole old can of worms," he says. "Old friend was trying to get back in. Like an old donkey coming through a new door again."

Haggard first came through this part of California in 1953, when he was sixteen, running away to Oregon with a girl he had met that day, making love all the way on the train. He saw Lake Shasta in the moonlight, and it stayed with him. Haggard settled up here in 1977, but for most of the next ten years he lived on his houseboat on Lake Shasta. He and Theresa moved off the boat in 1989 because their daughter had started to walk and the water worried them. At first they moved into a cabin on the back end of the property—a cabin Haggard didn't even know he owned; the first time he went to see it, there was a cow standing in the front room.

They've had trouble with mold over the years at various houses on the property, but he clearly loves it here and talks passionately about how he has fashioned the land as a sanctuary for animals and birds. It is also the home of his inspiration, as he explained to a visiting IRS agent. He says that after he walked the agent around and detailed how each bit of the landscape had fed into his songs, the IRS agreed it should be a tax write-off and told him that their visit had cost them $93,000.

Today, Haggard asks the band to listen to a scratchy old Bob Wills boogie tune from the 1940s, and then they try to duplicate it, his eyes lighting up whenever they come close. After a few more songs, they break. We talk about UFOs; Merle is a firm believer in these and in various conspiracy theories, and he espouses a kind of random, angry libertarian politics. Eventually, I ask what is the most important thing aliens might learn if they listened to Merle Haggard records.

"That I'm a contrary old son of a bitch, I guess," he says.

He, in turn, has a question for me.

"Do you like peach pie?" he asks. "Let's have peach pie."

.   .   .

Haggard was married for the first time before he went into San Quentin. It was a marriage full of tempestuous incidents, including the time his wife Leona jumped out of the car at fifty miles an hour after he moved to hit her. The marriage didn't survive a terrible day that ended with Haggard choking Leona after she'd taunted him in front of a new boyfriend. ("I remember thinking in my mind: *Well, I know where I'll be going—I'll be going to death row, San Quentin.* But I was so upset with her. . . . Then I came back to reality.") He was married three more times before he met Theresa. She was dating his guitarist at the time, Clint Strong, but Haggard says that Strong was rude to her, and so he felt justified in asking Theresa to meet him in his hotel room after a show and telling Strong to go away when he came banging on the door. If his behavior was poor, his instincts were good—it is a night that has lasted twenty-one years so far.

I ask Haggard what, over the years, five marriages have taught him.

"It's kind of like the study they did on the largemouth bass," he replies. "Some students from a university put 140 largemouth bass in a lake down in Southern California and had an implant in each one of them, and they tracked their habits for one year. And, for example, they had this big roped-off cove just to the right of the launching ramp, and this big fourteen-pound largemouth stayed in there six days a week and on Mondays, when there was no traffic, came out to feed. Then most of the fish stayed along the shore, like most people live in New York, but some bass went straight out into the middle of the lake and lived about seven feet underwater their entire lives. So what it showed was absolutely nothing. That bass are like people, and what makes them so interesting to fish for in America is because they're unpredictable. I don't know any more about women than I did to begin with."

•   •   •

Over the years, San Quentin has returned to him—and he to it—only in his nightmares. For a while, he had thought he was finally past them, but he had another about fifteen months ago. "It was always the same dream," he says. "I was back in jail, and I really didn't know what for. But I was back there again, and I knew nobody would understand why I was there. I had known the taste of freedom, and now I was back again. I had somehow stumbled."

Was the dream really specific?

"Oh, it was an *awful* feeling. It's like being lost, like being in a railroad station with your parents and being four years old, and you look around and they're not there. It can't be described—it's the most horrible feeling in the world. You, without any help. No one can help you. Once again you've screwed up, and you're behind bars, and anybody that cares can't get to you. . . . That incarceration, that awful feeling that comes from losing one's freedom. Not having the right to be heard. You can scream all night and beat on the walls and rack the bars with a tin cup . . . and nobody will come."

•   •   •

That last morning, it is a more fragile Haggard who sits with me. Some of it is my fault, churning up the sediments he would rather have stayed settled. "When you become my age, hopefully your life will be worth as much to someone else—they'll come and ask you the things you're asking me," he says. "And only then will you know what I'm going through." Some of it is the way he has been feeling. Yesterday, in the middle of a meal, he began to notice something he has felt seven or eight times before in recent years, a kind of stomach disorder that makes him shake inside and his eyes twitch.

I don't ask many questions today. I think he figures that as I'm here, he might as well explain how it really is.

"You know, I woke up this morning in a wimpy mood," he says. "Men don't like to be wimps. But I have reached the point, it's really sad to mention, I have reached the point where . . . They always say you'll know when it's time. Speaking of the place in your life when you finally say: Do you want to die on a highway or do you want to die in bed? I'm tired of it. I'm tired of it. I'm tired of singing 'Okie from Muskogee.' I'm tired of the whole gig. Somewhere around my age, people begin to feel insignificant and small and unnecessary and not so much in demand." There is plenty of work out there for him, but its attraction is waning. "I guess I've come to a point in my life where . . . I hate to admit fear. I hate to even admit fear's part of my reasoning. But I have some dementia that's coming around, and there's a bit of a nervous tic—I don't know what that's about; I guess it's growing old. And I don't feel as bulletproof as I should feel. I've traveled all over the world without a seat belt for forty-two years. Forty-three. And I'm a bit of a gambler and have a feel for odds. The odds are really against me."

He says nearly all his heroes are dead. He tried to call the remaining two—Johnny Gimble and Gordon Terry, both fiddle players—this morning, but he couldn't get hold of either. He says he feels like a guy who just watched the *Titanic* sink, and almost everybody he knows is dead. And he's asking himself, Why should I swim anymore?

I ask what he most cherishes the idea of doing if he stays at home.

"*Doing* is out of the picture," he says. "When you get to a certain age, you reach a place where you say, Look, I'm all right. I'm not in pain unless I have to do something. Anything I do—if I have to get up and walk over there—it hurts. When you get old, everything that you take for granted goes away, and it's not by choice. And it finally boils down to how much pain can you stand?" He says that it has hurt onstage for a while now. "I could probably let my hair fall out, and quit dyeing my hair, and just go on out there and look stupid and finally fall onstage. The only thing is, I'd be the one who loses. If I go ahead and stay onstage until I become totally senile, well, I don't know, it seems to me somewhat silly. Why not stop when you're still knocking people out? Why wait until you get knocked out? The last few years, I've been faking it. I've been in pain—the pains of growing old, I guess. The only thing I can attribute it to."

I say that surely he'll carry on making records, but he says he needs to stay in shape to do that, and that he's hardly written any songs this year. "I've recorded an album that I've put forth my very best on, and it's truly good," he says of his latest, *Chicago Wind*, "but I don't think there's a hit song on it. In fact, I'm sure there's not. It's all good, but I don't believe they're of the quality to pull me out of the aging slump. I thought maybe there would be a song like 'All of Me' for me, coming in the later years like it did for Frank Sinatra. I'm beginning to doubt that'll happen. I spent just about all the extra energy I had on this last project." His voice cracks. "These are very sad words. But they're honest." This is what he wants to say. "You know, I'm not young anymore. And I don't like it. I don't like it."

There's a steel and sadness in his face, a proud combination of force and frailty; whatever the gracious opposite of serenity is, that is what Merle Haggard oozes. He smiles. "There comes a time when you can't do it anymore. It's a double-edged sword: If I can manage to get over the wimpiness and continue to go, I'll probably live longer and probably enjoy it. But I'm at that pivot point in my life where I can swing that way and give my last bit of strength to the music of my life, or I can give it to my little family here." He gestures toward the open kitchen, empty now, but through which his wife and children are constantly flowing, past the post on which their heights over the years have been marked. "And music has supported my little family; my little family knows what music means to me. I am music. Music is me, and I am music. But which one is which? Which one do you favor in the latter moments?"

.   .   .

One of the band members wanders in. "We're doing the last of the article here," Haggard tells him. "It's maybe the article that'll put me on the goddamned shelf." He laughs. "They're gonna jump on Chris, say, 'What did you do—kill fucking Haggard?'"

It is as the random business of the day encroaches upon him that his mood seems to lighten, or to at least leave wimpiness far behind. First there's a fuss about a fence being cut and some building being done on the property—"If you want to bust somebody's head, go ahead," he encourages a man who works for him—and then some concern about the 1,200 crawfish being delivered to his ponds this morning. The phone rings. He is being asked to do something for those who suffered in a local fire. "Well, I don't do autographs," he tells the caller, "but I will play and sing and try to raise some money for you—that's what I do." He hands the call over to Theresa. His attitude seems to be that he doesn't much want to play an extra concert but that he wouldn't dream of not doing it. When Theresa is done on the phone, Haggard tells her, "Satan is in charge of fires, he's in charge of harming those people up there, and he's in charge of that call. We're gonna surprise his ass. What an asshole. Goddamn the Devil in Jesus's name."

The news that really gets him going is that his goats have been at the outside of his tour bus overnight, ripping the rub rails off.

He's out of his chair. Those goats have picked the wrong man on the wrong day. "The sun won't set on the same problem," he says. "These goats will be out of our life. I'm tired of that fucking shit."

As I prepare to leave, Haggard's son is putting gel in his hair, and somehow Haggard gets encouraged by his son and wife to join in. Soon his hair is spiking outward in every direction, and he sits in a rocking chair with a goofy grin, like some kind of hillbilly Einstein. More band members walk in, each offering a double take and then looking bemused. "We're going punk rock," he announces. That is how I leave him: his hair heading to heaven, a wink in his eye, and a final word of explanation. "I am not an ordinary man," he declares.

·   ·   ·

When I arrive this last morning, there is a sheet of paper lying by Haggard's chair. It is the lyric to one of the songs he has written this year, a song to which Toby Keith, the current superstar of country, will be adding his vocal alongside Haggard's this afternoon in Nashville. Haggard wrote it quickly this spring with Bob Dylan in mind: "He was on my mind. I'd just met him. We'd just gone into the first venue, and I asked him for a song. I wanted a great Bob Dylan song to record myself. And he said to me, 'I don't write anymore—I don't have any more songs.' And in some strange way that inspired it. I thought, Well, I'll go write the song that I wanted him to write."

He lifts his guitar onto his lap and starts. It's a song of measured hope, humility, and the inevitable:

But there's one common thread in the scheme of it all.
Some of us fly, all of us fall.

Afterward, he will ask me whether I think this song could be a hit. It's the only one he thinks might have a chance. There's nothing I know about how the country charts work in 2005, but I hope I know a little bit more about songs and about beauty and about honesty, and about why this one has played over and over in my head ever since.

> Some play it smart. . . . I had a ball.
> Some of us fly, all of us fall.

"I looked at it," he tells me, "and I couldn't tell what it was about."

For now, Merle Haggard is still flying. Sure, it gets harder to stay aloft. And sure, he can see the ground below, a little clearer and closer each year, patiently waiting for him. But long may it have to wait. Long may we hear the cantankerous flapping of his wings, and the whisper of truth he gives to the wind. And long may it be before even Merle Haggard has to fall in final, glorious protest.

The Oxford American

FINALIST—
FEATURE WRITING

In "Love and Death in the Cape Fear Serpentarium," Wendy Brenner introduces us to Dean Ripa, a misanthropic snake collector with a flair for painting, writing, and crooning Sinatra standards. With restrained objectivity, keen observation, and selective interpretation, the writer brings to life a man who is even more compelling and surprising than the shape-shifting creatures who slither front and center.

Wendy Brenner

Love and Death in the Cape Fear Serpentarium

*S*ome passions are more dangerous than others.

He is a fool who injures himself by amassing things. And no one knows why people cannot help but do it. **—Danse Macabre**

Fortunately, I number among my friends a young man named Dean Ripa, who could have stepped from the pages of a Joseph Conrad novel. **—William S. Burroughs, *The Western Lands***

One day in 1971 in Wilmington, North Carolina, fourteen-year-old Dean Ripa was at home performing surgery on a cottonmouth snake, and it bit him. This was unfortunate for a couple of reasons. He knew enough about snakes to know he would probably not die, but he did need a ride to the hospital, which meant his parents were going to find out about the fifty snakes he was keeping in their spare room: rattlesnakes, the water moccasins he'd caught in local swamps, even several cobras he had purchased via mail-order—he had a king cobra years before he had his driver's license.

The bite landed him in Intensive Care for two weeks—with fever, a grossly swollen arm, blistering skin—during which time his father donated Dean's entire snake collection to a local roadside zoo, a seemingly apocalyptic setback that might have ended any normal person's love affair with snakes. But Dean turned out to be another kind of person, the kind who, after a full recovery, quickly began amassing more snakes, breeding his own snakes, and making extra money to buy snakes by collecting snakes for the same zoo that had adopted his earlier snakes. A year after the cottonmouth episode, one of his new cobras got loose and the whole Ripa family had to move out of the house for five days until it could be found and shot.

Thirty-one years later, in what might be the ultimate fantasy of young snake lovers everywhere, Dean Ripa opened the Cape Fear Serpentarium, and, most thrilling of all to a twelve-year-old acquaintance of mine, he lives there, too.

The Serpentarium is no roadside attraction, but an elegant, bi-level, 6,300-square-foot gallery overlooking the Cape Fear River in gentrified downtown Wilmington, exhibiting one of the largest collections of live exotic venomous snakes in the U.S. About a hundred are on public display at any given time, dozens of different species, almost all of which were captured by Dean himself in jungles and marshes around the world. He specializes in the rarest and deadliest: Gaboon vipers, black mambas, spitting cobras, puff adders, and bushmasters, of which he has the biggest known collection anywhere. In fact, Dean was the first person ever to breed the rare blackheaded bushmaster in captivity (he continues to supply them internationally to zoos and researchers), and once even reproduced a bushmaster hybrid, in effect recreating an extinct ancestor of the existing species. He has also survived four bushmaster bites—*envenomings* is the herpetologist's Orwellian term—despite the fact that almost all bushmaster victims die, even with antivenom treatment.

The Serpentarium was built by Dean's father, a local contractor, who has presumably forgiven Dean for his adolescence (or perhaps is just happy to have survived it). The Serpentarium's neighbors include antique stores and historic bed and breakfasts and Thai restaurants and art galleries. Snakes do not seem especially popular around here; the local attitude is perhaps best summed up by a resident of a snake-plagued Wilmington apartment complex, quoted in a recent story in the *Wilmington Star-News*: "I don't like those fellows with no shoulders." Yet Dean has gotten no complaints from his neighbors (he says they're grateful for the business he brings to the area), with the sole exception of a group of cat lovers who once confronted him after hearing a rumor that Dean stalks downtown alleys at dawn, collecting cats in a basket to feed to his snakes. "Ludicrous," he tells me. "I never get up before 10 A.M."

The Serpentarium snakes live in lush enclosures built to Dean's specifications by set designers from Screen Gems (Frank Capra Jr.'s Wilmington film studios), featuring stalactites and stalagmites and twisted roots and vines, real animal skulls and bones, moss-draped grottos and cypress knees, and running waterfalls and ponds. Each snake is rated by skulls-and-bones to indicate its deadliness level (two skulls mean life-threatening to children and the elderly, possible mild disfigurement; five skulls mean survival unlikely), and placards on the exhibits give detailed descriptions, especially popular with children, of exactly how you will die if bitten by each particular snake.

I learn that the Egyptian cobra, whose festive yellow and black stripes evoke Charlie Brown's shirt, is believed to be the asp that killed Cleopatra; in ancient Egypt, the sign reads, these snakes were awarded to royal prisoners as a means of suicide. The Asiatic spitting cobras, meanwhile, which never seem to run out of venom, are like a "SORT OF ENDLESS POISONOUS SQUIRT GUN." The bite of the Central American fer-de-lance feels like having your hand slammed in a car door and then seared with a blow torch. As the placard helpfully elaborates, "THE BITTEN EXTREMITY SWELLS TO MASSIVE PROPORTIONS, THE SKIN BURSTS OPEN, AND YOUR EYES WEEP BLOOD." The fifteen-foot king cobra, the longest venomous snake in the world, can kill an elephant with a single bite, and is known to rear up six feet in the air, hood flared, and look a man in the eye while growling like a dog. For some reason, perhaps a primal one, the male king cobra's eerie, flat dirt color is scarier to me than some of the flashier patterns on display here. Likewise the look of the steely black mambas, who are long, skinny, and, according to their description, "EXCITABLE"—and indeed each time I've visited they were wide awake and slicing around their enclosure like a gang looking for some action. Most disturbing of all, perhaps, are the puff adders, whose odd, fat cigar-shaped bodies make them grotesquely evocative, like nightmare shape-shifter snakes. *We are snakes,* they seem to say, *but we are on the verge of becoming something else.*

The Serpentarium also exhibits a few nonvenomous reptiles, including a 250-pound python named Sheena, some ethereally beautiful emerald tree boas, and a nine-foot, man-eating crocodile, which, like every crocodile, alligator, or lizard I've ever seen, looks fake, prehistoric, and improbable. One day while I was visiting Dean, the girl at the front desk reported that a worried visitor claimed the beaded lizard looked dead. "It always looks dead," Dean said irritably. "That's how it looks." We went to check on the lizard, which was fine. It resembled a large, exotic purse. The placard noted that "THESE LIZARDS MAKE EXCELLENT—IF UNRESPONSIVE—PETS."

For the truly obsessive, the Serpentarium gift shop offers a huge assortment of fetishes: toy snakes, snake-decorated T-shirts, and snake stickers and snake books, Viper Blast spray candy (and, inexplicably, Skittles), watercolor paintings by Dean's mother, carved Peruvian rainsticks, and the occasional display of traditional African art and sculpture, available for purchase from a local importer. A sign on the front desk warns against tapping on the snakes' enclosures: IF YOU KNEW THAT THE ONLY THING STANDING BETWEEN YOU AND DEATH WAS A PANE OF GLASS, WOULD YOU RISK BREAKING IT? This is not P.T. Barnum–style hyperbole. One day I was taking flash photos of an apparently pissed-off cobra (she was waving menacingly about, hood flared), my face as close as my camera lens would allow, when she finally had enough and struck at me, hitting the glass. I had the delayed jolt you get right after a fender-bender—*did that really just happen?*

Though this is the kind of safe thrill one might expect at a zoo, weekend feedings at the Serpentarium go one step further. Suddenly the barriers between audience and predator disappear: a few comically symbolic plastic yellow chains are hooked up to keep people out of the way, the glass enclosures propped wide open. Dean (or his curator, Scott) uses barbecue tongs to deliver dead rats, jiggling them to provoke a strike, sometimes even climbing in with the snakes to prevent fights. (One might imagine the feeders wear something like astronaut suits, but the day I saw Dean break up a tussle between two bushmasters, he was wearing only a polo shirt and cargo shorts.) The yellow chains are, it turns out, unnecessary—men the size of linebackers dart to the back of the crowd, pretending they're just joking: *Ha! I think I'll stand back here.* Some people can't even bear the sight of Dean handling the dead rodents. During one feeding a woman murmured, "He's touching that rat like it ain't nothing."

· · ·

People who devote their careers to animals—veterinarians, zoologists—are often quite different in temperament from garden-variety animal lovers, taking a flat-footed, unsentimental approach to their subjects, skeptical of any anthropomorphism. My mother worked as a docent at Chicago's Lincoln Park Zoo for twenty-five years, and has an enormous collection of butterflies she traveled all over the world to catch; my father is a lifelong birdwatcher, getting up before dawn every weekend to search for rare shorebirds at landfills and sewerage plants. And yet neither of my parents is particularly romantic about the animals they love. They love them for perplexingly literal reasons—because they're such fascinating examples of evolution, or because they have "unusual plumage." My parents do not seem especially interested in talking or thinking about what animals are like, what they evoke or suggest, what they *mean*—all the things that are most compelling to me, the writer in the family.

My favorite novelist, Joy Williams, once said in an interview that the Bible had influenced her as a child because "all those wonderful stories—about snakes and serpents and mysterious seeds and trees—didn't mean what they seemed. They meant some other thing." In Williams's short story "Lu-Lu," the characters do nothing but sit around discussing the meaning of a giant snake (Lu-Lu)—whether she has a soul, how she seems to materialize and dematerialize at will, how she can occupy herself doing nothing. The snake continues to accrue symbolic weight until the story finally ends, hauntingly, with a young woman trying to coax the stoic Lu-Lu into her car: "How do you beckon to something like this, she wondered; something that can change everything, your life?" When I was twelve, my mother gave my father a pet boa constrictor for their anniversary, and never once in all the subsequent years we owned Jaws (we got and named her in 1978) did it occur to me that she could change anything, let alone our lives. We did not discuss her symbolism. We talked about whether she was going to shed her skin soon, or whether she was ready to move up from mice to rats.

So even before I meet Dean Ripa, I think I know what kind of person he will be: another scientist. Though he has no advanced degree, his snake collection is internationally recognized, his research on bushmasters published in herpetological journals.

But then he gives me a copy of his essay, "Confessions of a Gaboon Viper Lover," which appeared in Gary Indiana's 1994 anthology *Living with the Animals*. It is a paean to Ripa's own late Gaboon viper, Madame Zsa Zsa. "Morphologically, she seems halfway to some unspeakable transformation that may or may not include a human head," he writes. "Her pattern might have been lifted from a Persian carpet," he says, and also suggests skeletons. "One can *see* into the pattern," a Tanzanian witch priest told Dean, but then declined to say what it was he saw. The snake's design brings to mind "Kandinsky zigzags," the "meretricious skulls" of Georgia O'Keeffe; its face suggests Bosch, or Dürer's engraving of *The Fall of Man*. Seeing the Gaboon viper, Dean writes, "seems largely participatory, on a parallel with perception itself. Like Dalí's paranoiac-critical method of the hidden face, there arises that 'magic' effect of audience creation." Watching a Gaboon viper "literally materialize before you from the debris of the forest floor," he concludes, "is perhaps the closest one can ever come among live creatures to the fright of encountering an actual ghost."

I notice that I am feeling slightly in love.

．　　　．　　　．

"It's definitely not like TV," Dean says, somewhat defiantly, about the Serpentarium experience. Dean has been invited by various animal-related TV programs to bring his snakes out into the jungle, set them loose, and then pretend to discover them on camera, and he declines all such invitations on principle. In the wild, he says, snakes are nearly impossible to find—you will go years without finding the one you want, unless, like Dean, you know where to look.

He is telling me this in his apartment, the entrance to which is an unmarked door on the Serpentarium's second level; he lives alone with his tiny, eleven-year-old Maltese dog, Wednesday (whom he also calls, variously, "Winky" and "Pinky"), and several aquariums full of deadly bushmasters in his bedroom. He has been married and divorced three times, but claims his snakes played no part in his romantic misfortunes. "I'm just not somebody who can be halved," he says, enigmatically. I suggest that it must be hard to find women who will sleep in a room with snakes—or maybe some women think it's a turn-on? "You get both kinds," Dean says. Either way, it occurs to me, if one were going to sleep with Dean Ripa, one would need a great deal of faith in Dean Ripa.

Not long after he quit high school ("for dramatic effect," he says), Dean moved to Italy to study painting under the portraitist Pietro Annigoni, whose work he had discovered in an art magazine. For a number of years, then, collecting and selling snakes became secondary, a way to support his art career. He enjoyed relative success, spending time with Salvador Dalí and selling a couple of paintings to the writer William S. Burroughs (these now hang on the walls of Dean's apartment, on loan from the Burroughs estate). His style is blackly surreal—muddy-hued portraits and still lifes with hidden messages, faces, and severed limbs floating to their dark, dreamy surfaces. "Ripa's painting depicts biologic fragmentation," Burroughs wrote. "The artist is giving birth to his selves on canvas." I think of *Rosemary's Baby*, the paintings Mia Farrow sees on the corridor walls as she's being carried into her Satanic neighbors' apartment, and I ask Dean why he so admired Annigoni, a more traditional, Renaissance-inspired realist. "I wanted to learn the secrets of the Old Masters," he says. "I've always been on a quest for hidden things, occult things. It's like the snakes. Certain things, to me, always seemed to promise more than they outwardly were."

In 1975, when Dean was eighteen, he sent Burroughs the manuscript of a children's book he was writing called *Johnny Zimb*. He didn't know Burroughs but was a fan of his work, its renegade exoticism seeming to speak directly to the "voices in my head," he says. *Johnny Zimb*'s plot was "a scarecrow-boy type of thing," he tells me. "You know, a surrealistic thing." Burroughs replied to Dean, "I think you have written a very good children's book, though perhaps a little too complex and literate for juvenile reading." Over the years that followed, their correspondence and friendship escalated, Burroughs sending letters to Dean in Ecuador, Ghana, Suriname, and Costa Rica, giving advice on writing and asking Dean's advice on art, inviting him to visit at his home in Lawrence, Kansas. They exchanged knives, guns, snakes, and, at one point, a human skull Dean claimed to have robbed from a grave as a teenager. ("I did indeed receive Helen with open arms," Burroughs wrote in thanks. "I know how difficult it was for you to part with her.") One time Dean brought Burroughs a suitcase full of snakes; another time he set a cobra loose in Burroughs's living room. While I'm reading through their letters, Dean goes into his room and brings out a .357 Magnum that Burroughs gave him, mentioning off-handedly as he sets it on the table before me that it's loaded. (*Jesus,* I think, *how many different things that can kill you can one person keep in his bedroom?*)

Burroughs's letters to Dean are full of fond and cryptic personal counsel: "Oh and as for Madame Whosit and her Oath of Secrecy I would caution you to stay well away from her dubious emanations. She sounds like bad news." In the mid '80s, Burroughs asked Dean to write a letter about centipede venom that he could include in his novel, *The Western Lands*; it appears in the text unedited, and Dean is thanked in the book's acknowledgments. "Have you thought of writing your memoirs as a snake catcher?" Burroughs wrote Dean in 1986. And again in 1988, Burroughs suggested, "Why not write a book about your experiences as a snake catcher? Your letters to me would be a good start." Then, as now, however, Dean was more interested in writing fiction and collecting snakes.

When Burroughs died of heart failure in 1997, Dean was at his bedside; he happened to be visiting that month ("I don't think it was a coincidence," he says). He had never seen someone die before, and stayed at Burroughs's house for days afterward—even sleeping in his bed—while fans came and went, leaving flowers on the door.

Nowadays, in between endless interruptions from the Serpentarium downstairs, Dean is working on a couple of novels, at least parts of which are based on his own experiences. He shows me the thick manuscript of one, *Succumbu (Mama Sleep)*, but then will only let me read its first line: "The beauty of Hell is that it is self-regenerating."

It is impossible to meet Dean Ripa and not think of John Laroche, the ragged, eccentric outlaw orchid breeder Susan Orlean wrote about in *The Orchid Thief*, portrayed by Chris Cooper so brilliantly in *Adaptation*. But the similarities are only in kind, not physical. For one thing, Dean still has all his teeth, and he is darkly, boyishly handsome, looking much younger than his age. The only off-note is his slightly malevolent grin. And while the orchid thief's various obsessions "arrived unannounced and ended explosively, like car bombs" (he had already abandoned orchids by the time Orlean finished writing about him), Dean's passions—painting, writing, and, most especially, snakes—seem eternal. "I'm doing the exact same things now that I was doing when I was ten years old," he says.

Dean dreams about snakes all the time. Sometimes they are good dreams: that he discovers he owns snakes he didn't know about, that aliens abduct him and take him to a secret part of North Carolina that was incompletely glaciated (there is always a scientific explanation in Dean's dreams), revealing a colony of rare snakes. He also has nightmares that his snakes are dying, that they're eating one another, that he forgot to feed them, that he must protect them from some unseen danger. He almost never dreams that his snakes bite or kill him; it is always the snakes that are in jeopardy, that he must save.

"The greater the value of a collection, the greater the risk of loss that it represents," Philipp Blom writes in *To Have and to Hold: An Intimate History of Collectors and Collecting*. To collect is to continually negotiate with the afterlife, with the fact that you can't take it with you. Even worse, if you collect living things you must also confront their mortality. In *The Orchid Thief*, Susan Orlean calls collecting "a sort of love sickness." Because orchids die, "to desire orchids," Orlean says, "is to have a desire that will never be, can never be, fully requited." So what kind of person devotes his life to collecting something both mortal and deadly? A collection that is both hard to keep alive and that might at any moment kill you?

Dean insists his romance has always been with danger, not death. He has eleven times endured the bites of potentially lethal snakes, including the cottonmouth that bit him when he was fourteen. "Some Greek said that men give themselves more trouble than is ordained by the Gods," Burroughs wrote to Dean in 1989. "A parish priest would tell you that your trouble is scruples. Like you make things more complicated than they need to be and more categorical. . . . So take things philosophic and remember you have reached a point where antivenom is almost more dangerous than snake bite." Dean claims Burroughs meant this last comment literally, since antivenom really can be as deadly as the snakebite itself. Still, it strikes me as beautiful, Zen-like advice.

I ask whether he suffers lingering effects from the envenomings. "I don't know about lingering effects, but I don't feel so great," he says, and laughs weakly, like he's not exactly joking. He claims he has a headache, and so I offer him something (I've got every kind of painkiller in my purse, I tell him, thanks to a recent dental procedure). "Well, then you'll lead a long life," he says wearily. He does admit he's more easily fatigued these days, but that it may be a result of the malaria, schistosomiasis, dysentery, and miscellaneous other tropical ailments he contracted during his travels. His hands are weaker from the bites, he says, and he has a greater tolerance for pain. Also, he fears death less than he used to, but this is not necessarily a good thing. "Actually what scares me isn't death," he clarifies, "but that I'll forget to fear death." He doesn't mean this figuratively or philosophically. He means: during feeding times.

Religious snake handlers sometimes try to buy snakes from Dean, but he won't sell to them, claiming his snakes are just too deadly ("They don't have enough faith for my snakes, believe me," he says). Yet he has no objection to what the handlers do, and even declares, "If I had a religion, that would probably be it. At least they're willing to test, to prove what they believe." He adds, "Actually, I might be a magic animist, if I'm anything. I'm interested in voodoo, but I would never call myself a voodooist. I don't like organized things, groups, mobs. The most frightening thing in the world is a group of people just *standing* there."

When too many visitors pack the Serpentarium, Dean hides out here in his apartment. But, I ask, I thought your purpose with the Serpentarium was to educate people. "I'm not here to educate people," he says. "I couldn't give a damn what happens to them." But then he adds, grudgingly, "Well, there are some people worth something, and ideally they'd get something out of it." By now I've grown accustomed (and rather devoted) to Dean's rhetorical style—outrageous overstatement, subsequent qualification—but I think I recognize something else, something authentic here: a certain strain of introverted misanthropy that often leads people to commit their lives to animals, something I think I know about from my family. Introverts and loners love animals. It runs the spectrum, I think, from my father's boyhood shyness to full-fledged autism—Temple Grandin and all those like her who understand animals better than people. Whether it's a quirk of personality or a genuine disorder, it's a trait I find familiar and strangely comforting.

.   .   .

It's Friday night in Wilmington and I'm at Alleigh's, a bright, horrifying "entertainment complex" featuring a warehouse-sized, earsplitting arcade, but I'm in a low-lit back room with a delighted, dressed-up crowd of about a hundred, watching the allegedly hermitic Dean Ripa perform beautiful renditions of Sinatra romantic standards, backed by a seventeen-piece orchestra which has come from miles away for this gig (out-of-state license plates in the parking lot read SAXAFON and STRAUSS). Dean organized the entire evening himself—sorting musical arrangements, assembling band members, advertising with flyers in the Serpentarium lobby: COME HEAR DEAN RIPA, 'THE VOICE,' SINGING SINATRA, BOBBY DARIN & OTHER FAVORITES FROM YEARS GONE BY! MONSTER ENTERTAINMENT!!

I feel disoriented, like I've crashed someone's wedding in, say, 1963. Dean does "Mack the Knife," "Fly Me to the Moon," "Best Is Yet to Come." He dances with the microphone; he gets down on one knee; he keeps up a mild, unintrusive patter with the audience in between songs. He does "I've Got You Under My Skin," "Witchcraft," "Come Fly with Me." During "New York, New York," three tipsy women spontaneously join him on the dance floor, kick off their shoes, and perform a cancan, cheered on by the crowd. There is no sign or mention anywhere of snakes.

My friends and I came expecting Vegas-style camp (and, in fact, a poster at the entrance advertises an upcoming Elvis impersonator's show), but Dean's performance is sincere, his delivery charged and charming, his voice accomplished and smooth. He's not making fun of Sinatra, nor trying to be Sinatra. He's just singing. He's so good I doubt my own ears and double-check with my friends—maybe it's the Percocet?—but no, they're equally excited. None of us can shake the odd, giddy feeling that we've stepped into a parallel Wilmington. Where did all these people come from? Who *is* Dean Ripa, anyway?

I'm a little breathless when I compliment him after the show, but I worry I'm insulting him by sounding so surprised. "I thought it was going to be like Lawrence Welk," I say.

"What you need to know about me," he says, "is that Lawrence Welk is my arch-enemy."

He does not elaborate.

"Well, so, what is all this?" I ask. "A hobby?"

"I don't have hobbies," Dean says. "Everything I do is work."

In fact, a few months after this show, he will be hired on as the lead vocalist with the Tommy Dorsey Orchestra and go on the road throughout the South, getting glowing reviews from the local papers—"a handsome hunk with a voice to match," "abducted the audience from their mundane existences," "dares us to experience ecstasy again!" For the moment, he allows that his snakes don't provide quite the same adrenaline rush they used to, that these days he finds a live audience scarier and hence more thrilling than the possibility of death by snakebite. Like his hero Sinatra, Dean has never learned to read music, because, he says, "it was too boring." I recall what he told me about his brief stint in the Peace Corps, teaching industrial arts in Liberian villages on the eve of a violent coup in which the country's president was overthrown: "It was the boringest thing you could imagine." He left long before his assignment was over. "I could never complete a job or do anything anyone told me to, never take orders from anyone," he says, then adds sheepishly, and unconvincingly, "Except people I love."

A few days later, I'm sitting on Dean's living-room floor, a sudden downpour roaring onto the tin roofs outside, before me on the coffee table a clutter of art books and herpetology journals, as well as a luminescent dead dragonfly Dean found on his balcony and dropped absently into my palm while pacing around the room answering my questions. It occurs to me to ask if he is a Scorpio, or perhaps born in the Chinese Year of the Snake. No, he says—but then it turns out we have *the same birthday*.

Things are getting creepy.

Dean goes on a fierce hunt for his birth certificate, because what if we were also born at the *same time*! He drags out files and manila envelopes but finally gives up. (He finds it a few days later: we were born a couple hours, not to mention nine years, apart. So what, he says, they could have made a mistake—were they holding a stopwatch or what?) When I manage to breathe again, I quiz Dean about Capricorn traits: stubborn (check), obsessive (check), respect for the traditional (check). "I have a lot of respect for tradition," he says, "even though I'm constantly trying to smash it."

•   •   •

Not long after this, I'm zipping down Eastwood Road, the busy four-lane highway that leads to Wrightsville Beach, when, improbably, I see a little box turtle attempting to cross right in my path: I will be the one to kill him. Without even deliberating, I brake and put on my blinkers, jump out, grab the turtle, and run down the embankment to deposit him safely by a pond at the edge of somebody's yard—and there's an alligator sitting there. (I set the turtle down *away* from the alligator.) I get an incredible rush, the wild overpowering urge to leave my car idling with its door open in the middle of the road and just keep walking, keep going, because surely right around the bend lies something even bigger, waiting just for me. It's like I'm being handed some exhilarating responsibility I can't begin to name. "Once you make that bargain," I recall Dean telling me one day, apropos of nothing as we drove along in his truck, "the assignments start coming faster and faster." He might have been talking about snakes, art, life—he never said. But right now I'm sure I know what he meant.

Field & Stream

FINALIST—
COLUMNS AND
COMMENTARY

How does a multitasking father sneak hunting and fishing into his suburban life? With great difficulty, humor, and insight. Bill Heavey uses his column, "A Sportsman's Life," to contemplate the everyday pleasures and torments of modern America.

Bill Heavey

Girl Meets Bluegill

How I (Nearly) Taught My Daughter to Love Fishing

The first rule of introducing a kid to fishing is that you absolutely must catch fish. Later on, he or she may be open to the idea of "enjoying the experience." But at five, believe me, they are out for blood. You get two, maybe three shots before even the dumbest *Clifford the Big Red Dog* DVD beats the hell out of watching a bobber do nothing. And then you have lost your child to all sorts of horrors: gangs, methamphetamines, violin lessons.

The first time I take Emma fishing, she is psyched right up until she steps into the canoe. Normally, water holds no terror for her. But now, just as we are about to shove off, her lower lip starts to tremble. "Gustave," she whispers.

Gustave is an all-too-real Nile crocodile we have recently seen on a National Geographic special. He is more than twenty feet long and in the past few decades has eaten over 200 people, mostly fishermen in a river near Lake Tanganyika. The story of the French naturalist trying to trap Gustave for study made for a riveting documentary. The only problem was that he failed. Gustave is still out there.

"Don't worry, Monk-a-lula," I tell Emma. "Gustave never comes here. It's too cold." Emma checks the shoreline for crocs. I can almost see the machinery in her brain weighing her father's perfect record (so far) of keeping her safe versus the primordial reptilian monster. The first tear streaks her cheek. Game over.

The second time, I decide to fish from shore. Emma has already shown remarkable casting potential with her little Tigger-themed push-button outfit, recently putting so much wrist into a cast with the yellow "fishy" practice plug that she snapped the line. I bait a No. 6 Eagle Claw hook with a worm just below the bobber. Emma attempts three casts, none of which reach the water. I gently take over, but the rig is so light that even I can barely get it out there. Fishless after two minutes, she starts throwing gravel into the water. "Monk, that scares the fish," I tell her.

"That's okay," she assures me brightly. I change locations, wanting at least to produce a fish so she understands the goal here. She follows, with larger handfuls of gravel.

"I'm fishing here," I say. There is a silence.

"Can we go home?" she asks. Zero for two.

•　　　•　　　•

It's the bottom of the ninth inning. Unless we get on fish quickly the next time, my daughter will be lost to me forever. She will become an animal rights activist and be trampled to death by hogs while attempting to liberate the stockyard at a Jimmy Dean plant.

The day of reckoning finds us at a shallow bass pond. I am prepared with two Shimano kids' outfits (one for backup), a bucket of minnows, juice boxes, string cheese, SPF 50 sunblock, insect repellent, and spare underwear. Emma works up the nerve to stick her hand in the bait bucket. When a minnow brushes her fingers, she giggles and yells, "They like me!" I bait one through the lips and toss it to a fishy-looking corner. It dances around for five minutes, nudging the bobber this way and that, and I am sure we are about to nail one. But it never happens. This is evidently bluegill water.

We go looking for worms and hit pay dirt by uprooting sod near a seep downhill from the pond. Emma cannot believe the abundance of the earth. Each new worm sends her into near delirium. "Another one!" she squeals. We put two dozen worms in a cigarette pack we find on the ground.

Three minutes later, the bobber heads south like a share of Enron stock, and we have our first bluegill. "That is a huge fish!" I say of the five-incher flapping at the end of the line. "A humongous-bungus fish! And you caught it!" All thirty-four pounds of my daughter are squirming with excitement. I ask if she wants to let it go.

"No! I want to keep it! I want to eat it! Let's catch some more!" We do.

I'm sure there will be other memorable moments in my youngest daughter's life: kindergarten, a first date, graduation, marriage. But I will keep forever the image of Emma's face, of the pure and triumphant delight as she lifted that snapping fish up into the air.

Family life does not linger long upon such summits. That very night, Emma and I tangle over the number of Barbie dolls allowed in the bathtub. I set the bag limit at ten to delay the inevitable clogging of the drain with synthetic hair. Furious at such tyranny, my daughter screams the worst insult she can think of: "Stupid. Little. DADDY!" Ten minutes later, as I am tucking in the still-damp light of my life, she stirs in her half-sleep and mumbles. "Daddy. Go again tomorrow?"

"Fishing?" I ask.

"Yeah," answers a small voice falling back into slumber. "But first digging worms."

The New Yorker

Elizabeth Kolbert brings to the complexity of global warming the clarity and synthesis that only a gifted writer can summon: The unfailing intelligence and irresistible sanity of Kolbert's narrative become a call to arms for all of us to confront the climate catastrophe we are leaving for our children.

Elizabeth Kolbert

The Climate
of Man—I

*Disappearing islands, thawing
permafrost, melting polar ice. How
the earth is changing.*

The Alaskan village of Shishmaref sits on an island
known as Sarichef, five miles off the coast of the Seward
Peninsula. Sarichef is a small island—no more than a
quarter of a mile across and two and a half miles long—and
Shishmaref is basically the only thing on it. To the north is the
Chukchi Sea, and in every other direction lies the Bering Land
Bridge National Preserve, which probably ranks as one of the least
visited national parks in the country. During the last ice age, the
land bridge—exposed by a drop in sea levels of more than three
hundred feet—grew to be nearly a thousand miles wide. The preserve occupies that part of it which, after more than ten thousand
years of warmth, still remains above water.

Shishmaref (pop. 591) is an Inupiat village, and it has been in-
habited, at least on a seasonal basis, for several centuries. As in
many native villages in Alaska, life there combines—often discon-
certingly—the very ancient and the totally modern. Almost everyone in Shishmaref still lives off subsistence hunting, primarily for
bearded seals but also for walrus, moose, rabbit, and migrating

birds. When I visited the village one day last April, the spring thaw was under way, and the seal-hunting season was about to begin. (Wandering around, I almost tripped over the remnants of the previous year's catch emerging from storage under the snow.) At noon, the village's transportation planner, Tony Weyiouanna, invited me to his house for lunch. In the living room, an enormous television set tuned to the local public-access station was playing a rock soundtrack. Messages like "Happy Birthday to the following elders . . ." kept scrolling across the screen.

Traditionally, the men in Shishmaref hunted for seals by driving out over the sea ice with dogsleds or, more recently, on snowmobiles. After they hauled the seals back to the village, the women would skin and cure them, a process that takes several weeks. In the early 1990s, the hunters began to notice that the sea ice was changing. (Although the claim that the Eskimos have hundreds of words for snow is an exaggeration, the Inupiat make distinctions among many different types of ice, including *sikuliaq*, "young ice," *sarri*, "pack ice," and *tuvaq*, "landlocked ice.") The ice was starting to form later in the fall, and also to break up earlier in the spring. Once, it had been possible to drive out twenty miles; now, by the time the seals arrived, the ice was mushy half that distance from shore. Weyiouanna described it as having the consistency of a "slush puppy." When you encounter it, he said, "your hair starts sticking up. Your eyes are wide open. You can't even blink." It became too dangerous to hunt using snowmobiles, and the men switched to boats.

Soon, the changes in the sea ice brought other problems. At its highest point, Shishmaref is only twenty-two feet above sea level, and the houses, many built by the U.S. government, are small, boxy, and not particularly sturdy-looking. When the Chukchi Sea froze early, the layer of ice protected the village, the way a tarp prevents a swimming pool from getting roiled by the wind. When the sea started to freeze later, Shishmaref became more vulnerable to storm surges. A storm in October 1997, scoured away a hundred-and-twenty-five-foot-wide strip from the town's northern edge; several houses were destroyed, and more than a dozen had to be relocated. During another storm, in October 2001, the village was threatened by twelve-foot waves. In the summer of 2002, residents of Shishmaref voted, a hundred and sixty-one to twenty, to move the entire village to the mainland. Last year, the federal government completed a survey of possible sites for a new village. Most of the spots that are being considered are in areas nearly as remote as Sarichef, with no roads or nearby cities, or even settlements. It is estimated that a full relocation will cost at least a hundred and eighty million dollars.

People I spoke to in Shishmaref expressed divided emotions about the proposed move. Some worried that, by leaving the tiny island, they would give up their connection to the sea and become lost. "It makes me feel lonely," one woman said. Others seemed excited by the prospect of gaining certain conveniences, like running water, that Shishmaref lacks. Everyone seemed to agree, though, that the village's situation, already dire, was likely only to get worse.

Morris Kiyutelluk, who is sixty-five, has lived in Shishmaref almost all his life. (His last name, he told me, means "without a wooden spoon.") I spoke to him while I was hanging around the basement of the village church, which also serves as the unofficial headquarters for a group called the Shishmaref Erosion and Relocation Coalition. "The first time I heard about global warming, I thought, I don't believe those Japanese," Kiyutelluk told me. "Well, they had some good scientists, and it's become true."

．　　　．　　　．

The National Academy of Sciences undertook its first rigorous study of global warming in 1979. At that point, climate modeling was still in its infancy, and only a few groups, one led by Syukuro Manabe, at the National Oceanic and Atmospheric Administration, and another by James Hansen, at NASA's Goddard Institute for Space Studies, had considered in any detail the effects of adding carbon dioxide to the atmosphere. Still, the results of their work were alarming enough that President Jimmy Carter called on the academy to investigate. A nine-member panel was appointed, led by the distinguished meteorologist Jule Charney, of MIT.

The Ad Hoc Study Group on Carbon Dioxide and Climate, or the Charney panel, as it became known, met for five days at the National Academy of Sciences' summer study center, in Woods Hole, Massachusetts. Its conclusions were unequivocal. Panel members had looked for flaws in the modelers' work but had been unable to find any. "If carbon dioxide continues to increase, the study group finds no reason to doubt that climate changes will result and no reason to believe that these changes will be negligible," the scientists wrote. For a doubling of CO_2 from preindustrial levels, they put the likely global temperature rise at between two and a half and eight degrees Fahrenheit. The panel members weren't sure how long it would take for changes already set in motion to become manifest, mainly because the climate system has a built-in time delay. It could take "several decades," they noted. For this reason, what might seem like the most conservative approach—waiting for evidence of warming in order to assess the models' accuracy—actually amounted to the riskiest possible strategy: "We may not be given a warning until the CO_2 loading is such that an appreciable climate change is inevitable."

It is now twenty-five years since the Charney panel issued its report, and, in that period, Americans have been alerted to the dangers of global warming so many times that volumes have been written just on the history of efforts to draw attention to the problem. (The National Academy of Sciences alone has issued nearly 200 reports on global warming; the most recent, "Radiative Forcing of Climate Change," was published just last month.) During this same period, worldwide carbon-dioxide emissions have continued to increase, from five billion billion metric tons a year to seven billion, and the earth's temperature, much as predicted by Manabe's and Hansen's models, has steadily risen. The year 1990 was the warmest year on record until 1991, which was equally hot. Almost every subsequent year has been warmer still. The year 1998 ranks as the hottest year since the instrumental temperature record began, but it is closely followed by 2002 and 2003, which are tied for second; 2001, which is third; and 2004, which is fourth. Since climate is innately changeable, it's difficult to say when, exactly, in this sequence natural variation could be ruled out as the sole cause. The American Geophysical Union, one of the nation's largest and most respected scientific organizations, decided in 2003 that the matter had been settled. At the group's annual meeting that year, it issued a consensus statement declaring, "Natural influences cannot explain the rapid increase in global near-surface temperatures." As best as can be determined, the world is now warmer than it has been at any point in the last two millennia, and, if current trends continue, by the end of the century it will likely be hotter than at any point in the last two million years.

In the same way that global warming has gradually ceased to be merely a theory, so, too, its impacts are no longer just hypothetical. Nearly every major glacier in the world is shrinking; those in Glacier National Park are retreating so quickly it has been estimated that they will vanish entirely by 2030. The oceans are becoming not just warmer but more acidic; the difference between day and nighttime temperatures is diminishing; animals are shifting their ranges poleward; and plants are blooming days, and in some cases weeks, earlier than they used to. These are the warning signs that the Charney panel cautioned against waiting for, and while in many parts of the globe they are still subtle enough to be overlooked, in others they can no longer be ignored. As it happens, the most dramatic changes are occurring in those places, like Shishmaref, where the fewest people tend to live. This disproportionate effect of global warming in the far north was also predicted by early climate models, which forecast, in column after column of FORTRAN-generated figures, what today can be measured and observed directly: the Arctic is melting.

· · ·

Most of the land in the Arctic, and nearly a quarter of all the land in the Northern Hemisphere—some five and a half billion acres—is underlaid by zones of permafrost. A few months after I visited Shishmaref, I took a trip through the interior of Alaska with Vladimir Romanovsky, a geophysicist and permafrost expert at the University of Alaska. I flew into Fairbanks, where Romanovsky lives, and when I arrived the whole city was enveloped in a dense haze that looked like fog but smelled like burning rubber. People kept telling me that I was lucky I hadn't come a couple of weeks earlier, when it had been much worse. "Even the dogs were wearing masks," one woman I met said. I must have smiled. "I am not joking," she told me.

Fairbanks, Alaska's second-largest city, is surrounded on all sides by forest, and virtually every summer lightning sets off fires in these forests, which fill the air with smoke for a few days or, in bad years, weeks. This past summer, the fires started early, in June, and were still burning two and a half months later; by the time of my visit, in late August, a record 6.3 million acres—an area roughly the size of New Hampshire—had been incinerated. The severity of the fires was clearly linked to the weather, which had been exceptionally hot and dry; the average summertime temperature in Fairbanks was the highest on record, and the amount of rainfall was the third lowest.

On my second day in Fairbanks, Romanovsky picked me up at my hotel for an underground tour of the city. Like most permafrost experts, he is from Russia. (The Soviets more or less invented the study of permafrost when they decided to build their gulags in Siberia.) A broad man with shaggy brown hair and a square jaw, Romanovsky as a student had had to choose between playing professional hockey and becoming a geophysicist. He had opted for the latter, he told me, because "I was little bit better scientist than hockey player." He went on to earn two master's degrees and two Ph.D.'s. Romanovsky came to get me at 10 A.M.; owing to all the smoke, it looked like dawn.

Any piece of ground that has remained frozen for at least two years is, by definition, permafrost. In some places, like eastern Siberia, permafrost runs nearly a mile deep; in Alaska, it varies from a couple of hundred feet to a couple of thousand feet deep. Fairbanks, which is just below the Arctic Circle, is situated in a region of discontinuous permafrost, meaning that the city is freckled with regions of frozen ground. One of the first stops on Romanovsky's tour was a hole that had opened up in a patch of permafrost not far from his house. It was about six feet wide and five feet deep. Nearby were the outlines of other, even bigger holes, which, Romanovsky told me, had been filled with gravel by the local public-works department. The holes, known as thermokarsts, had appeared suddenly when the permafrost gave way, like a rotting floorboard. (The technical term for thawed permafrost is talik, from a Russian word meaning "not frozen.") Across the road, Romanovsky pointed out a long trench running into the woods. The trench, he explained, had been formed when a wedge of underground ice had melted. The spruce trees that had been growing next to it, or perhaps on top of it, were now listing at odd angles, as if in a gale. Locally, such trees are called "drunken." A few of the spruces had fallen over. "These are very drunk," Romanovsky said.

In Alaska, the ground is riddled with ice wedges that were created during the last glaciation, when the cold earth cracked and the cracks filled with water. The wedges, which can be dozens or even hundreds of feet deep, tended to form in networks, so that when they melt they leave behind connecting diamond- or hexagonal-shaped depressions. A few blocks beyond the drunken forest, we came to a house where the front yard showed clear signs of ice-wedge melt-off. The owner, trying to make the best of things, had turned the yard into a miniature-golf course. Around the corner, Romanovsky pointed out a house—no longer occupied—that had basically split in two; the main part was leaning to the right and the garage toward the left. The house had been built in the sixties or early seventies; it had survived until almost a decade ago, when the permafrost under it started to degrade. Romanovsky's mother-in-law used to own two houses on the same block. He had urged her to sell them both. He pointed out one, now under new ownership; its roof had developed an ominous-looking ripple. (When Romanovsky went to buy his own house, he looked only in permafrost-free areas.)

"Ten years ago, nobody cared about permafrost," he told me. "Now everybody wants to know." Measurements that Romanovsky and his colleagues at the University of Alaska have made around Fairbanks show that the temperature of the permafrost has risen to the point where, in many places, it is now less than one degree below freezing. In places where permafrost has been disturbed, by roads or houses or lawns, much of it is already thawing. Romanovsky has also been monitoring the permafrost on the North Slope and has found that there, too, are regions where the permafrost is very nearly thirty-two degrees Fahrenheit. While the age of permafrost is difficult to determine, Romanovsky estimates that most of it in Alaska probably dates back to the beginning of the last glacial cycle. This means that if it thaws it will be doing so for the first time in more than a hundred and twenty thousand years. "It's really a very interesting time," he said.

. . .

The next morning, Romanovsky picked me up at seven. We were going to drive from Fairbanks nearly 500 miles north to the town of Deadhorse, on Prudhoe Bay, to collect data from electronic monitoring stations that Romanovsky had set up. Since the road was largely unpaved, he had rented a truck for the occasion. Its windshield was cracked in several places. When I suggested this could be a problem, Romanovsky assured me that it was "typical Alaska." For provisions, he had brought along an oversized bag of Tostitos.

The road that we were traveling on had been built for Alaskan oil, and the pipeline followed it, sometimes to the left, sometimes to the right. (Because of the permafrost, the pipeline runs mostly aboveground, on pilings.) Trucks kept passing us, some with severed caribou heads strapped to their roofs, others advertising the Alyeska Pipeline Service Company. About two hours outside Fairbanks, we started to pass through tracts of forest that had recently burned, then tracts that were still smoldering, and, finally, tracts that were still, intermittently, in flames. The scene was part Dante, part *Apocalypse Now*. We crawled along through the smoke. Beyond the town of Coldfoot—really just a gas station—we passed the tree line. An evergreen was marked with a plaque that read "Farthest North Spruce Tree on the Alaska Pipeline: Do Not Cut." Predictably, someone had taken a knife to it. A deep gouge around the trunk was bound with duct tape. "I think it will die," Romanovsky said.

Finally, at around five in the afternoon, we reached the turnoff for the first monitoring station. Because one of Romanovsky's colleagues had nursed dreams—never realized—of traveling to it by plane, it was near a small airstrip, on the far side of a river. We pulled on rubber boots and forded the river, which, owing to the lack of rain, was running low. The site consisted of a few posts sunk into the tundra; a solar panel; a 200-foot-deep borehole with heavy-gauge wire sticking out of it; and a white container, resembling an ice chest, that held computer equipment. The solar panel, which the previous summer had been mounted a few feet off the ground, was now resting on the scrub. At first, Romanovsky speculated that this was a result of vandalism, but after inspecting things more closely he decided that it was the work of a bear. While he hooked up a laptop computer to one of the monitors inside the white container, my job was to keep an eye out for wildlife.

For the same reason that it is sweaty in a coal mine—heat flux from the center of the earth—permafrost gets warmer the farther down you go. Under equilibrium conditions—which is to say, when the climate is stable—the very warmest temperatures in a borehole will be found at the bottom and they will decrease steadily as you go higher. In these circumstances, the lowest temperature will be found at the permafrost's surface, so that, plotted on a graph, the results will be a tilted line. In recent decades, though, the temperature profile of Alaska's permafrost has drooped. Now, instead of a straight line, what you get is shaped more like a sickle. The permafrost is still warmest at the very bottom, but instead of being coldest at the top it is coldest somewhere in the middle, and warmer again toward the surface. This is an unambiguous sign that the climate is heating up.

"It's very difficult to look at trends in air temperature, because it's so variable," Romanovsky explained after we were back in the truck, bouncing along toward Deadhorse. It turned out that he had brought the Tostitos to stave off not hunger but fatigue—the crunching, he said, kept him awake—and by now the bag was more than half empty. "So one year you have around Fairbanks a mean annual temperature of zero"—thirty-two degrees Fahrenheit— "and you say, 'Oh yeah, it's warming,' and other years you have a mean annual temperature of minus six"—twenty-one degrees Fahrenheit—"and everybody says, 'Where? Where is your global warming?' In the air temperature, the signal is very small compared to noise. What permafrost does is it works as a low-pass filter. That's why we can see trends much easier in permafrost temperatures than we can see them in atmosphere." In most parts of Alaska, the permafrost has warmed by three degrees since the early 1980s. In some parts of the state, it has warmed by nearly six degrees.

•   •   •

When you walk around in the Arctic, you are stepping not on permafrost but on something called the "active layer." The active layer, which can be anywhere from a few inches to a few feet deep, freezes in the winter but thaws over the summer, and it is what supports the growth of plants—large spruce trees in places where conditions are favorable enough and, where they aren't, shrubs and, finally, just lichen. Life in the active layer proceeds much as it does in more temperate regions, with one critical difference. Temperatures are so low that when trees and grasses die they do not fully decompose. New plants grow out of the half-rotted old ones, and when these plants die the same thing happens all over again. Eventually, through a process known as cryoturbation, organic matter is pushed down beneath the active layer into the permafrost, where it can sit for thousands of years in a botanical version of suspended animation. (In Fairbanks, grass that is still green has been found in permafrost dating back to the middle of the last ice age.) In this way, much like a peat bog or, for that matter, a coal deposit, permafrost acts as a storage unit for accumulated carbon.

One of the risks of rising temperatures is that this storage process can start to run in reverse. Under the right conditions, organic material that has been frozen for millennia will break down, giving off carbon dioxide or methane, which is an even more powerful greenhouse gas. In parts of the Arctic, this is already happening. Researchers in Sweden, for example, have been measuring the methane output of a bog known as the Stordalen mire, near the town of Abisko, for almost thirty-five years. As the permafrost in the area has warmed, methane releases have increased, in some spots by up to 60 percent. Thawing permafrost could make the active layer more hospitable to plants, which are a sink for carbon. Even this, though, probably wouldn't offset the release of greenhouse gases. No one knows exactly how much carbon is stored in the world's permafrost, but estimates run as high as four hundred and fifty billion metric tons.

"It's like ready-use mix—just a little heat, and it will start cooking," Romanovsky told me. It was the day after we had arrived in Deadhorse, and we were driving through a steady drizzle out to another monitoring site. "I think it's just a time bomb, just waiting for a little warmer conditions." Romanovsky was wearing a rain suit over his canvas work clothes. I put on a rain suit that he had brought along for me. He pulled a tarp out of the back of the truck.

Whenever he has had funding, Romanovsky has added new monitoring sites to his network. There are now sixty of them, and while we were on the North Slope he spent all day and also part of the night—it stayed light until nearly eleven—rushing from one to the next. At each site, the routine was more or less the same. First, Romanovsky would hook up his computer to the data logger, which had been recording permafrost temperatures on an hourly basis since the previous summer. (When it was raining, he would perform this step hunched under the tarp.) Then he would take out a metal probe shaped like a "T" and poke it into the ground at regular intervals, measuring the depth of the active layer. The probe was a meter long, which, it turned out, was no longer quite long enough. The summer had been so warm that almost everywhere the active layer had grown deeper, in some spots by just a few centimeters, in other spots by more than that; in places where the active layer was particularly deep, Romanovsky had had to work out a new way of measuring it using the probe and a wooden ruler. Eventually, he explained, the heat that had gone into increasing the depth of the active layer would work its way downward, bringing the permafrost that much closer to the thawing point. "Come back next year," he advised me.

On the last day I spent on the North Slope, a friend of Romanovsky's, Nicolai Panikov, a microbiologist at the Stevens Institute of Technology, in New Jersey, arrived. Panikov had come to collect cold-loving microorganisms known as psychrophiles. He was planning to study these organisms in order to determine whether they could have functioned in the sort of conditions that, it is believed, were once found on Mars. Panikov told me that he was quite convinced that Martian life existed—or, at least, had existed. Romanovsky expressed his opinion on this by rolling his eyes; nevertheless, he had agreed to help Panikov dig up some permafrost.

That day, I also flew with Romanovsky by helicopter to a small island in the Arctic Ocean, where he had set up yet another monitoring site. The island, just north of the seventieth parallel, was a bleak expanse of mud dotted with little clumps of yellowing vegetation. It was filled with ice wedges that were starting to melt, creating a network of polygonal depressions. The weather was cold and wet, so while Romanovsky hunched under his tarp I stayed in the helicopter and chatted with the pilot. He had lived in Alaska since 1967. "It's definitely gotten warmer since I've been here," he told me. "I have really noticed that."

When Romanovsky emerged, we took a walk around the island. Apparently, in the spring it had been a nesting site for birds, because everywhere we went there were bits of eggshell and piles of droppings. The island was only about ten feet above sea level, and at the edges it dropped off sharply into the water. Romanovsky pointed out a spot along the shore where the previous summer a series of ice wedges had been exposed. They had since melted, and the ground behind them had given way in a cascade of black mud. In a few years, he said, he expected more ice wedges would be exposed, and then these would melt, causing further erosion. Although the process was different in its mechanics from what was going on in Shishmaref, it had much the same cause and, according to Romanovsky, was likely to have the same result. "Another disappearing island," he said, gesturing toward some freshly exposed bluffs. "It's moving very, very fast."

·　　·　　·

On September 18, 1997, the *Des Groseilliers*, a 318-foot-long ice-breaker with a bright-red hull, set out from the town of Tuktoy-aktuk, on the Beaufort Sea, and headed north under overcast skies. Normally, the *Des Groseilliers*, which is based in Québec City, is used by the Canadian Coast Guard, but for this particular journey it was carrying a group of American geophysicists, who were planning to jam it into an ice floe. The scientists were hoping to conduct a series of experiments as they and the ship and the ice floe all drifted, as one, around the Arctic Ocean. The expedition had taken several years to prepare for, and during the planning phase its organizers had carefully consulted the findings of a previous Arctic expedition, which took place back in 1975. Based on those findings, they had decided to look for a floe averaging nine feet thick. But when they reached the area where they planned to overwinter—at seventy-five degrees north latitude— they found that not only were there no floes nine feet thick but there were barely any that reached six feet. One of the scientists on board recalled the reaction on the *Des Groseilliers* this way: "It was like 'Here we are, all dressed up and nowhere to go.' We imagined calling the sponsors at the National Science Foundation and saying, 'Well, you know, we can't find any ice.'"

Sea ice in the Arctic comes in two varieties. There is seasonal ice, which forms in the winter and then melts in the summer, and perennial ice, which persists year-round. To the untrained eye, all sea ice looks pretty much the same, but by licking it you can get a good idea of how long a particular piece has been floating around. When ice begins to form in seawater, it forces out the salt, which has no place in the crystal structure. As the ice gets thicker, the rejected salt collects in tiny pockets of brine too highly concentrated to freeze. If you suck on a piece of first-year ice, it will taste salty. Eventually, if the ice survives, these pockets of brine drain out through fine, vein-like channels, and the ice becomes fresher. Multiyear ice is so fresh that if you melt it you can drink it.

The most precise measurements of Arctic sea ice have been made by NASA, using satellites equipped with microwave sensors. In 1979, the satellite data show, perennial sea ice covered 1.7 billion acres, or an area nearly the size of the continental United States. The ice's extent varies from year to year, but since then the overall trend has been strongly downward. The losses have been particularly great in the Beaufort and Chukchi Seas, and also considerable in the Siberian and Laptev Seas. During this same period, an atmospheric circulation pattern known as the Arctic Oscillation has mostly been in what climatologists call a "positive" mode. The positive Arctic Oscillation is marked by low pressure over the Arctic Ocean, and it tends to produce strong winds and higher temperatures in the far north. No one really knows whether the recent behavior of the Arctic Oscillation is independent of global warming or a product of it. By now, though, the perennial sea ice has shrunk by roughly two hundred and fifty million acres, an area the size of New York, Georgia, and Texas combined. According to mathematical models, even the extended period of a positive Arctic Oscillation can account for only part of this loss.

The researchers aboard the *Des Groseilliers* knew that the Arctic sea ice was retreating; that was, in fact, why they were there. At the time, however, there wasn't much data on trends in sea-ice depth. (Since then, a limited amount of information on this topic—gathered, for rather different purposes, by nuclear submarines—has been declassified.) Eventually, the researchers decided to settle for the best ice floe they could find. They picked one that stretched over some thirty square miles and in some spots was six feet thick, in some spots three. Tents were set up on the floe to house experiments, and a safety protocol was established: anyone venturing out onto the ice had to travel with a buddy and a radio. (Many also carried a gun, in case of polar-bear problems.) Some of the scientists speculated that, since the ice was abnormally thin, it would grow during the expedition. The opposite turned out to be the case. The *Des Groseilliers* spent twelve months frozen into the floe, and, during that time, it drifted some 300 miles north. Nevertheless, at the end of the year, the average thickness of the ice had declined, in some spots by as much as a third. By August 1998, so many of the scientists had fallen through that a new requirement was added to the protocol: anyone who set foot off the ship had to wear a life jacket.

·　　·　　·

Donald Perovich has studied sea ice for thirty years, and on a rainy day last fall I went to visit him at his office in Hanover, New Hampshire. Perovich works for the Cold Regions Research and Engineering Laboratory, or CRREL (pronounced "crell"), a division of the U.S. Army established in 1961 in anticipation of a very cold war. (The assumption was that if the Soviets invaded they would probably do so from the north.) He is a tall man with black hair, very black eyebrows, and an earnest manner. His office is decorated with photographs from the *Des Groseilliers* expedition, for which he served as the lead scientist; there are shots of the ship, the tents, and, if you look closely enough, the bears. One grainy-looking photo shows someone dressed up as Santa Claus, celebrating Christmas out on the ice. "The most fun you could ever have" was how Perovich described the expedition to me.

Perovich's particular area of expertise, in the words of his CRREL biography, is "the interaction of solar radiation with sea ice." During the *Des Groseilliers* expedition, he spent most of his time monitoring conditions on the floe using a device known as a spectroradiometer. Facing toward the sun, a spectroradiometer measures incident light, and facing toward earth it measures reflected light. If you divide the latter by the former, you get a quantity known as albedo. (The term comes from the Latin word for "whiteness.") During April and May, when conditions on the floe were relatively stable, Perovich took measurements with his spectroradiometer once a week, and during June, July, and August, when they were changing more rapidly, he took measurements every other day. The arrangement allowed him to plot exactly how the albedo varied as the snow on top of the ice turned to slush, and then the slush became puddles, and, finally, some of the puddles melted through to the water below.

An ideal white surface, which reflected all the light that shone on it, would have an albedo of one, and an ideal black surface, which absorbed all the light, would have an albedo of zero. The albedo of the earth, in aggregate, is 0.3, meaning that a little less than a third of the sunlight that hits it gets reflected back out. Anything that changes the earth's albedo changes how much energy the planet absorbs, with potentially dramatic consequences. "I like it because it deals with simple concepts, but it's important," Perovich told me.

At one point, Perovich asked me to imagine that we were looking down at the earth from a spaceship above the North Pole. "It's springtime, and the ice is covered with snow, and it's really bright and white," he said. "It reflects over 80 percent of the incident sunlight. The albedo's around 0.8, 0.9. Now, let's suppose that we melt that ice away and we're left with the ocean. The albedo of the ocean is less than 0.1; it's like 0.07.

"Not only is the albedo of the snow-covered ice high; it's the highest of anything we find on earth," he went on. "And not only is the albedo of water low; it's pretty much as low as anything you can find on earth. So what you're doing is you're replacing the best reflector with the worst reflector." The more open water that's exposed, the more solar energy goes into heating the ocean. The result is a positive feedback, similar to the one between thawing permafrost and carbon releases, only more direct. This so-called ice-albedo feedback is believed to be a major reason that the Arctic is warming so rapidly.

"As we melt that ice back, we can put more heat into the system, which means we can melt the ice back even more, which means we can put more heat into it, and, you see, it just kind of builds on itself," Perovich said. "It takes a small nudge to the climate system and amplifies it into a big change."

·   ·   ·

A few dozen miles to the east of CRREL, not far from the Maine–New Hampshire border, is a small park called the Madison Boulder Natural Area. The park's major—indeed, only—attraction is a block of granite the size of a two-story house. The Madison Boulder is thirty-seven feet wide and eighty-three feet long and weighs about ten million pounds. It was plucked out of the White Mountains and deposited in its current location eleven thousand years ago, and it illustrates how relatively minor changes to the climate system have, when amplified, yielded cataclysmic results.

Geologically speaking, we are now living in a warm period after an ice age. Over the past two million years, huge ice sheets have advanced across the Northern Hemisphere and retreated again more than twenty times. (Each major glaciation tended, for obvious reasons, to destroy the evidence of its predecessors.) The most recent advance, called the Wisconsin, began roughly a hundred and twenty thousand years ago, when ice began to creep outward from centers in Scandinavia, Siberia, and the highlands near Hudson Bay. By the time the sheets had reached their maximum southern extent, most of New England and New York and a good part of the upper Midwest were buried under ice nearly a mile thick. The ice sheets were so heavy that they depressed the crust of the earth, pushing it down into the mantle. (In some places, the process of recovery, known as isostatic rebound, is still going on.) As the ice retreated, it deposited, among other landmarks, the terminal moraine called Long Island.

It is now known, or at least almost universally accepted, that glacial cycles are initiated by slight, periodic variations in the earth's orbit. These orbital variations alter the distribution of sunlight at different latitudes during different seasons according to a complex pattern that takes a hundred thousand years to complete. But orbital variations in themselves aren't nearly sufficient to produce the sort of massive ice sheet that moved the Madison Boulder.

The crushing size of that ice sheet, the Laurentide, which stretched over some five million square miles, was the result of feedbacks, more or less analogous to those now being studied in the Arctic, only operating in reverse. As ice built up, albedo increased, leading to less heat absorption and the growth of yet more ice. At the same time, for reasons that are not entirely understood, as the ice sheets advanced CO_2 levels declined: during each of the most recent glaciations, carbon-dioxide levels dropped almost precisely in synch with falling temperatures. During each warm period, when the ice retreated, CO_2 levels rose again. Ice cores from Antarctica contain a record of the atmosphere stretching back more than four glacial cycles—minute samples of air get trapped in tiny bubbles—and researchers who have studied these cores have concluded that fully half the temperature difference between cold periods and warm ones can be attributed to changes in the concentrations of greenhouse gases. Antarctic ice cores also show that carbon-dioxide levels today are significantly higher than they have been at any other point in the last 420 thousand years.

While I was at CRREL, Perovich took me to meet a colleague of his named John Weatherly. Posted on Weatherly's office door was a bumper sticker designed to be pasted—illicitly—on SUVs. It said, "I'm Changing the Climate! Ask Me How!" For the last several years, Weatherly and Perovich have been working to translate the data gathered on the *Des Groseilliers* expedition into computer algorithms to be used in climate forecasting. Weatherly told me that some climate models—worldwide, there are about fifteen major ones in operation—predict that the perennial sea-ice cover in the Arctic will disappear entirely by the year 2080. At that point, although there would continue to be seasonal ice that forms in winter, in summer the Arctic Ocean would be completely ice-free. "That's not in our lifetime," he observed. "But it is in the lifetime of our kids."

Later, back in his office, Perovich and I talked about the long-term prospects for the Arctic. Perovich noted that the earth's climate system is so vast that it is not easily altered. "On the one hand, you think, It's the earth's climate system, it's big; it's robust. And, indeed, it has to be somewhat robust or else it would be changing all the time." On the other hand, the climate record shows that it would be a mistake to assume that change, when it comes, will come slowly. Perovich offered a comparison that he had heard from a glaciologist friend. The friend likened the climate system to a rowboat: "You can tip and then you'll just go back. You can tip it and just go back. And then you tip it and you get to the other stable state, which is upside down."

Perovich said that he also liked a regional analogy. "The way I've been thinking about it, riding my bike around here, is, You ride by all these pastures and they've got these big granite boulders in the middle of them. You've got a big boulder sitting there on this rolling hill. You can't just go by this boulder. You've got to try to push it. So you start rocking it, and you get a bunch of friends, and they start rocking it, and finally it starts moving. And then you realize, Maybe this wasn't the best idea. That's what we're doing as a society. This climate, if it starts rolling, we don't really know where it will stop."

• • •

As a cause for alarm, global warming could be said to be a 1970s idea; as pure science, however, it is much older than that. In 1859, a British physicist named John Tyndall, experimenting with a machine he had built—the world's first ratio spectrophotometer—set out to study the heat-trapping properties of various gases.

Tyndall found that the most common elements in the air—oxygen and nitrogen—were transparent to both visible and infrared radiation. Gases like carbon dioxide, methane, and water vapor, by contrast, were not. Tyndall was quick to appreciate the implications of his discovery: the imperfectly transparent gases, he declared, were largely responsible for determining the earth's climate. He likened their impact to that of a dam built across a river: just as a dam "causes a local deepening of the stream, so our atmosphere, thrown as a barrier across the terrestrial rays, produces a local heightening of the temperature at the earth's surface."

The phenomenon that Tyndall identified is now referred to as the "natural greenhouse effect." It is not remotely controversial; indeed, it's an essential condition of life on earth as we know it. To understand how it works, it helps to imagine the planet without it. In that situation, the earth would constantly be receiving energy from the sun and, at the same time, constantly radiating energy back out to space. All hot bodies radiate, and the amount that they radiate is a function of their temperature. In order for the earth to be in equilibrium, the quantity of energy it sends into space must equal the quantity it is receiving. When, for whatever reason, equilibrium is disturbed, the planet will either warm up or cool down until the temperature is once again sufficient to make the two energy streams balance out.

If there were no greenhouse gases, energy radiating from the surface of the earth would flow away from it unimpeded. In that case, it would be comparatively easy to calculate how warm the planet would have to get to throw back into space the same amount of energy it absorbs from the sun. (This amount varies widely by location and time of year; averaged out, it comes to some 235 watts per square meter, or roughly the energy of four household light bulbs.) The result of this calculation is a frigid zero degrees. To use Tyndall's Victorian language, if the heat-trapping gases were removed from the air for a single night "the warmth of our fields and gardens would pour itself unrequited into space, and the sun would rise upon an island held fast in the iron grip of frost."

Greenhouse gases alter the situation because of their peculiar absorptive properties. The sun's radiation arrives mostly in the form of visible light, which greenhouse gases allow to pass freely. The earth's radiation, meanwhile, is emitted mostly in the infrared part of the spectrum. Greenhouse gases absorb infrared radiation and then reemit it—some out toward space and some back toward earth. This process of absorption and reemission has the effect of limiting the outward flow of energy; as a result, the earth's surface and lower atmosphere have to be that much warmer before the planet can radiate out the necessary 235 watts per square meter. The presence of greenhouse gases is what largely accounts for the fact that the average global temperature, instead of zero, is actually a far more comfortable fifty-seven degrees.

By the end of the nineteenth century, Tyndall's work on the natural greenhouse effect had been extended to what would today be called the "enhanced greenhouse effect." In 1894, the Swedish chemist Svante Arrhenius became convinced that humans were altering the earth's energy balance. Much as Tyndall had tried to imagine what the world would be like in the absence of green- house gases, Arrhenius tried to imagine what it would be like in the presence of more of them. Starting on Christmas Eve, he set out to calculate what would happen to the earth's temperature if CO_2 levels were doubled. Arrhenius described the calculations as some of the most tedious of his life. He routinely worked on them for fourteen hours a day, and was not finished for nearly a year. Finally, in December 1895, he announced his results to the Royal Swedish Academy of Sciences.

Like the natural greenhouse effect, the enhanced green- house effect is—in theoretical terms, at least—uncontroversial. If greenhouse-gas levels in the atmosphere increase, all other things being equal, the earth's temperature will rise. The key uncertain- ties concern how this process will play out in practice, since in the real world all things rarely are equal. For several decades after Arrhenius completed his calculations, scientists were unsure to what extent mankind was even capable of affecting atmospheric carbon-dioxide levels; the general assumption was that the oceans would absorb just about everything humans could emit. Arrhenius himself predicted that it would take three thousand years of coal burning to double the CO_2 in the air, a prediction, it is now known, that was off by roughly twenty-eight centuries.

.   .   .

Swiss Camp is a research station set up in 1990 on a platform drilled into the Greenland ice sheet. Because the ice sheet is moving—ice flows like water, only more slowly—the camp is always in motion: in fifteen years, it has migrated by more than a mile, generally in a westerly direction. Every summer, the whole place gets flooded, and every winter its contents solidify. The cumulative effect of all this is that almost nothing at Swiss Camp functions anymore the way it was supposed to. To get into it, you have to clamber up a snowdrift and descend through a trapdoor in the roof, as if entering a ship's hold or a space module. The living quarters are no longer habitable, so now the scientists at the camp sleep outside, in tents. (The one assigned to me was the same sort used by Robert Scott on his ill-fated expedition to the South Pole.) By the time I arrived at the camp, late last May, someone had jackhammered out the center of the workspace but had left the desks encased in three-foot-high blocks of ice. Inside them I could dimly make out a tangle of wires, a bulging plastic bag, and an old dustpan.

Konrad Steffen, a professor of geography at the University of Colorado, is the director of Swiss Camp. A native of Zurich, Steffen is tall and lanky, with pale-blue eyes, blondish hair, and a blondish-gray beard. He fell in love with the Arctic when, as a graduate student in 1975, he spent a summer on Axel Heiberg

Island, 400 miles northwest of the north magnetic pole. A few years later, for his doctoral dissertation, he lived for two winters on the sea ice off Baffin Island. (Steffen told me that for his honeymoon he had wanted to take his wife to Spitsbergen, an island 500 miles north of Norway, but she demurred, and they had ended up driving across the Sahara instead.)

When Steffen planned Swiss Camp—he built much of the place himself—it was not with global warming in mind. Rather, he was interested in meteorological conditions on what is known as the ice sheet's "equilibrium line." Along this line, winter snow and summer melt are supposed to be precisely in balance. But, in recent years, "equilibrium" has become an increasingly elusive quality. In the summer of 2002, the ice sheet melted to an unprecedented extent. Satellite images taken by NASA showed that snow had melted up to an elevation of 6,500 feet. In some of these spots, ice-core records revealed, liquid water had not been seen for hundreds, perhaps thousands, of years. The following winter, there was an unusually low snowfall, and in the summer of 2003 the melt was so great that, around Swiss Camp, five feet of ice were lost.

When I arrived at the camp, the 2004 melt season was already under way. This, to Steffen, was a matter of both intense scientific interest and serious practical concern. A few days earlier, one of his graduate students, Russell Huff, and a postdoc, Nicolas Cullen, had driven out on snowmobiles to service some weather stations closer to the coast. The snow there was melting so fast that they had had to work until five in the morning, and then take a long detour back, to avoid getting caught in the quickly forming rivers. Steffen wanted to get everything that needed to be done completed ahead of schedule, in case everyone had to pack up and leave early. My first day at Swiss Camp he spent fixing an antenna that had fallen over in the previous year's melt. It was bristling with equipment, like a high-tech Christmas tree. Even on a relatively warm day on the ice sheet, which this was, it never gets more than a few degrees above freezing, and I was walking around in a huge parka, two pairs of pants plus long underwear, and two pairs of gloves. Steffen, meanwhile, was tinkering with the antenna with his bare hands. He has spent fourteen summers at Swiss Camp, and I asked him what he had learned during that time. He answered with another question.

"Are we disintegrating part of the Greenland ice sheet over the longer term?" he asked. He was sorting through a tangle of wires that to me all looked the same but must have had some sort of distinguishing characteristics. "What the regional models tell us is that we will get more melt at the coast. It will continue to melt. But warmer air can hold more water vapor, and at the top of the ice sheet you'll get more precipitation. So we'll add more snow there. We'll get an imbalance of having more accumulation at the top, and more melt at the bottom. The key question now is: What is the dominant one, the more melt or the increase?"

.   .   .

Greenland's ice sheet is the second-largest on earth. (Antarctica's is the largest.) In its present form, the Greenland ice sheet is, quite literally, a relic of the last glaciation. The top layers consist of snow that fell recently. Beneath these layers is snow that fell centuries and then millennia ago, until, at the very bottom, there is snow that fell 130,000 years ago. Under current climate conditions, the ice sheet probably would not form, and it is only its enormous size that has sustained it for this long. In the middle of the island, the ice is so thick—nearly two miles—that it creates a kind of perpetual winter. Snow falls in central Greenland year-round and it never melts, although, over time, the snow gets compacted into ice and is pressed out toward the coast. There, eventually, it either calves off into icebergs or flows away. In summertime, lakes of a spectacular iridescent blue form at the ice sheet's lower elevations; these empty into vast rivers that fan out toward the sea. Near Swiss

Camp—elevation 3,770 feet—there is a huge depression where one such lake forms each July, but by that point no one is around to see it: it would be far too dangerous.

Much of what is known about the earth's climate over the last 100,000 years comes from ice cores drilled in central Greenland, along a line known as the ice divide. Owing to differences between summer and winter snow, each layer in a Greenland core can be individually dated, much like the rings of a tree. Then, by analyzing the isotopic composition of the ice, it is possible to determine how cold it was at the time each layer was formed. (Although ice cores from Antarctica contain a much longer climate record, it is not as detailed.) Over the last decade, three Greenland cores have been drilled to a depth of 10,000 feet, and these cores have prompted a rethinking of how the climate operates. Where once the system was thought to change, as it were, only glacially, now it is known to be capable of sudden and unpredictable reversals. One such reversal, called the Younger Dryas, after a small Arctic plant—*Dryas octopetala*—that suddenly reappeared in Scandinavia, took place roughly 12,800 years ago. At that point, the earth, which had been warming rapidly, was plunged back into glacial conditions. It remained frigid for twelve centuries and then warmed again, even more abruptly. In Greenland, average annual temperatures shot up by nearly twenty degrees in a single decade.

As a continuous temperature record, the Greenland ice cores stop providing reliable information right around the start of the last glacial cycle. Climate records pieced together from other sources indicate that the last interglacial, which is known as the Eemian, was somewhat warmer than the present one, the Holocene. They also show that sea levels during that time were at least fifteen feet higher than they are today. One theory attributes this to a collapse of the West Antarctic Ice Sheet. A second holds that meltwater from Greenland was responsible. (When sea ice melts, it does not affect sea level, because the ice, which was floating, was already displacing an equivalent volume of water.) All told, the Greenland ice sheet holds enough water to raise sea levels world-wide by twenty-three feet. Scientists at NASA have calculated that throughout the 1990s the ice sheet, despite some thickening at the center, was shrinking by twelve cubic miles per year.

· · ·

Jay Zwally is a NASA scientist who works on a satellite project known as ICESat. He is also a friend of Steffen's, and about ten years ago he got the idea of installing global-positioning-system receivers around Swiss Camp to study changes in the ice sheet's elevation. Zwally happened to be at the camp while I was there, and the second day of my visit we all got onto snowmobiles and headed out to a location known as JAR 1 (for Jakobshavn Ablation Region) to reinstall a GPS receiver. The trip was about ten miles. Midway through it, Zwally told me that he had once seen spy-satellite photos of the region we were crossing, and that they had shown that underneath the snow it was full of crevasses. Later, when I asked Steffen about this, he told me that he had had the whole area surveyed with bottom-seeking radar, and no crevasses of any note had been found. I was never sure which one of them to believe.

Reinstalling Zwally's GPS receiver entailed putting up a series of poles, a process that, in turn, required drilling holes thirty feet down into the ice. The drilling was done not mechanically but thermally, using a steam drill that consisted of a propane burner, a steel tank to hold snow, and a long rubber hose. Everyone—Steffen, Zwally, the graduate students, me—took a turn. This meant holding onto the hose while it melted its way down, an activity reminiscent of ice fishing. Seventy-five years ago, not far from JAR 1, Alfred Wegener, the German scientist who proposed the theory of continental drift, died while on a meteorological expedition. He was buried in the ice sheet, and there is a running joke at Swiss Camp about stumbling onto his body. "It's Wegener!" one of the graduate students exclaimed, as the drill worked its way downward. The first hole was finished relatively quickly, at which point everyone decided—prematurely, as it turned out—that it was time for a midday snack. Unless a hole stays filled with water, it starts to close up again, and can't be used. Apparently, there were fissures in the ice, because water kept draining out of the next few holes that were tried. The original plan had been for three holes, but, some six hours later, only two had been drilled, and it was decided that this would have to suffice.

Although Zwally had set out to look for changes in the ice sheet's elevation, what he ended up measuring was, potentially, even more significant. His G.P.S. data showed that the more the ice sheet melted the faster it started to move. Thus in the summer of 1996, the ice around Swiss Camp moved at a rate of thirteen inches per day, but in 2001 it had sped up to twenty inches per day. The reason for this acceleration, it is believed, is that meltwater from the surface makes its way down to the bedrock below, where it acts as a lubricant. (In the process, it enlarges cracks and forms huge ice tunnels, known as moulins.) Zwally's measurements also showed that, in the summer, the ice sheet rises by about six inches, indicating that it is floating on a cushion of water.

At the end of the last glaciation, the ice sheets that covered much of the Northern Hemisphere disappeared in a matter of a few thousand years—a surprisingly short time, considering how long it had taken them to build up. At one point, about 14,000 years ago, they were melting so fast that sea levels were rising at the rate of more than a foot a decade. Just how this happened is not entirely understood, but the acceleration of the Greenland ice sheet suggests yet another feedback mechanism: once an ice sheet begins to melt, it starts to flow faster, which means it also thins out faster, encouraging further melt. Not far from Swiss Camp, there is a huge river of ice known as the Jakobshavn Isbrae, which probably was the source of the iceberg that sank the *Titanic*. In 1992, the Jakobshavn Isbrae flowed at a rate of three and a half miles per hour; by 2003, its velocity had increased to 7.8 miles per hour. Similar findings were announced earlier this year by scientists measuring the flow of ice streams on the Antarctic Peninsula.

Over the last century, global sea levels have risen by about half a foot. The most recent report of the U.N.'s Intergovernmental Panel on Climate Change, issued in 2001, predicts that they will rise anywhere from four inches to three feet by the year 2100. This prediction includes almost no contribution from Greenland or Antarctica; it is based mostly on the physics of water, which, as it warms up, expands. Two climatologists at Pennsylvania State University, Richard Alley and Byron Parizek, recently issued new predictions that take into account the observed acceleration of the ice sheets; this effect in Greenland alone, they estimate, will cause up to two and half inches of additional sea-level rise over the coming century. James Hansen, the NASA official who directed one of the initial 1970s studies on the effects of carbon dioxide, has gone much further, arguing that if greenhouse-gas emissions are not controlled the total disintegration of the Greenland ice sheet could be set in motion in a matter of decades. Although the process would take hundreds, perhaps thousands, of years to fully play out, once begun it would become self-reinforcing, and hence virtually impossible to stop. In an article published earlier last year in the journal *Climatic Change*, Hansen, who is now the head of the Goddard Institute for Space Studies, wrote that he hoped he was wrong about the ice sheet, "but I doubt it."

.　　　.　　　.

As it happened, I was at Swiss Camp just as last summer's global-warming disaster movie, *The Day After Tomorrow*, was opening in theatres. One night, Steffen's wife called on the camp's satellite phone to say that she had just taken the couple's two teenage children to see it. Everyone had enjoyed the film, she reported, especially because of the family connection.

The fantastic conceit of *The Day After Tomorrow* is that global warming produces global freezing. At the start of the film, a chunk of Antarctic ice the size of Rhode Island suddenly melts. (Something very similar to this actually happened in March 2002, when the Larsen B ice shelf collapsed.) Most of what follows—an instant ice age, cyclonic winds that descend from the upper atmosphere—is impossible as science but not as metaphor. The record preserved in the Greenland ice sheet shows that over the last 100,000 years temperatures have often swung wildly—so often that it is our own relatively static experience of climate that has come to look exceptional. Nobody knows what caused the sudden climate shifts of the past; however, many climatologists suspect that they had something to do with changes in ocean-current patterns that are known as the thermohaline circulation.

"When you freeze sea ice, the salt is pushed out of the pores, so that the salty water actually drains," Steffen explained to me one day when we were standing out on the ice, trying to talk above the howl of the wind. "And salty water's actually heavier, so it starts to sink." Meanwhile, owing both to evaporation and to heat loss, water from the tropics becomes denser as it drifts toward the Arctic, so that near Greenland a tremendous volume of seawater is constantly sinking toward the ocean floor. As a result of this process, still more warm water is drawn from the tropics toward the poles, setting up what is often referred to as a "conveyor belt" that moves heat around the globe.

"This is the energy engine for the world climate," Steffen went on. "And it has one source: the water that sinks down. And if you just turn the knob here a little bit"—he made a motion of turning the water on in a bathtub—"we can expect significant temperature changes based on the redistribution of energy." One way to turn the knob is to heat the oceans, which is already happening. Another is to pour more freshwater into the polar seas. This is also occurring. Not only is runoff from coastal Greenland increasing; the volume of river discharge into the Arctic Ocean has been rising. Oceanographers monitoring the North Atlantic have documented that in recent decades its waters have become significantly less salty. A total shutdown of the thermohaline circulation is considered extremely unlikely in the coming century. But, if the Greenland ice sheet started to disintegrate, the possibility of such a shutdown could not be ruled out. Wallace Broecker, a professor of geochemistry at Columbia University's Lamont-Doherty Earth Observatory, has labeled the thermohaline circulation the "Achilles' heel of the climate system." Were it to halt, places like Britain, whose climate is heavily influenced by the Gulf Stream, could become much colder, even as the planet as a whole continued to warm up.

For the whole time I was at Swiss Camp, it was "polar day," and so the sun never set. Dinner was generally served at ten or eleven P.M., and afterward everyone sat around a makeshift table in the kitchen, talking and drinking coffee. (Because it is not—strictly speaking—necessary, alcohol was in short supply.) One night, I asked Steffen what he thought conditions at Swiss Camp would be like in the same season a decade hence. "In ten years, the signal should be much more distinct, because we will have added another ten years of greenhouse warming," he said.

Zwally interjected, "I predict that ten years from now we won't be coming this time of year. We won't be able to come this late. To put it nicely, we are heading into deep doo-doo."

Either by disposition or by training, Steffen was reluctant to make specific predictions, whether about Greenland or, more generally, about the Arctic. Often, he prefaced his remarks by noting that there could be a change in atmospheric-circulation patterns that would dampen the rate of temperature increase or even—temporarily at least—reverse it entirely. But he was emphatic that "climate change is a real thing.

"It's not something dramatic now—that's why people don't really react," he told me. "But if you can convey the message that it will be dramatic for our children and our children's children—the risk is too big not to care."

The time, he added, "is already five past midnight."

On the last night that I spent at Swiss Camp, Steffen took the data he had downloaded off his weather station and, after running them through various programs on his laptop, produced the mean temperature at the camp for the previous year. It was the highest of any year since the camp was built.

That night, dinner was unusually late. On the return trip of another pole-drilling expedition, one of the snowmobiles had caught on fire, and had to be towed back to camp. When I finally went out to my tent to go to bed, I found that the snow underneath it had started to melt, and there was a large puddle in the middle of the floor. I got some paper towels and tried to mop it up, but the puddle was too big, and eventually I gave up.

•   •   •

No nation takes a keener interest in climate change, at least on a per-capita basis, than Iceland. More than 10 percent of the country is covered by glaciers, the largest of which, Vatnajökull, stretches over 3,200 square miles. During the so-called Little Ice Age, the advance of the glaciers caused widespread misery; it has been estimated that in the mid-eighteenth century nearly a third of the country's population died of starvation or associated ills. For Icelanders, many of whom can trace their genealogy back a thousand years, this is considered to be almost recent history.

Oddur Sigurdsson heads up a group called the Icelandic Glaciological Society. One day last fall, I went to visit him in his office, at the headquarters of Iceland's National Energy Authority, in Reykjavík. Little towheaded children kept wandering in to peer under his desk. Sigurdsson explained that Reykjavík's public schoolteachers were on strike, and his colleagues had had to bring their children to work.

The Icelandic Glaciological Society is composed entirely of volunteers. Every fall, after the summer-melt season has ended, they survey the size of the country's 300-odd glaciers and then file reports, which Sigurdsson collects in brightly colored binders. In the organization's early years—it was founded in 1930—the volunteers were mostly farmers; they took measurements by building cairns and pacing off the distance to the glacier's edge. These days, members come from all walks of life—one is a retired plastic surgeon—and they take more exacting surveys, using tape measures and iron poles. Some glaciers have been in the same family, so to speak, for generations. Sigurdsson became head of the society in 1987, at which point one volunteer told him that he thought he would like to relinquish his post.

"He was about ninety when I realized how old he was," Sigurdsson recalled. "His father had done this at that place before and then his nephew took over for him." Another volunteer has been monitoring his glacier, a section of Vatnajökull, since 1948. "He's eighty," Sigurdsson said. "And if I have some questions that go beyond his age I just go and ask his mother. She's a hundred and seven."

In contrast to glaciers in North America, which have been shrinking steadily since the 1960s, Iceland's glaciers grew through the 1970s and 1980s. Then, in the mid-1990s, they, too, began to decline, at first slowly and then much more rapidly. Sigurdsson pulled out a notebook of glaciological reports, filled out on yellow forms, and turned to the section on a glacier called Sólheimajökull, a tongue-shaped spit of ice that sticks out from a much larger glacier, called Mýrdalsjökull. In 1996, Sólheimajökull crept back by ten feet. In 1997, it receded by another thirty-three feet, and in 1998 by ninety-eight feet. Every year since then, it has retreated even more. In 2003, it shrank by 302 feet and in 2004 by 285 feet. All told, Sólheimajökull—the name means "sun-home glacier" and refers to a nearby farm—is now 1,100 feet shorter than it was just a decade ago. Sigurdsson pulled out another notebook, which was filled with slides. He picked out some recent ones of Sólheimajökull. The glacier ended in a wide river. An enormous rock, which Sólheimajökull had deposited when it began its retreat, stuck out from the water, like the hull of an abandoned ship.

"You can tell by this glacier what the climate is doing," Sigurdsson said. "It is more sensitive than the most sensitive meteorological measurement." He introduced me to a colleague of his, Kristjana Eythórsdóttir, who, as it turned out, was the granddaughter of the founder of the Icelandic Glaciological Society. Eythórsdóttir keeps tabs on a glacier named Leidarjökull, which is a four-hour trek from the nearest road. I asked her how it was doing. "Oh, it's getting smaller and smaller, just like all the others," she said. Sigurdsson told me that climate models predicted that by the end of the next century Iceland would be virtually ice-free. "We will have small ice caps on the highest mountains, but the mass of the glaciers will have gone," he said. It is believed that there have been glaciers on Iceland for the last few million years. "Probably longer," Sigurdsson said.

. . .

In October 2000, in a middle school in Barrow, Alaska, officials from the eight Arctic nations—the U.S., Russia, Canada, Denmark, Norway, Sweden, Finland, and Iceland—met to talk about global warming. The group announced plans for a three-part, two-million-dollar study of climate change in the region. This past fall, the first two parts of the study—a massive technical document and a 140-page summary—were presented at a symposium in Reykjavík.

The day after I went to talk to Sigurdsson, I attended the symposium's plenary session. In addition to nearly 300 scientists, it drew a sizable contingent of native Arctic residents—reindeer herders, subsistence hunters, and representatives of groups like the Inuvialuit Game Council. In among the shirts and ties, I spotted two men dressed in the brightly colored tunics of the Sami and several others wearing sealskin vests. As the session went on, the subject kept changing—from hydrology and biodiversity to fisheries and on to forests. The message, however, stayed the same. Almost wherever you looked, temperatures in the Arctic were rising, and at a rate that surprised even those who had expected to find clear signs of climate change. Robert Corell, an American oceanographer and a former assistant director at the National Science Foundation, coordinated the study. In his opening remarks, he ran through its findings—shrinking sea ice, receding glaciers, thawing permafrost—and summed them up as follows: "The Arctic climate is warming rapidly now, with an emphasis on now." Particularly alarming, Corell said, were the most recent data from Greenland, which showed the ice sheet melting much faster "than we thought possible even a decade ago."

Global warming is routinely described as a matter of scientific debate—a theory whose validity has yet to be demonstrated. This characterization, or at least a variant of it, is offered most significantly by the Bush administration, which maintains that there is still insufficient scientific understanding to justify mandatory action. The symposium's opening session lasted for more than nine hours. During that time, many speakers stressed the uncertainties that remain about global warming and its effects—on the thermohaline circulation, on the distribution of vegetation, on the survival of cold-loving species, on the frequency of forest fires. But this sort of questioning, which is so basic to scientific discourse, never extended to the relationship between carbon dioxide and rising temperatures. The study's executive summary stated, unequivocally, that human beings had become the "dominant factor" influencing the climate. During an afternoon coffee break, I caught up with Corell. "Let's say that there's 300 people in this room," he told me. "I don't think you'll find five who would say that global warming is just a natural process."

The third part of the Arctic-climate study, which was still unfinished at the time of the symposium, was the so-called "policy document." This was supposed to outline practical steps to be taken in response to the scientific findings, including—presumably—reducing greenhouse-gas emissions. The policy document remained unfinished because American negotiators had rejected much of the language proposed by the seven other Arctic nations. (A few weeks later, the U.S. agreed to a vaguely worded statement calling for "effective"—but not obligatory—actions to combat the problem.) This recalcitrance left those Americans who had traveled to Reykjavík in an awkward position. A few tried—halfheartedly—to defend the administration's stand to me; most, including many government employees, were critical of it. At one point, Corell observed that the loss of sea ice since the late 1970s was equal to "the size of Texas and Arizona combined. That analogy was made for obvious reasons."

That evening, at the hotel bar, I talked to an Inuit hunter named John Keogak, who lives on Banks Island, in Canada's Northwest Territories, some five hundred miles north of the Arctic Circle. He told me that he and his fellow-hunters had started to notice that the climate was changing in the mid-eighties. A few years ago, for the first time, people began to see robins, a bird for which the Inuit in his region have no word.

"We just thought, Oh, gee, it's warming up a little bit," he recalled. "It was good at the start—warmer winters, you know—but now everything is going so fast. The things that we saw coming in the early nineties, they've just multiplied.

"Of the people involved in global warming, I think we're on top of the list of who would be most affected," Keogak went on. "Our way of life, our traditions, maybe our families. Our children may not have a future. I mean, all young people, put it that way. It's just not happening in the Arctic. It's going to happen all over the world. The whole world is going too fast."

The symposium in Reykjavík lasted for four days. One morning, when the presentations on the agenda included "Char as a Model for Assessing Climate Change Impacts on Arctic Fishery Resources," I decided to rent a car and take a drive. In recent years,

Reykjavík has been expanding almost on a daily basis, and the old port city is now surrounded by rings of identical, European-looking suburbs. Ten minutes from the car-rental place, these began to give out, and I found myself in a desolate landscape in which there were no trees or bushes or really even soil. The ground—fields of lava from some defunct, or perhaps just dormant, volcanoes—resembled macadam that had recently been bulldozed. I stopped to get a cup of coffee in the town of Hveragerdi, where roses are raised in greenhouses heated with steam that pours directly out of the earth. Farther on, I crossed into farm country; the landscape was still treeless, but now there was grass, and sheep eating it. Finally, I reached the sign for Sólheimajökull, the glacier whose retreat Oddur Sigurdsson had described to me. I turned off onto a dirt road. It ran alongside a brown river, between two crazily shaped ridges. After a few miles, the road ended, and the only option was to continue on foot.

By the time I got to the lookout over Sólheimajökull, it was raining. In the gloomy light, the glacier looked forlorn. Much of it was gray—covered in a film of dark grit. In its retreat, it had left behind ridged piles of silt. These were jet black and barren—not even the tough local grasses had had a chance to take root on them. I looked for the enormous boulder I had seen in the photos in Sigurdsson's office. It was such a long way from the edge of the glacier that for a moment I wondered if perhaps it had been carried along by the current. A raw wind came up, and I started to head down. Then I thought about what Sigurdsson had told me. If I returned in another decade, the glacier would probably no longer even be visible from the ridge where I was standing. I climbed back up to take a second look.

(*This is the first part of a three-part article.*)

GQ

"Upon This Rock" is both a hilarious, picaresque tale of a trip to a Christian-rock festival and a deeply moving exploration of belief. Encompassing everything from one of the most cogent criticisms of Christian rock in print to instructions on how to cook frog legs over a campfire, John Jeremiah Sullivan's recklessly paced narrative is modern gonzo at its best, but the ultimate bittersweet note of hope is what makes this piece resonate.

John Jeremiah Sullivan

Upon This Rock

*Rock music used to be a safe
haven for degenerates and rebels.
Until it found Jesus. Now
Christian-rock concerts are pulling
in a new generation of true
believers. John Jeremiah Sullivan
went deep into the biggest festival
of them all and found that the
Lord rocks in mysterious ways.*

It is wrong to boast, but in the beginning, my plan was perfect.
I was assigned to cover the Cross-Over Festival in Lake of
the Ozarks, Missouri, three days of the top Christian bands
and their backers at an isolated Midwestern fairground or something. I'd stand at the edge of the crowd and take notes on the
scene, chat up the occasional audience member ("What's
harder—homeschooling or regular schooling?"), then flash my
pass to get backstage, where I'd rap with the artists themselves:
"This Christian music—it's a phenomenon. What do you tell
your fans when they ask you why God let Creed break up?" The
singer could feed me his bit about how all music glorifies Him,
when it's performed with a loving spirit, and I'd jot down every
tenth word, inwardly smiling. Later that night, I might sneak

some hooch in my rental car and invite myself to lie with a prayer group by their fire, for the fellowship of it. Fly home, stir in statistics. Paycheck.

But as my breakfast-time mantra says, I am a professional. And they don't give out awards for that sort of toe-tap, J-school foolishness. I wanted to know what these people are, who claim to love this music, who drive hundreds of miles, traversing states, to hear it live. Then it came, my epiphany: I would go with them. Or rather, they would go with me. I would rent a van, a plush one, and we would travel there together, I and three or four hard-core buffs, all the way from the East Coast to the implausibly named Lake of the Ozarks. We'd talk through the night, they'd proselytize at me, and I'd keep my little tape machine working all the while. Somehow I knew we'd grow to like and pity one another. What a story that would make—for future generations.

The only remaining question was: how to recruit the willing? But it was hardly even a question, because everyone knows that damaged types who are down for whatever's clever gather in "chat rooms" every night. And among the Jesusy, there's plenty who are super f'd up. He preferred it that way, evidently.

So I published my invitation, anonymously, at youthonthe rock.com, and on two Internet forums devoted to the good-looking Christian pop-punk band Relient K, which had been booked to appear at Cross-Over. I pictured that guy or girl out there who'd been dreaming in an attic room of seeing, with his or her own eyes, the men of Relient K perform their song "Gibberish" from *Two Lefts Don't Make a Right . . . But Three Do.* How could he or she get there, though? Gas prices won't drop, and Relient K never plays North Florida. Please, Lord, make it happen. Suddenly, here my posting came, like a great light. We could help each other. "I'm looking for a few serious fans of Christian rock to ride to the festival with me," I wrote. "Male/female doesn't matter, though you shouldn't be older than, say, 28, since I'm looking at this primarily as a youth phenomenon."

They seem like harmless words. Turns out, though, I had failed to grasp how "youth" the phenomenon is. Most of the people hanging out in these chat rooms were teens, and I don't mean nineteen, friends, I mean fourteen. Some of them, I was about to learn, were mere tweens. I had just traipsed out onto the World Wide Web and asked a bunch of twelve-year-old Christians if they wanted to come for a ride in my van.

It wasn't long before the little fuckers rounded on me. "Nice job cutting off your email address," wrote "mathgeek29," in a tone that seemed not at all Christlike. "I doubt if anybody would give a full set of contact information to some complete stranger on the Internet. . . . Aren't there any Christian teens in Manhattan who would be willing to do this?"

"Oh, I should hope not," I blubbered.

A few of the children were credulous. "Riathamus" said, "i am 14 and live in indiana plus my parents might not let me considering it is a stranger over the Internet. but that would really be awsome." A girl by the name of "LilLoser" even tried to be a friend:

> I doubt my parents would allow their baby girl to go with some guy they don't and I don't know except through email, especially for the amount of time you're asking and like driving around everywhere with ya. . . . I'm not saying you're a creepy petifile, lol, but i just don't think you'll get too many people interested . . . cuz like i said, it spells out "creepy" . . . but hey—good luck to you in your questy missiony thing. lol.

The luck that she wished me I sought in vain. The Christians stopped chatting with me and started chatting among themselves, warning one another about me. Finally one poster on the official Relient K site hissed at the others to stay away from my scheme, as I was in all likelihood "a 40 year old kidnapper." Soon I logged on and found that the moderators of the site had removed my post and its lengthening thread of accusations altogether, offering no explanation. Doubtless at that moment they were faxing alerts to a network of moms. I recoiled in dread. I called my lawyer, in Boston, who told me to "stop using computers."

In the end, the experience inspired in me a distaste for the whole Cross-Over Festival, and I resolved to refuse the assignment. I withdrew.

•   •   •

The problem with a flash mag like the *Gentlemen's Quarterly* is that there's always some overachieving assistant, sometimes called Greg, whom the world hasn't beaten down yet and who, when you phone him, out of courtesy, just to let him know that "the Cross-Over thing fell through" and that you'll be in touch when you "figure out what to do next," hops on that mystical boon the Internet and finds out that the festival you were planning to attend was in fact not "the biggest one in the country," as you'd alleged. The biggest one in the country—indeed, in Christendom—is the Creation Festival, inaugurated in 1979, a regular Godstock. And it happens not in Missouri but in ruralmost Pennsylvania, in a green valley, on a farm called Agape. This festival did not end a month ago; it starts the day after tomorrow. Already they are assembling, many tens of thousands strong. *But hey— good luck to you in your questy missiony thing. lol.*

I made one demand: that I not be forced to camp. I'd be given some sort of vehicle with a mattress in it, one of these pop-ups, maybe. "Right," said Greg. "Here's the deal. I've called around. There are no vans left within a hundred miles of Philly. We got you an RV, though. It's a twenty-nine-footer." Once I reached the place, we agreed (for he led me to think he agreed), I would certainly be able to downgrade to something more manageable.

The reason twenty-nine feet is such a common length for RVs, I presume, is that once a vehicle gets much longer, you need a special permit to drive it. That would mean forms and fees, possibly even background checks. But show up at any RV joint with your thigh stumps lashed to a skateboard, crazily waving your hooks-for-hands, screaming you want that twenty-nine-footer out back for a trip to you *ain't sayin' where*, and all they want to know is: Credit or debit, tiny sir?

Two days later, I stood in a parking lot, suitcase at my feet. Debbie came toward me. She was a lot to love, with a face as sweet as a birthday cake beneath spray-hardened bangs. She raised a meaty arm and pointed, before either of us spoke. The thing she pointed at was the object about which I'd just been saying, "Not that one, Jesus, okay?" It was like something the ancient Egyptians might have left behind in the desert.

"Hi, there," I said, "Listen, all I need is, like, a camper van or whatever. It's just me, and I'm going 500 miles . . ."

She considered me. "Where ya headed?"

"To this thing called Creation. It's, like, a Christian-rock festival."

"You and everybody!" she chirped. "The people who got our vans are going to that same thing. There's a *bunch o' ya.*"

Her coworker Jack emerged—tattooed, squat, gray-mulleted, spouting open contempt for MapQuest. He'd be giving me real directions. "But first let's check 'er out."

We toured the outskirts of my soon-to-be mausoleum. It took time. Every single thing Jack said, somehow, was the only thing I'd need to remember. White water, gray water, black water (drinking, showering, *le devoir*). Here's your this, never ever that. Grumbling about "weekend warriors." I couldn't listen, because listening would mean accepting it as real, though his casual mention of the vast blind spot in the passenger-side mirror squeaked through, as did his description of the "extra two feet on each side"—the bulge of my living quarters—which I wouldn't be able to see but would want to "be conscious of" out there. Debbie followed us with a video camera, for insurance purposes. I saw my loved ones gathered in a mahogany-paneled room to watch this footage; them being forced to hear me say, "What if I never use the toilet—do I still have to switch on the water?"

Mike pulled down the step and climbed aboard. It was really happening. The interior smelled of spoiled vacations and amateur porn shoots wrapped in motel shower curtains and left in the sun. I was physically halted at the threshold for a moment. Jesus had never been in this RV.

What should I tell you about my voyage to Creation? Do you want to know what it's like to drive a windmill with tires down the Pennsylvania Turnpike at rush hour by your lonesome, with darting bug-eyes and shaking hands; or about Greg's laughing phone call "to see how it's going"; about hearing yourself say "no No NO NO!" every time you try to merge; or about thinking you detect—beneath the mysteriously comforting blare of the radio—faint honking sounds, then checking your passenger-side mirror only to find you've been straddling the lanes for an unknown number of miles (those two extra feet!) and that the line of traffic you've kept pinned stretches back farther than you can see; or about stopping at Target to buy sheets and a pillow and peanut butter but then practicing your golf swing in the sporting-goods aisle for a solid twenty-five minutes, unable to stop, knowing that when you do, the twenty-nine-footer will be where you left her, alone in the side lot, hulking and malevolent, waiting for you to take her the rest of the way to your shared destiny?

She got me there, as Debbie and Jack had promised, not possibly believing it themselves. Seven miles from Mount Union, a sign read CREATION AHEAD. The sun was setting; it floated above the valley like a fiery gold balloon. I fell in with a long line of cars and trucks and vans—not many RVs. Here they were, all about me: the born again. On my right was a pickup truck, its bed full of teenage girls in matching powder blue T-shirts; they were screaming at a Mohawked kid who was walking beside the road. I took care not to meet their eyes—who knew but they weren't the same fillies I had solicited days before? Their line of traffic lurched ahead, and an old orange Datsun came up beside me. I watched as the driver rolled down her window, leaned halfway out, and blew a long, clear note on a ram's horn.

Oh, I understand where you are coming from. But that is what she did. I have it on tape. She blew a ram's horn. Quite capably. Twice. A yearly rite, perhaps, to announce her arrival at Creation.

My turn at the gate. The woman looked at me, then past me to the empty passenger seat, then down the whole length of the twenty-nine-footer. "How many people in your group?" she asked.

.   .   .

I pulled away in awe, permitting the twenty-nine-footer to float. My path was thronged with excited Christians, most younger than eighteen. The adults looked like parents or pastors, not here on their own. Twilight was well along, and the still valley air was sharp with campfire smoke. A great roar shot up to my left—something had happened onstage. The sound bespoke a multitude. It filled the valley and lingered.

I thought I might enter unnoticed—that the RV might even offer a kind of cover—but I was already turning heads. Two separate kids said, "I feel sorry for him" as I passed. Another leaped up on the driver's-side step and said, "Jesus Christ, man," then fell away running. I kept braking—even idling was too fast. Whatever spectacle had provoked the roar was over now: The roads were choked. The youngsters were streaming around me in both directions, back to their campsites, like a line of ants around some petty obstruction. They had a disconcerting way of stepping aside for the RV only when its front fender was just about to graze their backs. From my elevated vantage, it looked as if they were waiting just a tenth of a second too long, and that I was gently, forcibly parting them in slow motion.

The Evangelical strata were more or less recognizable from my high school days, though everyone, I observed, had gotten better looking. Lots were dressed like skate punks or in last season's East Village couture (nondenominationals); others were fairly trailer (rural Baptists or Church of God); there were preps (Young Life, Fellowship of Christian Athletes—these were the ones who'd have the pot). You could spot the stricter sectarians right away, their unchanging anti-fashion and pale glum faces. When I asked one woman, later, how many she reckoned were white, she said, "Roughly 100 percent." I did see some Asians and three or four blacks. They gave the distinct impression of having been adopted.

I drove so far. You wouldn't have thought this thing could go on so far. Every other bend in the road opened onto a whole new cove full of tents and cars; the encampment had expanded to its physiographic limits, pushing right up to the feet of the ridges. It's hard to put across the sensory effect of that many people living and moving around in the open: part family reunion, part refugee camp. A tad militia, but cheerful.

The roads turned dirt and none too wide: Hallelujah Highway, Street Called Straight. I'd been told to go to "H," but when I reached H, two teenage kids in orange vests came out of the shadows and told me the spots were all reserved. "Help me out here, guys," I said, jerking my thumb, pitifully indicating my mobile home. They pulled out their walkie-talkies. Some time went by. It got darker. Then an even younger boy rode up on a bike and winked a flashlight at me, motioning I should follow.

It was such a comfort to yield up my will to this kid. All I had to do was not lose him. His vest radiated a warm, reassuring officialdom in my headlights. Which may be why I failed to comprehend in time that he was leading me up an almost vertical incline—"the Hill Above D."

I'm not sure which was first: the little bell in my spine warning me that the RV had reached a degree of tilt she was not engineered to handle, or the sickening knowledge that we had begun to slip back. I bowed up off the seat and crouched on the gas. I heard yelling. I kicked at the brake. With my left hand and foot I groped, like a person drowning, for the emergency brake (had Jack's comprehensive how-to sesh not touched on its whereabouts?). We were losing purchase; she started to shudder. My little guide's eyes looked scared.

I'd known this moment would come, of course, that the twenty-nine-footer would turn on me. We had both of us understood it from the start. But I must confess, I never imagined her hunger for death could prove so extreme. Laid out below and behind me was a literal field of Christians, toasting buns and playing guitars, fellowshipping. The aerial shot in the papers would show a long scar, a swath through their peaceful tent village. And that this gigantic psychopath had worked her vile design through the agency of a child—an innocent, albeit impossibly stupid, child . . .

My memory of the next five seconds is smeared, but logic tells me that a large and perfectly square male head appeared in the windshield. It was blond and wearing glasses. It had wide-open eyes and a Chaucerian West Virginia accent and said rapidly that I should "JACK THE WILL TO THE ROT" while applying the brakes. Some branch of my motor cortex obeyed. The RV skidded briefly and was still. Then the same voice said, "All right, hit the gas on three: one, two . . ."

She began to climb—slowly, as if on a pulley. Some freakishly powerful beings were pushing. Soon we had leveled out at the top of the hill.

There were five of them, all in their early twenties. I remained in the twenty-nine-footer; they gathered below.

"Thank you," I said.

"Aw, hey," shot back Darius, the one who'd given the orders. He talked very fast. "We've been doing this all day—I don't know why that kid keeps bringing people up here—we're from West Virginia—listen, he's retarded—there's an empty field right there."

I looked back and down at what he was pointing to: pastureland.

Jake stepped forward. He was also blond, but slender. And handsome in a feral way. His face was covered in stubble as pale as his hair. He said he was from West Virginia and wanted to know where I was from.

"I was born in Louisville," I said.

"Really?" said Jake. "Is that on the Ohio River?" Like Darius, he both responded and spoke very quickly. I said that in fact it was.

"Well, I know a dude that died who was from Ohio. I'm a volunteer fireman, see. Well, he flipped a Chevy Blazer nine times. He was spread out from here to that ridge over there. He was dead as four o'clock."

"Who are you guys?" I said.

Ritter answered. He was big, one of those fat men who don't really have any fat, a corrections officer—as I was soon to learn—and a former heavyweight wrestler. He could burst a pineapple in his armpit and chuckle about it (or so I assume). Haircut: military. Mustache: faint. "We're just a bunch of West Virginia guys on fire for Christ," he said. "I'm Ritter, and this is Darius, Jake, Bub, and that's Jake's brother, Josh. Pee Wee's around here somewhere."

"Chasin' tail," said Darius disdainfully.

"So you guys have just been hanging out here, saving lives?"

"We're from West Virginia," said Darius again, like maybe he thought I was thick. It was he who most often spoke for the group. The projection of his jaw from the lump of snuff he kept there made him come off a bit contentious, but I felt sure he was just high-strung.

"See," Jake said, "well, our campsite is right over there." With a cock of his head he identified a car, a truck, a tent, a fire, and a tall cross made of logs. And that other thing was . . . a PA system?

"We had this spot last year," Darius said. "I prayed about it. I said, 'God, I'd just really like to have that spot again—you know, if it's Your will.'"

I'd assumed that my days at Creation would be fairly lonely and end with my ritual murder. But these West Virginia guys had such warmth. It flowed out of them. They asked me what I did and whether I liked sassafras tea and how many others I'd brought with me in the RV. Plus they knew a dude who died horribly and was from a state with the same name as the river I grew up by, and I'm not the type who questions that sort of thing.

"What are you guys doing later?" I said.

Bub was short and solid; each of his hands looked as strong as a trash compactor. He had darker skin than the rest—an olive cast—with brown hair under a camouflage hat and brown eyes and a full-fledged dark mustache. Later he would share with me that friends often told him he must be "part N-word." He was shy and always looked like he must be thinking hard about something. "Me and Ritter's going to hear some music," he said.

"What band is it?"

Ritter said, "Jars of Clay."

I had read about them; they were big. "Why don't you guys stop by my trailer and get me on your way?" I said. "I'll be in that totally empty field."

Ritter said, "We just might do that." Then they all lined up to shake my hand.

$\bullet \qquad \bullet \qquad \bullet$

While I waited for Ritter and Bub, I lay in bed and read *The Silenced Times* by lantern light. This was a thin newsletter that had come with my festival packet. It wasn't really a newsletter; it was publisher's flackery for *Silenced*, a new novel by Jerry Jenkins, one of the minds behind the multi-hundred-million-dollar Left Behind series—twelve books so far, all about what happens after the Rapture, to people like me. His new book was a futuristic job, set in 2047. The dateline on the newsletter read: "March 2, 38." You get it? Thirty-seven years have passed since they wiped Jesus from history. *The Silenced Times* was laid out to look like a newspaper from that coming age.

It was pretty grim stuff. In the year 38, an ancient death cult has spread like a virus and taken over the "United Seven States of

America." Adherents meet in "cell groups" (nice touch: a bit of old Commie lingo); they enlist the young and hunger for global hegemony while striving to hasten the end of the world. By the year 34—the time of the last census—44 percent of the population had professed membership in the group; by now the figure is closer to half. This dwarfs any other surviving religious movement in the land. Even the president (whom they mobilized to elect) has been converted. The most popular news channel in the country openly backs him and his policies; and the year's most talked-about film is naked propaganda for the cult, but in a darkly brilliant twist, much of the population has been convinced that the media are in fact controlled by . . .

I'm sorry! That's all happening now. That's Evangelicalism. *The Silenced Times* describes Christians being thrown into jail, driven underground, their pamphlets confiscated. A dude wins an award for ratting out his sister, who was leading a campus Bible study (you know how we do). Jerry Jenkins must blow his royalties on crack. I especially liked the part in *The Silenced Times* where it reports that antireligion forces have finally rounded up Jenkins himself—in a cave. He's ninety-seven years old but has never stopped typing, and as they drag him away, he's bellowing Scripture.

Ritter beat on the door. He and Bub were ready to hear some Jars of Clay. Now that it was night, more fires were going; the whole valley was aromatic. And the sky looked like a tin punch lantern—thousands of stars were out. There were so many souls headed toward the stage, it was hard to walk, though I noticed the crowd tended to give Ritter a wider berth. He kind of leaned back, looking over people's heads, as if he expected to spot a friend. I asked about his church in West Virginia. He said he and the rest of the guys were Pentecostal, speaking in tongues and all that—except for Jake, who was a Baptist. But they all went to the same "sing"—a weekly Bible study at somebody's house with food and guitars. Did Ritter think everyone here was a Christian? "No, there's some who probably aren't saved. With this many people, there has to be." What were his feelings on that? "It just opens up opportunities for witnessing," he said.

Bub stopped suddenly—a signal that he wished to speak. The crowd flowed on around us for a minute while he chose his words. "There's Jewish people here," he said.

"Really?" I said. "You mean, Jew Jews?"

"Yeah," Bub said. "These girls Pee Wee brung around. I mean, they're Jewish. That's pretty awesome." He laughed without moving his face; Bub's laugh was a purely vocal phenomenon. Were his eyes moist?

We commenced walking.

I suspect that on some level—say, the conscious one—I didn't want to be noticing what I noticed as we went. But I've been to a lot of huge public events in this country during the past five years, writing about sports or whatever, and one thing they all had in common was this weird implicit enmity that American males, in particular, seem to carry around with them much of the time. Call it a laughable generalization, fine, but if you spend enough late afternoons in stadium concourses, you feel it, something darker than machismo. Something a little wounded, and a little sneering, and just plain ready for bad things to happen. It wasn't here. It was just . . . not. I looked for it, and I couldn't find it. In the three days I spent at Creation, I saw not one fight, heard not one word spoken in anger, felt at no time even mildly harassed, and in fact met many people who were exceptionally kind. I realize they were all of the same race, all believed the same stuff, and weren't drinking, but there were also 100,000 of them. What's that about?

We were walking past a row of portable toilets, by the food stands. As we came around the corner, I saw the stage, from off to the side. And the crowd on the hill that faced the stage. Their bodies rose till they merged with the dark. "Holy crap," I said.

Ritter waved his arm like an impresario. He said, "This, my friend, is Creation."

.   .   .

For their encore, Jars of Clay did a cover of U2's "All I Want Is
You." It was *bluesy*.

That's the last thing I'll be saying about the bands.

Or, no, wait, there's this: The fact that I didn't think I heard a
single interesting bar of music from the forty or so acts I caught or
overheard at Creation shouldn't be read as a knock on the acts
themselves, much less as contempt for the underlying notion of
Christians playing rock. These were not Christian bands, you see;
these were Christian-rock bands. The key to digging this scene lies
in that one-syllable distinction. Christian rock is a genre that exists to edify and make money off of evangelical Christians. It's
message music for listeners who know the message cold, and,
what's more, it operates under a perceived *responsibility*—one the
artists embrace—to "reach people." As such, it rewards both obvi-
ousness and maximum palatability (the artists would say clarity),
which in turn means *parasitism*. Remember those perfume dis-
pensers they used to have in pharmacies—"If you like Drakkar
Noir, you'll love Sexy Musk"? Well, Christian rock works like that.
Every successful crappy secular group has its Christian off-brand,
and that's proper, because culturally speaking, it's supposed to
serve as a stand-in for, not an alternative to or an improvement on,
those very groups. In this it succeeds wonderfully. If you think it
profoundly sucks, that's because your priorities are not its priorities; you want to hear something cool and new, it needs to play
something proven to please . . . while praising Jesus Christ. That's
Christian rock. A Christian band, on the other hand, is just a band
that has more than one Christian in it. U2 is the exemplar, held
aloft by believers and nonbelievers alike, but there have been others through the years, bands about which people would say, "Did
you know those guys were Christians? I know—it's freaky. They're
still fuckin' good, though." The Call was like that; Lone Justice was
like that. These days you hear it about indie acts like Pedro the Lion
and Damien Jurado (or P.O.D. and Evanescence—de gustibus). In

most cases, bands like these make a very, very careful effort not to be seen as playing "Christian rock." It's largely a matter of phrasing: Don't tell the interviewer you're born-again; say faith is a very important part of your life. And here, if I can drop the open-minded pretense real quick, is where the stickier problem of *actually being any good* comes in, because a question that must be asked is whether a hard-core Christian who turns nineteen and finds he or she can write first-rate songs (someone like Damien Jurado) would ever have anything whatsoever to do with Christian rock. Talent tends to come hand in hand with a certain base level of subtlety. And believe it or not, the Christian-rock establishment sometimes expresses a kind of resigned approval of the way groups like U2 or Switchfoot (who played Creation while I was there and had a monster secular-radio hit at the time with "Meant to Live" but whose management wouldn't allow them to be photographed onstage) take quiet pains to distance themselves from any unambiguous Jesus-loving, recognizing that this is the surest way to connect with the world (you know that's how they refer to us, right? We're "of the world"). So it's possible—and indeed seems likely—that Christian rock is a musical genre, the only one I can think of, that has excellence-proofed itself.

. . .

It was late, and the Jews had sown discord. What Bub had said was true: There were Jews at Creation. These were Jews for Jesus, it emerged, two startlingly pretty high school girls from Richmond. They'd been sitting by the fire—one of them mingling fingers with Pee Wee—when Bub and Ritter and I returned from seeing Jars of Clay. Pee Wee was younger than the other guys, and cute, and he gazed at the girls admiringly when they spoke. At a certain point, they mentioned to Ritter that he would writhe in hell for having tattoos (he had a couple); it was what their people believed. Ritter had not taken the news all that well. He was fairly confident about his position among the elect. There was debate;

Pee Wee was forced to escort the girls back to their tents, while Darius worked to calm Ritter. "They may have weird ideas," he said, "but we worship the same God."

The fire had burned to glowing coals, and now it was just we men, sitting on coolers, talking late-night hermeneutics blues. Bub didn't see how God could change His mind, how He could say all that crazy shit in the Old Testament—like don't get tattoos and don't look at your uncle naked—then take it back in the New.

"Think about it this way," I said. "If you do something that really makes Darius mad, and he's pissed at you, but then you do something to make it up to him, and he forgives you, that isn't him changing his mind. The situation has changed. It's the same with the old and new covenants, except Jesus did the making up."

Bub seemed pleased with this explanation. "I never heard anyone say it like that," he said. But Darius stared at me gimlet-eyed across the fire. He knew my gloss was theologically sound, and he wondered where I'd gotten it. The guys had been gracefully dancing around the question of what I believed—"where my walk was at," as they would have put it—all night.

We knew one another fairly well by now. Once Pee Wee had returned, they'd eagerly showed me around their camp. Most of their tents were back in the forest, where they weren't supposed to be; the air was cooler there. Darius had located a small stream about thirty yards away and, using his hands, dug out a basin. This was supplying their drinking water.

It came out that these guys spent much if not most of each year in the woods. They lived off game—as folks do, they said, in their section of Braxton County. They knew all the plants of the forest, which were edible, which cured what. Darius pulled out a large piece of cardboard folded in half. He opened it under my face: a mess of sassafras roots. He wafted their scent of black licorice into my face and made me eat one.

Then he remarked that he bet I liked weed. I allowed as how I might not *not* like it. "I used to love that stuff," he told me. Seeing that I was taken aback, he said, "Man, to tell you the truth, I wasn't even convicted about it. But it's socially unacceptable, and that was getting in the way of my Christian growth."

The guys had put together what I did for a living—though, to their credit, they didn't seem to take this as a reasonable explanation for my being there—and they gradually got the sense that I found them exotic (though it was more than that). Slowly, their talk became an ecstasy of self-definition. They were passionate to make me see *what kind of guys they were.* This might have grown tedious, had they been any old kind of guys. But they were the kind of guys who believed that God had personally interceded and made it possible for four of them to fit into Ritter's silver Chevrolet Cavalier for the trip to Creation.

"Look," Bub said, "I'm a pretty big boy, right? I mean, I'm stout. And Darius is a big boy"—here Darius broke in and made me look at his calves, which were muscled to a degree that hinted at deformity; "I'm a freak," he said; Bub sighed and went on without breaking eye contact—"and you know Ritter is a big boy. Plus we had two coolers, guitars, an electric piano, our tents and stuff, all"—he turned and pointed, turned back, paused—"in that Chevy." He had the same look in his eyes as earlier, when he'd told me there were Jews. "I think that might be a miracle," he said.

In their lives, they had known terrific violence. Ritter and Darius met, in fact, when each was beating the shit out of the other in middle-school math class. Who won? Ritter looked at Darius, as if to clear his answer, and said, "Nobody." Jake once took a fishing pole that Darius had accidentally stepped on and broken and beat him to the ground with it. "I told him, 'Well, watch where you're stepping,' " Jake said. (This memory made Darius laugh so hard he removed his glasses.) Half of their childhood friends had been murdered—shot or stabbed over drugs or nothing. Others had killed themselves. Darius's grandfather, great-uncle, and onetime best friend had all committed suicide. When Darius was growing up, his father was in and out of jail; at least once, his father had done hard time. In Ohio he stabbed a man in the chest (the man had refused to stop "pounding on" Darius's grandfather). Darius caught a lot of grief—"Your daddy's a jailbird!"—during those years. He'd carried a chip on his shoulder from that.

"You came up pretty rough," I said.

"Not really," Darius said. "Some people ain't got hands and feet." He talked about how much he loved his father. "With all my heart—he's the best. He's brought me up the way that I am."

"And anyway," he added, "I gave all that to God—all that anger and stuff. He took it away."

God had left him enough to get by on. Earlier in the evening, the guys had roughed up Pee Wee a little and tied him to a tree with ratchet straps. Some other Christians must have reported his screams to the staff, because a guy in an orange vest came stomping up the hill. Pee Wee hadn't been hurt much, but he put on a show of tears, to be funny. "They always do me like that," he said. "Save me, mister!"

The guy was unamused. "It's not them you got to worry about," he said. "It's me."

Those were such foolish words! Darius came forward like some hideously fast-moving lizard on a nature show. "I'd watch it, man," he said. "You don't know who you're talking to. This'n here's as like to shoot you as shake your hand."

The guy somehow appeared to move back without actually taking a step. "You're not allowed to have weapons," he said.

"Is that right?" Darius said. "We got a conceal 'n' carry right there in the glove box. Mister, I'm from West Virginia—I know the law."

"I think you're lying," said the guy. His voice had gone a bit warbly.

Darius leaned forward, as if to hear better. His eyes were leaving his skull. "How would you know that?" he said. "Are you a prophet?"

"I'm Creation staff!" the guy said.

All of a sudden, Jake stood up—he'd been watching this scene from his seat by the fire. The fixed polite smile on his face was indistinguishable from a leer. "Well," he said, "why don't you go somewhere and *create* your own problems?"

I realize that these tales of the West Virginia guys' occasional truculence might appear to gainsay what I claimed earlier about "not one word spoken in anger," etc. But look, it was playful. Darius, at least, was performing a bit for me. And if you take into account what the guys have to be on guard for all the time back home, the notable thing becomes how effectively they checked their instincts at Creation.

In any case, we operated with more or less perfect impunity from then on.

This included a lot of very loud, live music between two and three o'clock in the morning. The guys were running their large PA off the battery in Jake's truck. Ritter and Darius had a band of their own back home, First Verse. They were responsible for the music at their church. Ritter had an angelic tenor that seemed to be coming out of a body other than his own. And Josh was a good guitar player; he had a Les Paul and an effects board. We passed around the acoustic. I had to dig to come up with Christian tunes. I did "Jesus," by Lou Reed, which they liked okay. But they really enjoyed "Redemption Song." When I finished, Bub said, "Man, that's really Christian. It really is." Darius made me teach it to him; he said he would take it home and "do it at worship."

Then he jumped up and jogged to the electric piano, which was on a stand ten feet away. He closed his eyes and began to play. I know enough piano to know what good technique sounds like, and Darius played very, very well. He improvised for an hour. At one point, Bub went and stood beside him with his hands in his pockets, facing the rest of us, as if guarding his friend while the latter was in this vulnerable trance state. Ritter whispered to me that Darius had been offered a music scholarship to a college in West Virginia; he went to visit a friend, and a professor heard him messing around on the school's piano. The dude offered him a full ride then and there. Ritter couldn't really explain why Darius had turned it down. "He's kind of our Rain Man," Ritter said.

At some juncture, I must have taken up my lantern and crept back down the hill, since I sat up straight the next morning, fully dressed in the twenty-nine-footer. The sound that woke me was a barbaric moan, like that of an army about to charge. Early mornings at Creation were about "Praise and Worship," a new form of Christian rock in which the band and the audience sing, all together, as loud as they can, directly to God. It gets rather intense.

·　　　·　　　·

The guys had told me they meant to spend most of today at the main stage, checking out bands. But hey, fuck that. I'd already checked out a band. Mine was to stay in this trailer, jotting impressions.

It was hot, though. As it got hotter, the light brown carpet started to give off fumes from under its plastic hide. I tumbled out the side hatch and went after Darius, Ritter, and Bub. In the light of day, one could see there were pretty accomplished freaks at this thing: a guy in a skirt wearing lace on his arms; a strange little androgynous creature dressed in full cardboard armor, carrying a sword. They knew they were in a safe place, I guess.

The guys left me standing in line at a lemonade booth; they didn't want to miss Skillet, one of Ritter's favorite bands. I got my drink and drifted slowly toward where I thought they'd be standing. Lack of food, my filthiness, impending sunstroke: These were ganging up on me. Plus the air down here smelled faintly of poo. There were a lot of blazing-hot portable toilets wafting miasma whenever the doors were opened.

I stood in the center of a gravel patch between the food and the crowd, sort of gumming the straw, quadriplegically probing with it for stubborn pockets of meltwater. I was a ways from the stage, but I could see well enough. Something started to happen to me. The guys in the band were middle-aged. They had blousy shirts and half-hearted arena-rock moves from the mid-eighties.

What was . . . this feeling? The singer kept grinning between lines, like if he didn't, he might collapse. I could just make out the words:

> There's a higher place to go
> (beyond belief, beyond belief),
> Where we reach the next plateau,
> (beyond belief, beyond belief) . . .

The straw slipped from my mouth.

"Oh, shit. It's Petra."

$$\cdot \qquad \cdot \qquad \cdot$$

It was 1988. The guy who brought me in we called Verm (I'll use people's nicknames here; they don't deserve to be dragooned into my memory-voyage). He was a short, good-looking guy with a dark ponytail and a devilish laugh, a skater and an ex-pothead, which had got him kicked out of his house a year or so before we met. His folks belonged to this nondenominational church in Ohio, where I went to high school. It was a movement more than a church—thousands of members, even then. I hear it's bigger now. "Central meeting" took place in an empty warehouse, for reasons of space, but the smaller meetings were where it was at: home church (fifty people or so), cell group (maybe a dozen). Verm's dad said, Look, go with us once a week and you can move back in.

Verm got saved. And since he was brilliant (he became something of a legend at our school because whenever a new foreign student enrolled, he'd sit with her every day at lunch and make her give him language lessons till he was proficient), and since he was about the most artlessly gregarious human being I've ever known, and since he knew loads of lost souls from his druggie days, he became a champion evangelizer, a golden child.

I was new and nurturing a transcendent hatred of Ohio. Verm found out I liked the Smiths, and we started swapping tapes. Before long, we were hanging out after school. Then the moment came that always comes when you make friends with a born-again: "Listen, I go to this thing on Wednesday nights. It's like a Bible study—no, listen, it's cool. The people are actually really cool."

They were, that's the thing. In fifteen minutes, all my ideas about Christians were put to flight. They were smarter than any bunch I'd been exposed to (I didn't grow up in Cambridge or anything, but even so), they were accepting of every kind of weirdness, and they had that light that people who are pursuing something higher give off. It's attractive, to say the least. I started asking questions, lots of questions. And they loved that, because they had answers. That's one of the ways Evangelicalism works. Your average agnostic doesn't go through life just *primed* to offer a clear, considered defense of, say, intratextual Scriptural inconsistency. But born-agains train for that chance encounter with the inquisitive stranger. And when you're a fourteen-year-old carting around some fairly undernourished intellectual ambitions, and a charismatic adult sits you down and explains that if you transpose this span of years onto the Hebrew calendar, and multiply that times seven, and plug in a date from the reign of King Howsomever, then you plainly see that this passage predicts the birth of Christ almost to the hour, despite the fact that the Gospel writers didn't have access to this information! I, for one, was dazzled.

But also powerfully stirred on a level that didn't depend on my naïveté. The sheer passionate engagement of it caught my imagination: Nobody had told me there were Christians like this. They went at the Bible with grad-seminar intensity, week after week. Mole was their leader (short for Moloch; he had started the whole thing, back in the '70s). He had a wiry, dark beard and a pair of nail-gun cobalt eyes. My Russian-novel fantasies of underground gatherings—shared subversive fervor—were flattered and, it seemed, embodied. Here was counterculture, without sad hippie trappings.

Verm hugged me when I said to him, in the hallway after a meeting, "I think I might believe." When it came time for me to go all the way—to "accept Jesus into my heart" (in that time-honored formulation)—we prayed the prayer together.

Three years passed. I waxed strong in spirit. Verm and I were sort of heading up the high school end of the operation now. Mole had discovered (I had discovered, too) that I was good with words, that I could talk in front of people; Verm and I started leading Bible study once a month. We were saving souls like mad, laying up treasure for ourselves in heaven. I was never the recruiter he was, but I grasped subtlety; Verm would get them there, and together we'd start on their heads. Witnessing, it's called. I had made some progress socially at school, which gave us access to the popular crowd; in this way, many were brought to the Lord. Verm and I went to conferences and on "study retreats"; we started taking classes in theology, which the group offered—free of charge—for promising young leaders. And always, underneath but suffusing it all, there were the cell-group meetings, every week, on Friday or Saturday nights, which meant I could stay out till morning. (My Episcopalian parents were thoroughly mortified by the whole business, but it's not easy telling your kid to *stop spending so much time at church.*)

Cell group was typically held in somebody's dining room, somebody pretty high up in the group. You have to understand what an honor it was to be in a cell with Mole. People would see me at central meeting and be like, "How is that, getting to rap with him every week?" It was awesome. He really got down with the Word (he had a wonderful old hippie way of talking; everything was something *action*: "time for some fellowship action . . . let's get some chips 'n' salsa action"). He carried a heavy "study Bible"—no King James for the nondenominationals; too many inaccuracies. When he cracked open its hand-tooled leather cover, you knew it was on. And no joke: The brother was gifted. Even handicapped by the relatively pedestrian style of the New American Standard version, he could twist a verse into your conscience like a bone screw, make you think Christ was standing there nodding approval. The prayer session alone would last an hour. Afterward, there was always a fire in the backyard. Mole would sit and whack a machete into a chopping block. He smoked cheap cigars; he let us smoke cigarettes. The guitar went around. We'd talk about which brother was struggling with sin—did he need counsel? Or about the end of the world: It'd be soon. We had to save as many as we could.

I won't inflict on you all my reasons for drawing away from the fold. They were clichéd, anyway, and not altogether innocent. Enough to say I started reading books Mole hadn't recommended. Some of them seemed pretty smart—and didn't jibe with the Bible. The defensive theodicy he'd drilled into me during those nights of heady exegesis developed cracks. The hell stuff: I never made peace with it. Human beings were capable of forgiving those who'd done them terrible wrongs, and we all agreed that human beings were maggots compared with God, so what was His trouble, again? I looked around and saw people who'd never have a chance to come to Jesus; they were too badly crippled. Didn't they deserve—more than the rest of us, even—to find His succor, after this life?

Belief and nonbelief are two giant planets, the orbits of which don't touch. Everything about Christianity can be justified *within the context of Christian belief.* That is, if you accept its terms. Once you do, your belief starts modifying the data (in ways that are *themselves* defensible, see?), until eventually the data begin to reinforce belief. The precise moment of illogic can never be isolated and may not exist. Like holding a magnifying glass at arm's length and bringing it toward your eye: Things are upside down, they're upside down, they're right side up. What lay between? If there was something, it passed too quickly to be observed. This is why you can never reason true Christians out of the faith. It's not, as the adage has it, because they were never reasoned into it—many were—it's that faith is a logical door which locks behind you. What looks like a line of thought is steadily warping into a circle, one that closes with you inside. If this seems to imply that no apostate was ever a true Christian and that therefore, I was never one, I think I'd stand by both of those statements. Doesn't the fact that I can't write about my old friends without an apologetic tone just show that I never deserved to be one of them?

The break came during the winter of my junior year. I got a call from Verm late one afternoon. He'd promised Mole he would do this thing, and now he felt sick. Sinus infection (he always had sinus infections). Had I ever heard of Petra? Well, they're a Christian-rock band, and they're playing the arena downtown. After their shows, the singer invites anybody who wants to know more about Jesus to come backstage, and they have people, like, waiting to talk to them.

The promoter had called up Mole, and Mole had volunteered Verm, and now Verm wanted to know if I'd help him out. I couldn't say no.

The concert was upsetting from the start; it was one of my first encounters with the other kinds of Evangelicals, the hand-wavers and the weepers and all (we liked to keep things "sober" in the group). The girl in front of me was signing all the words to the songs, but she wasn't deaf. It was just horrifying.

Verm had read me, over the phone, the pamphlet he got. After the first encore, we were to head for the witnessing zone and wait there. I went. I sat on the ground.

Soon they came filing in, the seekers. I don't know what was up with the ones I got. I think they may have gone looking for the restroom and been swept up by the stampede. They were about my age and wearing hooded brown sweatshirts—mouths agape, eyes empty. I asked them the questions: What did they think about all they'd heard? Were they curious about anything Petra talked about? (There'd been lots of "talks" between songs.)

I couldn't get them to speak. They stared at me like they were waiting for me to slap them.

This was my opening. They were either rapt or retarded, and whichever it was, Christ called on me to lay down my testimony.

The sentences wouldn't form. I flipped though the list of dogmas, searching for one I didn't essentially think was crap, and came up with nothing.

There might have ensued a nauseating silence, but I acted with an odd decisiveness to end the whole experience. I asked them if they wanted to leave—it was an all but rhetorical question—and said I did, too. We walked out together.

I took Mole and Verm aside a few nights later and told them my doubts had overtaken me. If I kept showing up at meetings, I'd be faking it. That was an insult to them, to God, to the group. Verm was silent; he hugged me. Mole said he respected my reasons, that I'd have to explore my doubts before my walk could be strong again. He said he'd pray for me. Unless he's undergone some radical change in character, he's still praying.

· · ·

Statistically speaking, my bout with Evangelicalism was probably unremarkable. For white Americans with my socioeconomic background (middle to upper-middle class), it's an experience commonly linked to one's teens and moved beyond before one reaches twenty. These kids around me at Creation—a lot of them were like that. How many even knew who Darwin was? They'd learn. At least once a year since college, I'll be getting to know someone, and it comes out that we have in common a high school "Jesus phase." That's always an excellent laugh. Except a phase is supposed to end—or at least give way to other phases—not simply expand into a long preoccupation.

Bless those who've been brainwashed by cults and sent off for deprogramming. That makes it simple: You put it behind you. But this group was no cult. They persuaded; they never pressured, much less threatened. Nor did they punish. A guy I brought into the group—we called him Goog—is still a close friend. He leads meetings now and spends part of each year doing pro bono dental work in Cambodia. He's never asked me when I'm coming back.

My problem is not that I dream I'm in hell or that Mole is at the window. It isn't that I feel psychologically harmed. It isn't even that I feel like a sucker for having bought it all. It's that I love Jesus Christ.

"The latchet of whose shoes I am not worthy to unloose." I can barely write that. He was the most beautiful dude. Forget the Epistles, forget all the bullying stuff that came later. Look at what He said. Read *The Jefferson Bible*. Or better yet, read *The Logia of Yeshua*, by Guy Davenport and Benjamin Urrutia, an unadorned translation of all the sayings ascribed to Jesus that modern scholars deem authentic. There's your man. His breakthrough was the aestheticization of weakness. Not in what conquers, not in glory, but in what's fragile and what suffers—there lies sanity. And salvation. "Let anyone who has power renounce it," he said. "Your father is compassionate to all, as you should be." That's how He talked, to those who knew Him.

Why should He vex me? Why is His ghost not friendlier? Why can't I just be a good Enlightenment child and see in His life a sustaining example of what we can be, as a species?

Because once you've known Him as God, it's hard to find comfort in the man. The sheer sensation of life that comes with a total, all-pervading notion of being—the pulse of consequence one projects onto even the humblest things—the pull of that won't slacken.

And one has doubts about one's doubts.

•   •   •

"D'ye hear that mountain lion last night?"

It was dark, and Jake was standing over me, dressed in camouflage. I'd been hunched over on a cooler by the ashes for a number of hours, waiting on the guys to get back from wherever they'd gone.

I told him I hadn't heard anything. Bub came up from behind, also in camo. "In the middle of the night," he said. "It woke me up."

Jake said, "It sounded like a baby crying."

"Like a little bitty baby," Bub said.

Jake was messing with something at my feet, in the shadows, something that looked alive. Bub dropped a few logs onto the fire and went to the Chevy for matches.

I sat there trying to see what Jake was doing. "You got that lantern?" he said. It was by my feet; I switched it on.

He started pulling frogs out of a poke. One after another. They strained in his grip and lashed at the air.

"Where'd you get those?" I asked.

"About half a mile that way," he said. "It ain't private property if you're in the middle of the creek." Bub laughed his high expressionless laugh.

"These ain't too big," Jake said. "In West Virginia, well, we got ones the size of chickens."

Jake started chopping their bodies in half. He'd lean forward and center his weight on the hand that held the knife, to get a clean cut, tossing the legs into a frying pan. Then he'd stab each frog in the brain and flip the upper parts into a separate pile. They kept twitching, of course—their nerves. Some were a little less dead than that. One in particular stared up at me, gulping for air, though his lungs were beside him, in the grass.

"Could you do that one in the brain again?" I said. Jake spiked it, expertly, and grabbed for the next frog.

"Why don't you stab their brains before you take off the legs?" I asked.

He laughed. He said I cracked him up.

Darius, when he got back, made me a cup of hot sassafras tea. "Drink this, it'll make you feel better," he told me. I'd never said I felt bad. Jake lightly sautéed the legs in butter and served them to me warm. "Eat this," he said. The meat was so tender, it all but dissolved on my tongue.

Pee Wee came back with the Jews, who were forced to tell us a second time that we were damned. (Leviticus 11:12, "Whatsoever hath no fins nor scales in the waters, that shall be an abomination unto you.") Jake, when he heard this, put on a show, making the demi-frogs talk like puppets, chewing the legs with his mouth wide open so all could see the meat.

The girls ran off again. Pee Wee went after them, calling, "Come on, they're just playin'!"

Darius peered at Jake. He looked not angry but saddened. Jake said, "Well, if he wants to bring them girls around here, they oughtn't to be telling us what we can eat."

"Wherefore, if meat make my brother to offend," Darius said, "I will eat no flesh while the world standeth."

"First Corinthians," I said.

"8:13," Darius said.

.   .   .

I woke without having slept—that evil feeling—and lay there steeling myself for the strains of Praise and Worship. When it became too much to wait, I boiled water and made instant coffee and drank it scalding from the lid of the peanutbutter jar. My body smelled like stale campfire. My hair had leaves and ash and things in it. I thought about taking a shower, but I'd made it two days without so much as acknowledging any of the twenty-nine-footer's systems; it would have been stupid to give in now.

I sat in the driver's seat and watched, through tinted glass, little clusters of Christians pass. They looked like people anywhere, only gladder, more self-contained. Or maybe they just looked like people anywhere. I don't know. I had no pseudo-anthropological moxie left. I got out and wandered. I sat with the crowd in front of the stage. There was a redheaded Christian speaker up there, pacing back and forth. Out of nowhere, he shrieked, "MAY YOU BE COVERED IN THE ASHES OF YOUR RABBI JESUS!" If I were to try to convey to you how loudly he shrieked this, you'd think I was playing wordy games.

I was staggering through the food stands when a man died at my feet. He was standing in front of the funnel-cake window. He was big, in his early sixties, wearing shorts and a short-sleeve button-down shirt. He just . . . died. Massive heart attack. I was standing there, and he fell, and I don't know whether there's some primitive zone in the brain that registers these things, but the second he landed, I knew he was gone. The paramedics jumped on him so fast, it was weird—it was like they'd been waiting. They pumped and pumped on his chest, blew into his mouth, ran IVs. The ambulance showed up, and more equipment appeared. The man's broad face had that slightly disgruntled look you see on the newly dead.

Others had gathered around; some thought it was all a show. A woman standing next to me said bitterly, "It's not a show. A man has died." She started crying. She took my hand. She was small with silver hair and black eyebrows. "He's fine, he's fine," she said. I looked at the side of her face. "Just pray for his family," she said. "He's fine."

·   ·   ·

I went back to the trailer and had, as the ladies say where I'm from, a colossal fucking go-to-pieces. I kept starting to cry and then stopping myself, for some reason. I felt nonsensically raw and lonely. What a dickhead I'd been, thinking the trip would be a lark. There were too many ghosts here. Everyone seemed so strange and so familiar. Plus I suppose I was starving. The frog meat was superb but meager—even Jake had said as much.

In the midst of all this, I began to hear, through the shell of the twenty-nine-footer, Stephen Baldwin giving a talk on the Fringe Stage—that's where the "edgier" acts are put on at Creation. If you're shaky on your Baldwin brothers, he's the vaguely troglodytic one who used to comb his bangs straight down and wear dusters. He's come to the Lord—I don't know if you knew. I caught him on cable a few months ago, some religious talk show. Him and Gary Busey. I don't remember what Baldwin said, because Busey was saying shit so weird the host got nervous. Busey's into "generational curses." If you're wondering what those are, too bad. I was born-again, not raised on meth.

Baldwin said many things; the things he said got stranger and stranger. He said his Brazilian nanny, Augusta, had converted him and his wife in Tucson, thereby fulfilling a prophecy she'd been given by her preacher back home. He said, "God allowed 9/11 to happen," that it was "the wrath of God," and that Jesus had told him to share this with us. He also said the Devil did 9/11. He said God wanted him "to make gnarly cool Christian movies." He said that in November we should vote for "the man who has the greatest faith." The crowd lost it; it seemed like the trailer might shake.

When Jake and Bub beat on the door, I'd been in there for hours, rereading *The Silenced Times* and the festival program. In the program, it said the candle-lighting ceremony was tonight. The guys had told me about it—it was one of the coolest things about Creation. Everyone gathered in front of the stage, and the staff handed out a candle to every single person there. The media handlers said there was a lookout you could hike to, on the mountain above the stage. That was the way to see it, they said.

When I opened the door, Jake was waving a newspaper. Bub stood behind him, smiling big. "Look at this," Jake said. It was

Wednesday's copy of *The Valley Log*, serving Southern Huntingdon County—"It is just a rumor until you've read it in *The Valley Log*."

The headline for the week read MOUNTAIN LION NOT BE-LIEVED TO BE THREAT TO CREATION FESTIVAL CAMPERS.

"Wha'd we tell you?" Bub said.

"At least it's not a threat," I said.

"Well, not to us it ain't," Jake said.

I climbed to their campsite with them in silence. Darius was sitting on a cooler, chin in hands, scanning the horizon. He seemed meditative. Josh and Ritter were playing songs. Pee Wee was listening, by himself; he'd blown it with the Jewish girls.

"Hey, Darius," I said.

He got up. "It's fixin' to shower here in about ten minutes," he said.

I went and stood beside him, tried to look where he was looking.

"You want to know how I know?" he said.

He explained it to me, the wind, the face of the sky, how the leaves on the tops of the sycamores would curl and go white when they felt the rain coming, how the light would turn a certain "dead" color. He read the landscape to me like a children's book. "See over there," he said, "how that valley's all misty? It hasn't poured there yet. But the one in back is clear—that means it's coming our way."

Ten minutes later, it started to rain, big, soaking, percussive drops. The guys started to scramble. I suggested we all get into the trailer. They looked at each other, like maybe it was a sketchy idea. Then Ritter hollered, "Get 'er done!" We all ran down the hillside, holding guitars and—in Josh's case—a skillet wherein the fried meat of some woodland creature lay ready to eat.

There was room for everyone. I set my lantern on the dining table. We slid back the panes in the windows to let the air in. Darius did card tricks. We drank spring water. Somebody farted; the conversation about who it had been lasted a good twenty minutes. The rain on the roof made a solid drumming. The guys were impressed with my place. They said I should fence it. With the money I'd get, I could buy a nice house in Braxton County.

We played guitars. The RV rocked back and forth. Jake wasn't into Christian rock, but as a good Baptist he loved old gospel tunes, and he called for a few, God love him. Ritter sang one that killed me. Also, I don't know what changed, but the guys were up for secular stuff. It turned out that Pee Wee really loved Neil Young; I mean, he'd never heard Neil Young before, but when I played "Powderfinger" for him, he sort of curled up like a kid, then made me play it again when I was done. He said I had a pretty voice.

We all told each other how good the other ones were, how everybody else should really think about a career in music. Josh played "Stairway to Heaven," and we got loud, singing along. Darius said, "Keep it down, man! We don't need everybody thinking this is the sin wagon."

The rain stopped. It was time to go. Two of the guys had to leave in the morning, and I needed to start walking if I meant to make the overlook in time for the candlelighting. They went with me as far as the place where the main path split off toward the stage. They each embraced me. Jake said to call them if I ever had "a situation that needs clearing up." Darius said God bless me, with meaning eyes. Then he said, "Hey, man, if you write about us, can I just ask one thing?"

"Of course," I said.

"Put in there that we love God," he said. "You can say we're crazy, but say that we love God."

The climb was long and steep. At the top was a thing that looked like a backyard deck. It jutted out over the valley, commanding an unobstructed view. Kids hung all over it like lemurs or something.

I pardoned my way to the edge, where the cliff dropped away. It was dark and then suddenly darker—pitch. They had shut off the lights at the sides of the stage. Little pinpricks appeared, moving along the aisles. We used to do candles like this at church, when I was a kid, on Christmas Eve. You light the edges, and the edges spread inward. The rate of the spread increases exponentially, and the effect is so unexpected, when, at the end, you have half the group lighting the other half's candles, it always seems like somebody flipped a switch. That's how it seemed now.

The clouds had moved off—the bright stars were out again. There were fireflies in the trees all over, and spread before me, far below, was a carpet of burning candles, tiny flames, many ten thousands. I was suspended in a black sphere full of flickering light.

And sure, I thought about Nuremberg. But mostly I thought of Darius, Jake, Josh, Bub, Ritter, and Pee Wee, whom I doubted I'd ever see again, whom I'd come to love, and who loved God—for it's true, I would have said it even if Darius hadn't asked me to, it may be the truest thing I will have written here: They were crazy, and they loved God—and I thought about the unimpeachable dignity of that love, which I never was capable of. Because knowing it isn't true doesn't mean you would be strong enough to believe if it were. Six of those glowing specks in the valley were theirs.

I was shown, in a moment of time, the ring of their faces around the fire, each one separate, each one radiant with what Paul called, strangely, "assurance of hope." It seemed wrong of reality not to reward such souls.

These are lines from a Czeslaw Milosz poem:

> And if they all, kneeling with poised palms,
> millions, billions of them, ended together with their
> illusion?
> I shall never agree. I will give them the crown.
> The human mind is splendid; lips powerful, and the
> summons so great it must open Paradise.

That's so exquisite. If you could just mean it. If one could only say it and mean it.

They all blew out their candles at the same instant, and the valley—the actual geographical feature—filled with smoke, there were so many.

I left at dawn, while creation slept.

Vanity Fair

Whatever the issue, columnist James Wolcott is both an unabashed moralist and a sublime stylist. With his bracing wit and boundless outrage, he skewers public figures who deceive and dissemble (tossing the occasional bouquet to those who live up to his exacting standards). His observations are original, his arguments persuasive, his energy unflagging.

James Wolcott

Caution:
Women Seething

*Why such outrage over Harvard
president Larry Summers's hazy
musing that women might be
innately less gifted at science?
Why such vitriol toward Michael
Kinsley over the dearth of female
bylines on the L.A. Times's op-ed
page? If the war between the
sexes is heating up again, there's
a good reason.*

Nothing clears the air and brings the fans alive like a rollicking battle between the sexes. Not the sort of cryptic, glacial psychosexual torture experiments that playwright Neil LaBute perpetrates, which pit passive-aggressive men against blank-canvas women, or the snippy rivalries between studs and starlets on reality TV, but a dramatic blowup that exposes seismic fault lines buried under the carpet. In James Thurber's cartoon fracas "The War Between Men and Women," the penguin-shaped foes engage in pitched battle on the staircase and hurl canned goods in the grocery store, but these days words are the weapons of choice, and only egos get bruised. We haven't had a real barn burner since Anita Hill vs. Clarence Thomas in

1991 (Thomas barely won the bout and has been bitter ever since), and so far this year we've been treated to a twin bill—Harvard president Larry Summers vs. Madame Curie, and the pesky writer-professor "Bruisin'" Susan Estrich vs. writer-editor Michael "the Mauler" Kinsley. I suspect these are only preliminary matches, with much more stormy petrel heading our way.

Readers relatively new to the planet never experienced or witnessed the visceral intensity of the civil war waged between the sexes in the late 60s–early 70s, when angry women and surly men squared off and wounded marriages were carried out on stretchers. (One typical memoir of the period was titled *Combat in the Erogenous Zone*.) Radical feminism had come steaming out of the political and social upheaval that produced Black Power, the anti-war movement, Students for a Democratic Society, the Young Lords, and the trippy counterculture, fueled in part by frustration with a male-dominated left as sexist as the worst chauvinist pigpen (typified by black radical Stokely Carmichael's gibe that "the only position for women in [the movement] is prone"). It was the time of Valerie Solanas's SCUM Manifesto (named for the Society for Cutting Up Men, of which Solanas was founder and sole member); the protest at the 1968 Miss America pageant, where feminists dumped girdles and brassieres into trash cans, inspiring the urban legend of bra burning; the feminist sit-in at the editorial offices of *Ladies' Home Journal*; and the flurry over Kate Millett's polemic *Sexual Politics*, which brought Norman Mailer into the gladiator ring, where he excited the mob with comments he later regretted, such as "women should be kept in cages." Feminist debate degenerated into fight night on television's *David Susskind Show*, hosted by a woolly liberal mystified by all the fuss. In her memoir *In Our Time*, Susan Brownmiller recalls being on a Susskind broadcast with the Amazonian Australian feminist and self-proclaimed "Intellectual Superwhore" Germaine Greer where "[Greer] had stripped to a sexy tank top, the male and female guests were trading insults as expected, and the invited audience of movement women was keeping up the heat by screaming at Susskind to take his hands off Germaine's bare shoulder." That never happens on *The Charlie Rose Show*, though he occasionally peers into the Andes.

Heated debate was a contact sport back then, but it wasn't all kung fu quarreling. Beyond and below the histrionics, intellectual breakthroughs and political progress were made in advancing equal-pay-for-equal-work, abortion rights, and rape awareness, and in combating sexual discrimination. In 1977, after the hostilities had tapered off enough to permit him to poke his head up for a look-see, essayist Wilfrid Sheed observed that the educated upper middle class had welcomed women's liberation with "reasonably open arms," but cautioned that this semi-embrace might not endure as "those rarest of plums, *interesting* jobs," became fewer in the workplace. He presciently warned, "The best and brightest who brought you women's lib may be the first to abandon it and start clawing each other the old way, man, woman, and black alike. . . . Already the most bitter fights take place on the most enlightened campuses. Even in graduate school, that cradle of civilization, women can usually count on an elbow in the eye right along with the lip service."

Enter Harvard president Lawrence H. Summers and chorus of faculty members nearly three decades later, grumbling across the quadrangle.

·　　·　　·

In January, Summers, who was treasury secretary under President Clinton, mused aloud at an academic conference that perhaps "intrinsic aptitude" helped account for the scarcity of women in the highest ranks of science and engineering, along with other factors. Two little words can undo so much, and this pair would usher in Summers's winter of discontent. Even before the full text of his remarks was made available, his hazy hypothesis tornado'd into the news and across the punditsphere, becoming an instant cause célèbre in the culture wars. A casualty of self-inflicted sound bite, Summers executed emergency damage control, back-pedaling like a punt returner and apologizing and appointing not one but two task forces to investigate how to attract more women into academic careers in science and engineering. This failed to placate the home team. In March, the Harvard faculty of arts and sciences, in a secret ballot, voted in favor of a motion for censure that read, "The faculty lacks confidence in the leadership of Lawrence H. Summers." The Furies had been unleashed and the gallop to judgment was on.

The intellectual caliber of the first responders barely rose above a popgun level. Sally Quinn, playing cute in *The Washington Post*, confessed that she was crummy at math herself and no great shakes in the natural sciences: "I took botany as my science requirement thinking it was flower arranging." George F. Will, also grooming in the pages of the *Post*, began his column with the *O.E.D.* definition of "hysteria" to diagnose M.I.T. biology professor Nancy Hopkins, who hyperventilated when she heard Summers's remarks. "My heart was pounding and my breath was shallow," she said afterward, adding that if she hadn't left the room she would have either thrown up or blacked out. Will pronounced Hopkins not only hysterical but delusional: "Hopkins's hysteria was a sample of America's campus-based indignation industry, which churns out operatic reactions to imagined slights." The erudite columnist neglected to include the etymology of the word "hysteria," from the Greek *hystera*, for womb, reflecting the ancient belief that women's emotional spasms were attributable to disturbances in their womb. He was, in short, slinging one of the oldest misogynist put-downs in the book: the poor things can't help behaving irrationally—nature just built them that way.

Taking their cue from Monsignor Will, conservative publications predictably portrayed the debate as political correctness run amok, the first move in a power coup. "A less-examined aspect of the Summers's soap opera is how the anti-Summers campaign fits in to the larger feminist game plan," wrote Carrie Lukas, director of policy at the Independent Women's Forum, privy to the secret minutes of the ballbusters' executive council. "Feminists are looking for opportunities to prove their relevance and power. Toppling Larry Summers would fit the bill nicely." Harvey Mansfield, a professor of government at Harvard, saw nothing quite so sinister in this witches' Sabbath. To him, Summers's detractors were just a batch of mixed-up dames, a bunch of silly hotheads too thin-skinned for manly differences of opinion in the billiard room. You know how sensitive these high-strung women can be. The least little thing, and they get all upset. "Feminists do not like to argue, and they consider you a case if you do not immediately agree with them," he wrote. " 'Raising consciousness' is their way of getting you to fall in with their plans, and 'tsk, tsk' is the only signal you should need and will get. Anyone who requires evidence and argument is already an enemy because he is considering a possibility hurtful to women."

> *Maureen Connolly (Coalition for Anti-Sexist Harvard):* I want Harvard to become a university that is supportive for women, for minorities, for it to stop being an old boys' club. And Larry Summers has not shown me . . .
> *Sean Hannity:* Oh, good grief.
> *Connolly:* It is not his job to guide the intellectual inquiry that happens at this university. It is the scholar's job to do that
> *Hannity:* You're overreacting, Maureen.
> —*Hannity and Colmes,*
> Fox News Channel, February 23, 2005.

•   •   •

Amid the hubbub, the original flash point of the controversy was nearly forgotten. A couple months after Summers's trip of the tongue, a front-page story in the *Wall Street Journal* by Jeanne

Whalen and Sharon Begley reported on studies of the new methods of teaching math in British classrooms that found girls closing the gender gap and even pulling ahead of the boys. These early results tended to refute the "intrinsic aptitude" theory Summers had floated. "The English experience with math education suggests that gender differences, even those that seem innate and based in biology, do not lead inevitably to any particular outcome," reported the *Journal*. "That view fits into a broader current sweeping over how scientists think of genetics. Many now believe that traits that seem intrinsic—meaning those grounded in the brain or shaped by a gene—are subject to cultural and social forces, and that these forces determine how a biological trait actually manifests itself in a person's behavior or abilities. An 'intrinsic' trait, in other words, does not mean an inevitable outcome, as many scientists had long thought." So put that in your Popeye pipe and smoke it, armchair he-men.

If the *Wall Street Journal* article didn't receive the notice it should have, it may be because the hellzapoppin' at Harvard was never primarily over innate aptitude and gender difference—Summers's comments were simply the spark that ignited the gunpowder barrels. His obstreperous, imperious manner made much of the faculty bristle (see Richard Bradley's book, *Harvard Rules*), and his pattern of governance at Harvard suggested that he had a larger problem with diversity and minority representation. Eugene Robinson pointed out in the *Washington Post*, "When Summers arrived at Harvard, one of his first acts was to dress down one of the university's best-known black scholars, Cornel West, for spending too much time on outside projects and not enough on research. Offended, West decamped to Princeton University [a bitter saga recounted by Sam Tanenhaus in *Vanity Fair*, June 2002]. But Harvard is lousy with peripatetic rock-star professors. One of Summers's most vocal defenders is Harvard Law School professor Alan Dershowitz, who found time amid his busy academic schedule to serve on the O. J. Simpson defense team, for heaven's sake. Why start with West? Was he doing anything his white colleagues don't do?" Well, he was cutting rap records, but in a democracy even a Harvard professor should be allowed to express his groove thang.

I don't discount these contributing factors, but they don't explain the ferocity of the media frenzy. What exploded, methinks, was a protracted buildup of exasperation over the persistent underrepresentation of women in positions of prominence and authority, and the mulish inability of powerful men to recognize the scope of the problem, or their tendency instead to rationalize it with voodoo genetics and Victorian-parlor sociology. Women are sick of hearing the same old sea chanteys. They've had their fill of men who insist on protecting their privileges and pretend it's the natural order of things.

·   ·   ·

Exasperation turned asp-tongued in the second card on the bill, an e-mail duel between former classmates at Harvard Law School, Susan Estrich and Michael Kinsley. More acrimonious and *ad hominem* than the Summers hoedown, this conflict blurred the usual left-right divisions largely because of the personalities involved. (There's something about Susan Estrich—some ineffable quality she possesses that, should it ever become effable, would peel paint off battleships—that annoys people of all faiths and political creeds.) A professor of law at the University of Southern California and campaign manager for Democratic presidential contender Michael Dukakis (oy), Estrich assigned her students to tally the number of female contributors to the *Los Angeles Times* op-ed page and discovered a lopsided ratio of men to women. In one nine-week stretch, only 20 percent of the bylines belonged to women. Estrich began to lobby Kinsley, the founding editor of *Slate*, who assumed editorship of the *Times*'s op-ed page in 2004, barraging him with e-mails. And what e-mails. Estrich castigated

Kinsley for his "arrogance," called him a "jerk," and threatened to bad-mouth him at a charity event—"You want me to work that dinner about what a [expletive deleted] you are?" But the unkindest cut was when she posited that Kinsley's medical condition—Parkinson's disease—might be eroding his mental capacity, sneering, "People are beginning to think that your illness may have affected your brain, your judgment and your ability to do this job." Kinsley, demonstrating that his mind hadn't lost its saber swash, filleted Estrich's pretensions to crusaderhood without losing his cool. "If Susan wants to boycott media institutions that don't adequately reflect her progressive feminist values, maybe she should start by resigning from Fox News, where she is a commentator," he wrote in Washington's *Examiner* newspaper.

A personal note. I worked under Kinsley in the early 80s when he was the editor of *Harper's*; his managerial style was casual and collegial, not autocratic and rigid. I never heard anything different about his tenures at *The New Republic* and *Slate*. But it is also true that just because it's Susan Estrich creating an almighty stink doesn't mean the stinker may not have a legitimate gripe. More than a month before Estrich started hitting the "Send" button, Helena Cobban, a columnist for the *Christian Science Monitor*, had been running a scoreboard on her blog, Just World News, counting the number of male and female contributors to the op-ed page of the *Washington Post*. From December 21, 2004, to February 14, 2005, Cobban counted only 26 female bylines out of 260—a measly 10 percent. The *New York Times* op-ed page has only one female columnist, Maureen Dowd. The gender breakdown of the op-ed pages of the leading organs of manufactured consent can't be ascribed to women's being consensus seekers and tremulous wallflowers. The numbers are too indicting.

•   •   •

As columnist Katha "Bone Crusher" Pollitt wrote in *The Nation*, "Feminine psychology doesn't explain why all five of *USA Today*'s political columnists are male, or why *Time*'s eleven columnists are male—down to the four in Arts and Entertainment—or why at *Newsweek* it's one out of six in print and two out of thirteen on the Web. According to *Editor and Publisher*, the proportion of female syndicated columnists (one in four) hasn't budged since 1999." Pollitt ridiculed the notion that outreach efforts for female writers required some wild-country safari. "How hard could it be to 'find' Barbara Ehrenreich, who filled in for Thomas Friedman for one month last summer and wrote nine of the best columns the *Times* has seen in a decade? Or Dahlia Lithwick, legal correspondent for *Slate*, another Friedman fill-in, who actually possesses a deep grasp of the field she covers—which cannot always be said for John Tierney, who begins his *Times* column in April? . . . And, not to be one of those shrinking violets everyone's suddenly so down on, What about me? Am I a potted plant?"

A personal note. I have met Katha Pollitt, and she is neither a potted plant nor chopped liver.

.   .   .

Broadcast media aren't much better than their print elders. Fairness and Accuracy in Reporting—FAIR—took a spin across the dial and discovered . . . well, the title of its press release tells the story: "Women's Opinions Also Missing on Television." Once again men monopolize the blather. "An upcoming FAIR study has found that on television, as in print, female pundits are in short supply." FAIR focused its study on the Sunday-morning panel shows, crediting only NBC's *The Chris Matthews Show* with achieving gender equity, but even here there were problems. "While the *Chris Matthews Show* did well on gender parity, every one of its 49 female panelists was white." If it weren't for Gwen Ifill and Donna Brazile, the other shows would have been as lily-white as a Confederate ball, too. FAIR: "The dearth of women pundits (and particularly women of color) on television can also be traced in part to the overall underrepresentation of women in the newsroom. In a 2004 survey, women made up only 37 percent of the staff at newspapers across the country (and only 34 percent of supervisors); women of color represented a paltry 6 percent (American Society of Newspaper Editors, 4/20/04)." Moreover, the skinny-assed white women who do populate Sunday panels tend to be politically neutered: "While a number of hard-right men are regularly featured on these shows—George Will, Charles Krauthammer, Robert Novak, Fred Barnes, Bill Kristol [some presumably harder than others, but let's not be prurient]—most of the women tapped are political correspondents who primarily provide analysis from a less openly opinionated viewpoint." It cites as an example National Public Radio political correspondent Mara Liasson, who's booked on Fox News pundit panels as the token liberal but in truth ladles out lukewarm mush, which still doesn't spare her from being interrupted and patronized by Fred Barnes and Brit Hume, who must have taken a graduate course in harrumphing together.

.   .   .

Make no mistake. A paucity of female pundits isn't the most burning issue on the ramparts. The real war between the sexes is waged out of the spotlight and in the trenches, a shadowy war of deprivation and restriction where women—particularly poor women—are increasingly denied access to contraception and family-planning information; blocked from advancing into management positions at mega-chains such as Wal-Mart (which is facing a huge class-action suit over sexual discrimination); shut out of the major action in Wall Street trading houses; brutalized body and soul as the primary victims of domestic violence (the Violence Against Women Act, enacted in 1994, comes up for renewal this year, its passage by no means certain); threatened by the Bush administration's stealth attempt to undermine Title IX, which was a boon to women's college athletics; and forced to bear the brunt of the class-warfare bankruptcy "reform" bill. ("Even without the reform, more than 1 million women will find themselves in bankruptcy court this year, outnumbering men by about 150,000, if past trends hold, says Jill Miller, chief executive officer of Women Work! in Washington, D.C."—*Christian Science Monitor*, April 4, 2005.) As religious values are imposed on the polity, this grinding rollback will only worsen, since fundamentalist religion of every flavor since the dawn of dust is based upon patriarchy and dominion over women's lives and bodies. Only when more women are visible in the opinionsphere will a cry be raised over this campaign of attrition, given that the men on *Imus* and Sunday-morning panels would rather talk war and football.

The rub is that if more women are picked for the op-ed pages and pundit roundups, they will most likely be chosen from the same incestuous Beltway-media clique that treats the rest of America as a giant appendix to their schmoozy careers. That was the lesson some of us took away when Kinsley said that one of the writers he had nabbed for his op-ed page was Margaret Carlson (of *Time* and a regular on CNN's *The Capital Gang*). Carlson, who has redefined mediocrity in every venue she's worked in, is no answer to anything. The real war between the sexes is a class war, a war that will remain under the radar as long as the self-perpetuating media and political establishment maintain the fiction that the country doesn't have a class system, that they all got where they are on "merit." All you have to do is listen to most of them to know that isn't so.

Wyatt Mason

A World
Unto Himself

The Rewards of Waiting
for a Debut Novel

First novels tend to share two traits: their authors typically are young when they write them, and their enduring virtues prove scarce if we seek them. Going back to
read, say, *Childhood*, Tolstoy's autobiographical debut at the age
of twenty-four, is an experience that lovers of *Anna Karenina* and
War and Peace cannot undertake with comparable rapture. Simi-
larly, a frequent visitor to Yoknapatawpha County, exploring
Faulkner's first novel, *Soldiers' Pay*, will find little to suggest its
twenty-nine-year-old maker capable of an *Absalom, Absalom!* (or,
for that matter, of winning a Nobel Prize). Flip through the inau-
gural efforts of a few, more recent titles: twenty-six-year-old Joyce
Carol Oates's hyperventilatory *With Shuddering Fall*; twenty-
eight-year-old Salman Rushdie's sci-fi folk yarn, *Grimus*; twenty-
nine-year-old E. L. Doctorow's western-by-numbers, *Welcome to
Hard Times* . . . If the lasting yield for readers of these books is
surely slight, their initial importance for their authors cannot be
overstated. However derivative or deeply flawed, immature or un-
derfed, the books were taken seriously enough to be published
and, therefore, to foster a fledgling readership for their unknown
authors. These young writers received a gift that few of their routinely unpublished peers will ever claim: they were offered encouragement to continue writing and developing before time and
unsuccess left them too discouraged to go on.

Other novelists, however, do not have to grow up in public. Apprentice works they produce in their twenties do not find their way into print, nor do the uneven gems they discharge in their early thirties. Instead, in solitude, absent editorial encouragement, denied the typically small but no less sustaining perks of publication (a reading here, a notice there), they nonetheless continue to burrow inward and invest further in their creations. Most of these investors yield nothing and are never heard from, an uncountable many. Some, though, with fortitude and luck, continue to confront themselves daily, second-guessing and redrafting through the years. And then, pale and pushing middle age, they emerge from the darkness of basement apartments bearing, of all things, masterpieces in manuscript boxes—suggesting that the gift of early publication can be the most mixed of blessings.

For wasn't it worth the wait when Joseph Heller, at the ripe age of thirty-eight, came to fruition with *Catch-22*; or Ralph Ellison, nearing forty, came of age with *Invisible Man*; or William Golding, at forty-three, turned up with *Lord of the Flies*; or Walker Percy, at forty-five, at last arrived with *The Moviegoer*? However unique, each of these novels shares a maturity of form and thought that products of the young, in most every case, can only feign. What sustained their makers through the dark years? From what place did these stalwarts draw such enduring resourcefulness? James Joyce, who suffered some on the road to himself and to us, ventured an answer that tidily acknowledges the fear that every aging author, unpublished, must face down: "Youth has an end: the end is here. It will never be. You know that well. What then? Write it, damn you, write it! What else are you good for?"

.   .   .

At seventy-two years old, Charles Chadwick, lately of London, has found any number of things to be "good for" during the course of his life. He has worked as a hotel houseman and valet; a campground clerk and a post-office sorter; a teacher at an Indian set-tlement; an assistant librarian at a museum; a civil servant offici-ating rural regions of Zambia; a lecturer in the proper adminis-tration of such regions; an assistant director for British Council installations in Kenya and Nigeria; and a director for same in Brazil, Canada, and Poland. Since his retirement from twenty-five years of international service, he has also served as an occasional election observer in Ghana, Pakistan, Cameroon, South Africa, Bosnia, and Uganda. And across fifty years of weekends around the world, Chadwick has been writing fiction—an endeavor, as he said in a recent interview, that he has long viewed as equivalent to "being an amateur watercolorist."

The fruits of this so-called amateurism are now on display. Al-though Chadwick has said that he had written four novels by the time he was thirty-five, as well as a fifth after he retired in 1992, it is only now—the month before Chadwick's seventy-third birthday—that a sixth novel has become the first of his books to find its way to readers. Weighing in at almost 700 oversized pages and running to 300,000 words (*Ulysses* is 267,000 words), *It's All Right Now* was written sporadically over the course of the last twenty-eight years, and the novel itself is a sporadic chronicle that spans those same three decades: the early 1970s through to the end of the millennium.

Chadwick's narrator, when we first meet him, is a forty-something Englishman named Tom Ripple. A husband of seven-teen years, a father of a boy and a girl, Ripple is exceptionally un-exceptional. He describes himself as a dedicated reader of "thrillers and lives of the great explorers mainly"; a devoted watcher of "es-capist tough stuff like *Starsky and Hutch, Hawaii Five-O, Kojak, The Avengers* and so forth"; and a dutiful adherent to a daily lunchtime ritual involving pornographic magazines. Ripple works for "a large trading company with offices throughout the world. My job is to produce tables and charts showing trends in sales and the like. . . . My boss is younger than I am and one can almost hear

him panting in his efforts to get to the top." Ripple has no illusions
about the significance of his employment: "There is nothing remotely interesting or important I could [say] about my job without lying." His responsibilities are limited; so long as he provides
his younger superior with the mutually acceptable minimum,
Ripple's job is secure:

> Conveniently for both of us, I'm his willing vassal. I turn in
> my work on time and he's never faulted it. He therefore
> thinks I'm a good chap and does not make enquiries of me
> that would lead him to conclude my job is overpaid and
> otherwise a complete doddle. I arm him with immaculate
> tables and charts and other data which he passes off as his
> own. I am quite happy with this state of affairs. I am glad he
> can depend on me because I have no choice but to depend
> on him. The thought of having to find another job puts me
> into a panic. He is my protector, for as long as I serve him
> well. It is a feudal relationship.

As with his workplace, so, too, his home: equally ordinary, sim-
ilarly stultifying. There, in a small house located in an "unnote-
worthy north London suburb," he feels himself to be at the whim
of another ruling hand, one belonging to his wife. "Seen upside
down," he remarks when recalling a family picnic, "she had the
look of a bearded tyrant caught in an off moment." Her "tyranni-
cal" reign over him, though, is hardly that of a needling sitcom
harpy; rather, "she is an impossible woman to fault. She knows
her own mind, is useful to the community, occupies her time
gainfully, is an admirable parent, in short, God knows (she
knows), is everything that I am not." Ripple's parenthetical "(she
knows)," poking through the otherwise perfunctory portrait of
Wife As Upstanding Citizen, suggests another register to Ripple's
voice. Although initially relegated to staccato asides, this more
candid, more engaging slice of self will become, as the book un-
folds, a defining feature of both Ripple and his book.

At the outset, though, Ripple is defined less by how he views himself than by how the world responds to him. The indifference of his children, twelve-year-old Virginia and Adrian, who is a few years younger, matters perhaps most of all; Ripple feels it every evening he returns from his work:

> As I hang up my coat in the hall I shout a word or two of greeting through to the living room where my children are watching the news. I try to vary the greeting but doubt if they notice it. "Hi there!" "Hallo, chaps!" "Home again!" "Evening, folks!" are about the extent of my range. There seldom being a response, I put my head round the door and repeat myself. My children glance up, sometimes raise a hand, sometimes smile, what is known as a ghost of one. . . .
> If my wife is there too, she says, "Hallo, dear," and to the children, "Say hallo to your father." Whereupon they say "Hi!" in chorus without looking away from the television for even a split second.

Ripple himself doesn't know how to act around his children; even when his adolescent daughter offers a rare display of spontaneous affection, he is so uneasy with her transformation from girlhood to womanhood that he can't allow himself to touch her: "My daughter ran over to hug me when I told her and I held her arms wide to prevent any such thing." He is no more able to touch her than reach out to his son when, on a weekend his wife is away, the boy has difficult news he needs to share; a panicky Ripple meets the moment with an inner "Shit. Shit. Shit. Now I had to hear it."

As brazenly as Ripple admits to his own haplessness as a parent, initially he only hints at the emptiness such incapacity has hollowed in him: "So when I look down at my children before pouring myself a glass of sweet, cheap sherry to take up to my bath, I may fleetingly regret the days when they were all over me when I came back from work, my son prodding me with a weapon and ordering me to fall about all over the place, my daughter hugging my legs and begging to be lifted up on to my shoulders." As the book progresses, the profundity of this loss is more clearly sounded: "I sometimes think I'd like to hold him for a long time in my arms in silence, his head against my chest, as used to happen when he was very young and had come to some minor harm in body or spirit." He notes how holidays seem to be

> the only time we feel like a complete family. . . . My children have gone back to calling me Daddy, have asked my permission as well as my wife's to do things, have cavorted about with me at the water's edge and have occasionally held my hand when walking along the beach or wherever. . . . I see other families like us and it occurs to me we compare well with them. We have a healthy look about us. Our inner voices seem to have gone silent.

. . .

However sympathetic one might well be to the plight of a white-collar father, bored at work and estranged from wife and children, it must be said that this has become rather familiar fictional terrain. Chadwick, for his part, has been candid about a derivative element to his enterprise. The inspiration for *It's All Right Now*, he has said, is a "wonderful book" he read while living in Nigeria in the 1970s: Joseph Heller's *Something Happened*. "I think that triggered the style. It really impressed me. It was simply about a man who wrote about his life. I thought, 'How can this be, that somebody can write a wonderful book, about a man talking about rather ordinary circumstances?' "

Although there are stylistic echoes between Chadwick's and Heller's books—compare Chadwick's "My son has stopped asking me about my work. A long time ago he stopped asking me how strong I am" with Heller's "My boy has stopped talking to me, and I don't think I can stand it. (He doesn't seem to like me.)"; or Chadwick's "Without adding (thinking?)" with Heller's "each of these women (girls?)"—they are only similarities of surface, the thinnest veneer. For Chadwick is up to something patently different from merely offering an English variation on the American theme of suburban ennui. Rather than present a character from the outside, as Updike did ("Rabbit Angstrom, coming up the alley in a business suit, stops and watches . . . "), or allow us to snoop on the carefully calibrated stream of consciousness of Heller's Slocum (whose sentences contain allusions that seem less within the reach of a mid-range corporate executive than an erudite literary novelist: "Both our children are unhappy, each in his (or her) separate way . . ."), Chadwick is presenting Ripple presenting himself—with convincing transparency. For if we can never forget when reading Updike's pleasurable prose that we are mulling an aesthetic experience; or, when reading Heller's, with his humor and careful plotting, that we are enjoying a literary one; when reading *It's All Right Now*, we have the uncommon experience that we are observing the inner workings of a real, rather than a conspicuously constructed, being. Nor does Ripple appear to be a novel's narrator, or even a literary character at all. A man suspicious of, and uninterested in, literature, he has elected to sit down and write down what is unfolding in his life, the book we have in our hands: "Well, one has to begin somewhere, on any old scrap of paper. I'm not sure what the point of it is. We shall have to see. It may take quite a time."

A question that will lurk beneath and at times bubble up from each word Ripple writes over the next three decades is, then, precisely why he has undertaken this project, why he "has to begin" writing at all on his present "scrap of paper" and then on the countless more to come. Ripple ventures an early answer:

It occurs to me to ask myself . . . why I have started writing about my life like this—except that I have time in the office to do it and it helps to make me look busy. I suppose I might be curious to know where it will take me and want to try some exploring of my own perhaps, not knowing what I'll find until I get there. In the meantime it gives clarity to, and saves the repetition of, all the talking to myself I do—no more or less than other people I don't suppose.

With the conspicuous innocence of Ripple's "I might be curious"; with his desire to supplement the reading of famous explorers in favor of doing "some exploring" of his own; with his claim of "not knowing what I'll find until I get there": it is nearly impossible not to feel the impulse to question his motives—and his reliability. After all, readers have learned that the history of the novel is studded with similar, seemingly offhand musings by narrators, such as those of Ford Madox Ford's Dowell in *The Good Soldier*, who posed his own "You may well ask why I write. And yet my reasons are quite many . . ."—"reasons" the innocence of which we come to understand are not to be relied on: there will, we assume, be a catch. For the reader, playing the game of trying to fish for the truthfulness of the storyteller can become—in books ranging from *Lolita* in the deep end to *The Remains of the Day* in the wading pool—a significant feature of the fun: such narrators are confessing (we grow increasingly sure), but to what (we increasingly wonder)?

Nevertheless, while reading *It's All Right Now* we soon arrive at the understanding that no such game is being played: we can dispense with the effort required to distinguish the false from the true, for Ripple isn't another unreliable narrator, quite the opposite. He is a man striving to be more and more reliable. Shortly after we meet Ripple, his wife leaves, taking their children with her, for she cannot rely on her husband's capacities as a father. What proves moving about Ripple's shortcomings is how clearly good his intentions are, their goodness nonetheless outpaced by the badness of the encroaching world.

Ripple's manner of dealing with adversities big and small, however, is to deny them. When he senses, among a group of people, that "there was discomfort in the air," and he wishes "there was a game we could all play," he is unable to find a game, or act in any outward way, that might reduce the tension. In those instances when he does manage to take action, it is invariably in the form of humor: he relentlessly tries to joke his way past suffering. Take this routine he delivers for his daughter's "benefit":

> "People have funny beliefs in Germany, some of them. I was at this party and heard this bloke next to me going on about little round red Jesus, smelly blue Jesus, smooth holy Jesus, Jesus for mice and Jesus that keeps you awake at night and cauliflower Jesus . . ."
> She got it then and began to giggle which made her cry again.

Jesus, cheeses: funny, no? Well, not so much if the daughter in question is, in fact, lying in a hospital bed after a car accident that happened with her soon-to-be stepfather at the wheel. And less funny still if the reason Ripple was trying to make her giggle was not to cheer her up at all but because he predicted that, with the emotional wound from her parents' separation fresh, her father's familiar foolishness would cause her to cry—from which he would gain confirmation that she still loved him: "That's my only excuse for the greed of my love and makes me no less ashamed of it."

"Will I ever learn," Ripple wonders, "the limits of humour?" Much of the drama of *It's All Right Now* lies in the friction created by the limits of Ripple's two very different selves: the irresponsible outer self, so indefensibly and frequently glib, and the thoughtful, responsible inner self we meet on the page. As we come to appreciate the overtures that the latter is making to us, we cannot help but feel remorse for the former's unstinting tendency to supply still more miserable grist.

In the hands of another novelist, such as a dark comedian like Martin Amis, this onslaught of harrowing material would be a forced death march that no reader could endure, yet Ripple's inner world blossoms on the page with writing that drives a reader onward. Although Ripple will not again enjoy the caring of a wife (or even the companionability of a lasting friendship), the world that opens up to him while he writes becomes a refuge. Seated at his desk, he can act appropriately by memorializing inappropriate moments lived. Quite early on, however, Ripple notes how difficult even this act can be. "The problem," he writes, "is how not to alter what happened in the light, or shadow, of what happened later":

> how not to impose a pattern on it so as to feel wise after the event, get increasing satisfaction the more one writes from the composition itself, make a fiction of it in fact so that if a change occurred from the first to the third person singular you'd hardly notice the difference. By then anything goes and you don't have to worry about the real and the true, a yarn is being spun and all for the sake of the finished cloth to be fashioned at will, which isn't anything like the snagged and tattered and altogether scruffy garment you were wearing and picking nervously at at the time.

Attentive to the truth, Ripple packs his language with telling surprises. Although he remarks, while married, that he prefers his wife to talk to their children because she could get across "my point of view with complete fairness, which is remarkable since I'm not at all sure I've got one, not to speak of," Ripple's once unspoken point of view begins to resonate with all the intensity of years of rumination. His sentences are consistent, in their hoarded compression, with a man who has been silent in his home life for far too long. Of a woman he dates after his marriage ends, he writes, "She worked in banking, a teller, and how"—managing with two commas to express everything we need to know about their relationship: brief, tedious, failed. And of a night spent with a woman he meets through the personal ads: "Someone listening in would have heard the noises of a small, unselective but contented zoo shortly after feeding time." And of his wife's and his own very different images of their maturing daughter: "I saw my daughter dressed as a nun being seized by cannibals. My wife saw her as a young woman with a dawning conscience."

As satisfactory as these lines may be, Ripple often proves unsatisfied with them. "So what is the truth?" he will write after an account of another lived debacle. "Now, some time later, I can say calmly . . . " before then going on to give us the far from calm account he "wrote at the time." When his daughter comes for a brief visit during which Ripple meets her husband-to-be and then makes a big production about lending them money, Ripple concludes his account of the visit not on a fleeting note of bitterness but on a resounding chord of sorrow after he watches her drive away: "it suddenly wasn't all right at all: my daughter traveling away from me, the things I hadn't said and didn't know how to say and never would." This would seem to say it, and yet Ripple has his doubts. "Perhaps that should come at the end," he writes. "Other things have happened since,"

but one remembers things simultaneously and brings them to a close each time in a different way as if asking: if this moment were to be my last, how would I choose to sum up? Waving goodbye to my daughter, a breath of warmth in the air at the end of winter, a patch of sunlight on a dark, unpainted wall, some bird singing alone long before daybreak—these things or things like them instead of the guilt, the failed joke, the thoughtlessness, the self-pity, the fear in the early hours

of being dead. . . . No, these won't do either as last words. . . .
There is far too much unraveling still to be undergone.

All these doubts about sequence and content, though, are not
those of someone trying to put a story together; they belong to
someone who is pulling a life apart. Ripple is not trying to spin a
yarn; he is, as he says, attempting an "unraveling" of his life's
knotted threads by combing through them. He may say, "I like
books to have a happy ending. . . . Because life isn't like that. It's
all separation and loss and everything gets taken away in the end,"
but he isn't trying to create a story that resolves a suffering past
through a revisionist version (unlike the writer/protagonist of Ian
McEwan's *Atonement*, for instance, a novel Ripple would likely
enjoy if he read novels). In his own book, Ripple refuses to provide an antidote to that separation and loss. Looking at his account's accumulating contents, he remarks of an early, not particularly kind assessment of his wife: "Why did I make her out all
those years ago to be so humourless, such a prig? Why do I not go
back and cancel all that out, rewrite it with hindsight and kindness, begin all over again? Is the truth so much less important
than truthfulness?" A distinction is being made here between the
"truth" that is accessible through hindsight and kindness and the
"truthfulness" that comes through in a moment of frustration;
that Ripple finds room for both offers an answer to the question
asked in many different ways throughout the book: "Why am I
writing this down," he wonders again and again, "if there's not the
slightest chance anyone else will read it and if there were I
wouldn't be writing it? For myself, then? But why shouldn't it be
enough simply to think things? It is for most people. Thoughts.
Words. All vanishing alike into thin air." Such thoughts do not
vanish, however; worded and marked down they remain, and we
come to appreciate their function: they measure distances between what we once thought and what we now do, a route that

describes the dimensions of the world we create within us, the world that is experienced, felt, and lived.

．　　　．　　　．

As Ripple lives through *It's All Right Now*'s quartet of parts—the emotional isolation of family life in part one; the literal isolation he endures alone in a small house in the Suffolk countryside, in his fifties, in part two; its perpetuation in a top-floor north London flat, in his sixties, in part three; and its continuance in his last little home by the seashore, at seventy, in part four—we live through his story with him. Ripple in his glacial change through thirty years and hundreds of thousands of words becomes fully human. We begin to believe in a Tom Ripple who is writing of his life, and that somewhere by the English seaside where he finishes out his days he is marking it all down.

This transubstantiation of the word made flesh is a pleasingly pagan magic, one that Ripple's humbleness puts within reach of any one of us. But perhaps it is less a matter of divination or conjury than of simple faith. In Ripple's case it is seclusion that, in time, yields a faith in what he harvests; seen from the point of its inception, his endeavor was little more than a desperate act. He spoke to himself for want of any other listener. It was out of loneliness that he wrote, and it was out of loneliness that another border opened up, one that Montaigne crossed four centuries ago, when he advised, "We must maintain a place for ourselves alone, a free zone where we can cultivate our liberty and our peace of mind and our solitude. . . . In solitude, be a world unto yourself."

The novelist is a creator of worlds, of course, and the commitment required to populate their continents frequently demands certain sacrifices, many of them sizable. As William Gass has noted, "It is not often one begins a sand castle on a lazy summer morning—pattybaking by the blue lagoon—only to—by gosh!—

achieve—thanks to a series of sandy serendipities—an Alhambra with all its pools by afternoon." Who knows what seaside sparked Charles Chadwick's Ripple, or what privations were required to keep him blazing through many a weekend afternoon? It is enough for a reader to know, upon completing *It's All Right Now*, that the world within it is alive and the life that is lived through its pages is as warm and quick as flesh. And so, as Chadwick, self-professed amateur, is bringing his three decades of creation to a close, if he allows himself a wink at the reader, a single moment when he parts the curtain on the stage behind poor Tom Ripple to tip his hat, it's a very minor break of form:

> Curiosity about living people cannot be confined within the covers of any book. Nothing can be invented. Wherever you look there is that universe of lives that can never be known. Novels are such a relief really, not that I have read many of them. People say they are an escape. Just so. Nothing wrong with that. Reality is there to be escaped from, or so it feels much of the time. I haven't the faintest idea how one would go about writing a novel, inventing people and imposing limits on them. Not that it matters if it's just fiction. It's not like having to do justice to real people.

Justice, in this case, has been served. Ripple is real.

Virginia Quarterly Review

WINNER—FICTION

Joyce Carol Oates explores the fallibility of memory in "Smother"

Joyce Carol Oates

Smother

nly a doll, Alva! Like you.

That's what they told her. Their voices were a single voice.

She was very young then. It had to be 1974 because she was in second grade at Buhr Elementary School, which was the faded-red-brick building set back from the busy street; she has forgotten the name of the street and much of her life at that time, but she remembers the school, she remembers a teacher who was kind to her, she remembers Rock Basin Park, where the child was smothered.

This was in Upper Darby, Pennsylvania. A long time ago.

●　　　●　　　●

Can't sleep. Can't breathe. Hurriedly dresses, leaves for the Arts College. On the bus her head rattles. A man is peering at her from behind a raised newspaper, eyes she feels crawling on her, disrobing her, poking fingers, prying open. *Cunt* is a nasty word she'd first heard at the faded-red-brick school long ago. No idea what it meant. No idea why the older boys laughed. No idea why she ran away to hide her face. No idea why her teacher spoke so carefully to her. *Alva, have you been hurt? Alva, have you been touched?* Holding out her left arm where the purplish-yellow bruise had blossomed in the night.

Alva pulls the cord. Next stop! Can't breathe in the crowded bus. Eyes crawling over her like lice. She has disguised herself in swaths of muslin, like a nun, like a Muslim woman, wrappings of saffron material, mist-colored, soiled-white. And her waist-long hair that needs washing, spilling from a makeshift velvet cowl.

Alva's long narrow bony feet. In need of washing.

Venus de Milo, it's been said of Alva, unclothed.

Botticelli Venus, in a voice of (male) marveling.

.   .   .

Tells herself, she is 1,200 miles from Rock Basin Park. She is thirty-seven years old, not seven.

Thirty-seven, Alva? You must be joking.

Alva doesn't joke. Taking cues from others, Alva is able to laugh on cue—a high-pitched, little-girl, startled sound like glass breaking—but doesn't understand the logic of jokes.

Alva sometimes laughs if (somehow) she's tickled. Breasts and abdomen palpated by an examining gynecologist at the Free Clinic, "echo" exam where the technician moves a device around, and around, and pushes into, the thinly flesh-cushioned bone protecting the heart.

Yet why is it, you can't tickle yourself? Alva wonders.

Sometimes even in mirrors, nobody's there.

Can't be more than, what—twenty-five?

Alva won't contest the point. Alva doesn't lie, but if people, predominately men, wish to believe that she's younger than her age, as young as she appears, Alva won't protest.

The transparent tape they'd wrapped around her head, over her face, to smother her, to shut her mouth and eyes, shut her terrified screams inside, Alva hadn't protested. Too exhausted, when finally the tape was torn off.

Tearing off eyelashes, much of her eyebrows, clumps of hair.

Hadn't protested. Never told. Who to tell?

Alva has learned: to modulate her voice like wind chimes, to smell like scented candles, to shake her long streaked-blond hair like a knotted waterfall past her slender shoulders. Her smile is shyly trusting. Her eyes are warm-melting caramel. Men have fallen in love with that smile. Men have fallen in love with those eyes. The exotic layers of cloth Alva wraps herself in, gauze, see-through, thin muslins, sometimes sprinkled with gold dust. An unexpected glimpse of Alva's bare flesh (is she naked, beneath?) inside the swaths of fabric, midriff, inside of a forearm, creamy-translucent breast.

Men follow Alva. Alva knows to hide.

.   .   .

Almost, she can see the man's face.

A perspiring face, red-flushed face, furious eyes.

Never tell! What we did to her, we'll do to you.

For a long time she forgot. Now, she's remembering. Why?

She's 1,200 miles from Rock Basin Park and Upper Darby, Pennsylvania. Has not returned in many years. Maybe the man who claimed to be her father has died. Maybe it's her mother who continues to send checks, whose signature Alva avoids looking at.

Guilt money, this is. But Alva needs money.

Lately, she can think of nothing else except *Only a doll, Alva. Like you.* Can't sleep, can't breathe. These terrible days of early warm spring when everyone else walks in the sunshine coatless and smiling. Airborne pollen, maple seeds madly swirling in the wind, a rich stupefying scent of lilac.

Lilac! In Rock Basin Park. Where she ran. Where she hid. Maybe he'd crushed her face in it: lilac. If not Alva's face, the other girl's.

.   .   .

Alva has never had a child. Alva has never been pregnant.

Men have tried to make Alva pregnant. Many times.

Children frighten Alva; she looks quickly away from them. If by accident she glances into a stroller, a baby buggy, a crib, quickly she turns her gaze aside.

It's just a doll, Alva. Like you.

Amnesia is a desert of fine white sun-glaring sand to the horizon. Amnesia isn't oblivion. Amnesia is almost-remembering. Amnesia is the torment of almost-remembering. Amnesia is the dream from which you have only just awakened, hovering out of reach below the surface of bright rippling water. Amnesia is the paralyzed limb into which one day, one hour, feeling may begin suddenly to flow.

·　　·　　·

This Alva fears. Amnesia has been peace, bliss. Waking will be pain.

·　　·　　·

Alva dear is something wrong, Alva tell me please?

. . . know you can trust me, Alva? Don't you?

Alva is childlike and trusting, but in fact Alva is not childlike and not trusting. Alva certainly isn't one to tell. Not any man, of the many who've befriended her.

Teachers. Social workers. Psychologists. Therapists. Older men eager to help Alva, who so mysteriously seems unable to help herself. *Some secret in your life, Alva? That has held you back, kept you from fulfilling your promise.*

This is true. This is true! Alva knows. Long ago she was a "promising" young dancer. She has been "promising" as a student, a singer, an actress. "Promising" as a spiritual being, and "promising" as an artist/sculptor/jeweler. Alva's most ambitious project was stringing together glass beads—hundreds, thousands of beads!—into exotic "Indian" necklaces and bracelets sold at a crafts fair in Grand Rapids, Michigan. Alva has received payment for intermittent work in Christian campus groups, feminist centers, Buddhist centers, organic food co-ops, neighborhood medical clinics. She has worked in photo shops, frame shops. She has passed out flyers on street corners. She has worked in cafeterias. She has waitressed. She has been a model.

Alva never accepts money. On principle.

Alva will accept money sometimes. Only if necessary.

If desperate, Alva will accept: meals, winter clothing, places to stay. (Alva never stays in one place for long. Alva slips away without saying good-bye.)

Like exotic glass beads, Alva's life. But there is no one to string the glass beads together.

Men who've loved Alva have asked, *What is it, a curse, a jinx, something in your childhood? Who are your parents? Where are you from? Are you close to your mother, your father . . . ?*

Alva is mute. Alva's head is wrapped in transparent tape. Alva's screams are shut up inside.

Alva removes the envelope from the post office box. Opens it, tosses aside the accompanying letter, keeps only the check made out to *Alva Lucille Ulrich.* Guilt money, this is. But Alva needs money.

Alva needs her medications. Alva has qualified for public health assistance, but still Alva must pay a minimal fee, usually ten dollars, for her meds.

Alva takes only prescription drugs. Alva has been clean for years.

You saw nothing. You are a very bad little girl.

Hiding in plain view. Nude model. The girl who'd been morbidly shy in school. Calmly removing her layers of exotic fabric, kicking off her sandals, slipping into a plain cotton robe to enter the life studies room. Taking her place at the center of staring strangers at whom she never looks.

The instructor, usually male. Staring at Alva, too. At whom Alva never looks.

Venus de Milo, it's been remarked of Alva. *Botticelli Venus.* Alva scarcely hears what is said of her at such times, for it isn't said of her but of her body.

Alva prefers large urban university campuses. Alva prefers academic art departments, not freelance artists or photographers.

Alva is an artist's model. Alva is not available for porn—"erotic art." Alva is not sexual.

Saw nothing. Bad girl.

. . .

It's early May. It's a sprawling university campus close by the Mississippi River. Far from Rock Basin Park. Far from Upper Darby, Pennsylvania.

Early May, too warm. Even Alva, naked, is warm. Students have shoved windows up as high as they can in the third-floor room in the old building on University Avenue. Alva has been sleepless, Alva has had difficulty breathing. Alva is uneasy, these windows open to the sky. There are noises from the busy street outside, but still there is airborne pollen, swirling maple seeds, a smell of lilac from somewhere on campus.

Smother!

Alva shudders. Alva stares into a corner of the ceiling. Alva holds herself so very still seated on the swath of velvet draped over a chair, Alva doesn't appear to be breathing.

The child! In a soiled pink eyelet nightgown smelling of her pan-icked body. Eyes open and staring, sightless. Where the hand has clamped there is the reddened impress of fingers in the ivory skin. A bubble of saliva tinged with blood glistens at the small bruised mouth. They are wrapping her in the blanket that had been Alva's. They are wrapping her tight so that if she comes awake, if she comes alive again, she won't be able to kick and struggle. At dusk they will drive to Rock Basin Park, they will abandon her in a desolate place where there are no footpaths and lilac is growing wild.

·   ·   ·

Phone rang. Friday evening. Believing it to be a friend, she lifted the receiver without checking the ID.

The voice was a stranger's. Low-pitched, somehow insinuating. "Mrs. Ulrich?"

Here was the wrong note. To her students and younger colleagues at the institute she was *Dr. Ulrich*. To friends and acquaintances, *Lydia*. No one called her *Mrs. Ulrich* any longer. No one who knew her.

She felt a stab of apprehension. Even as she tensed, she spoke warmly and easily into the phone: "Yes, who is it?"

By the age of sixty-three she'd acquired a social personality that was warm, easy, welcoming. You might call it a maternal personality. You would not wish to call it a manipulative personality. She was a professional woman of several decades. Her current position was director of a psychology research institute at George Mason University. She'd been a professor at the university for eighteen years, much admired for her collegiality and ease with students. Her deepest self, brooding and still as dark water at the bottom of a deep well, was very different.

". . . of the Upper Darby Police Department. I have a few questions to ask you, preferably in person."

Upper Darby! She'd moved away nearly twenty-five years ago. Lydia, her husband Hans, and their young daughter Alva.

Her friendships of that time, when she'd been an anxious young wife and mother, had long since faded. Her husband had had professional ties in the Philadelphia area, but long ago.

"But—why? What do you have to ask me?"

"Your husband is deceased, Mrs. Ulrich? Is that correct?"

This was correct. Hans had died in 2000. Already five years had passed. For seven years in all, Lydia and Hans had not been living together. They had not divorced or even formally separated because Hans had not believed in any outward acknowledgment of failure on his part.

The detective, whose name Lydia hadn't quite heard, was asking if he and an associate could come to her residence in Bethesda to speak with her the following day, at about 2 P.M. They would drive from Upper Darby for an interview of possibly forty minutes or an hour.

The next day was Saturday. This was to have been a day of solitude. When she needn't be *Dr. Ulrich*. In the evening she was going out with a friend; through the long hours of the day she intended to work, with an afternoon break for a long, vigorous walk. As a professional woman she had learned to hoard her privacy, her aloneness, while giving the impression, in public, of being warmly open and available.

It was difficult to keep the edge out of her voice: "Why must it be in person? Can't we speak over the phone?"

"Mrs. Ulrich, we prefer not on the phone."

Again *Mrs. Ulrich*. Spoken with an insinuating authority. As if the police officer knew *Mrs. Ulrich* intimately, it was *Mrs. Ulrich* he wanted.

In this way Lydia understood: the subject of the inquiry would be family. Whatever it was, it would have nothing to do with her professional identity and reputation.

She could not avoid asking this question, with dread: "Is this—about my daughter?"

Lydia strained to hear, behind the detective's low-pitched voice, background voices, muffled sound. The man was calling from Upper Darby police headquarters. His intrusion into her life, into the solitude and privacy of her apartment (a tenth-floor

condominium overlooking a shimmering green oasis of park-
land), was impersonal, as if random. He didn't know her, had no
care of her. He was pursuing a goal that had nothing to do with
her. And of course it couldn't be random, but calculated. He'd acquired her (unlisted) home telephone number in Bethesda,
Maryland. He knew about Hans's death. This meant he probably
knew other facts about her. That he might know facts about Lydia
Ulrich she didn't know about herself caused her to feel dizzy suddenly, as if a net were being closed around her.

The detective hadn't said yes, nor had he said no. Was this call
about Alva?

"Is Alva in trouble? Is she—ill?"

*Has she been arrested, is she in police custody, has she overdosed
on a drug, is she in a hospital, is she . . .*

Since answering the phone, Lydia had been placating herself
with the thought that, so far as she knew, Alva was in Illinois, not
Pennsylvania. Since they'd moved from Upper Darby, Alva had
never been back. Lydia was sure.

The detective whose name Lydia hadn't caught was telling her,
in a voice that didn't sound friendly, that their daughter was not
ill, so far as he knew. But the subject of his inquiry had to do with
her, Alva Ulrich, as a possible witness in a criminal investigation.

Criminal investigation! Lydia's heart stopped.

It would be drugs. Since the age of fourteen Alva had been involved with drugs. Like malaria, the disease persisted. Lydia
jammed her fist against her mouth. The detective's words had
struck her like an arrow. Damned if she would cry out in pain.

No doubt, many more times than her parents knew, Alva had
been arrested for drug possession. She'd been taken into police
custody, briefly jailed, discharged to rehab, discharged "clean."
Drifting on then to the next state, another sprawling university
campus. Another improvised fringe life, in pursuit of some sort
of artistic career . . . The last time, a call jarring as this had come
from a stranger, years ago when she and Hans had been living in

Georgetown, their thirty-year-old daughter from whom they'd long been estranged had been hospitalized in East Lansing, Michigan, after a drug overdose. She'd been comatose, near death. Dumped by her druggie friends on the pavement outside the ER, one night in winter 1997.

Immediately, Lydia had flown to East Lansing. Hans had refused to accompany her.

The detective was asking wasn't Lydia in contact with her daughter? Lydia wondered if the question wasn't a trick, for already he knew the answer, from Alva. Quickly Lydia said yes, of course she was in contact with her daughter: "Alva is an art student, a painter, at . . ." But was it Illinois State University at Carbondale or Springfield? Alva had provided Lydia with post office box numbers in both cities recently. "I just wrote to her, about two weeks ago. I sent her a check, as I often do, and she seems to have cashed it. Please tell me if something has happened to my daughter . . ."

"When is the last time you spoke with her, Mrs. Ulrich?"

Lydia could not answer. She was being humiliated, eviscerated.

Yet the stranger at the other end of the line continued, with a pretense of solicitude. Asking hadn't Lydia a street address for her daughter, either?—so Lydia was forced to admit no, "Just a post office box; it's been that way since she left home. Alva has wanted her privacy. She's an artist . . ."

Lydia's voice was weak now, faltering. Not the self-assured voice of Dr. Lydia Ulrich, director of the Pratt Institute for Research in Cognitive and Social Psychology at George Mason University, but the broken, defeated, bewildered voice of Hans Ulrich's wife.

". . . Springfield, is it? Alva is studying art there . . ."

The detective murmured something ambiguous. Maybe yes, maybe no.

". . . don't seem to have her street address, officer. Maybe, if you know it, you could tell me?"

"Sorry, Mrs. Ulrich. Your daughter has requested that we not inform you of her exact location at this time."

"Oh. I see."

This hurt. This was unmistakable. An insult. Shame.

Not my fault. How is it my fault! I tried to love her. I do love her.

Now Lydia was broken, defeated. Quickly now she gave in. Of course the detectives could come to see her, next day. The net was tightening, her breath came short. Before they hung up Lydia heard herself ask, "If a—a crime has been committed—Alva isn't in danger, is she? Alva is being protected—is she?"

The detective's answer was terse, enigmatic; she would ponder its meaning through much of the night: "At the present time, ma'am, it appears, yes, she is."

. . .

Of course, Alva was in Carbondale, not Springfield! Lydia knew this.

A few minutes after her conversation with the Upper Darby detective, she realized.

. . .

She would cancel her plans for the weekend. Both Saturday and Sunday. She knew, seemed to know, the Upper Darby detectives would not be bringing her good news.

"My daughter. Alva. Something has happened. She has become involved in a 'criminal case' out in Illinois, I think. She's a 'witness' . . ."

Witness to what? Lydia shuddered to think.

She was rehearsing what she would say, telephoning friends. To cancel their plans for dinner, a play. To explain her state of mind. (Agitated, anxious.) In the turbulent years of her marriage to a demanding and difficult man, Lydia hadn't time for the cultivation of friends, but now her life was spacious and aerated as a cloudless sky, she'd acquired a circle of remarkable friends. Most of them were women her age, divorcees, widows. A few remained married. Their children were grown and gone. All were professional women nearing retirement age but, like Lydia, in no hurry to retire. They did not wish to speak of it.

Not yet! Not yet! The women clung to their work, at which they excelled, with a maternal possessiveness.

Their children had not only grown and gone but in some cases had disappeared. Like Alva, they were of the legion of walking wounded, drifting into a drug culture as into a vast American inland sea. The women did not speak of these children except in rare, raw moments. Lydia's friends knew about Alva, and knew not to ask after Alva. The son of Lydia's closest friend had committed suicide several years ago in a particularly gruesome way; only Lydia knew among their circle of friends. But never spoke of it.

The women had come to these friendships late in life, but not too late. Theirs was the most precious sisterhood: no blood ties between them.

. . .

Genes are the cards we're all dealt. What we do with the cards is our lives.

This was a remark of Hans Ulrich's, frequently cited in intellectual journals.

. . .

"I tried. I have never given up on . . ."

He had given up. The father.

And how painful for Lydia to realize that, long after Hans had coolly detached himself from their daughter, refusing even to hear from Lydia what Alva's latest problems, crises, predicaments were, Alva still preferred him to Lydia: the powerful elusive father.

Seductive even when elusive. Especially when absent.

"But where is Daddy, why isn't Daddy with you? Are you keeping Daddy from me? Are you lying to Daddy about me? Does Daddy know that I almost died? I don't want you here, I want Daddy. *I don't trust you, I hate you.*"

It was a child's accusation. Hateful, unthinking, intended purely to hurt.

In the hospital in East Lansing, at Alva's bedside, Lydia had tried to disguise her horror, seeing her daughter so haggard and sallow-skinned, her eyes bloodshot, sunk deep into their sockets. Alva had been too weak to sit up, to eat solids, to speak except in a low hoarse broken voice, almost inaudible and terrible to hear. Lydia wanted to believe it was Alva's sickness that spoke, not Alva. For how could Alva hate *her*!

"Darling, I'm your mother. I love you, I'm here to help you . . ."

"You're wrong. You're stupid. It's Daddy I trust. His judgment."

Lydia was stunned. Thinking, *Even in her sickness, she knows.*

Not Lydia's judgment but Hans's judgment was to be trusted. Hans's moral repugnance at what he called the slow train wreck of their daughter's life. Not a mother's unconditional love and forgiveness the wounded daughter craved but a father's righteous fury, unforgiving.

You disgust me. You and your kind. If your mother can stomach you, good for her. Not me.

Hans had refused to come with Lydia to East Lansing, and he would refuse to discuss the arrangements Lydia made for Alva to be admitted to a drug rehabilitation clinic after her discharge from the hospital. He was departing for Europe. Medical conferences in Berlin, Rome. Hans Ulrich was a consultant to the UN and would be named to the president's advisory board on matters of health and public welfare. His life was a worldly one; he'd become one of the preeminent epidemiologists of his generation. Not the effluvia of family life but the grandeur of public life would define him. Not fatherhood, not marriage. Not love, but professional achievement and renown. Hans was a man who, when he died (prematurely, aged sixty-one, of cardiac arrest, thousands of miles from Lydia), would be eulogized in prominent obituaries for his "seminal" work in this crucial field. *Survived by wife; daughter* was the perfunctory afterthought.

In the hospital in East Lansing, at her daughter's bedside, Lydia had seemed finally to understand. It had to be a fact others knew, to which Lydia had come late: to love unconditionally is fraudulent, a lie. There is a time for love, and there is a time for the repudiation of love. Yet Lydia protested, "I can't change my love for you, Alva, even if . . ."

Even if you don't love me.

Alva grimaced and shut her eyes. A shudder passed over her thin body. She could not have weighed more than ninety pounds. Her skin looked jaundiced but was coolly clammy to the touch. An IV tube drained liquid into her bruised forearm. The hair that had been a beautiful ashy blond through Alva's girlhood was coarse, matted, threaded now with silver like glinting wires. A sour odor lifted from her that Lydia would carry away from the hospital in her clothing, her hair. She thought this must be the odor of dissolution, impending death.

She returned to her hotel room. She showered, washed her hair. She left a message for Hans with his assistant. *You must try to come! Our daughter may be dying.*

But Alva had not died. Another time, Alva recovered.

So quickly, one day she checked out of the hospital and eluded her mother. It was a bleakly comic scene Lydia would long recall: her astonishment at Alva's vacated bed, her naive query put to one of the floor nurses, "But—didn't my daughter leave any word for me?"

No word. Only the hospital bill.

A considerable bill, for eight full days.

That had been the last time Lydia had seen her daughter or spoken with her. Terrible to realize, when the detective from Upper Darby called her, it had been more than seven years.

Seven years. A child's lifetime.

Genes are the cards we're all dealt. What we do with the cards is our lives.

Hans Ulrich was denounced in some circles as cold, unfeeling, a statistician and not a medical man. In other circles, politically conservative, he was honored as a seer.

In fact it had been more than seven years that Lydia had been sending checks to Alva in care of post office boxes in the Midwest. After dropping out of college for the third and final time, Alva had drifted westward to Ohio, Indiana, Iowa. To Michigan, Minnesota. To Missouri. To Illinois. Impossible to determine if Alva traveled alone or with others; if she acquired, in her itinerant life, some sort of family; if she'd even married, and if so, if she'd remained with her husband or drifted away from him as she'd drifted away from her parents. Lydia sent checks, and Alva cashed them. At the outset, she and Hans were still living together in Georgetown, where both had academic appointments; Hans disapproved but never interfered, so long as the money Lydia sent was clearly her own, from her salary. With the checks Lydia never failed to enclose a handwritten letter or card. She would wish one day that she'd kept a record of these, as a kind of journal or diary of her own life, the crucial facts of her life offered to her daughter in a relentlessly upbeat tone, for words are the easiest of deceits, so long as they aren't spoken aloud. To write a thing is to make it true, Lydia thought.

Alva rarely replied to Lydia's letters, except from time to time to notify her of another change of address, on the printed form provided by the post office. But Alva never failed to cash the checks.

"She reads my letters, at least. That's how we keep in touch."

This had to be so. Lydia would explain to the prying detectives.

.   .   .

"Not an interrogation, Mrs. Ulrich. An interview."

Mrs. Ulrich. The wife, the mother. She was their subject.

Lydia's nervous offer of coffee? tea? soda? was politely declined. A woman whose home is entered, a woman who can't provide some gesture of hospitality, is a woman disoriented, disadvantaged like one suffering from that infection of the inner ear that determines our ability to keep our balance.

Lydia's offer of a smile was politely declined.

Their names were Hahn and Panov. Lydia stared at the cards handed to her. Already she had forgotten which man was which.

Hahn, Panov. Was Hahn the elder? He led the interview.

". . . won't mind, will you, if we tape this . . ."

Lydia invited them to sit down. It must have been choreographed; the detectives took seats in chairs facing her but at a little distance from each other. Lydia would glance at one of the men, and at the other; back to the first, and again the other. While Hahn questioned her, Panov studied her in profile.

Alva was in danger, Lydia thought. It had to be drug-related, and it had to be a serious crime.

How she, the mother, was connected, Lydia could not imagine. Wanting to cry, *Please tell me! Don't torment me.*

It was unnerving to think that these strangers glancing about casually at Lydia's attractive living room flooded with May sunshine, making no comment on it as other visitors would naturally have done, seemingly not very impressed, knew something about Alva, and something about Lydia, that Lydia didn't know.

Unnerving to think that these men, who'd driven from the Philadelphia area to Bethesda to speak with Lydia, had flown to Carbondale, Illinois, to speak with Alva.

Yet more unnerving, Alva had been the one to contact the detectives. Alva who feared and despised figures of authority like police, social welfare officials, judges!

Lydia was told that her daughter had been encouraged to contact the Upper Darby Police Department by a therapist whom she'd been seeing, as well as a faculty member at the state university, because in recent weeks she had been haunted by memories of having witnessed a violent crime as a child. Alva had come to believe that she had crucial information to offer police, to aid in the investigation of a homicide of 1974 that had recently been re-opened by Upper Darby police.

Homicide! Lydia was astonished.

"This can't be. Alva couldn't have been more than seven at that time . . ."

Not drugs? Not Illinois?

Lydia smiled nervously. Looking from Hahn to Panov, from Panov to Hahn, thinking this had to be a misunderstanding. Surely not a joke?

Alva had never been one to joke. You couldn't reason with Alva by speaking playfully. Couldn't coax her, even as a little girl, out of a mood by making her laugh because Alva couldn't be made to laugh. Instead, Alva would stare at you. Blankly.

So the detectives regarded Lydia, not exactly blankly but with professional detachment, a kind of clinical curiosity. They were seeing a sixty-three-year-old woman who looked much younger than her age, a widow, a professional woman, obviously educated and well-spoken and not the Mrs. Ulrich they might have expected, having first met her daughter.

They were seeing a woman who needed to be assured her daughter wasn't ill, wasn't in danger.

". . . for some reason I have only a post office address for Alva in Carbondale. I would so appreciate it, if you could give me her street address before you leave."

A reasonable voice. Not exactly begging. A mother concerned for her child, though the child is thirty-seven.

"She moves so often, that's why I seem to have lost . . ."

Lydia had forgotten she'd been told that Alva didn't want her to know her street address. You'd have thought she had forgotten.

Neither Hahn nor Panov acknowledged her remark. Lydia wanted to think, *They're being kind, they feel sorry for me. They are on my side.*

So you yearn to think when investigators enter your home.

The detectives would have recognized Alva at once: one of the walking wounded, casualties of the drug culture. Young people whose early promise had been destroyed by drugs as by a virulent disease.

They would recognize Lydia, the brave left-behind mother.

". . . a witness, you say? Alva? As a child of . . ."

Lydia spoke respectfully of her daughter though also skeptically. She would not suggest that her daughter had to be fantasizing, as so often, through the years, Alva had done.

Hahn was telling Lydia that the newly reopened case was a notorious one: "Pink Bunny Baby." Did she remember it?

A very young child, believed to be about two, had been found dead in a remote area of Rock Basin Park. She'd been tightly swaddled in a blanket, bruised but not visibly injured, having been smothered to death. The little girl wore an article of clothing with pink bunnies on it, and so in the media she was the Pink Bunny Baby. A police sketch of her doll-like face as it must have been before her death had been replicated many thousands of times in the press, for weeks, months.

Pink Bunny Baby had never been identified. Her murderer or murderers had never been identified.

Lydia was stunned. Whatever she'd been expecting, it could not have been this.

"Of course I remember. That nightmare. We lived only a few miles from Rock Basin Park. Alva was in second grade at the time. We tried to shield her from . . ."

It came back to Lydia, the clutch of fear she'd felt then. A mother's fear that something terrible might happen to her child.

When your child is an infant, you're in terror that somehow she will die, simply cease breathing, you must check her constantly, compulsively. When she's older and often out of your sight, you worry that a madman might steal her away.

Though it was widely believed that Pink Bunny Baby had been killed by a parent or parents, not a roving madman.

For who else would wish to kill a child so young, except a deranged parent? That was the nightmare.

Lydia spoke slowly at first, with a kind of recalled dread. By degrees she began speaking more rapidly, as if a mechanism had been sprung in her brain.

". . . for months, every day it was 'Pink Bunny Baby' in newspapers, on TV. There were flyers and posters. Everyone spoke of it. You couldn't escape it. We censored everything that came into the house, and we never let Alva watch TV alone, but still she was badly frightened by older children at school. She was a highstrung, nervous child. Extremely intelligent, with a talent for drawing and music, but too restless to sit still for more than a few minutes. Today she would be diagnosed as 'ADD,' but in the 1970s no one had identified 'attention deficit disorder,' and the only medication for hyperactive children would have been tranquilizers. We took Alva—that is, I took her—to pediatricians, child psychiatrists, neurologists. Hans was outraged when she was diagnosed as 'borderline autistic'—we knew this couldn't be accurate. Alva was a bright, communicative, verbal child who could look you in the eye when she wanted to. Even before the child's body was found she'd had nightmares, and these got worse. She did astonishing crayon drawings of the 'little pink baby' she called her baby sister. She begged us to let her sleep with us at night—but she was too old, Hans insisted. She begged us to take her to the place where Pink Bunny Baby was found."

Words spilled from Lydia, leaving her breathless. The detectives listened without commentary and without the usual encouraging smiles and head signals that accompany conversation.

This wasn't a conversation, of course. This was an interview.

The elder detective asked, "And did you take your daughter to the park, Mrs. Ulrich?"

"Of course not! You can't be serious."

"Did your husband take her?"

"Certainly not."

"Neither of you, ever, alone or together, took your daughter to Rock Basin Park?"

Lydia looked from one detective to the other. Hahn, Panov.

She was confused, she was speaking incoherently. Wanting to plead with them, *What did my daughter see? What has she told you about me?*

"Well, yes. Before the child's body was found. But not to that terrible place."

"You knew where the 'place' was, then? You were familiar with that part of the park?"

Lydia hesitated. It had been so long: thirty years. "Only just from the newspaper. There were countless stories, photographs of the park. Even maps."

"How long did you live in Upper Darby, Mrs. Ulrich?"

"Five years. Hans had an academic appointment at . . ."

"In all those years you'd never been to that part of Rock Basin Park where the child was found? Yet you could recognize it from the newspaper?"

Lydia tried not to speak sharply. Knowing, as an administrator, that a sudden break in civility, a breach in decorum, can never really be amended. "Yes, probably we'd been there. It was a hiking area, wasn't it? A very beautiful part of Rock Basin Park, a stony creek, wild-growing lilac, wood-chip paths through a pine forest, massive outcroppings of granite . . . When I took Alva to the park by myself, which was most of the time, while Hans was working, we kept to the playground area, where there were other children, but when Hans was with us, on Sundays usually, he wanted to hike along the creek. Once, when Alva was about four, very bright and precocious, she slipped away from Hans and me, and we'd thought she was lost, or abducted, we were searching for her everywhere, calling for her, terrified she might have drowned in the creek, but it turned out that Alva was only just hiding from us, a kind of demon got into her sometimes, she was hiding from us inside a hedge of lilac, she was feverish-looking, giggling at us, and when Hans caught up with her he was furious, lost control and grabbed Alva by the shoulders and shook her hard, like a rag doll, shouted into her face, she was paralyzed with fear, I wasn't able to stop Hans in time, I think . . ." Lydia paused, trembling. She had never told anyone this. She had never entirely acknowledged this. Between Hans and her there had been patches of blank, lacunae to which no language accrued, therefore no knowledge. Perhaps Hans had hurt Alva; the child was white-faced with terror, mute. That Daddy had turned on her, Daddy whom she adored. And the truth was, Lydia hadn't dared intervene, she'd been frightened of Hans herself. Wondering afterward if Alva had known how her mother had failed her at that crucial moment. "I tried to hold her, comfort her, but . . . Ever afterward, if I took Alva to the park, to the playground area, she was anxious, frightened. She began to have a thing about dolls, not her own dolls, Alva hadn't wanted dolls, but dolls left behind in the playground, lost and broken dolls, she was fascinated by them and frightened, 'Look at the baby, look at the baby.' She'd laugh, hide her mouth with her hand as if there was something naughty, something obscene, about the doll, or about seeing it, and I would say, 'Alva, it's only a doll, you know what a doll is, Alva, don't be silly, it's only a doll.' And this went on for years." Lydia paused, not liking her anxious, eager voice. She stared at the tape recorder. The slow-turning cassette inside. What was she revealing, to strangers, that could never be retracted! "But none of this has anything to do with the little girl found in the park in 1974. This happened years before. Alva was seven when the child was found. She was in second grade at Buhr Elementary. As I said, she became morbidly fascinated with 'Pink Bunny Baby.' At this time, Hans began traveling often. He's a—he was a—prominent scientist, and ambitious. When he was away, Alva became particularly anxious. It was 'Daddy'—'Daddy'—'Where is Daddy, is Daddy coming back?' As if Alva could foresee, many years later, that Daddy would leave us—leave me. Of course, Hans was flattered by our daughter's fixation on him, but he couldn't tolerate any sort of household upset. Emotions have very little to do with science, I mean with the methods of science. If you're a psychologist, like me, you might study emotions—but not in an emotional way. As I grew out of being a mother, I grew into being a scientist. But not a scientist like Hans Ulrich. Not of his originality, genius. Not of his stature. Hans was a quintessential male scientist—he needed a domestic household, he needed a wife who was in no way a rival. He'd been born in Frankfurt, he was contemptuous of the ways in which Americans spoil their children. Not all Americans—just the affluent, the privileged. He hadn't been a child of privilege, and he didn't want a child of his to be one, either. So he wasn't the sort of father to indulge a child so imaginative and headstrong and sensitive as Alva. He believed that she was exaggerating her fears—her nightmares—to manipulate us. Especially Daddy. I found it hard to discipline Alva, even to scold her. Like tossing a lighted match onto flammable material! I was afraid my daughter wouldn't love me. Maybe Hans was right, I wasn't a good mother, something went terribly wrong. Already in middle school she began to grow away from us, and in high school the drugs began. So Alva left me, anyway. Whatever I did, it must have been a mistake."

Lydia paused. She was breathless, agitated. Yet awaiting assurance—*Of course you aren't to blame, how wrong you are to blame yourself, obviously your daughter has a biochemical imbalance, you are wrong to blame yourself, Mrs. Ulrich!*—but the detectives from Upper Darby, PA, allowed the moment to pass.

. . .

Is it a cliché of speech, a sinking heart? Yet Lydia felt a sinking sensation in her chest at this moment. They aren't kind men. They don't feel sorry for me. They are not on my side.

. . .

Now the interview must conclude, for Lydia had told the detectives all she knew.

"Mrs. Ulrich, your daughter was adopted, yes?"

"No, Alva isn't adopted. I'm sorry."

Sorry my daughter misled you. Sorry a daughter wishes not to be a daughter.

She went away to bring the birth certificate to show the detectives. Moving stiffly like one with knee or spinal pain. Moving stiffly like an elderly woman.

The detectives studied the document without comment. *Alva Lucille Ulrich.* Parents *Lydia Moore Ulrich, Hans Stefan Ulrich.* The certificate had been signed by an obstetrician at the University of Pennsylvania Medical School Hospital, Philadelphia, Pennsylvania, February 19, 1968.

". . . a common fantasy, adoption. In imaginative children. It isn't considered pathological unless carried to extremes. Just a fantasy, a kind of comfort. That you've been adopted, your real parents are . . ."

Somewhere else. Someone else.

Lydia recalled the birth pains. Excruciating labor that had lasted nearly ten hours. She had wanted, she'd thought, a natural childbirth, what's called, bluntly, "vaginal." Her obstetrician and her husband had not thought this a very good idea. And so it had not been a very good idea.

In the end, Lydia had had a C-section. An ugly razor-scar in the pit of her now sagging belly she might show to the detectives if they were skeptical of her credentials as a biological mother.

"Alva had asked if she'd been adopted. We told her no. Yet the fantasy persisted. Except, as an adult, she should have grown out of it."

They were asking Lydia if she'd adopted another child. A younger child. Or had she had another child, younger than Alva.

A younger sister to Alva. Who had died.

"No. I did not."

It was bewildering to contemplate the shadow figure who was somehow Mrs. Ulrich, in Alva's imagination. Mrs. Ulrich whom the detectives were pursuing.

While she, Lydia, recalled through a haze of pain someone bringing her a squirming wet red-faced baby, *hers.* The astonishment of this baby so naturally in her arms, sucking at her milk-heavy breast. It had seemed to transpire in a dream. The dream could not have been her own, for it was too wonderful for Lydia to have imagined. Out of the massive labor, the exhilaration of the baby, the nursing. The eager young father who'd loved her then.

Detectives' questions are circular, tricky. Another time Lydia was asked if she'd adopted a child, any child, and Lydia explained no, never. And another time she was asked if she'd had any other children apart from Alva, and she said no. Any other children apart from Alva who had died.

"No. I'm sorry."

In their marriage it was Lydia who had wanted more children and Hans who had not. All marriages are fairy tales—*Once upon a time there was a man and a woman*—and the Ulrichs' tale was of a man who'd pursued a career and a woman who'd delayed her career to be a devoted mother to a difficult daughter who would repudiate her and break her heart. In fact, Lydia hadn't really wanted another child. She had allowed Hans to think so; in a way it was flattering to Hans to think a woman would wish to have a second child with him after the stresses of the first, perhaps a son this time, to perpetuate the Ulrich name, but truly, in the most secret recesses of her heart, Lydia had not wanted another child, not a son, certainly not another daughter, after the first.

·　　·　　·

Wishing in secret, in weak moments, *If Alva had never been born.*

Lydia's own mother had suggested an abortion, when Lydia was newly pregnant. Before Hans had known. For Lydia and Hans weren't yet married. They had not even been living together. Hans was finishing his doctorate at Penn, Lydia was only midway in her graduate studies. She was twenty-three. She was a very young twenty-three. She was a brilliant but self-doubting student whose professors had encouraged her to continue, but she'd fallen in love with Hans Ulrich, how difficult not to fall in love with Hans Ulrich, though her mother warned her she was too young to be a mother, she had so much life before her, children might wait, marriage might wait, to another man perhaps, for Hans Ulrich was not a man to give comfort but only to take comfort, and in the spell of sexual enchantment she'd defied her mother, married Hans Ulrich, and had his child.

He had loved her, then. Lydia, and their daughter.

For Alva had been a beautiful child, at first.

The child of Lydia's destiny. That seemed clear.

Really, Lydia couldn't imagine her life without Alva. Never!

Very easily, she could imagine her life without Alva. The life she was living now, if you subtracted all thoughts of Alva in the way that, despairing over being able to wash clean a grimy wall, you simply painted it over.

Lydia's friends who were mothers like herself, some of them grandmothers, never spoke of such things. They spoke of other things but never this. No one dared to acknowledge a lost life, if she had not married and had children exactly as she had. You did not speak of it. You dared not speak of it. In fact, it was pointless to speak of it.

You did not even think of it, with children near. For children hear what is not said, more keenly than what is.

Only a doll, Alva. Like you.

As a research psychologist Dr. Ulrich had tested numberless subjects. She was particularly interested in the relationship between consciousness and the brain: "self-identifying." There is a magical period of self-recognition in two-year-olds, utterly missing in younger children. To recognize the self (in a mirror, in reflective surfaces, in photographs) is taken for granted in normal individuals. Self-identity resides in a certain region of the brain that, if destroyed, can't be replaced. The self is in the brain: the soul is in the brain cells. To be an academic scientist is to test hypotheses. You perform experiments, you tally results, you publish papers, by degrees you accumulate a public career. Dr. Ulrich, the psychological tester, was without affect. In her role as tester she smiled cordially, to manipulate and comfort. But no one could read her heart. Subjects are to be manipulated, otherwise there is no experiment and there is no accumulated wisdom. Now the detectives from Upper Darby, PA, were the testers and Dr. Ulrich, seated on an ottoman in her own living room, was the subject. She understood the detectives' cordial expressions. The steely calculation in their eyes.

To be innocent of wrongdoing is to be vulnerable as one whose skin has been peeled back. To stand so naked, exposed. Every word sounds like an admission of guilt.

But guilt for what, Lydia had no idea.

Forty minutes into the interview—forty minutes! it had seemed like hours—as the detectives were asking her another time to tell them what she could remember of her daughter's "medical record" as a child living in Upper Darby, the telephone rang. Lydia had intended to remove the receiver from the hook but had forgotten. Now she was grateful for the interruption. This summons to another life.

Within earshot of the detectives she said, in a voice her friend would not have identified as anxious, "Dolores, I'm sorry, I will have to call you back in about twenty minutes."

Wanting the intruders to hear. Twenty minutes. No more.

Wanting them to hear. My life. My real life. To which you have no access.

·   ·   ·

It was then they told her.

Why they'd come to speak with her. Why her daughter had called the Upper Darby PD. What claims her daughter was making that involved her and her husband in the smothering death of the unidentified child found in Rock Basin Park.

Stunned, Lydia looked from one detective to the other. Their names were lost to her now. Their faces were blurred as faces reflected in water.

Lydia began to stammer, "I don't understand—my daughter has accused my husband and me—"

Smothering? Murder? A baby sister? The child in the tightly swaddled blanket, the soiled jumper said to be decorated with a row of pink bunnies?

"... the murder? That murder? The little girl? In Rock Basin Park? My daughter Alva has ..."

Now the net was tightening around her, she could not breathe. A band tightening around her forehead. She was stammering, trying to speak. To deny, to explain. *My daughter is sick. My daughter has blamed me. I don't know why.* But she could not explain. She could not speak. One of the detectives caught her arm, she'd begun to faint. The other went quickly away to bring her a glass of ice water.

Ice water! At such a time, the detective had brought her ice water. Seeing that Lydia had, in her compact kitchen, a refrigerator that dispenses ice cubes.

"... don't believe this. Can't ..."

Afterward she would not recall what they'd said. What they'd said next. She had assured them she was fine, she would not faint. She could hear their voices, though at a distance. She could see them as if through the wrong end of a telescope. Her vision bizarrely narrowed, edged in black. For part of her brain, its visual field, had darkened. *My daughter hates me. Blames me. But I am blameless.*

Her voice was begging. Her voice was near inaudible.

"Please, I want to speak with her. My daughter. Please . . ."

But she could not speak with her daughter, for her daughter did not wish to speak with her. So it was explained to Mrs. Ulrich, another time.

". . . a misunderstanding! My daughter isn't well. If you've spoken with her, you must know. Alva has a history of . . ."

But she could not accuse her daughter, could she!

These men on a mission. Regarding her steely-eyed, assessing.

A sixty-three-year-old woman. A professional woman. Accused of having smothered a child thirty years before. A child who'd possibly been her own daughter. Unless an adopted daughter. Two-year-old younger sister of the seven-year-old daughter. Unless the seven-year-old was also adopted. Unless Mrs. Urlich had not herself smothered the child but had aided and abetted Hans Ulrich. Conspired with Hans Ulrich to commit the murder. Thirty years ago.

". . . why? Why now? Why on earth now? I've just sent her a check, Alva cashed. For $500. I have the canceled check, I can show you. I've saved all the checks. Thousands of dollars. Why would she turn on me? Why now, so long after . . ."

She didn't want to think, *These are men on a mission. Mrs. Ulrich is their prey.*

Pink Bunny Baby was a high-profile cold case. Suddenly you read of "cold cases" everywhere in America. As crime rates decline. As old unsolved cases are reactivated. Old detectives, some of them coming back from retirement, are reactivated.

Reinspired. Mrs. Ulrich was in their gun sights.

". . . if I could just talk with Alva, if you could arrange for me to speak with her, please! In person . . ."

"Your daughter doesn't want to speak with you, Mrs. Ulrich. We've explained."

"But . . ."

Men with a mission. You could see.

Possibly they pitied her. The trembling sixty-three-year-old woman whose life was shattering around her.

Yet she was in their gun sights, she was their prey. "Mrs. Ulrich."

They'd driven in pursuit of her this morning from Upper Darby, PA, to Bethesda, MD. As they'd flown, last week, to Carbondale, IL. To interview her accuser. To tape the accuser's statement.

Her life shattered. Her professional life destroyed. Now she would retire: forced to retire. Even if not arrested, not formally accused. Her photograph in the papers, on TV. *Lydia Ulrich. Director of. Questioned by police. Smothering murder, 1974. Two-year-old victim. Body left in park.*

Was she arrested? She was not arrested. Not yet.

Should she call a lawyer? That was up to Mrs. Ulrich.

Still her vision was radically diminished: a tunnel rimmed with black. The detectives' blurred faces at the end of the tunnel. If, one day, you open your eyes and can't see one side of the room, it's a brain tumor you have. Tunnel vision, it's panic.

Panic that your life is being taken from you. Tattered and flapping like flags in the wind.

Body left in park. Believed younger daughter of. Smothered.

The detectives were saying they would play a tape of her daughter's statement, recorded the previous week in Carbondale. If Mrs. Ulrich wished.

Yes. No. She could not bear it.

She would call a lawyer, she would save herself. As Hans would have fought to save himself.

Her life passing before her eyes, something tattered and torn flapping in the wind. Pitiful.

The detectives were regarding her with pity. Suspicion but also pity. Perhaps they would be kind. Perhaps they did not want to destroy her. In their mission to solve the notorious "cold case"— in their zeal for TV celebrity—they would not want to destroy an innocent sixty-three-year-old woman.

Not arrested. Not arrested. Not yet!

Her heartbeat was rapid but weak. It could not pump enough blood to her brain.

If Hans were here! It was Hans they sought. The smotherer.

If Hans were here, as soon as the detectives entered the apartment, even as he was shaking their hands, he would allow them to know, *This is a home, I am the authority here.*

As a mother she'd taken the sorrow of her life and transformed it into love for her daughter. By an act of pure will she'd transformed it. Evidently, it hadn't been enough.

She would explain. She could not explain.

There were no words. Language was being taken from her.

The infant greedily sucking at her breast. Tugging at the raw nipple. Oh! it had hurt, as if the infant girl had teeth. But how lovely, the most sensual experience of Lydia's life.

A woman's secret, erotic life. A mother's life.

Hans had not known. Hans would have been astonished and revulsed if he'd known. But Hans had not known.

". . . a tape of your daughter's statement, Mrs. Ulrich? Would you like to hear?"

She could not accuse her daughter, could she. Her daughter she loved, she could not.

Could not plead, *She is cruel, she hates us. Blames me, I don't know why. My only child. She is evil.*

The history of her nightmares. The history of her fantasizing. Delusions, hallucinations. Accusing others. Blaming others. Sex, molestations, rape. Threats against her life. Stalking. "Plundering" of her soul.

She wasn't sure she could bear it, hearing her daughter's voice. The voice she hadn't heard in years. Gripping her daughter's thin clammy-cold hand, in the hospital room in East Lansing. Vowing to save her. Not to abandon her, as Hans had done. *Trade my life for yours if I could.*

History of nightmares. How was it the mother's fault?

History of accusations. Causing wreckage in lives then moving on. How was it the mother's fault?

Not under arrest. Her name would not (yet) be released to any news media. Certainly she might call an attorney. Cooperation with the investigation was advised.

Witnesses would be interviewed. Records and documents would be checked. Mrs. Ulrich might provide names. Mrs. Ulrich might take a polygraph if wished. The body of Pink Bunny Baby would very likely be exhumed for DNA analysis.

A match to Mrs. Ulrich?

Unless the child had been adopted.

Unless the child had been abducted.

". . . never spoke of this, Mrs. Ulrich? That you can recall?"

"Spoke of . . . ?"

"Having seen your husband 'smothering' a child. Telling your daughter it was 'only a doll.' "

"Of course not."

"This is entirely new to you."

"Yes! It is."

Wanting to scream at him. The enemy.

Lydia was speaking more calmly now. A sob in her voice.

She would not cry. Swiping at her eyes that stung as if she'd been staring into a blinding sun.

They would be impressed with Lydia's integrity. Her honesty. She'd taken a seat on the ottoman. Backless, because her posture was so impressive. *She would not cry.*

"She began taking drugs in middle school, I think. She was fourteen, wouldn't come downstairs to dinner one evening when Hans was home, he called her, insisted that she come eat with us, there was a wild stomping on the stairs, Alva had wound transparent tape around her head, over her face, she'd made a grotesque mask of her own face, distorted, hellish, she was laughing and flinging herself around as if she wanted to hurt herself, Hans and I were terrified . . . She'd taken methamphetamine, we'd hardly known such a drug existed. Hans couldn't deal with it. I had to calm Alva, try to calm her, her skin was burning, I managed to unwind and cut the horrible tape away from her head, her eyebrows and eyelashes, clumps of hair were pulled out, what a nightmare! Hans, the most agnostic of men, who hadn't a shred of belief in anything supernatural, said of our daughter, 'A devil gets into her,' sometimes, 'A devil is in her.' But he never hurt her. Except once, that time in the park. The lilac bushes were in bloom, it should have been a beautiful time. Stands of lilac growing wild. That rich smothering smell, there's a kind of madness in it. Hans hadn't meant to hurt her. She was a torment to us. 'A devil, a devil is in her.' But after that he rarely touched her even to hug her, kiss her. He was frightened, I think. Of what he might do to her. I was the one who loved her. I've never given up."

Yes, she would be calling an attorney: This very day.

Yes, she would cooperate with their investigation, for she had no reason not to cooperate. Her daughter's charges were absurd. Her daughter was mentally unstable. There was a medical history, there were medical records.

The good that came of this would be: Alva would receive medical treatment. In Carbondale, or here in Bethesda. Lydia would make arrangements.

Would not cry. Would not be destroyed.

Yes, she would hear the tape of her daughter's accusations. She was prepared for the shock of it. She believed.

Then, as one of the detectives moved to change the cassettes, Lydia asked him to wait a minute. She would be right back.

Rising shakily to her feet. One of the detectives helped her. How brittle her bones felt! For the first time, she was feeling her age.

·   ·   ·

In her bathroom Lydia ran cold water from a faucet, distracted by the stricken face in the mirror. Perhaps she did look sixty-three. Perhaps the detectives had not been surprised. The capacity to recognize the self is located in the left brain hemisphere, but in Lydia, so wounded, the capacity seemed to be damaged. *Why is that woman so old? I remember her young.*

She could not bear it, the woman's eyes.

In the medicine cabinet were numerous little bottles of pills. Old prescriptions she'd never thrown away. You never know when you might need sleeping pills, painkillers. She'd amassed a considerable quantity.

Running water, Lydia opened the bathroom door stealthily.

She'd hoped that, through the mirror, which would pick up a reflecting surface in the dining room, she could see slantwise into the living room, where the detectives were. By now one was probably on his feet, stretching. Perhaps both. In lowered tones they would be speaking of their suspect. The mask-faces were animated now. They were alive now, scenting their prey. Their teeth were bared in exhilaration. Yet: they were uncertain of the woman, she was nothing like they'd expected. The daughter's story was so far-fetched. Much of it was unverifiable. Much of it was common knowledge, widely reported in the media. The defense attorney would rebut their case. There was the daughter's medical history, they would investigate.

But Lydia couldn't see into the living room. The glass door of a breakfront reflected only a doorway, a wall.

Lydia was thinking of the famous experiment in childhood truth-telling and deception. Pandora's box, some called it.

Several children of about the age of three were left alone together in a room, emphatically instructed not to look into a shut box. Through a hidden camera, the children were videotaped. Nearly 90% of the children looked into the box, but, when questioned, less than 33% confessed to having looked. When five-year-olds were tested, nearly 100% disobeyed and tried, often very convincingly, to deceive. Demonstrating that, as children mature, their capacity for deception increases.

Curious, Hans had wanted to test Alva at age two. Her disobeying, and her insistence upon her innocence afterward, had been so charming, Hans had only laughed. His beautiful little girl, so precocious! In a variant of the test, Hans offered a chocolate treat to Alva if she "really, really" told the truth. Some children, stricken with doubt, would have demurred at this. Not Alva.

Lydia had laughed with Hans, though saddened by the child's precocious duplicity. And, somehow, the innocence of it. But Hans had been charmed. *In Homo sapiens the talent for deception is our strong evolutionary advantage.*

No trust. Preemptive war. The only wisdom.

Summoning her strength to walk back into the living room, even to smile at her tormentors, Lydia saw that, as she'd envisioned, one of the detectives was strolling about, admiring the view from Lydia's windows. "Twelfth floor? Must be nice." Gently Lydia corrected him: "Tenth floor."

They asked Lydia if she was prepared to hear her daughter's statement, and Lydia said yes.

Contributors

JAMES BAMFORD is the former Washington, D.C., investigative producer for ABC's *World News Tonight* and is the author of the books *The Puzzle Palace, Body of Secrets,* and *A Pretext For War: 9/11, Iraq, and the Abuse of America's Intelligence Agencies.* His articles have appeared in dozens of publications, including cover stories for the *New York Times Magazine, The Washington Post Magazine,* and the *Los Angeles Times Magazine.* He is based in Washington, D.C.

SVEN BIRKERTS is the author of six books, including *The Gutenberg Elegies: The Fate of Reading in an Electronic Age* and *My Sky Blue Trades: Growing Up Counter in a Contrary Time,* and the editor of three others. His numerous awards include a National Book Critics Circle Award for excellence in reviewing and the PEN/Spielvogel-Diamonstein Award for the best book of essays. Since 2002 Birkerts has edited the journal *Agni.*

WENDY BRENNER is the author of two collections of stories, *Phone Calls from the Dead* (Algonquin, 2001) and *Large Animals in Everyday Life* (W. W. Norton, 1997), which won the Flannery O'Connor Award. She is the recipient of a National Endowment for the Arts Fellowship, the Henfield Award, and the AWP Intro Award for her fiction. Her stories and essays have appeared in *Seventeen, Allure, Travel and Leisure, Story, Ploughshares, Mississippi Review, New England Review,* and other magazines. She is a contributing writer for *Oxford American.* Brenner is coordinator of the MFA program in creative writing at University of North Carolina–Wilmington.

GRAYDON CARTER has been editor of *Vanity Fair* since July 1992. He has won seven National Magazine Awards, including two for general excellence. Mr. Carter has been named *Advertising Age's* editor of the year and is the first editor ever to be twice named *Adweek* magazine's editor of the year. Before joining *Vanity Fair*, Mr. Carter was the editor of the *New York Observer*, which he completely revamped, making it the paper it is today. He came to the *New York Observer* from *Spy*, which he cofounded in 1986. He worked as a staff writer for *Time*, where he covered business, law, and entertainment for five years before joining *Life* as a staff writer in 1983. Mr. Carter was an executive producer of *9/11*, the highly acclaimed film about the World Trade Center attacks, which aired on CBS. Mr. Carter received an Emmy Award for *9/11* as well as a Peabody Award. He also produced the acclaimed documentary *The Kid Stays in the Picture*. Mr. Carter is the author of *What We've Lost* (Farrar, Straus and Giroux, September 2004), a comprehensive critical examination of the Bush administration. He edited the best-selling *Vanity Fair's Hollywood* (Viking Studio, October 2000), as well as *Oscar Night* (Knopf, October 2004). Born in Toronto, Canada, Mr. Carter resides in Manhattan with his wife, Anna. He has four children.

CHRIS HEATH joined *GQ* as a correspondent in 2003. Heath has provided in-depth profiles of celebrity subjects such as James Gandolfini, Russell Crowe, and Colin Farrell. Prior to joining *GQ*, he was a regular writer for many publications, including *Rolling Stone*, *Details*, and the *Sunday Times*. Heath is also the author of *Feel: Robbie Williams*, Britain's best-selling work of biography in 2004.

BILL HEAVEY is an editor-at-large for *Field and Stream* and writes the monthly Sportsman's Life column that appears the back page. He became an obsessed fisherman after landing his first bluegill at age five and has never really been right since. He took up hunting in his thirties, much to the disappointment of his parents, who had raised him better. Eventually, he descended into bow hunting, grew gaunt, and lost all his hair. He will try anything once, keep at it until he realizes he will never attain proficiency, then decide to stick with it forever. His work has appeared in *Men's Journal, Outside, National Geographic Traveler, Reader's Digest,* the *Washington Post,* and the *Los Angeles Times.*

HENDRIK HERTZBERG is a senior editor and staff writer at *The New Yorker.* He returned to the magazine in 1992—having been a staff writer from 1969 to 1977—and has served as both editorial director and executive editor of the magazine. Hertzberg came to *The New Yorker* from *The New Republic,* where he served two terms as editor, from 1981 until 1985, and then again from 1988 until 1991. He spent his hiatus from that magazine as a fellow at the Kennedy School of Government and at the Joan Shorenstein Barone Center on the Press, Politics, and Public Policy at Harvard University. While at *The New Republic,* Hertzberg also held the positions of contributing editor, national political correspondent, senior editor, and columnist. From 1979 until 1981, he was the chief speechwriter for President Carter and served on the White House staff throughout the Carter administration. Hertzberg began his career as a San Francisco correspondent for *Newsweek.*

JESSE KATZ is a senior writer at *Los Angeles Magazine.* His work has appeared in the *Los Angeles Times Magazine,* the *New York Times Magazine, Rolling Stone,* and *Texas Monthly.*

ELIZABETH KOLBERT has been a staff writer at *The New Yorker* since January 1999. She came to the magazine from the *New York Times,* where she wrote the Metro Matters column. Previously, from 1992 to 1997, she was a political and media reporter for the paper. She has also contributed articles to the *New York Times Magazine* on subjects ranging from the use of focus groups in elections to the New York water supply. From 1988 to 1991, she was the *New York Times* Albany bureau chief. Kolbert began working for the *Times* in 1984 as a stringer based in Germany and moved to the metro desk in 1985. Kolbert's first book, *The Prophet of Love: And Other Tales of Power and Deceit* was published by Bloomsbury in 2004.

PRISCILLA LONG is the author of *Where the Sun Never Shines: A History of America's Bloody Coal Industry*, as well as poems, stories, and essays. She serves as senior editor of the online encyclopedia of Washington State history, Historylink.org.

WYATT MASON is a contributing editor of *Harper's* magazine, where his essays regularly appear. He has also written for *The New Yorker*, *The New Republic*, *The Nation*, *The London Review of Books*, *Slate*, and the *New York Times*. Modern Library has published, in three volumes, his translations of the complete works of Arthur Rimbaud. In 2004, he was a fellow of the Dorothy and Lewis B. Cullman Center for Scholars and Writers at the New York Public Library. The National Book Critics Circle awarded him the 2005 Nona Balakian Citation for excellence in criticism.

JOYCE CAROL OATES is a stunningly prolific and accomplished writer—fourteen O. Henry Awards, six Pushcart Prizes, and a National Book Award. Her novel *We Were the Mulvaneys* was an Oprah Book Club selection and went to number one on the *New York Times* best-seller list, and her most recent book, *The Falls*, was praised by *Kirkus Reviews* as "her best ever and a masterpiece."

ERIK REECE is writer-in-residence at the University of Kentucky, where he is also codirector of the Summer Environmental Writing Program. His article "Death of a Mountain" won the John B. Oakes Award for Distinguished Environmental Journalism. His work has appeared in *Harper's* magazine, *The Nation*, *Orion*, the *Oxford American*, and other places.

JOHN JEREMIAH SULLIVAN is currently a *GQ* correspondent. He is a former senior editor at *Harper's* magazine. His writing has also appeared in the *Paris Review* and in the *Oxford American*. His essay "Feet in Smoke," written for the latter, was included in the *Best of the Oxford American* anthology, published in 2001. Sullivan is the winner of the 2003 National Magazine Award for best feature writing, the 2003 Eclipse Award for magazine writing, and the 2004 Whiting Writers' Award for nonfiction. His first book, *Blood Horses: Notes of a Sportswriter's Son*, was published in April 2004 by Farrar, Straus and Giroux.

DAVID FOSTER WALLACE is the author of *Infinite Jest*, *The Broom of the System*, and *Girl With Curious Hair*. His essays and stories have appeared in *Harper's*, *The New Yorker*, *Playboy*, and *Paris Review*, among others. Wallace has received the Whiting Award, the Lannan Award for Fiction, the Paris Review Prize for humor, the QPB Joe Savago New Voices Award, and an O. Henry Award.

MARJORIE WILLIAMS was born in Princeton, N.J., in 1958 and died in Washington, D.C., in 2005. At the time she was diagnosed with liver cancer, Williams was writing a weekly op-ed column for the *Washington Post*; frequent political profiles for *Vanity Fair*, where she was a contributing editor; and regular book reviews for *Slate*. "A Matter of Life and Death," which was assembled after Williams' death from portions of an unfinished memoir, appeared in the October 2005 issue of *Vanity Fair*. A longer version of the essay can be found under the title "Hit By Lightning" in *The Woman at the Washington Zoo: Writings on Politics, Family, and Fate*. The book earlier this year won PEN's Martha Albrand Award for First Nonfiction.

JAMES WOLCOTT has been a contributing editor at *Vanity Fair* since 1997. His monthly column covers pop culture, media, and the literary scene. In 2003, Wolcott received a National Magazine Award for three articles in the Reviews and Criticism category. He began his career in the circulation department at the *Village Voice* in 1972. He first joined *Vanity Fair* in 1983 and wrote the "Mixed Media" column, then worked as staff writer at *The New Yorker* for four years, before returning to *Vanity Fair*. His work has appeared in *Esquire, Harper's,* and the *Wall Street Journal* to name a few. His first novel, *The Catsitters,* was published in 2001.

2006 National Magazine Award Finalists

NOTE: All nominated issues are dated 2005 unless otherwise specified. The editor whose name appears in connection with finalists for 2006 held that position, or was listed on the masthead, at the time the issue was published in 2005. In some cases, another editor is now in that position.

General Excellence

This category recognizes overall excellence in magazines. It honors the effectiveness with which writing, reporting, editing, and design all come together to command readers' attention and fulfill the magazine's unique editorial mission.

Under 100,000 Circulation

Aperture: Melissa Harris, editor in chief, for Spring, Fall, Winter issues.
The Believer: Heidi Julavits, Ed Park, Vendela Vida, founding editors; Andrew Leland, managing editor, for February, June/July, September issues.
Legal Affairs: Lincoln Caplan, editor and president, for January/February, March/April, September/October issues.
ReadyMade: Shoshana Berger, editor in chief, for January/February, October/November, December/January issues.
The Virginia Quarterly Review: Ted Genoways, editor, for Winter, Summer, Fall issues.

100,000 to 250,000 Circulation

Chicago: Richard Babcock, editor, for June, September, December issues.
Foreign Policy: Moisés Naím, editor in chief, for May/June, September/October, November/December issues.
Harper's magazine: Lewis H. Lapham, editor, for May, November, December issues.
Harvard Business Review: Thomas A. Stewart, editor, for March, September, December issues.
Town and Country Travel: Pamela Fiori, editor in chief, for Spring, Fall, Winter issues.

250,000 to 500,000 Circulation

The Atlantic Monthly: Cullen Murphy, managing editor, for January/February, November, December issues.

Backpacker: Jonathan Dorn, editor in chief; for May, June, October issues.

New York Magazine: Adam Moss, editor in chief, for April 4, July 18, September 19 issues.

Technology Review: Jason Pontin, editor in chief and publisher, for January, July, August issues.

Texas Monthly: Evan Smith, editor, for July, November, December issues.

500,000 to 1,000,000 Circulation

Esquire: David Granger, editor in chief, for March, September, November issues.

Everyday Food: Margaret Roach, editorial director; Melissa Morgan, executive editor, for May, July/August, December issues.

House and Garden: Dominique Browning, editor, for January, June, October issues.

Marie Claire: Lesley Jane Seymour, editor in chief, for July, September, October issues.

Runner's World: David Willey, editor in chief, for April, June, August issues.

Wired: Chris Anderson, editor in chief, for July, November, December issues.

1,000,000 to 2,000,000 Circulation

ESPN: The Magazine: Gary Hoenig, editor in chief, for June 6, November 7, November 21 issues.

Fortune: Eric Pooley, managing editor, for September 19, October 17, November 28 issues.

Martha Stewart Living: Martha Stewart, founder; Margaret Roach, editorial director, for May, October, November issues.

The New Yorker: David Remnick, editor, for February 14 and 21, September 19, December 19 issues.

Vogue: Anna Wintour, editor in chief, for March, September, December issues.

Over 2,000,000 Circulation

Glamour: Cynthia Leive, editor in chief, for August, September, December issues.

National Geographic: Chris Johns, editor in chief, for September, October, November issues.

O: The Oprah Magazine: Oprah Winfrey, founder and editorial director; Amy Gross, editor in chief, for July, October, November issues.

Prevention: Rosemary Ellis, editorial director, for February, March, April issues.

Time: James Kelly, managing editor, for June 20, September 12, October10 issues.

Personal Service

This category recognizes excellence in service journalism. The advice or instruction presented should help readers improve the quality of their personal lives.

Field and Stream: Sid Evans, editor in chief, for *How to Raise a Hunter*, by Keith McCafferty, December/January.

Men's Health: David Zinczenko, editor in chief, for a three-part series, "Death Threats"; part 1: "Hunting My Father's Killer," by William G. Phillips, September; part 2: "How to Dismantle an Anatomic Bomb," by Hamilton Cain, November; part 3: "The Greatest Medical Revolution of the Century is About to Begin," by Christopher McDougall, December.

National Geographic: Chris Johns, editor in chief, for "The Secrets of Long Life," by Dan Buettner, November.

O: The Oprah Magazine: Oprah Winfrey, founder and editorial director; Amy Gross, editor in chief, for "Money: The Million Dollar Question," March.

Self: Lucy S. Danziger, editor in chief, for its breast cancer handbook, "Keep Your Breasts, Healthy for Life," October.

Leisure Interests

This category recognizes excellent service journalism about leisure-time pursuits. The practical advice or instruction presented should help readers enjoy hobbies or other recreational interests.

Bicycling: Stephen Madden, editor in chief, for "Hey, Big Fella," September.

Condé Nast Traveler: Klara Glowczewska, editor in chief, for "The Fabulous 50," by Wendy Perrin, December.

Golf Magazine: David M. Clarke, editor, for "The New Way to Putt," October.

GQ: Jim Nelson, editor in chief, for "The 20 Hamburgers You Must Eat Before You Die," by Alan Richman, July.

Men's Health: David Zinczenko, editor in chief, for its special section "Play Hard for Life"; part 1: "The Indestructible Man," by Jim Thornton; part 2: "101 Ways to Stay in the Game"; part 3, "This is Your Brain on Multiple Concussions," by Bob Drury, July/August.

Reporting

This category recognizes excellence in reporting. It honors the enterprise, exclusive reporting, and intelligent analysis that a magazine exhibits in covering an event, a situation, or a problem of contemporary interest and significance.

The Atlantic Monthly: Cullen Murphy, managing editor, for "In a Ruined Country," by David Samuels, September.

The Atlantic Monthly: Cullen Murphy, managing editor, for "The Wrath of Khan," by William Langewiesche, November.

Harper's magazine: Lewis H. Lapham, editor, for "Death of a Mountain," by Erik Reece, April.

The New Yorker: David Remnick, editor, for three articles by Jane Mayer: "Outsourcing Torture," February 14 and 21; "The Experiment," July 11 and 18; "A Deadly Interrogation," November 14.

Rolling Stone: Jann S. Wenner, editor and publisher; Will Dana, managing editor, for "The Man Who Sold the War," by James Bamford, December 1.

Public Interest

This category recognizes journalism that has the potential to affect national or local policy or lawmaking. It honors investigative reporting or groundbreaking analysis that sheds new light on an issue of public importance.

The Atlantic Monthly: Cullen Murphy, managing editor, for "Why Iraq Has No Army," by James Fallows, December.

Legal Affairs: Lincoln Caplan, editor and president, for "The Gentle People," by Nadya Labi, January/February.

Mother Jones: Russ Rymer, editor in chief, for "Climate of Denial," a special report on global warming, big money, and junk science, May/June.

The New Yorker: David Remnick, editor, for "The Climate of Man," a three-part series by Elizabeth Kolbert, part 1, April 25; part 2, May 2; part 3, May 9.

Texas Monthly: Evan Smith, editor, for "Hurt? Injured? Need a Lawyer? Too Bad!" by Mimi Swartz, November.

Feature Writing

This category recognizes excellence in feature writing. It honors the stylishness, flair, and originality with which the author treats his or her subject.

The American Scholar: Robert Wilson, editor, for "Genome Tome," by Priscilla Long, Summer.

The Atlantic Monthly: Cullen Murphy, managing editor, for "Countdown to a Meltdown," by James Fallows, July/August.

GQ: Jim Nelson, editor in chief, for "Upon This Rock," by John Jeremiah Sullivan, February.

Outside: Hal Espen, editor, for "Raising the Dead," by Tim Zimmermann, August.

The Oxford American: Marc Smirnoff, editor and publisher, for "Love and Death in the Cape Fear Serpentarium," by Wendy Brenner, Winter.

Profile Writing

This category recognizes excellence in profile writing. It honors the vividness and perceptiveness with which the writer brings his or her subject to life.

The Atlantic Monthly: Cullen Murphy, managing editor, for "Host," by David Foster Wallace, April.

Esquire: David Granger, editor in chief, for "Into the Light," by Robert Kurson, June.

GQ: Jim Nelson, editor in chief, for "The Last Outlaw," by Chris Heath, November.

Los Angeles Magazine: Kit Rachlis, editor in chief, for "The Recruit," by Jesse Katz, March.

The New Yorker: David Remnick, editor, for "The Crossing," by Alec Wilkinson, June 27.

Rolling Stone: Jann S. Wenner, editor and publisher; Will Dana, managing editor, for "Bono: The Rolling Stone Interview," by Jann S. Wenner, November 3.

Essays

This category recognizes excellence in essay writing on topics ranging from the personal to the political. Whatever the subject, it honors the author's eloquence, perspective, fresh thinking, and unique voice.

Harper's magazine: Lewis H. Lapham, editor, for "Don't Watch the News," by Frederick Busch, November.

Harper's magazine: Lewis H. Lapham, editor, for "The Christian Paradox," by Bill McKibben, August.

Vanity Fair: Graydon Carter, editor, for "A Matter of Life and Death," by Marjorie Williams, October.

The Virginia Quarterly Review: Ted Genoways, editor, for "The Wagon," by Martin Preib, Summer.

The Virginia Quarterly Review: Ted Genoways, editor, for "Dead Enough? The Paradox of Brain Death," by Pauline W. Chen, Fall.

Columns and Commentary

This category recognizes excellence in short-form political, social, economic, or humorous commentary. The award honors the eloquence, force of argument, and succinctness with which the writer presents his or her views.

Field and Stream: Sid Evans, editor in chief, for "A Sportsman's Life," by Bill Heavey, "Girl Meets Bluegill," August; "Aging Ungracefully," September; "One Moment, Please . . . ," November.

Inc.: John Koten, editor, for "Street Smarts," by Norm Brodsky and Bo Burlingham, "Subcontracting Made Easy," February; "Why the Union Can't Win," March; "Let the (Political) Games Begin," June.

The New Yorker: David Remnick, editor, for three columns by Hendrik Hertzberg, "Landmarks," February 14 and 21; "Mired," August 22; "Bah Humbug," December 26 and January 2.

Scientific American: John Rennie, editor in chief, for "Relief is Not Enough," March; "Okay, We Give Up," April; "Fill This Prescription," October.

Vanity Fair: Graydon Carter, editor, for three columns by James Wolcott, "Caution: Women Seething," June; "To Live and Die in Iraq," August; "Flooding the Spin Zone," November.

Reviews and Criticism

This category recognizes excellence in criticism of art, books, movies, television, theater, music, dance, food, dining, fashion, products, and the like. It honors the knowledge, persuasiveness, and original voice that the critic brings to his or her reviews.

The Atlantic Monthly: Cullen Murphy, managing editor, for three reviews by Sandra Tsing Loh, "Marshal Plan," March; "Kiddie Class Struggle," June; "The Great Escape," September.

GQ: Jim Nelson, editor in chief, for three reviews by Tom Carson, "I Love a Crusade," May; "Skin Flicks," June; "The Art of Darkness," October.

Harper's magazine: Lewis H. Lapham, editor, for three reviews by Wyatt Mason, "Make it Newish," May; "A World Unto Himself," July; "White Knees," October.

New York Magazine: Adam Moss, editor in chief, for three columns by Mark Stevens, "Curtain Up," February 28; "Surrealism U.S.A.," June 20; "Way Outside the Box," October 24.

The Virginia Quarterly Review: Ted Genoways, editor, for two pieces by Sven Birkerts, "Humboldt's Gift," Summer; "A Weekend at Montauk," Winter.

Magazine Section

This category recognizes excellence of a regular department or editorial section of a magazine, either front- or back-of-book, and composed of a variety of elements, both text and visual. Finalists are selected based on the section's voice, originality, design, and packaging.

Backpacker: Jonathan Dorn, editor in chief, for its "Basecamp" section, June, September, December.

Condé Nast Traveler: Klara Glowczewska, editor in chief, for its front-of-book section "Stop Press: Star Power," September; "Orient Express," October; "The Great Escape," November.

Entertainment Weekly: Rick Tetzeli, managing editor, for "The Must List," its back-of-book reviews section, December 9, December 16, December 23.

Men's Health: David Zinczenko, editor in chief, for its front-of-book section "Male-grams," September, October, December.

New York Magazine: Adam Moss, editor in chief, for its "Strategist" section, January 10, October 17, December 12.

Single-Topic Issue

This category recognizes magazines that have devoted an issue to an in-depth examination of one topic. It honors the ambition, comprehensiveness, and imagination with which a magazine treats its subject.

National Geographic: Chris Johns, editor in chief, for "Africa: Whatever You Thought, Think Again," September.

The Oxford American: Marc Smirnoff, editor and publisher, for its Southern Music Issue, Summer.

Saveur: Colman Andrews, editor in chief, for its special issue "American Cheese," April.

Scientific American: John Rennie, editor in chief, for "Crossroads for Planet Earth," September.

Time: James Kelly, managing editor, for "An American Tragedy," September 12.

Design

This category recognizes excellence in magazine design. It honors the effectiveness of overall design, artwork, graphics, and typography in enhancing a magazine's unique mission and personality.

Everyday Food: Margaret Roach, editorial director; Melissa Morgan, executive editor; Eric Pike, creative director; Scot Schy, design director, for May, July/August, December issues.

GQ: Jim Nelson, editor in chief; Fred Woodward, design director; Jim Moore, creative director, for March, July, December issues.

Kids: Fun Stuff To Do Together: Jodi Levine, editorial director; Melissa Morgan, executive editor; Deb Bishop, design director, Summer, Fall, Winter issues.

Martha Stewart Living: Martha Stewart, founder; Margaret Roach, editorial director; James Dunlinson and Joele Cuyler, art directors, for May, November, December issues.

New York Magazine: Adam Moss, editor in chief; Luke Hayman, design director, for July 25, November 21, December 19 issues.

Nylon: Marvin Scott Jarrett, editor; Patrick Mitchell, design director, for March, April, August issues.

Photography

This category recognizes excellence in magazine photography. It honors the effectiveness of photography, photojournalism, and photo illustration in enhancing a magazine's unique mission and personality.

Departures: Richard David Story, editor in chief; Bernard Scharf, creative director; Jennifer Martin, director of photography, for September, October, November/December issues.

Gourmet: Ruth Reichl, editor in chief; Richard Ferretti, creative director; Erika Oliveira, art director; Amy Koblenzer, photo editor, for May, July, September issues.

New York Magazine: Adam Moss, editor in chief; Luke Hayman, design director; Jody Quon, photography director; Chris Dixon, art director, for April 4, August 29–September 5, December 19 issues.

Texas Monthly: Evan Smith, editor; Scott Dadich, creative director; Leslie Baldwin, photography editor, for April, July, September issues.

Time: James Kelly, managing editor; Arthur Hochstein, art director; director of photography, Michele Stephenson, director of photography, for January 10, September 12, November 7 issues.

W: Patrick McCarthy, chairman and editorial director; Dennis Freedman, vice chairman and creative director; Edward Leida, executive vice president and group design director; Kirby Rodriguez, art director, for July, September, October issues.

Photo Portfolio/Photo Essay

This category recognizes a distinctive portfolio or photographic essay. It honors either photos that express an idea or a concept, or documentary photojournalism shot in real time.

Aperture: Melissa Harris, editor in chief; Yolanda Cuomo, art director, for "A Procession of Them: The Plight of the Mentally Disabled," by Eugene Richards, Spring.

Field and Stream: Sid Evans, editor in chief; Robert Perino, art director; Amy Berkley, photography editor, for "How We Hunt," a portfolio by Erika Larsen, December/ January.

National Geographic: Chris Johns, editor in chief; David Griffin, senior editor, photography and illustrations, for "Tracking the Next Killer Flu," by Tim Appenzeller, photographs by Lynn Johnson, October.

Rolling Stone: Jann S. Wenner, editor and publisher; Will Dana, managing editor; Amid Capeci, art director; Jodi Peckman, director of photography, for "The Edge of the World," by Sebastião Salgado, November 17.

Vanity Fair: Graydon Carter, editor; David Harris, design director; Susan White, photography director, for "Hell and High Water," by Jonas Karlsson, November.

W: Patrick McCarthy, chairman and editorial director; Dennis Freedman, vice chairman and creative director; Edward Leida, executive vice president and group design director; Kirby Rodriguez, art director, for "Domestic Bliss," by Steven Klein, July.

Fiction

This category recognizes excellence in magazine fiction writing. It honors the quality of a publication's literary selections.

The Atlantic Monthly: Cullen Murphy, managing editor, for "A Record Book for Small Farmers," by Anna North, January/February; "Bullheads," by Michael Lohre, April; "One of Our Whales is Missing," by Christopher Buckley, September.

McSweeney's: Dave Eggers and Eli Horowitz, editors, for "I Understand," by Roddy Doyle, January; "Mudder Tongue," by Brian Evenson, June; "Somoza's Dream," by Daniel Orozco, November.

The Virginia Quarterly Review: Ted Genoways, editor, for "Peacekeeper," by Alan Heathcock, Fall; "Smother," by Joyce Carol Oates, Fall; "Ina Grove," by R. T. Smith, Fall.

The Virginia Quarterly Review: Ted Genoways, editor, for "So Help Me God," by Joyce Carol Oates, Winter; "The Guggenheim Lovers," by Isabel Allende, Summer; "The Ghosts We Love," by Brock Clarke.

Zoetrope: All-Story: Michael Ray, editor, for "Blessing," by Charles D'Ambrosio, Winter; "Today I'm Yours," by Mary Gaitskill, Winter; "High Lonesome," by Joyce Carol Oates, Winter.

General Excellence Online

This category recognizes outstanding magazine Internet sites, as well as online-only magazines and Web logs that have a significant amount of original content. It honors sites that reflect an outstanding level of interactivity, journalistic integrity, service, and innovative visual presentation.

Beliefnet.com (www.beliefnet.com): Steven Waldman, cofounder and editor in chief.
CNET.com (www.cnet.com): Candice Meyers, senior vice president, and Jai Singh, editor in chief.
men.style.com (http://men.style.com): Jamie Pallot, editorial director, CondeNet.
National Geographic Online (www.ngm.com): Chris Johns, editor in chief.
Newsweek.com (www.newsweek.msnbc.com): Deidre Depke, editor.

National Magazine Award Winners, 1966–2006

Best Interactive Design

2001   SmartMoney.com

Columns and Commentary

2002   New York
2003   The Nation
2004   New York
2005   National Journal
2006   The New Yorker

Design

1980   Geo
1981   Attenzione
1982   Nautical Quarterly
1983   New York
1984   House and Garden
1985   Forbes
1986   Time
1987   Elle
1988   Life
1989   Rolling Stone
1990   Esquire
1991   Condé Nast Traveler
1992   Vanity Fair
1993   Harper's Bazaar
1994   Allure
1995   Martha Stewart Living
1996   Wired
1997   I.D.
1998   Entertainment Weekly
1999   ESPN The Magazine
2000   Fast Company
2001   Nest
2002   Details

2003   Details
2004   Esquire.
2005   Kids: Fun Stuff to Do Together
2006   New York

Essays

2000   The Sciences
2001   The New Yorker
2002   The New Yorker
2003   The American Scholar
2004   The New Yorker
2005   National Geographic
2006   Vanity Fair

Essays and Criticism

1978   Esquire
1979   Life
1980   Natural History
1981   Time
1982   The Atlantic
1983   The American Lawyer
1984   The New Republic
1985   Boston Magazine
1986   The Sciences
1987   Outside
1988   Harper's Magazine
1989   Harper's Magazine
1990   Vanity Fair
1991   The Sciences
1992   The Nation
1993   The American Lawyer
1994   Harper's Magazine
1995   Harper's Magazine
1996   The New Yorker

1997	*The New Yorker*
1998	*The New Yorker*
1999	*The Atlantic Monthly*

Feature Writing

1988	*The Atlantic*
1989	*Esquire*
1990	*The Washingtonian*
1991	*U.S. News and World Report*
1992	*Sports Illustrated*
1993	*The New Yorker*
1994	*Harper's Magazine*
1995	*GQ*
1996	*GQ*
1997	*Sports Illustrated*
1998	*Harper's Magazine*
1999	*The American Scholar*
2000	*Sports Illustrated*
2001	*Rolling Stone*
2002	*The Atlantic Monthly*
2003	*Harper's Magazine*
2004	*The New Yorker*
2005	*Esquire*
2006	*The American Scholar*

Fiction

1978	*The New Yorker*
1979	*The Atlantic Monthly*
1980	*Antaeus*
1981	*The North American Review*
1982	*The New Yorker*
1983	*The North American Review*
1984	*Seventeen*
1985	*Playboy*
1986	*The Georgia Review*
1987	*Esquire*

1988	*The Atlantic*
1989	*The New Yorker*
1990	*The New Yorker*
1991	*Esquire*
1992	*Story*
1993	*The New Yorker*
1994	*Harper's Magazine*
1995	*Story*
1996	*Harper's Magazine*
1997	*The New Yorker*
1998	*The New Yorker*
1999	*Harper's Magazine*
2000	*The New Yorker*
2001	*Zoetrope: All-Story*
2002	*The New Yorker*
2003	*The New Yorker*
2004	*Esquire*
2005	*The Atlantic Monthly*
2006	*The Virginia Quarterly Review*

Fiction and Belles Lettres

1970	*Redbook*
1971	*Esquire*
1972	*Mademoiselle*
1973	*The Atlantic Monthly*
1974	*The New Yorker*
1975	*Redbook*
1976	*Essence*
1977	*Mother Jones*

General Excellence

1973	*BusinessWeek*
1981	*ARTnews*
	Audubon
	BusinessWeek
	Glamour

1982	*Camera Arts*		1992	*Mirabella*
	Newsweek			*National Geographic*
	Rocky Mountain Magazine			*The New Republic*
	Science81			*Texas Monthly*
1983	*Harper's Magazine*		1993	*American Photo*
	Life			*The Atlantic Monthly*
	Louisiana Life			*Lingua Franca*
	Science82			*Newsweek*
1984	*The American Lawyer*		1994	*BusinessWeek*
	House and Garden			*Health*
	National Geographic			*Print*
	Outside			*Wired*
1985	*American Health*		1995	*Entertainment Weekly*
	American Heritage			*I.D. Magazine*
	Manhattan, Inc.			*Men's Journal*
	Time			*The New Yorker*
1986	*Discover*		1996	*BusinessWeek*
	Money			*Civilization*
	New England Monthly			*Outside*
	3–2-1- Contact			*The Sciences*
1987	*Common Cause*		1997	*I.D. Magazine*
	Elle			*Outside*
	New England Monthly			*Vanity Fair*
	People Weekly			*Wired*
1988	*Fortune*		1998	*DoubleTake*
	Hippocrates			*Outside*
	Parents			*Preservation*
	The Sciences			*Rolling Stone*
1989	*American Heritage*		1999	*Condé Nast Traveler*
	Sports Illustrated			*Fast Company*
	The Sciences			*I.D. Magazine*
	Vanity Fair			*Vanity Fair*
1990	*Metropolitan Home*		2000	*National Geographic*
	7 Days			*Nest*
	Sports Illustrated			*The New Yorker*
	Texas Monthly			*Saveur*
1991	*Condé Nast Traveler*		2001	*The American Scholar*
	Glamour			*Mother Jones*
	Interview			*The New Yorker*
	The New Republic			*Teen People*

2002	*Entertainment Weekly*
	National Geographic Adventure
	Newsweek
	Print
	Vibe
2003	*Architectural Record*
	The Atlantic Monthly
	ESPN The Magazine
	Foreign Policy
	Parenting
	Texas Monthly
2004	*Aperture*
	Budget Living
	Chicago Magazine
	Gourmet
	Newsweek
	Popular Science
2005	*Dwell*
	Glamour
	Martha Stewart Weddings
	The New Yorker
	Print
	Wired
2006	*ESPN The Magazine*
	Esquire
	Harper's Magazine
	New York
	Time
	The Virginia Quarterly Review

General Excellence in New Media

1997	*Money*
1998	*The Sporting News Online*
1999	*Cigar Aficionado*
2000	*BusinessWeek Online*

General Excellence Online

(formerly General Excellence in New Media)

2001	U.S. News Online
2002	National Geographic Magazine Online
2003	Slate
2004	CNET News.com
2005	Style.com
2006	National Geographic Online

Leisure Interests

(formerly Special Interests)

2002	*Vogue*
2003	*National Geographic Adventure*
2004	*Consumer Reports*
2005	*Sports Illustrated*
2006	*Golf*

Magazine Section

2005	*Popular Science*
2006	*Backpacker*

Personal Service

1986	*Farm Journal*
1987	*Consumer Reports*
1988	*Money*
1989	*Good Housekeeping*
1990	*Consumer Reports*
1991	*New York*
1992	*Creative Classroom*
1993	*Good Housekeeping*
1994	*Fortune*

1995	SmartMoney
1996	SmartMoney
1998	Glamour
1999	Men's Journal
2000	Good Housekeeping
2001	PC Computing
2002	National Geographic Adventure
2002	National Geographic Adventure
2003	Outside
2004	Men's Health
2005	BabyTalk
2006	Self

Photography

1985	Life
1986	Vogue
1987	National Geographic
1988	Rolling Stone
1989	National Geographic
1990	Texas Monthly
1991	National Geographic
1992	National Geographic
1993	Harper's Bazaar
1994	Martha Stewart Living
1995	Rolling Stone
1996	Saveur
1997	National Geographic
1998	W
1999	Martha Stewart Living
2000	Vanity Fair
2001	National Geographic
2002	Vanity Fair
2003	Condé Nast Traveler
2004	City
2005	Gourmet
2006	W

Photo Portoflio/Photo Essay

2004	W
2005	Time
2006	Rolling Stone

Profile Writing

2000	Sports Illustrated
2001	The New Yorker
2002	The New Yorker
2003	Sports Illustrated
2004	Esquire
2005	The New Yorker
2006	Esquire

Public Interest

1970	Life
1971	The Nation
1972	Philadelphia
1974	Scientific American
1975	Consumer Reports
1976	BusinessWeek
1977	Philadelphia
1978	Mother Jones
1979	New West
1980	Texas Monthly
1981	Reader's Digest
1982	The Atlantic
1983	Foreign Affairs
1984	The New Yorker
1985	The Washingtonian
1986	Science85
1987	Money
1988	The Atlantic
1989	California
1990	Southern Exposure
1991	Family Circle

1992	Glamour
1993	The Family Therapy Networker
1994	Philadelphia
1995	The New Republic
1996	Texas Monthly
1997	Fortune
1998	The Atlantic Monthly
1999	Time
2000	The New Yorker
2001	Time
2002	The Atlantic Monthly
2003	The Atlantic Monthly
2004	The New Yorker
2005	The New Yorker
2006	The New Yorker

Reporting

1970	The New Yorker
1971	The Atlantic Monthly
1972	The Atlantic Monthly
1973	New York
1974	The New Yorker
1975	The New Yorker
1976	Audubon
1977	Audubon
1978	The New Yorker
1979	Texas Monthly
1980	Mother Jones
1981	National Journal
1982	The Washingtonian
1983	Institutional Investor
1984	Vanity Fair
1985	Texas Monthly
1986	Rolling Stone
1987	Life
1988	The Washingtonian and Baltimore Magazine

1989	The New Yorker
1990	The New Yorker
1991	The New Yorker
1992	The New Republic
1993	IEEE Spectrum
1994	The New Yorker
1995	The Atlantic Monthly
1996	The New Yorker
1997	Outside
1998	Rolling Stone
1999	Newsweek
2000	Vanity Fair
2001	Esquire
2002	The Atlantic Monthly
2003	The New Yorker
2004	Rolling Stone
2005	The New Yorker
2006	Rolling Stone

Reviews and Criticism

2000	Esquire
2001	The New Yorker
2002	Harper's Magazine
2003	Vanity Fair
2004	Esquire
2005	The New Yorker
2006	Harper's Magazine

Service to the Individual

1974	Sports Illustrated
1975	Esquire
1976	Modern Medicine
1977	Harper's Magazine
1978	Newsweek
1979	The American Journal of Nursing
1980	Saturday Review

1982   *Philadelphia*
1983   *Sunset*
1984   *New York*
1985   *The Washingtonian*

Single Awards

1966   *Look*
1967   *Life*
1968   *Newsweek*
1969   *American Machinist*

Single-Topic Issue

1979   *Progressive Architecture*
1980   *Scientific American*
1981   *BusinessWeek*
1982   *Newsweek*
1983   *IEEE Spectrum*
1984   *Esquire*
1985   *American Heritage*
1986   *IEEE Spectrum*
1987   *Bulletin of the Atomic Scientists*
1988   *Life*
1989   *Hippocrates*
1990   *National Geographic*
1991   *The American Lawyer*
1992   *BusinessWeek*
1993   *Newsweek*
1994   *Health*
1995   *Discover*
1996   *Bon Appétit*
1997   *Scientific American*
1998   *The Sciences*
1999   *The Oxford American*
2002   *Time*
2003   *Scientific American*
2004   *The Oxford American*

2005   *Newsweek*
2006   *Time*

Special Awards

1976   *Time*
1989   Robert E. Kenyon, Jr.

Special Interests

1986   *Popular Mechanics*
1987   *Sports Afield*
1988   *Condé Nast Traveler*
1989   *Condé Nast Traveler*
1990   *Art and Antiques*
1991   *New York*
1992   *Sports Afield*
1993   *Philadelphia*
1994   *Outside*
1995   *GQ*
1996   *Saveur*
1997   *Smithsonian*
1998   *Entertainment Weekly*
1999   *PC Computing*
2000   *I.D. Magazine*
2001   *The New Yorker*

Specialized Journalism

1970   *Philadelphia*
1971   *Rolling Stone*
1972   *Architectural Record*
1973   *Psychology Today*
1974   *Texas Monthly*
1975   *Medical Economics*
1976   *United Mine Workers Journal*
1977   *Architectural Record*

1978	*Scientific American*
1979	*National Journal*
1980	*IEEE Spectrum*

Visual Excellence

1970	*Look*
1971	*Vogue*

1972	*Esquire*
1973	*Horizon*
1974	*Newsweek*
1975	*Country Journal*
	National Lampoon
1976	*Horticulture*
1977	*Rolling Stone*
1978	*Architectural Digest*
1979	*Audubon*

ASME Board of Directors

American Society of Magazine Editors
Mission Statement

ASME is the professional organization for editors of magazines published in the United States. ASME's mission is to:

- Uphold editorial integrity

- Encourage and reward outstanding and innovative achievement in the creation of magazines and their content

- Bring magazine editors together for networking

- Disseminate useful information on magazine editing to magazine staff members and others

- Attract talented young people to magazine editorial work

- Speak out on public policy issues, particularly those pertaining to the First Amendment; and to acquaint the general public with the work of magazine editors and the special character of magazines as a channel of communication

ASME was founded in 1963, and currently has 900 members nationwide.